THE TRUE NAME TORAH

The Five Books Of Moses
Genesis, Exodus, Leviticus, Numbers, Deuteronomy

Returning the Name of God to His Word

With edits by YoHanan – YeHoVaH's Writer

Introduction

This translation is based on the Ancient Hebrew Scriptures. It is considered the Word of God as given to Moses to record. The name YeHoVaH that has been removed for thousands of years has been returned.

Visit our website at www.TorahPublications.com

Printed in the United States of America

First Printing: February 2020
Torah Publications

ISBN-978-1-7345383-1-1

Torah Publications
We are rooted in the Torah

Dallas, Texas USA

ISBN: 978-1-7345383-1-1

CONTENTS

INTRODUCTION TO THE TORAH

A quick lesson in Hebrew

The **"Torah"** contains the 5 books of Moses (Genesis, Exodus, Leviticus, Numbers and Deuteronomy). The **"Pentateuch"** is Greek and means "Five Books", refers to the **Torah** i.e. the 5 Books of Moses.

~Original Hebrew had no punctuation, capitalization or paragraphs. All those were added by man.
~Hebrew is read from right to left. (left to right in English)
~There is no 'J' or 'W' in the 22 letter Hebrew alphabet.
~It is sometimes written with vowels or without.
~The Torah was not written in books, chapters and verses and had no verse and number markings such as 1:3. All those were added by man for ease of reading.

INTRODUCTION TO HIS NAME

Exodus 13 And Moses said to *Elohim*, Behold, when I come to the children of Israel, and say to them, The *Elohim* of your fathers has sent me to you; and they shall say to me, What is his name? what shall I say to them? *14* And *Elohim* said to Moses, I AM THAT I AM: *15* And *YeHoVaH* (See explanation below) said to Moses, Thus shall you say to the children of Israel, the *Elohim* of your fathers, the *Elohim* of Abraham, the *Elohim* of Isaac, and the *Elohim* of Jacob, has sent me to you: *this is my name forever*, *and this is my memorial to* **all generations**.

If you could read Hebrew and were reading the ancient Hebrew Scriptures you would notice one thing … the word God is never used as God's name but only to refer to other gods. So then why do we call our creator and the creator of the universe 'God'? How would you feel if someone removed your name and replaced it with what really amounts to nothing more than a mere title (LORD)?

What you would find in reading the Hebrew Scriptures is His Name: YHVH (without vowels) or YeHoVaH (with vowels). The Hebrew language in its original form was written without vowel points; after all, one wrote down what one heard and he could fill in the vowels when he spoke the name. Many reasons are given that the true name of God was removed from the bible. It was said it was too sacred to say out loud, some say the Romans forbid the use of the name, and others say it wasn't popular so it was left out in order to sell more bibles. Whatever the reason, none is excusable as it denies the reader (listener) their inalienable right. God is a title: YeHoVaH (Ye-Ho-VaH) is His name. YHVH is found over 6,800 times in the original Hebrew Scriptures. Biblical Hebrew was written only in consonants, as we see in the letters YHVH. Therefore, the main question of pronunciation concerns which vowel (points) to add to the consonants. The vowels can make a difference in the meaning. If we add the vowels - "e"-"o"-"a"- to the consonants, we have the name YeHoVaH. In this format, the "e" (sh'va) stands for the future tense, the "o" (holom) for the present tense, and the "a" (patach) refers to the past tense. That gives meaning to the name YeHoVaH as "**He will be, He is, He was**." In other words, the Eternal One. This meaning fits the understanding of the early patriarchs. Since every example of the YHVH root used in biblical names in this pattern shows the vowels as "e"-"o"-"a", one would have to show some other overwhelming evidence, textually or grammatically, to choose a different pronunciation. There is no other overpowering documentation great enough to refute the biblical and grammatical evidence. Simply stated, 1) the meaning of the vowels, 2) the grammatical form, and 3) the list of biblical examples*, all point to YeHoVaH. Reference: http://streamsinthenegev.com/school-of-fish/names-of-god/yehovah-or-yahweh-by-asher-intrater/ by Asher Intrater

Some English adaptations for His Name are Jehovah or Yehweh or YHWH but since there is no 'J' or 'W' in the Hebrew language, these would not be His true name but only adaptations.

The world-renown Hebrew scholar *Nehemia Gordon* has worked as a translator on the Dead Sea Scrolls, and as a researcher deciphering ancient Hebrew manuscripts. He and his research team over the last two years have been on a quest to identify and verify God's true name. As of this writing they have found YeHoVaH with full vowels in over 2,300 Hebrew

GENESIS

bible manuscripts in libraries around the world. Gordon holds a Master's Degree in Biblical Studies and a Bachelor's Degree in Archaeology from the Hebrew University of Jerusalem.

In his book *"Shattering the Conspiracy of Silence"*, available at Amazon.com, Nehemia explains that God's name YHVH derives from the exact same Hebrew root as 'I am." The name is a combination of three forms of the Hebrew root: Hayah, Hoveh, and Yihyeh. The three words mean, "He was," "He is," "He will be." So, "I am" is not His name but an explanation of His name. Nehemia states that when God said His name, YHVH, is le'olam, He meant that as long as the Universe continues to exist, this will be His name. Find more of Nehemia's work @ https://www.nehemiaswall.com/1000-manuscripts-yehovah

From Strong's Concordance H3068

Yĕhovah Yᵉhôvâh, yeh-ho-vaw'

GENESIS

H V H Y   HaVoHeY

Without vowels - With vowels

Hebrew is written and read from right to left as above. In English it is written YeHoVaH.

Why you don't see *Elohim*, YeHoVaH, YHVH, or Adonai in your Old Testament bible
In translating the Ancient Hebrew Scriptures, whenever the word ***Elohim*** appeared, translators *changed* it to 'God or G-d'. When YeHoVaH or YHVH appeared, they *changed* it to 'LORD' or 'Lᴏʀᴅ' or 'L-RD' (all caps). When Adonai was used they *changed* it to 'Lord' or 'L-rd'. ***Elohim*** and Adonai were titles, not His name. His name is YeHoVaH or YHVH.

True Name Torah & Hebrew Scriptures	Your Bible Today
Elohim (title)	God or G-d (title)
Adonai (title)	Lord or L-rd (not all caps) (title)
El Shaddai (title)	God Almighty
YeHoVaH (Name)	LORD or L-RD (ALL CAPS) (title)

The goal in The True Name Torah is to return His true name to its rightful place it deserves and to what He told Moses to record. Some will argue His Name but please don't argue His Word.

Now that you know His name you can say it loud and clear every time you see it.

BOOK LAYOUT

Since YeHoVaH did not name the books of the Torah nor assign chapter and verse numbers to his words (man did), we have grouped the verses into groups of 10 in order to make the reading flow better and allow room to write notes if you wish.

In synagogue there is a Parsha (a section of the Torah assigned for weekly reading in synagogue worship) reading that is studied for that week. The entire Torah then is read over a one year span. Hopefully your quest for His word will have you reading much quicker than that. The start and end of the weekly reading portions are 'marked' as below.

Reading 1 begins
These mark weekly readings for those following the Parsha Schedule
Reading 1 ends

Each book and chapter is preceded with a short description of the main events contained in each. These were added and are not part of YeHoVaH's Word.

Reading Plans

Reading Plan One: Each week, Torah Observant believers across the world read a section from the Torah (the five books of Moses). In Hebrew, this passage is called *Parashat HaShavua*, which means "portion of the week." Sometimes it is called the *parsha* or *sidra*. The community follows a schedule of readings based on the Hebrew calendar. Over the course of a year, the entire Torah is read. Each reading has a name based on one of the important Hebrew words in the first sentence of the passage. There are fifty-four portions in the regular cycle. The reading cycle for Genesis listed below is for Week 1 to week 12. For a different reading cycle year search Google 'Torah Portion Calendar'.

Reading Plan Two: Simply begin reading Genesis 1:1 and read as you can to the end of Deuteronomy and you will have read the complete Torah.

Reading Plan Three: Start anytime you want with the **Reading 1** and follow the reading sections in order as you are able. Following the readings in order is very important to understanding the whole story and purpose.

Average Reading Times
Times will vary depending on your reading style

Genesis – 3.5h
Exodus – 3h
Leviticus – 2h
Numbers – 3h
Deuteronomy – 2.5h
  Total 14 hours

~GENESIS~

Genesis, Exodus, Leviticus, Numbers, Deuteronomy

The 1st Book of Moses

Genesis in Hebrew is Bereishit (be-ray-SHEET) meaning "In the beginning." It deals with Creation; Adam and Eve; the Flood; the Patriarchs and the Matriarchs of the Jewish people, and ends with the descent of Jacob and his family to Egypt. It also contains the commandment of circumcision, and *Elohim*'s promise to Abraham that he would receive the Land of Israel and that his descendants would be a major, positive influence on the entire world.

READINGS FOR GENESIS

The name in (parentheses) is the Hebrew name for that week. For example: Week 1 'In the beginning' in Hebrew is 'B'reisheet'.

Reading 1 *"In the beginning"* (B'reisheet) *Usually starts in August* Genesis **1:1 - 6:8**
YeHoVaH creates the world. After Adam and Eve eat the forbidden fruit, they are banished from the Garden of Eden. Later Cain kills Abel. YeHoVaH then considers destroying all of Creation.

Reading 2 *"Noah"* (Noach) Genesis **6:9 - 11:32**
YeHoVaH punishes the wicked in the world by causing a giant flood. YeHoVaH saves Noah and his family, who will repopulate the world. We are also introduced to Abram and his wife, Sarai.

Reading 3 *"Go forth"* (Lech Lecha) Genesis **12:1 - 17:27**
YeHoVaH makes a covenant with Abram promising to make his descendants a great nation. YeHoVaH changes Abram's name to Abraham. Abraham has a child with Hagar and names him Ishmael. Elohim then promises Abraham's barren wife, Sarah, that she will have a child.

Reading 4 *"And he appeared"* (Vayeira) Genesis **18:1 - 22:24**
Three guests arrive at Abraham and Sarah's tent. They inform Abraham that YeHoVaH will give the elderly Sarah a child. The prophesy comes true, and they name their son Isaac. YeHoVaH informs Abraham that Sodom and Gomorrah will be destroyed, though Abraham attempts to convince YeHoVaH otherwise. YeHoVaH tells Abraham to sacrifice Isaac. Abraham obliges but is told that it was a test of faith and offers a ram to sacrifice instead.

Reading 5 *"Sarah's Life"* (Chayei Sarah) Genesis **23:1 - 25:18**
Sara dies at the age of 127. Abraham searches for a place to bury her and settles on Machpelah. Abraham searches for a wife for his son, Isaac. Abraham sends his servant to find a wife for Isaac. The servant meets Rebecca at a well, where she provides water for him and his camels. Abraham marries Keturah and has six more sons. He then dies at the age of 175.

Reading 6 *"Family history"* (Toldot) Genesis **25:19 - 28:9**
Rebecca and Isaac have twins, the smooth-skinned Jacob, whom Rebecca favors, and the hairy Esau, who Isaac favors. After returning from a hunting trip, Esau asks his brother for some lentil soup, but Jacob tells him he must trade him his birthright. Years later, when Isaac is old and blind, Jacob tricks their father into giving him the firstborn blessing. Jacob leaves home, fearing his brother will retaliate, and finds a wife at his uncle Laban's house.

Reading 7 *"He went out"* (Vayetze) Genesis **28:10 - 32:3**
Jacob has a dream in which angels go up and down a ladder connecting earth to heaven. YeHoVaH appears before Jacob and renews the covenant that YeHoVaH had made with Abraham. Jacob sees Rachel, Laban's daughter, tending sheep and wishes to marry her. Laban tricks Jacob into marrying his eldest daughter, Leah, after seven years of labor. In exchange for another seven years of work, Jacob is allowed to marry Rachel. Jacob has many sons with Leah, but Rachel is unable to conceive. Finally, YeHoVaH blesses Rachel, and she has a son, she names Joseph.

Reading 8 *"He sent "* (Vayishlach) Genesis **32:4 - 36:43**
YeHoVaH tells Jacob to return home. Worried that his brother Esau will kill him, Jacob divides his clan into two camps, so at least some will survive in case of a fight. Jacob sleeps alone in the desert and is awoken by an angel who wrestles him through the night. Jacob survives and is blessed by the angel and renamed Israel. Jacob meets his brother and, surprisingly, they embrace. Dinah, Jacob's daughter, is

raped by Shekhem, who then proposes to Jacob that he marry her. Shimeon and Levi brutally murder Shekhem and his clan. Rachel has another child, whom she and Jacob name Benjamin.

Reading 9 *"He settled"* (*Vayeshev*) Genesis 37:1 - 40:23
Jacob favors Joseph, and this angers Joseph's brothers. Joseph has dreams in which he predicts reigning over his brothers, provoking them further. They decide to sell Joseph into slavery in Egypt. Tamar disguises herself as a prostitute and sleeps with her father-in-law, Judah. In Egypt, the wife of Joseph's owner tries to seduce Joseph, and when he rejects her, she accuses him of trying to rape her and has him sent to prison. In prison, Pharaoh's baker and butler have dreams, and Joseph interprets them correctly.

Reading 10 *"From the end"* (*Miketz*) Genesis 41:1 - 44:17
Pharaoh has two troubling dreams, and at the suggestion of his baker, who remembers Joseph from prison, Pharaoh brings Joseph to interpret them. Pharaoh is so impressed by Joseph that he makes him his adviser. There is a famine, and Jacob sends his sons, minus Benjamin, to Egypt to buy food. The brothers do not recognize Joseph when they meet him, and Joseph tests them by accusing them of being spies. Joseph arrests Simeon and demands the brothers bring Benjamin to Egypt to prove they are not spies. When Benjamin arrives, Joseph puts a goblet in Benjamin's bag and accuses him of stealing it.

Reading 11 *"He approached"* (*Vayigash*) Genesis 44:18 - 47:27
Joseph's brothers refuse to return to Canaan without Benjamin, whom Joseph has falsely accused of theft. Joseph reveals his true identity and invites his brothers to return for their father, Jacob, and bring him and their families to Egypt to live. When they return, Joseph introduces his father to Pharaoh, and, at Pharaoh's suggestion, the family settles in Goshen, a particularly fertile region of Egypt.

Reading 12 *"He lived "* (*Vayechi*) Genesis 47:28 - 50:26
Joseph promises Jacob that he will bury him in Canaan. On his deathbed, Jacob blesses his grandchildren, Ephraim and Menashe, and then blesses each of his sons. Jacob dies and is embalmed. Joseph affirms to his brothers that he has forgiven them for their misdeeds. Ending the Book of Genesis, Joseph dies.

-End Torah Readings for Genesis-

CHAPTERS 1- 10

Chapter 1

Elohim creates the heavens and the earth and all that lives upon it. He makes mankind in his image, and puts them in charge over the earth.

Reading 1 begins

1 In the very beginning **Elohim** began to create the heavens and the earth. **2** Now the earth was unformed and void, and darkness was upon the face of the deep; and the *spirit* of **Elohim** hovered over the face of the waters. **3** And **Elohim** said: 'Let there be light' And there was light. **4** And **Elohim** saw the light that it was good; and **Elohim** divided the light from the darkness. **5** And **Elohim** called the light Day, and the darkness He called Night. There was evening and then morning, the **first** day. (This is why the Jewish day starts at sundown and ends 24 hours later at sundown) **6** And **Elohim** said: 'Let there be a separation (firmament*) in the midst of the waters, and let it divide the waters from the waters'. **7** And **Elohim** made the separation, and divided the waters that were under the separation from the waters that were above the separation; and it was so. **8** And **Elohim** called the separation heaven and there was evening and there was morning, a **second** day. **9** And **Elohim** said: 'Let the waters under the heaven be gathered together to one place, and let the dry land appear' And it was so. **10** And **Elohim** called the dry land Earth, and the gathering together of the waters He called the seas; and **Elohim** saw that it was good.

11 And **Elohim** said: 'Let the earth put forth grass, plants that yield seed, and fruit-trees bearing fruit after its kind, And seed, upon the earth' And it was so. **12** And the earth brought forth grass, herb yielding seed after its kind, and tree bearing fruit, wherein is the seed, after its kind; and **Elohim** saw that it was good. **13** And there was evening and there was morning, a **third** day. **14** And **Elohim** said: 'Let there be lights in the separation of the heaven to divide the day from the night; and let them be for signs, and for seasons, and for days and years; **15** and let them be for lights in the separation of the heaven to give light upon the earth' And it was so. **16** And **Elohim** made the two great lights: the greater light (sun) to rule the day, and the lesser light (moon) to rule the night; and the stars. **17** And **Elohim** set them in the separation of the heaven to give light upon the earth, **18** and to rule over the day and over the night, and to divide the light from the darkness; and **Elohim** saw that it was good. **19** And there was evening and there was morning, a **fourth** day. **20** And **Elohim** said: 'Let the waters swarm with swarms of living creatures, and let birds fly above the earth in the open separation of heaven'.

21 And **Elohim** created the great whales, and every living creature that creeps, wherever the waters swarmed, and every winged bird; and **Elohim** saw that it was good. **22** And **Elohim** blessed them, saying: 'Be fruitful, and multiply, and fill the waters in the seas, and let birds multiply in the earth'. **23** And there was evening and there was morning, a **fifth** day. **24** And **Elohim** said: 'Let the earth bring forth the living creature after its kind, cattle, and creeping things, and beast of the earth' And it was so. **25** And **Elohim** made the beast of the earth after its kind, and the cattle after their kind, and everything that creeps upon the ground after its kind; and **Elohim** saw that it was good. **26** And **Elohim** said: 'Let us make man in our image, after our likeness; and let them have dominion over the fish of the sea, and over the birds of the air, and over the cattle, and over all the earth, and over everything that creeps upon the earth'. **27** And **Elohim** created man in **His** own image, in the image of **Elohim** man was created; male and female He created them. **28** And **Elohim** blessed them; and **Elohim** said to them: 'Be fruitful, and multiply, and fill the earth, and master it; and have authority over the fish of the sea, and over the birds of the air, and over every living thing that creeps upon the earth'. *29* And *Elohim* said: 'Behold, I have given you every seed bearing plant, which is upon the face of all the earth, and every tree, in which is the fruit of a tree yielding seeds - to you it shall be for food; *30* and to every beast of the earth, and to every bird of the air, and to everything that creeps upon the earth, wherein there is a living soul, I have given every green plant for food'. And it was so.

31 And *Elohim* saw everything that He had made, and, behold, it was very good and there was evening and there was morning, the *sixth* day.

Chapter 2
Elohim places man in the garden and tells him not to eat from the tree of good and evil. Elohim saw that Adam needed a helpmate and created Eve as his partner (wife). Additional details of Elohim's creation.

1 And the heaven and the earth were finished, and all the host of them. *2* And on the *seventh* day *Elohim* finished the work that He had made; and He *rested (ceased work)* **on the seventh day** from all the work that He had made. *3* And *Elohim* blessed the *seventh* day, and set it apart; because that in it He rested from all the work that *Elohim* created and had made. *4* These are the generations of the heaven and of the earth when they were created; in the day that *Elohim* made earth and heaven. *5* No shrub of the field was yet in the earth, and no plant of the field had yet sprung up; for *Adonai Elohim* had not caused it to rain upon the earth, and there was not a man to till the ground; *6* but there went up a mist from the earth, and watered the whole face of the ground. *7* Then *Elohim* formed man of the dust of the ground, and breathed into his nostrils the breath of life; and man became a living soul. *8* And *Elohim* planted a garden in the east, in Eden; and there He put the man whom He had formed. *9* And out of the ground *Elohim* made to grow every tree that is pleasant to the sight, and good for food; the tree of life also in the midst of the garden, and the tree of the knowledge of good and evil. *10* And a river went out of Eden to water the garden; and from there it was parted, and became four rivers.

11 The name of the first is Pishon; that is it which includes the whole land of Havilah, where there is gold; *12* and the gold of that land is good; there is bdellium and the onyx stone. *13* And the name of the second river is Gihon; the same that includes the whole land of Cush. *14* And the name of the third river is Tigris; that is it that goes toward the east of Asshur. And the fourth river is the Euphrates. *15* And *Elohim* took the man, and put him into the Garden of Eden to dress it and to keep it. *16* And *Elohim* commanded the man, saying: 'Of every tree of the garden you may freely eat; *17* but of the tree of the knowledge of good and evil, you shall not eat of it; for in the day that you eat of it you shall surely die.' *18* And *Elohim* said: 'It is not good that the man should be alone; I will make him a helpmate (companion/wife).' *19* And out of the ground *Elohim* formed every beast of the field and every bird of the air; and brought them to the man to see what he would call them; and whatever the man would call every living creature, that was to be their name. *20* And the man gave names to all cattle and to the birds of the air, and to every beast of the field; but for **Adam** there was not found a helpmate for him.

21 And *Elohim* caused a deep sleep to fall upon the man, and he slept; and He took one of his ribs, and closed up the flesh there. *22* And the rib, which *Elohim* had taken from the man (*ish*),

He made a woman (*ishah*), and brought her to the man. *23* And the man said: 'This is now bone of my bones, and flesh of my flesh; she shall be called Woman, because she was taken out of Man.' *24* Therefore shall a man leave his father and his mother, and shall cling to his wife, and they shall be one flesh. *25* And they were both naked, the man and his wife, and were not ashamed.

Chapter 3

Adam and Eve let themselves be deceived by the serpent and they eat from the tree Elohim forbid them to eat. Elohim curses the serpent and the earth and bestows hardship on Adam and Eve before expelling them from the garden.

1 Now the serpent was craftier than any beast of the field which **Elohim** had made. And he said to the woman: 'Has **Elohim** really said: You shall not eat of any tree of the garden?' *2* And the woman said to the serpent: 'Of the fruit of the trees of the garden we may eat; *3* but of the fruit of the tree which is in the midst of the garden, **Elohim** has said: You shall not eat of it, neither shall you touch it, lest you die.' *4* And the serpent said to the woman: 'You shall not surely die; *5* for **Elohim** knows that in the day you eat of it, then your eyes shall be opened, and you shall be as **Elohim**, knowing good and evil.' *6* And when the woman saw that the tree was good for food, and that it was a delight to the eyes, and that the tree was to be desired to make one wise, she took of the fruit, and did eat it; and she gave also to her husband who was with her, and he did eat. *7* And the eyes of them both were opened, and they knew that they were naked; and they sewed fig leaves together, and made themselves covers. *8* And they heard the voice of **Elohim** walking in the garden toward the cool of the day; and the man and his wife hid themselves from the presence of **Elohim** among the trees of the garden. *9* And **Elohim** called to the man, and said to him: 'Where are you?' *10* And he said: 'I heard your voice in the garden, and I was afraid, because I was naked; and I hid myself.'

11 And **Elohim** said: 'Who told you that you were naked? Have you eaten of the tree that I commanded you should not eat?' *12* And the man said: 'The woman whom you gave to be with me, she gave me of the tree, and I did eat.' *13* And **Elohim** said to the woman: 'What is this you have done?' And the woman said: 'The serpent tricked me, and I did eat.' *14* And **Elohim** said to the serpent: 'Because you have done this, cursed are you from among all cattle, and from among all beasts of the field; upon your belly shall you go, and dust shall you eat all the days of your life. *15* And I will put hostility between you and the woman, and between your offspring and her offspring; they shall bruise your head, and you shall bruise their heel.' *16* To the woman He said: 'I will greatly multiply your pain and your conception; in pain you shall bring forth children; and your desire shall be to your husband, and he shall rule over you.' *17* And to Adam He said: 'Because you have listened to the voice of your wife, and have eaten of the tree, of which I commanded you, saying: You shall not eat of it; cursed is the ground for your sake; in toil shall you eat of it all the days of your life. *18* Thorns also and thistles shall it bring forth to you; and you shall eat the plants of the field. *19* In the sweat of your face shall you eat bread, till you return to the ground; for out of it you were taken; for dust you art, and to dust shall you return.' *20* And the man called his wife's name Eve: because she was the mother of all living.

21 And **Elohim** made for Adam and for his wife garments of skins, and clothed them. *22* And **Adonai Elohim** said: 'Behold, the man is become as one of us, to know good and evil; and now, what if he puts forth his hand, and take also of the tree of life, and eat, and live forever.' *23* Therefore **Elohim** sent him forth from the garden of Eden, to till the ground from where he was taken. *24* So He drove out the man; and He placed at the east of the Garden of Eden the cherubim (winged guardians), and the flaming sword that turned every way, to guard the way to the tree of life.

Chapter 4

Cain makes offerings to Elohim but only Abel's is acceptable, so Cain kills Able. Abel's blood cries out to Elohim and Cain is cursed and sent away. Men begin to call upon the name of YeHoVaH.

1 And Adam had relations with Eve his wife; and she conceived and bore **Cain**, and said: 'I have gained a son with the help of *Elohim*.' *2* And again she bore his brother **Abel**. And Abel was a keeper of sheep, but Cain was a tiller of the ground. *3* And in the process of time it came to pass, that Cain brought of the fruit of the ground an offering to *Elohim*. *4* And Abel, he also brought of the firstborn of his flock and of the fat thereof. And *Elohim* paid heed to Abel and to his offering; *5* but to Cain and to his offering He paid no heed. And Cain was very distressed, and his face fell. *6* And *Elohim* said to Cain: 'Why are you distressed? and why is your face fallen? *7* If you do well, shall it not be lifted up? and if you do not well, sin sits at the door; and to you is its desire, but you may rule over it.' *8* And Cain spoke to Abel his brother. And it came to pass, when they were in the field, that Cain rose up against Abel his brother, and killed him. *9* And *Elohim* said to Cain: 'Where is Abel your brother?' And he said: 'I know not; am I my brother's keeper?' *10* And He said: 'What have you done? the voice of your brother's blood cries to Me from the ground.

11 And now cursed are you from the ground, which has opened her mouth to receive your brother's blood from your hand. *12* When you till the ground, it shall no longer yield to you her strength; a fugitive and a wanderer shall you be in the earth.' *13* And Cain said to *Elohim*: 'My punishment is greater than I can bear. *14* Behold, You have driven me out this day from the face of the land; and from Your face shall I be hid; and I shall be a fugitive and a wanderer in the earth; and it will come to pass, that whoever finds me will kill me.' *15* And *Elohim* said to him: 'Therefore whoever slays Cain, vengeance shall be taken on him sevenfold.' And *Elohim* set a sign for Cain, if any finding him should kill him. *16* And Cain went out from the presence of *Elohim*, and dwelt in the land of Nod, on the east of Eden. *17* And Cain had relations with his wife and she conceived, and bore Enoch; and he built a city, and called the name of the city after the name of his son Enoch. *18* And to Enoch was born Irad; and Irad fathered Mehujael; and Mehujael fathered Methushael; and Methushael fathered Lamech. *19* And Lamech took two wives; the name of one was Adah, and the name of the other Zillah. *20* And Adah bore Jabal; he was the father of such as dwell in tents and have cattle.

21 And his brother's name was Jubal; he was the father of all that play instruments and music. *22* And Zillah, she also bore Tubal-cain, the forger of every cutting instrument of brass and iron; and the sister of Tubal-cain was Naamah. *23* And Lamech said to his wives: Adah and Zillah, hear my voice; you wives of Lamech, hear my speech; for I have slain a man for wounding me, and a young man for bruising me; *24* If Cain shall be avenged seven times, truly Lamech seventy-seven times. *25* And Adam had relations with his wife again; and Eve bore a son, and called his name **Seth**: 'for *Elohim* has appointed me another offspring in place of Abel; for Cain killed him.' *26* And to Seth, to him also there was born a son; and he called his name **Enosh**; it was **then** that men began to *call upon the name of YeHoVaH*.

Note* From this point forward, the Name YeHoVaH (YHVH) was written and spoken. But man felt His name was too sacred so changed it in bibles to LORD instead. *We now respectfully return His Name to where it belongs in this True Name Torah to YeHoVaH.*

Chapter 5

The line of Adam is: Seth, Enosh, Kenan, Mahalalel, Jared, Enoch, Methuselah, Lamech and Noah. Noah's sons were Shem, Ham and Japheth. Enoch walks with YeHoVaH.

1 This is the book of the generations of Adam. In the day that **Elohim** created man, in the likeness of **Elohim** He made him; *2* male and female He created, and blessed them, and called their name Adam, in the day when they were created. *3* And Adam lived 130 years, and *fathered a son in his own likeness, after his image; and called his name Seth.* *4* And the days of Adam after he fathered Seth were 800 years; and he fathered more sons and daughters. *5* And all the days that Adam lived were 930 years; and then he died. *6* And Seth lived 105 years, and fathered Enosh. *7* And Seth lived after he fathered Enosh 807 years, and fathered sons and daughters. *8* And all the days of Seth were 912 years; and he died. *9* And Enosh lived 90 years, and fathered Kenan. *10* And Enosh lived after he fathered Kenan 815 years, and fathered sons and daughters.

11 And all the days of Enosh were 905 years; and he died. *12* And Kenan lived 70 years, and fathered Mahalalel. *13* And Kenan lived after he fathered Mahalalel 840 years, and fathered sons and daughters. *14* And all the days of Kenan were 910 years; and he died. *15* And Mahalalel lived 65 years, and fathered Jared. *16* And Mahalalel lived after he fathered Jared 830 years, and fathered sons and daughters. *17* and all the days of Mahalalel were 895 years; and he died. *18* And Jared lived a 162 years, and fathered Enoch. *19* And Jared lived after he fathered Enoch 800 years, and fathered sons and daughters. *20* And all the days of Jared were 962 years; and he died.

21 And Enoch lived 65 years, and fathered **Methuselah**. *22* And Enoch **walked with** **Elohim** after he fathered Methuselah 300 years, and fathered sons and daughters. *23* And all the days of Enoch were 365 years. *24* And Enoch **walked with** **Elohim**, and then he was not; for **Elohim** took him and he was not seen again. *25* And Methuselah lived 187 years, and fathered Lamech. *26* And Methuselah lived after he fathered Lamech 782 years, and fathered sons and daughters. *27* And all the days of Methuselah were 969 years; and he died. *28* And Lamech lived 182 years, and fathered a son. *29* And he called his name **Noah**, saying: 'This same shall comfort us in our work and in the toil of our hands, which comes from the ground which **YeHoVaH** has cursed.' *30* And Lamech lived 595 years after he fathered Noah, and fathered sons and daughters.

31 And all the days of Lamech were 777 years; and he died. *32* And Noah was 500 years old; and Noah fathered **Shem**, **Ham**, and **Japheth**.

Chapter 6

Mankind has corrupted the earth with evil. YeHoVaH decides to destroy them. He instructs Noah to build an ark so he and his family are saved from the flood.

1 And it came to pass, when men began to multiply on the face of the earth, and daughters were born to them, *2* that the sons of **YeHoVaH** saw the daughters of men that they were fair;

and they took wives, whoever they chose. *3* And **YeHoVaH** said: 'My spirit shall not abide in man forever, for that he also is flesh; therefore shall his days be 120 years.' *4* The **Nephilim** were in the earth in those days, and also after that, when the sons of **YeHoVaH** had relations with the daughters of men, and they bore children to them; the same were the mighty men that were of old, the men of renown. *5* And **YeHoVaH** saw that the wickedness of man was great in the earth, and that every imagination of the thoughts of his heart was only evil continually. *6* And **YeHoVaH** regretted that He had made man on the earth, and it grieved Him at His heart. *7* And **YeHoVaH** said: 'I will blot out man whom I have created from the face of the earth; both man, and animal, and creeping things, and birds of the air; for I regret that I have made them.' *8* But **Noah** found grace in the eyes of **YeHoVaH**.

Reading 1 ends

Reading 2 begins

9 These are the generations of Noah. Noah was in his generations a man righteous and wholehearted; Noah walked with **YeHoVaH**. *10* And Noah fathered three sons, Shem, Ham, and Japheth.

11 And the earth was corrupt before **Elohim**, and the earth was filled with violence. *12* And **YeHoVaH** saw the earth, and, behold, it was corrupt; for all flesh had corrupted their way upon the earth. *13* And **YeHoVaH** said to Noah: 'The end of all flesh is come before Me; for the earth is filled with violence through them; and, behold, I will destroy them with the earth. *14* Make you an ark of gopher wood; with rooms, and you shall cover it within and without with pitch (tar-like substance). *15* And this is how you shall make it: the length of the ark is to be 300 cubits (approximately the length from a man's finger tips to his elbo), the breadth of it 50 cubits, and the height of it 30 cubits. *16* A light shall you make to the ark, and to a cubit shall you finish it upward; and the door of the ark shall you set in the side thereof; with lower, second, and third stories shall you make it. *17* And I, behold, I do bring the flood of waters upon the earth, to destroy all flesh, wherein is the breath of life, from under heaven; everything that is in the earth shall perish. *18* But I will establish My covenant with you; and you shall come into the ark, you, and your sons, and your wife, and your sons' wives with you. *19* And of every living thing of all flesh, two of every sort shall you bring into the ark, to keep them alive with you; they shall be male and female. *20* Of the birds after their kind, and of the cattle after their kind, of every creeping thing of the ground after its kind, two of every sort shall come to you, to keep them alive.

21 And take of all food that is eaten, and gather it to you; and it shall be for food for you, and for them.' *22* Thus Noah did; according to all that **Elohim** commanded him.

Chapter 7

Noah takes his family into the ark along with two/seven of each creature. The waters prevailed upon the earth a hundred and fifty days.

1 And **YeHoVaH** said to Noah: 'Come you and all your family into the ark; for you have I seen righteous before Me in this generation. *2* Of every **clean** beast you shall take to you **seven** and

seven, each with his mate; and of the beasts that are *not clean* **two** and **two**, each with his mate; *3* of the birds also of the air, **seven** and **seven**, male and female; to keep offspring alive upon the face of all the earth. *4* For yet seven days, and I will cause it to rain upon the earth forty days and forty nights; and every living substance that I have made will I blot out from off the face of the earth.' *5* And Noah did according to all that *YeHoVaH* commanded him. *6* And Noah was 600 years old when the flood of waters was upon the earth. *7* And Noah went in, and his sons, and his wife, and his sons' wives with him, into the ark, because of the waters of the flood. *8* Of clean beasts, and of beasts that are not clean, and of fowls, and of everything that creeps upon the ground, *9* there went in two and two and seven and seven to Noah into the ark, male and female, as *YeHoVaH* commanded Noah. *10* And it came to pass after the seven days that the waters of the flood were upon the earth.

11 In the six hundredth year of Noah's life, in the second month, on the 17th day of the month, on the same day were all the fountains of the great deep broken up, and the windows of heaven were opened. *12* And the rain was upon the earth forty days and forty nights. *13* In the same day entered Noah, and Shem, and Ham, and Japheth, the sons of Noah, and Noah's wife, and the three wives of his sons with them, into the ark; *14* they, and every beast after its kind, and all the cattle after their kind, and every creeping thing that creeps upon the earth after its kind, and every fowl after its kind, every bird of every sort. *15* And they went with Noah into the ark, two and two and seven and seven, of all flesh wherein is the breath of life. *16* And they that went in, went in male and female of all flesh, as *Elohim* commanded him; and *YeHoVaH* shut him in. *17* And the flood was forty days upon the earth; and the waters increased, and bore up the ark, and it was lifted up above the earth. *18* And the waters prevailed, and increased greatly upon the earth; and the ark went upon the face of the waters. *19* And the waters prevailed exceedingly upon the earth; and all the high mountains that were under the whole heaven were covered. *20* Fifteen cubits upward did the waters prevail; 15 cubits (22.5 ft. – 26.25 ft.) higher than the mountains.

21 And all flesh perished that moved upon the earth, both bird, and cattle, and beast, and every swarming thing that swarms upon the earth, and every man; *22* all in whose nostrils was the breath of the spirit of life, whatsoever was in the dry land, died. *23* And He blotted out every living substance which was upon the face of the ground, both man, and cattle, and creeping thing, and bird of the heaven; and they were blotted out from the earth; and Noah only was left, and they that were with him in the ark. *24* And the waters prevailed upon the earth 150 days (4.5 months).

Chapter 8
The rains stop. Noah sends out a raven and two doves. When the earth dries up YeHoVaH calls them out of the ark and Noah built an altar for sacrifice. YeHoVaH promises never to destroy all the earth by water again.

1 And *Elohim* remembered Noah, and every living thing, and all the animals that were with him in the ark; and *Elohim* made a wind to pass over the earth, and the waters subsided; *2* the fountains also of the deep and the windows of heaven were stopped, and the rain from heaven was restrained. *3* And the waters returned from off the earth continually; and after the end of a hundred and fifty days the waters decreased. *4* And the ark rested in the seventh month, on the seventeenth day of the month, upon the mountains of Ararat. *5* And the waters decreased continually until the tenth month; in the tenth month, on the first day of the month, were the tops of the mountains seen. *6* And it came to pass at the end of forty days, that Noah opened the window of the ark that he had made. *7* And he sent forth a *raven*, and it went forth to and fro, until the waters were dried up from off the earth. *8* And he sent forth a dove from him, to see if the waters were subsided from off the face of the ground. *9* But the dove found no rest for the sole of her foot, and she returned to him to the ark, for the waters were on the face of the whole earth; and he put forth his hand, and took her, and brought her in to him into the ark. *10* And he stayed yet another seven days; and again he sent forth the dove out of the ark.

11 And the dove came in to him at evening; and in her mouth was an olive-leaf freshly plucked; so Noah knew that the waters were decreased from off the earth. *12* And he stayed yet another seven days; and sent forth the dove; and she returned not again to him anymore. *13* And it came to pass in the six hundred and first year, in the first month, the first day of the month, the waters were dried up from off the earth; and Noah removed the covering of the ark, and looked, and behold, the face of the ground was dried. *14* And in the second month, on the seventh and twentieth day of the month, was the earth dry. *15* And **Elohim** spoke to Noah, saying: *16* 'Go forth from the ark, you, and your wife, and your sons, and your sons' wives with you. *17* Bring forth with you every living thing that is with you of all flesh, both bird, and cattle, and every creeping thing that creeps upon the earth; that they may swarm in the earth, and be fruitful, and multiply upon the earth.' *18* And Noah went forth, and his sons, and his wife, and his sons' wives with him; *19* every beast, every creeping thing, and every bird, whatsoever moves upon the earth, after their families; went forth out of the ark. *20* And Noah built an altar to **YeHoVaH**; and took of every **clean** beast, and of every **clean** bird, and offered burnt offerings on the altar.

21 And **YeHoVaH** smelled the sweet savor; and **YeHoVaH** said in His heart: 'I will not again curse the ground any more for man's sake; for the imagination of man's heart is evil from his youth; neither will I again destroy any more of everything living, as I have done. *22* While the earth remains, seedtime and harvest, and cold and heat, and summer and winter, and day and night shall not cease.'

Chapter 9
YeHoVaH blesses Noah and tells him to be fruitful and multiply. YeHoVaH establishes a covenant with Noah and every living creature, for perpetual generations.

1 And **Elohim** blessed Noah and his sons, and said to them: 'Be fruitful and multiply, and replenish the earth. *2* And the fear of you will be strong and shall be upon every beast of the earth, and upon every bird of the air, and upon all the fishes of the sea: into your hand are they delivered. *3* Every moving thing that lives shall be for food for you; as the green plants have I given you all. *4* Only flesh with the life thereof, which is the blood thereof, shall you **not** eat. *5* And surely your blood of your lives will I require; at the hand of every beast will I require it; and at the hand of man, even at the hand of every man's brother, will I require the life of man. *6* Whoever sheds man's blood, by man shall his blood be shed; for in the image of **YeHoVaH** he made man. *7* And you, be you fruitful, and multiply; swarm in the earth, and multiply therein.' *8* And **Elohim** spoke to Noah, and to his sons with him, saying: *9* 'As for Me, behold, **I establish My covenant with you**, and with **your offspring** after you; *10* and with every living creature that is with you, the birds, the cattle, and every beast of the earth with you; of all that go out of the ark, even every beast of the earth.

11 And I will establish My covenant with you; neither shall all flesh be cut off any more by the waters of the flood; neither shall there anymore be a flood to destroy the earth.' *12* And **Elohim** said: 'This is the token of the covenant which I make between Me and you and every living creature that is with you, for **perpetual** generations: *13* I have set My rainbow in the cloud, and it shall be for a token of a covenant between Me and the earth. *14* And it shall come to pass, when I bring clouds over the earth, and the rainbow is seen in the cloud, *15* that I will remember My covenant, which is between Me and you and every living creature of all flesh; and the waters *shall no more become a flood to destroy all flesh*. *16* And the rainbow shall be in the cloud; and I will look upon it, that I may remember the everlasting covenant between *Elohim* and every living creature of all flesh that is upon the earth.' *17* And *Elohim* said to Noah: 'This is the token of the covenant which I have established between Me and all flesh that is upon the earth.' *18* And the sons of Noah, that went forth from the ark, were Shem, Ham, and Japheth; and Ham is the father of Canaan. *19* These three were the sons of Noah, and of these was the whole earth covered. *20* And Noah the cultivator (husbandman) began, and planted a vineyard.

21 And he drank of the wine, and was drunk; and he was uncovered within his tent. *22* And Ham, the father of **Canaan**, saw the nakedness of his father, and told his two brethren outside. *23* And Shem and Japheth took a garment, and laid it upon both their shoulders, and went backward, and covered the nakedness of their father; and their faces were backward, and they saw not their father's nakedness. *24* And Noah awoke from his wine, and *knew what his youngest son had done to him*. *25* And he said: Cursed be Canaan; a servant of servants shall he be to his brethren. *26* And he said: Blessed be *YeHoVaH,* the *Elohim* of Shem; and let Canaan be their servant. *27* May *Elohim* enlarge Japheth, and he shall dwell in the tents of Shem; and let Canaan be their servant. *28* And Noah lived after the flood 350 years. *29* And all the days of Noah were 950 years; and he died.

Chapter 10
The generations of Noah and his sons.

1 Now these are the generations of the sons of Noah: Shem, Ham, and Japheth; and to them were sons born after the flood. *2* The sons of Japheth: Gomer, and Magog, and Madai, and Javan, and Tubal, and Meshech, and Tiras. *3* And the sons of Gomer: Ashkenaz, and Riphath, and Togarmah. *4* And the sons of Javan: Elishah, and Tarshish, Kittim, and Dodanim. *5* Of these were the isles of the nations divided in their lands, every one after his language, after their families, in their nations. *6* And the sons of Ham: Cush, and Mizraim, and Put, and Canaan. *7* And the sons of Cush: Seba, and Havilah, and Sabtah, and Raamah, and Sabteca; and the sons of Raamah: Sheba, and Dedan. *8* And Cush fathered **Nimrod**; he began to be a mighty one in the earth. *9* He was a mighty hunter before *YeHoVaH*; where it is said: 'Like Nimrod a mighty hunter before *YeHoVaH*.' *10* And the beginning of his kingdom was Babel, and Erech, and Accad, and Calneh, in the land of Shinar.

11 Out of that land went forth Asshur, and built Nineveh, and Rehoboth-ir, and Calah, *12* and Resen between Nineveh and Calah--the same is the great city. *13* And Mizraim fathered Ludim, and Anamim, and Lehabim, and Naphtuhim, *14* and Pathrusim, and Casluhim-- which went forth the Philistines--and Caphtorim. *15* And Canaan fathered Zidon his firstborn, and Heth; *16* and the Jebusite, and the Amorite, and the Girgashite; *17* and the Hivite, and the Arkite, and the Sinite; *18* and the Arvadite, and the Zemarite, and the Hamathite; and afterward were the families of the Canaanite spread abroad. *19* And the border of the Canaanite was from Zidon, as you go toward Gerar, to Gaza; as you go toward **Sodom and Gomorrah** and Admah and Zeboiim, to Lasha. *20* These are the sons of Ham, after their families, after their language, in their lands, in their nations.

GENESIS

21 And to Shem, the father of all the children of Eber, the elder brother of Japheth, to him also were children born. 22 The sons of Shem: Elam, and Asshur, and Arpachshad, and Lud, and Aram. 23 And the sons of Aram: Uz, and Hul, and Gether, and Mash. 24 And Arpachshad fathered Shelah; and Shelah fathered Eber. 25 And to Eber were born two sons; the name of the one was Peleg; for in his days was the earth divided; and his brother's name was Joktan. 26 And Joktan fathered Almodad, and Sheleph, and Hazarmaveth, and Jerah; 27 and Hadoram, and Uzal, and Diklah; 28 and Obal, and Abimael, and Sheba; 29 and Ophir, and Havilah, and Jobab; all these were the sons of Joktan. 30 And their dwelling was from Mesha, as you go toward Sephar, to the mountain of the east.

31 These are the sons of Shem, after their families, after their language, in their lands, after their nations. 32 These are the families of the sons of Noah, after their generations, in their nations; and of these were the nations divided in the earth after the flood.

CHAPTERS 11- 20

Chapter 11
Man decides to build a great tower to reach heaven. YeHoVaH is displeased and confuses their language so they cannot work. Shem's line includes Abram who married Sarai.

1 And the whole earth was of one language and of one speech. 2 And it came to pass, as they journeyed east, that they found a plain in the land of Shinar; and they dwelt there. 3 And they said one to another: 'Come, let us make brick, and burn them thoroughly.' And they had brick for stone, and slime for mortar. 4 And they said: 'Come, let us build a city, and a tower, with its top in heaven, and let us make us a name; if we be scattered abroad upon the face of the whole earth.' 5 And **YeHoVaH** came down to see the city and the tower, which the children of men built. 6 And **YeHoVaH** said: 'Behold, they are one people, and they have all one language; and this is what they begin to do; and now nothing will be withheld from them, which they try to do. 7 Come, let **us** go down, and confuse their language, that they may not understand one another's speech.' 8 So **YeHoVaH** scattered them abroad from there upon the face of all the earth; and they stopped building the city. 9 Therefore the name of it was called **Babel**; because **YeHoVaH** did confuse the language of all the earth; and from then on **YeHoVaH** scattered them abroad upon the face of all the earth. 10 These are the generations of Shem. Shem was 100 years old, and fathered Arpachshad two years after the flood.

11 And Shem lived after he fathered Arpachshad 500 years, and fathered sons and daughters. 12 And Arpachshad lived 35 years, and fathered Shelah. 13 And Arpachshad lived after he fathered Shelah 403 years, and fathered sons and daughters. 14 And Shelah lived 30 years, and fathered Eber. 15 And Shelah lived after he fathered Eber 403 years, and fathered sons and daughters. 16 And Eber lived 34 years, and fathered Peleg. 17 And Eber lived after he fathered Peleg 430 years, and fathered sons and daughters. 18 And Peleg lived 30 years, and fathered Reu. 19 And Peleg lived after he fathered Reu 209 years, and fathered sons and daughters. 20 And Reu lived 32 years, and fathered Serug.

21 And Reu lived after he fathered Serug 207 years, and fathered sons and daughters. *22* And Serug lived 30 years, and fathered Nahor. *23* And Serug lived after he fathered Nahor 200 years, and fathered sons and daughters. *24* And Nahor lived 29 years, and fathered Terah. *25* And Nahor lived after he fathered Terah at 119 years, and fathered sons and daughters. *26* And Terah lived 70 years, and fathered **Abram**, Nahor, and Haran. *27* Now these are the generations of Terah. Terah fathered **Abram**, Nahor, and Haran; and Haran fathered **Lot**. *28* And Haran died in the presence of his father Terah in the land of his nativity, in Ur of the Chaldees. *29* And **Abram** and Nahor took wives: the name of Abram's wife was **Sarai**; and the name of Nahor's wife, Milcah, the daughter of Haran, the father of Milcah, and the father of Iscah. *30* And Sarai was barren; she had no child.

31 And Terah took Abram his son, and Lot the son of Haran, his son's son, and Sarai his daughter-in-law, his son Abram's wife; and they went forth with them from Ur of the Chaldees, to go into the land of Canaan; and they came to Haran, and dwelt there. *32* And the days of Terah were 205 years; and Terah died in Haran.
  Reading 2 ends

Chapter 12

YeHoVaH tells Abram that He will make him a great nation. In Egypt Abram lies about Sarai being his sister and Pharaoh is cursed because of it.
  Reading 3 begins
1 Now **YeHoVaH** said to Abram: 'Get out of your country, and from your kindred, and from your father's house, to the land that I will show you. *2* And I will make of you a great nation, and I will bless you, and make your name great; and you will be a blessing. *3* And I will *bless them that bless you, and him that curses you will I curse*; and in you shall all the families of the earth be blessed.' *4* So Abram went, as **YeHoVaH** had spoken to him; and **Lot** went with him; and Abram was 75 years old when he departed out of Haran. *5* And Abram took Sarai his wife, and Lot *his brother's son*, and all their property that they had gathered, and the people that they had gotten in Haran; and they went forth to go into the land of Canaan; and into the land of Canaan they came. *6* And Abram passed through the land to the place of Shechem, to the trees of Moreh. And the Canaanite was then in the land. *7* And **YeHoVaH** appeared to Abram, and said: 'To your offspring will I give this land'; and he built there an altar to **YeHoVaH**, who appeared to him. *8* And he went from there to the mountain on the east of Beth-el, and pitched his tent, having Beth-el on the west, and Ai on the east; and he built there an altar to **YeHoVaH**, and called upon the name of **YeHoVaH**. *9* And Abram journeyed, going on still toward the South. *10* And there was a famine in the land; and Abram went down into Egypt to stay (sojourn) there; for the famine was severe in the land.

11 And it came to pass, when he came near to enter into Egypt that he said to Sarai his wife: 'Behold now, I know that you are a fair woman to look upon. *12* And it will come to pass, when the Egyptians shall see you that they will say: This is his wife; and they will kill me, but you they will keep alive. *13* Say, I pray you, you are my sister; that it may be well with me for your sake, and that my soul may live because of you.' *14* And it came to pass, that, when Abram came into Egypt, the Egyptians beheld the woman that she was very fair. *15* And the princes of Pharaoh saw her, and praised her to Pharaoh; and the woman was taken into Pharaoh's house. *16* And he dealt well with Abram for her sake; and he had sheep, and oxen, and he-donkeys, and men-servants, and maidservants, and she-donkeys, and camels. *17* And **YeHoVaH** plagued Pharaoh and his house with great plagues because of Sarai, Abram's wife. *18* And Pharaoh called

Abram, and said: 'What is this that you have done to me? Why did you not tell me that she was your wife? *19* Why did you say: She is my sister? so that I took her to be my wife; now therefore behold your wife, take her, and go your way.' *20* And Pharaoh gave men charge concerning him; and they sent him on the way, and his wife, and all that he had.

Chapter 13
Abram travels with his nephew Lot. They decide to go their separate ways so Lot goes to Sodom, and Abram to Canaan. YeHoVaH promises all the land to him and his offspring forever.

1 And Abram went up out of Egypt, he, and his wife, and all that he had, and Lot with him, into the south. *2* And Abram was very rich in cattle, in silver, and in gold. *3* And he went on his journeys from the South even to Beth-el, to the place where his tent had been at the beginning, between Beth-el and Ai; *4* to the place of the altar, which he had made there at the first; and Abram called there on the name of **YeHoVaH**. *5* And Lot also, who went with Abram, had flocks, and herds, and tents. *6* And the land was not able to bear them that they might dwell together; for their property and belongings were great, so that they could not dwell together. *7* And there was strife between the herdsmen of Abram's cattle and the herdsmen of Lot's cattle. And the Canaanite and the Perizzite dwelt then in the land. *8* And Abram said to Lot: 'Let there be no strife, I pray thee, between me and thee, and between my herdsmen and your herdsmen; for we are brethren. *9* Is not the whole land before thee? separate thyself, I pray thee, from me; if you will take the left hand, then I will go to the right; or if you take the right hand, then I will go to the left.' *10* And Lot lifted up his eyes, and beheld all the plain of the Jordan, that it was well watered everywhere, before **YeHoVaH** destroyed Sodom and Gomorrah, like the garden of **YeHoVaH**, like the land of Egypt, as you go to Zoar.

11 So Lot chose all the plain of the Jordan; and Lot journeyed east; and they separated themselves the one from the other. *12* Abram dwelt in the land of Canaan, and Lot dwelt in the cities of the Plain, and moved his tent as far as Sodom. *13* Now the men of Sodom were wicked and sinners against **YeHoVaH** exceedingly. *14* And **YeHoVaH** said to Abram, after that Lot was separated from him: 'Lift up now your eyes, and look from the place where you are, northward and southward and eastward and westward; *15* for all the land which you see, to you will I give it, and to your offspring forever. *16* And I will make your seed as the dust of the earth; so that if a man can number the dust of the earth, then shall your seed also be numbered. *17* Arise, walk through the land in the length of it and in the breadth of it; for to thee will I give it.' *18* And Abram moved his tent, and came and dwelt by the cashew trees (terebinths) of Mamre, which are in Hebron, and built there an altar to **YeHoVaH**.

Chapter 14
The kings go to war and take Lot captive. Abram rescues Lot. Melchizedek blesses Abram and gives him a tenth of everything he had taken.

1 And it came to pass in the days of Amraphel king of Shinar, Arioch king of Ellasar, Chedorlaomer king of Elam, and Tidal king of Goiim, *2* that they made war with Bera king of **Sodom**, and with Birsha king of **Gomorrah**, Shinab king of Admah, and Shemeber king of Zeboiim, and the king of Bela--the same is Zoar. *3* All these came as allies to the vale of Siddim-which is the same as the Salt Sea. *4* 12 years they served Chedorlaomer, and in the 13th year they rebelled. *5* And in the 14th year came Chedorlaomer and the kings that were with him, and killed the Rephaim in Ashteroth-karnaim, and the Zuzim in Ham, and the Emim in

GENESIS

Shaveh-kiriathaim, *6* and the Horites in their mount Seir, to El-paran, which is by the wilderness. *7* And they turned back, and came to En-mishpat—which is the same as Kadesh-- and destroyed all the country of the Amalekites, and also the Amorites, that dwelt in Hazazon-tamar. *8* And there went out the king of Sodom, and the king of Gomorrah, and the king of Admah, and the king of Zeboiim, and the king of Bela--the same is Zoar; and they set the battle in array against them in the vale of Siddim; *9* against Chedorlaomer king of Elam, and Tidal king of Goiim, and Amraphel king of Shinar, and Arioch king of Ellasar; four kings against the five. *10* Now the vale of Siddim was full of slime pits; and the kings of Sodom and Gomorrah fled, and they fell there, and they that remained fled to the mountain.

11 And they took all the goods of Sodom and Gomorrah, and all their provisions (victuals), and went their way. *12* And they took Lot, Abram's brother's son, who dwelt in Sodom, and his goods, and departed. *13* And there came one that had escaped, and told Abram the Hebrew-- now he dwelt in the plains of Mamre the Amorite, brother of Eshcol, and brother of Aner; and these were allies with Abram. *14* And when Abram heard that his nephew was taken captive, he led forth his 318 trained men, born in his house, and pursued as far as Dan. *15* And he divided himself against them by night, he and his servants, and killed them, and pursued them to Hobah, which is on the left hand of Damascus. *16* And he brought back all the goods, and also brought back his nephew Lot, and his goods, and the women also, and the people. *17* And the king of Sodom went out to meet him, after his return from the slaughter of Chedorlaomer and the kings that were with him, at the vale of Shaveh--the same is the King's Vale. *18* And **Melchizedek** king of Salem brought forth bread and wine; and he was priest of ***Elohim*** the Most High. *19* And he blessed him, and said: 'Blessed be Abram of ***Elohim*** Most High, Maker of heaven and earth; *20* and blessed be ***YeHoVaH*** the Most High, who has delivered your enemies into your hand.' And he (Melchizedek) gave him (Abram) a **tenth** of all he had taken. (This is often misread that Abram gave Melchizedek 10% but it was the other way around)

21 And the king of Sodom said to Abram: 'Give me the people, and take the goods to yourself.' *22* And Abram said to the king of Sodom: 'I have lifted up my hand to ***YeHoVaH Elohim*** Most High, maker of heaven and earth, *23* that I will not take a thread nor a sandal strap nor nothing that is yours, lest you should say: I have made Abram rich; *24* save only that which the young men have eaten, and the portion of the men which went with me, Aner, Eshcol, and Mamre, let them take their portion.'

Chapter 15
YeHoVaH promises Abram an heir and countless descendants. Abram doubts and asks how he will know he will inherit it so YeHoVaH gives him a sign.

1 After these things the word of ***YeHoVaH*** came to Abram in a vision, saying: 'Fear not, Abram, I am your shield, your reward shall be exceedingly great.' *2* And Abram said: 'O ***Adonai YeHoVaH***, what will You give me, seeing I go childless, and he that shall be possessor of my house is Eliezer of Damascus?' *3* And Abram said: 'Behold, to me You have given no offspring, and, one born in my house is to be my heir.' *4* And, behold, the word of ***YeHoVaH*** came to him, saying: 'This man shall not be my heir; but he that shall come forth out of my own bowels shall be my heir.' *5* And He brought him forth outside, and said: 'Look now toward heaven, and count the stars, if you be able to count them'; and He said to him: 'So shall your offspring be.' *6* And he believed in ***YeHoVaH***; and He credited it to him for righteousness. *7* And He said to him: 'I am ***YeHoVaH*** that brought you out of Ur of the Chaldees, to give you this land to inherit it.'

8 And he said: 'O **Adonai Elohim**, whereby shall I know that I shall inherit it?' *9* And He said to him: 'Take Me a heifer of three years old, and a she-goat of three years old, and a ram of three years old, and a turtle-dove, and a young pigeon.' *10* And he took him all these, and divided them in the midst, and laid each half over against the other; but the birds he did not divide.

11 And the birds of prey came down upon the carcasses, and Abram drove them away. *12* And it came to pass, that, when the sun was going down, a deep sleep fell upon Abram; and a dread, even a great darkness, fell upon him. *13* And He said to Abram: 'Know for certain that your offspring shall be a stranger in a land that is not theirs, and shall serve them; and they shall afflict them 400 years; *14* and also that nation, whom they shall serve, will I judge; and afterward shall they come out with great things. (The Exodus) *15* But you shall go to your fathers in peace; you shall be buried in a good old age. *16* And in the fourth generation they shall come back here; for the iniquity of the Amorite is not yet full.' *17* And it came to pass, that, when the sun went down, and there was thick darkness, behold a smoking furnace, and a flaming torch that passed between these pieces. *18* In that day **YeHoVaH** made a covenant with Abram, saying: 'To your offspring (heirs) have I given this land, from the river of Egypt to the great river, the river Euphrates; *19* the Kenite, and the Kenizzite, and the Kadmonite, *20* and the Hittite, and the Perizzite, and the Rephaim,

21 the Amorite, the Canaanite, the Girgashite, and the Jebusite.'

Chapter 16
Sarai tells Abram to have a child with Hagar. After Hagar conceives she runs away, but an angel sends her back. Abram calls the name of his son, whom Hagar bore, Ishmael

1 Now Sarai, Abram's wife bore him no children; and she had a handmaid, an Egyptian, whose name was **Hagar**. *2* And Sarai said to Abram: 'Behold now, **YeHoVaH** has restrained me from bearing children; go in, I pray you, have relations with my handmaid; so it may be that I shall be built up through her.' And Abram hearkened to the voice of Sarai. *3* And Sarai, Abram's wife took Hagar the Egyptian, her handmaid, after Abram had dwelt ten years in the land of Canaan, and gave her to Abram her husband to be his wife. *4* And he had relations with Hagar, and she conceived; and when Hagar saw that she had conceived, her mistress was despised in her eyes. *5* And Sarai said to Abram: "May the wrong done to me be upon you!: I gave my handmaid into your bosom; and when she saw that she had conceived, I was despised in her eyes: **YeHoVaH** judge between me and you.' *6* But Abram said to Sarai: 'Behold, your maid is in your hand; do to her that which is good in your eyes.' And Sarai dealt harshly with her, and she fled from her face. *7* And the messenger of **YeHoVaH** found her by a fountain of water in the wilderness, by the fountain in the way to Shur. *8* And he said: 'Hagar, Sarai's handmaid, where have you come from? and where do you go?' And she said: 'I flee from the face of my mistress Sarai.' *9* And the messenger of **YeHoVaH** said to her: 'Return to your mistress, and submit yourself under her hands.' *10* And the messenger of **YeHoVaH** said to her: 'I will greatly multiply your offspring (heirs), that it may not be numbered.

11 And the messenger of **YeHoVaH** said to her: 'Behold, you are with child, and shall bear a son; and you shall call his name **Ishmael**, because **YeHoVaH** has heard your suffering. *12* And he shall be a wild man: his hand shall be against every man, and every man's hand against him; and he shall dwell in the face of all his brothers.' *13* And she called the name of **YeHoVaH** that spoke to her; You are El-roi (god) of seeing; for she said: 'Have I even seen Him that sees

Me?' *14* Therefore the well was called 'Beer-lahai-roi; behold, it is between Kadesh and Bered. *15* And Hagar bore Abram a son; and Abram called the name of his son, whom Hagar bore, Ishmael. *16* And Abram was 86 years old, when Hagar bore Ishmael to Abram.

Chapter 17

YeHoVaH made a covenant with Abram and renamed him Abraham and renamed Sarai, Sarah and promised them a son. All the men were circumcised.

1 And when Abram was 99 years old, **YeHoVaH** appeared to him and said: 'I am **El Shaddi** (God Almighty); walk before Me, and be blameless. *2* And I will make My covenant between Me and you, and will multiply you exceedingly.' *3* And Abram fell on his face; and **Elohim** talked with him, saying: *4* 'As for Me, behold, My covenant is with you, and you shall be the father of a multitude of nations. *5* *Neither shall your name any more be called Abram, but your name shall be* **Abraham**; for the father of a multitude of nations have I made you. *6* And I will make you exceeding fruitful, and I will make nations of you, and kings shall come out of you. *7* And I will establish My covenant between Me and you and your heirs after you throughout their generations for an ***everlasting*** covenant, to be **Elohim** to you and to your offspring after you. *8* And I will give to you, and to your offspring after you, the land of your wanderings, all the land of Canaan, for an everlasting possession; and I will be their **Elohim**.' *9* And **Elohim** said to Abraham: 'And as for you, you shall keep My covenant, you, and **your offspring** after you **throughout their generations**. *10* This is My covenant, which you shall keep, between Me and you and your offspring after you: every male among you shall be **circumcised**.

11 And you shall be circumcised in the flesh of your foreskin; and it shall be a token of a covenant between Me and you. *12* And he that is **eight days old** shall be circumcised among you, **every male throughout your generations**, he that is born in the house, or bought with money of any foreigner, that is not of your offspring. *13* He that is born in your house, and he that is bought with your money, **must be circumcised**; and My covenant shall be in your flesh for an **everlasting** covenant. *14* And the uncircumcised male who is *not circumcised* in the flesh of his foreskin, **that soul shall be cut off from his people***;* he has broken My covenant.' *15* And **Elohim** said to Abraham: 'As for Sarai your wife, you shall not call her name Sarai, but **Sarah** shall her name be. *16* And I will bless her, and moreover I will give you a son by her; I will bless her, and she shall be a mother of nations; kings of peoples shall be of her.' *17* Then Abraham fell upon his face, and *laughed*, and said in his heart: 'Shall a child be born to him that is 100 years old? and shall Sarah, that is 90 years old, bear a child?' *18* And Abraham said to **Elohim**: 'Oh that Ishmael might live before You!' *19* And **Elohim** said: "No, but Sarah your wife shall bear you a son; and you shall call his name **Isaac**; and I will establish My covenant with him for an **everlasting** covenant for his offspring after him. *20* And as for Ishmael, I have heard you; behold, I have blessed him, and will make him fruitful, and will multiply him exceedingly; twelve princes shall he produce, and I will make him a great nation.

21 But My covenant will I establish with Isaac, whom Sarah shall bear to you at this set time next year.' *22* And He left off talking with him, and **Elohim** went up from Abraham. *23* And Abraham took Ishmael his son, and all that were born in his house, and all that were bought with his money, every male among the men of Abraham's house, and circumcised the flesh of their foreskin in the same day, as **Elohim** had said to him. *24* And Abraham was 99 years old, when he was circumcised in the flesh of his foreskin. *25* And Ishmael his son was 13 years old, when he was circumcised in the flesh of his foreskin. *26* In the same day was Abraham

circumcised, and Ishmael his son. *27* And all the men of his house, those born in the house, and those bought with money of a foreigner, were circumcised with him.
Reading 3 ends

Chapter 18

Three messengers (angels) come and say that Sarah would have a son next year. YeHoVaH says that Sodom is very evil and will be destroyed; Abraham pleads for the righteous in the city.
Reading 4 begins

1 And **YeHoVaH** appeared to him (through the messengers) by the trees (terebinths) of Mamre, as he sat in the tent door in the heat of the day; *2* and he lifted up his eyes and looked, and, behold, three **men** (*messengers/angels*) stood over near him; and when he saw them, he ran to meet them from the tent door, and bowed down to the earth, *3* and said: 'My lord, if now I have found favor in your sight, do not pass by me, I pray you, from your servant. *4* Let now a little water be fetched, and wash your feet, and recline under the tree. *5* And I will fetch a morsel of bread, and stay you your heart; after that you shall pass on; since you have come to your servant.' And they said: 'So do, as you have said.' *6* And Abraham hastened into the tent to Sarah, and said: 'Make ready quickly three measures of fine meal, knead it, and make cakes.' *7* And Abraham ran to the herd, and fetched a calf tender and good, and gave it to the servant; and he hastened to prepare it. *8* And he *took **curd, and milk, and the calf** that he had prepared, and set it before them; and he stood by them under the tree, and **they did eat**. (they **did** eat milk and meat **together**) *9* And they said to him: 'Where is Sarah your wife?' And he said: 'Behold, in the tent.' *10* And He said: 'I will certainly return to you when the season comes round; and, you will see, Sarah your wife shall have a son.' And Sarah heard in the tent door, which was behind him.

11 Now Abraham and Sarah were old, and well up in age; and Sarah had long ago ceased having menstrual cycles of woman. *12* And Sarah laughed within herself, saying: 'After I am grown old shall I have pleasure, my lord being old also?' *13* And **YeHoVaH** said to Abraham, *through the men*: 'Why did Sarah laugh, saying: Shall it be known in advance that I bear a child, I who am old? *14* And He said, 'Is anything too hard for **YeHoVaH**. At the set time I will return to you, when the season comes round, and Sarah shall have a son.' *15* Then Sarah denied, saying: 'I laughed not'; for she was afraid. And He said: 'Nay; but you did laugh.' *16* And the men rose up from there, and looked out toward Sodom; and Abraham went with them to bring them on the way. *17* And **YeHoVaH** said: 'Shall I hide from Abraham that which I am doing; *18* seeing that Abraham shall surely become a great and mighty nation, and all the nations of the earth shall be blessed in him? *19* For I have known him, to the end that he may command his children and his household after him, that they may keep the way of **YeHoVaH**, to do righteousness and justice; to the end that **YeHoVaH** may bring upon Abraham that which He has spoken of him.' *20* And **YeHoVaH** said: 'certainly, the cry of Sodom and Gomorrah is great, and, truly (verily), their sin is exceeding grievous.

21 I will go down now, and see whether their acts are as bad as the outcry against it, which has come to Me; and if not, I will know.' *22* And the (two) men turned from there, and went toward Sodom; but Abraham stood yet before **YeHoVaH**. *23* And Abraham drew near, and said: 'Will you indeed sweep away the righteous with the wicked? *24* If possibly there are 50 righteous within the city; will You indeed sweep away and not forgive the place for the 50 righteous that are therein? *25* That be far from You to do after this manner, to slay the righteous with the wicked, that so the righteous should be as the wicked; that be far from You; shall not the judge of all the earth do justly?' **26** And **YeHoVaH** said: 'If I find in Sodom 50 righteous within the city, then I will forgive all the place for their sake.' **27** And Abraham answered and said: 'Behold now, I have taken upon me to speak to Adonai, who is but dust and ashes. **28** If possibly there shall lack 45 of the 50 righteous; will You destroy all the city for lack of 45?' And He said: 'I will not destroy it, if I find there 45.' **29** And he spoke to Him yet again, and said: If possibly there shall be 40 found there.' And He said: 'I will not do it for the 40's sake.' **30** And he said: 'Oh, let not **YeHoVaH** be angry, and I will speak. If possibly there shall 30 be found there.' And He said: 'I will not do it, if I find 30 there.'

31 And he said: 'Behold now, I have taken upon me to speak to Adonai. If possibly there shall be 20 found there.' And He said: 'I will not destroy it for the 20's sake.' **32** And he said: 'Oh, let not **Adonai** be angry, and I will speak yet but this once. If possibly 10 shall be found there.' And He said: 'I will not destroy it for the 10's sake.' **33** And **YeHoVaH** went His way, as soon as He had left off speaking to Abraham; and Abraham returned to his place.

Chapter 19
YeHoVaH's, Messengers/Angels take Lot and his family out of Sodom. The city is destroyed by fire and Lot's wife was turned to salt for looking back. His daughters decide to preserve offspring through their father.

1 And the two messengers (angels) came to Sodom at evening; and **Lot** sat in the gate of Sodom; and Lot saw them, and rose up to meet them; and he fell down on his face to the earth; **2** and he said: 'Behold now, my lords, come, I pray you, into your servant's house, and stay all night, and wash your feet, and you shall rise up early, and go on your way.' And they said: 'No; but we will abide in the open place all night.' **3** And he urged them greatly; and they turned to him, and entered his house; and Lot made them a feast, and did bake unleavened bread, and they did eat. **4** But before they lay down, the men of the city, even the men of Sodom, surrounded the house, both young and old, all the people from every quarter. **5** And they called to Lot, and said to him: 'Where are the men that came to you this night? Bring them out to us, that we may know them.' **6** And Lot went out to them at the door, and shut the door behind him. **7** And he said: 'I pray you, my brethren, do not do wickedly. **8** Behold now, I have two daughters that have not known man; let me, I pray you, bring them out to you, and do you to them as is good in your eyes; only to these men do nothing; for they come under the shadow of my roof.' **9** And they said: 'Stand back.' And they said: 'This one man came in to stay (sojourn), and he acts to play the judge; now will we deal worse with you, than with them.' And they pressed hard upon Lot, and drew near to break the door. **10** But the men inside put forth their hands, and brought Lot into the house to them, and they shut the door tightly.

11 And the men (angels) inside covered the men that were at the door of the house with blindness, both small and great; so that they strained themselves to find the door. **12** And the men (angels) said to Lot: 'Is there anyone here besides yourself? son-in-law, and your sons, and your daughters, and whomever you have in the city; bring them out of the place; **13** for **we** will destroy this place, because the cry of them is growing great before **YeHoVaH**; and **YeHoVaH** has sent **us** to destroy it.' **14** And Lot went out, and spoke to his sons-in-law, who married his daughters, and said: 'Get up and get out of this place; for **YeHoVaH** will destroy the city.' But he seemed to his sons-in-law as one that joked. **15** And when the morning arose, then the angels prepared Lot, saying: 'Arise, take your wife, and your two daughters that are here; or you will be swept away in the wickedness of the city.' **16** But he lingered; and the men laid hold upon his hand, and upon the hand of his wife, and upon the hand of his two daughters; **YeHoVaH** being merciful to him. And they brought him forth, and set him outside the city. **17** And it came to pass, when they had brought them out that he said: 'Escape for your life; look not behind you, neither stay in all the Plain; escape to the mountain, or you be swept away.' **18** And Lot said to them: 'Oh, not so, my lord; **19** behold now, your servant has found grace in your sight, and you have magnified your mercy, which you have shown to me in saving my life; and I cannot escape to the mountain, or the evil will overtake me, and I will die. **20** Behold now, this city is near to flee to, and it is a little one; oh, let me escape there …and my soul shall live.'

21 And he said to Lot: 'See, I have accepted you concerning this thing also, that I will not overthrow the city of which you have spoken. **22** Hurry, escape there; for I cannot do anything until you arrive there.' The name of the city was called Zoar. **23** The sun had risen upon the earth when Lot arrived at Zoar. **24** Then **YeHoVaH** caused to rain upon Sodom and upon Gomorrah brimstone and fire from **YeHoVaH** out of heaven; **25** and He overthrew those cities, and all the Plain, and all the inhabitants of the cities, and that which grew upon the ground. **26** But when leaving, Lot's wife looked back from behind him, and she became a pillar of salt. **27** And Abraham got up early in the morning to the place where he had stood before **YeHoVaH**. **28** And he looked out toward Sodom and Gomorrah, and toward all the land of the Plain, and beheld, and, the smoke of the land went up as the smoke of a furnace. **29** And it came to pass, when **Elohim** destroyed the cities of the Plain, that **YeHoVaH** remembered Abraham, and sent Lot out of the midst of the overthrow, when He overthrew the cities in which Lot dwelt. **30** And Lot went up out of Zoar, and dwelt in the mountain and his two daughters with him; for he feared to dwell in Zoar; so he dwelt in a cave, he and his two daughters.

31 And Lot's first-born daughter said to the younger: 'Our father is old, and there is not a man in the earth to be a husband in a natural way. **32** Come, let us make our father drink wine, and we will lie with him, that we may preserve offspring of our father.' **33** And they made their father drink wine that night. And the first-born went in, and lay with her father; and he was not aware when she lay down, nor when she arose. **34** And it came to pass the next day that the first-born said to the younger: 'Behold, I lay last night with our father. Let us make him drink wine this night also; and you go in, and lie with him, that we may preserve offspring of our father.' **35** And they made their father drink wine that night also. And the younger arose, and lay with him; and he knew not when she lay down, nor when she arose. **36** Thus both the daughters of **Lot** became *with child by their father*. **37** And the first-born bore a son, and called his name **Moab**-- the same is the father of the Moabites to this day. **38** And the younger, she also bore a son, and called his name **Ben-ammi**--the same is the father of the children of Ammon to this day.

Chapter 20
Abraham claims, "Sarah is my sister," in order to save his life. King Abimelech takes Sarah but YeHoVaH warns him in a dream so he restores Sarah to Abraham.

1 And Abraham journeyed from there toward the land of the South, and dwelt between Kadesh and Shur; and he stayed in Gerar. **2** And Abraham told everyone of Sarah his wife: 'She is my sister.' And Abimelech king of Gerar sent, and took Sarah. **3** But **Elohim** came to Abimelech in a dream of the night, and said to him: 'Behold, you shall die, because of the woman whom you have taken; for she is a man's wife.' **4** Now Abimelech had not come near her; and he said: 'Adonai, will You slay even a righteous nation? **5** Didn't he say to me: She is my sister? and she, even she herself said: He is my brother. In the simplicity of my heart and the innocence of my hands have I done this.' **6** And **Elohim** said to him in the dream: 'Yes, I know that in the simplicity of your heart you have done this, and I also withheld you from sinning against Me. Therefore I kept you from touching her. **7** Now therefore restore the man's wife; for he is a prophet, and he shall pray for you, and you shall live; and if you do not restore her, know that you shall surely die, you, and all that are yours.' **8** And Abimelech rose early in the morning, and called all his servants, and told all these things to them to hear; and the men became very afraid. **9** Then Abimelech called Abraham, and said to him: 'What have you done to us? and where have I sinned against you that you have brought on me and on my kingdom a great sin? You have done deeds to me that should not be done.' **10** And Abimelech said to Abraham: 'What did you see, that you have done this thing?'

11 And Abraham said: 'Because I thought: Surely the fear of **Elohim** is not in this place; and they will slay me for my wife's sake. **12** And moreover she **is indeed my sister**, the daughter of my father, but **not** the daughter of my mother; and so she became my wife. **13** And it came to pass, when **Elohim** caused me to wander from my father's house that I said to her: This is your kindness which you shall show to me; at every place where we shall come, say of me: He is my brother.' **14** And Abimelech took sheep and oxen, and men-servants and women-servants, and gave them to Abraham, and restored him Sarah his wife. **15** And Abimelech said: 'Behold, my land is before you: dwell where it pleases you.' **16** And to Sarah he said: 'Behold, I have given your brother a thousand pieces of silver; behold, it is for you a covering of the eyes to all that are with you; and before all men you are righted.' **17** And Abraham prayed to **Elohim**; and **Elohim** healed Abimelech, and his wife, and his maidservants; and they bore children. **18** For **YeHoVaH** had closed up all the wombs of the house of Abimelech, because of Sarah, Abraham's wife.

CHAPTERS 21- 30

Chapter 21
Sarah had a son as promised and named him Isaac. She has Hagar and Ishmael sent away but YeHoVaH guides them. A treaty is made by Abraham and Abimelec.

1 And **YeHoVaH** remembered Sarah as He had said, and **YeHoVaH** did to Sarah as He had spoken. **2** And Sarah conceived, and bore Abraham a son in his old age, at the set time of which **Elohim** had spoken to him. **3** And Abraham called the name of his son whom Sarah bore to him, **Isaac**. **4** And Abraham circumcised his son Isaac when he was eight days old, as **Elohim** had commanded him. **5** And Abraham was 100 years old, when his son Isaac was born to him. **6** And Sarah said: **Elohim** has made laughter for me; every one that hears will laugh on account of me.' **7** And she said: 'Who would have said to Abraham, that Sarah should nurse children? for I have given him a son in his old age.' **8** And the child grew, and was weaned. And Abraham made a great feast on the day that Isaac was weaned. **9** And Sarah saw the son of Hagar the Egyptian, whom she had borne to Abraham, mocking. **10** Therefore she said to Abraham: 'Cast out this slave (bond) woman and her son; for the son of this slave woman shall not be heir with my son, Isaac.'

11 And the thing was very serious in Abraham's sight on account of his son. **12** And **Elohim** said to Abraham: 'Let it not be dreadful in your sight because of the lad, and because of your slave woman; in all that Sarah said to you, listen to her voice; for in Isaac shall offspring be called to you. *13* And also of the son of the slave woman will I make a nation, because he is your offspring.' *14* And Abraham arose up early in the morning, and took bread and a bottle of water, and gave it to Hagar, putting it on her shoulder, and the child, and sent her away; and she departed, and strayed in the wilderness of Beer-sheba. *15* And the water in the bottle was gone, and she hid the child under one of the shrubs. *16* And she went, and sat down near him but a good way off, as it were a bow-shot; for she said: 'Let me not look upon the death of the child.' And she sat over against him, and lifted up her voice, and wept. *17* And **Elohim** heard the voice of Ishmael; and the angel (messenger) of **Elohim** called to Hagar out of heaven, and said to her: 'What ails you, Hagar? fear not; for **Elohim** has heard the voice of the lad where he is. *18* Arise, lift up Ishmael, and hold him fast by your hand; for I will make him a great nation.' *19* And **Elohim** opened her eyes, and she saw a well of water; and she went, and filled the bottle with water, and gave him a drink. *20* And **Elohim** was with Ishmael, and he grew; and he dwelt in the wilderness, and became an archer.

21 And he dwelt in the wilderness of Paran; and his mother took him a wife out of the land of Egypt. *22* And it came to pass at that time that Abimelech and Phicol the captain of his host spoke to Abraham, saying: **Elohim** is with you in all that you do. *23* Now therefore swear to me here by **Elohim** that you will not deal falsely with me, nor with my son, nor with my son's son; but according to the kindness that I have done to you, you shall do to me, and to the land where you have stayed.' *24* And Abraham said: 'I will swear.' *25* And Abraham corrected Abimelech because of the well of water, which Abimelech's servants had violently taken away. *26* And Abimelech said: 'I know not who has done this thing; neither did you tell me, neither yet heard I of it, but today.' *27* And Abraham took sheep and oxen, and gave them to Abimelech; and they both made a covenant. *28* And Abraham set seven ewe-lambs of the flock by themselves. *29* And Abimelech said to Abraham: 'What do these seven ewe-lambs mean which you have set by themselves?' *30* And he said: 'Surely, these seven ewe-lambs shall you take of my hand, that it may be a witness to me, that I have dug this well.'

31 That place was called Beer-sheba; because there both of them swore. *32* So they made a covenant at Beer-sheba; and Abimelech rose up, and Phicol the captain of his host, and they returned into the land of the Philistines. *33* And Abraham planted a tamarisk-tree (small tree) in Beer-sheba, and called there on the name of **YeHoVaH**, the Everlasting **Elohim**. *34* And Abraham stayed (sojourned) in the land of the Philistines many days.

Chapter 22
YeHoVaH tells Abraham to sacrifice his son Isaac. Abraham obeyed but an angel stopped him before he kills Isaac and provides a ram instead and blesses Abraham.

1 And it came to pass after these things, that **Elohim** did test Abraham, and said to him: 'Abraham'; and he said: 'Here am I.' *2* And He said: 'Take now your son, your only son Isaac, whom you love, and go into the land of Moriah; and offer him there for a burnt-offering upon one of the mountains which I will tell you of.' *3* And Abraham rose early in the morning, and saddled his donkey, and took two of his young servants with him, and Isaac his son; and he chopped the wood for the burnt offering, and rose up, and went to the place of which **Elohim** had told him. *4* On the third day Abraham lifted up his eyes, and saw the place far off. *5* And Abraham said to his young men: 'Stay here with the donkey, and *I and Isaac* will go yonder; and **we will** worship, and **come back** to you.' *6* And Abraham took the wood of the burnt offering, and laid it upon Isaac his son; and he took in his hand the fire and the knife; and they both went together. *7* And Isaac spoke to Abraham his father, and said: 'My father.' And he said: 'Here am I, my son.' And he said: 'Behold the fire and the wood; but where is the lamb for a burnt-offering?' *8* And Abraham said: '**YeHoVaH** will provide Himself the lamb for a burnt-offering, my son.' So they both went together. *9* And they came to the place that **Elohim** had told him of; and Abraham built the altar there, and laid the wood in order, and bound Isaac his son, and laid him on the altar, upon the wood. *10* And Abraham stretched forth his hand, and took the knife to slay his son.

11 Then a messenger (angel) of **YeHoVaH** called to him out of heaven, and said: 'Abraham, Abraham.' And he said: 'Here am I.' *12* And he said: 'Lay not your hand upon the lad, neither do you anything to him; for now I know that you are a **Elohim** fearing man, seeing you have not withheld your son, your only son, from Me.' *13* And Abraham lifted up his eyes, and looked, and behold behind him was a ram caught in the thicket by his horns. And Abraham took the ram, and offered him up for a burnt offering in place of his son. *14* And Abraham called the name of that place Adonai-jireh; as it is said to this day: 'In the mount where **YeHoVaH** is seen.' *15* And the angel of **YeHoVaH** called to Abraham a second time out of heaven, *16* and said: 'By Myself have I sworn, says **YeHoVaH**, because you have done this thing, and have not withheld your son, your only son, *17* that in blessing I will bless you, and in multiplying I will multiply your offspring as the stars of the heaven, and as the sand which is upon the seashore; and your offspring shall possess the gate of his enemies; *18* and in your offspring shall all the nations of the earth be blessed; because you have listened to My voice.' *19* So Abraham returned to his servant men, and they rose up and went together to Beer-sheba; and Abraham dwelt at Beer-sheba. *20* And it came to pass after these things that it was told Abraham, saying: 'Behold, Milcah, she also has borne children to your brother Nahor:

21 Uz his first-born, and Buz his brother, and Kemuel the father of Aram; *22* and Chesed, and Hazo, and Pildash, and Jidlaph, and Bethuel.' *23* And Bethuel fathered **Rebekah**; these eight did Milcah bear to Nahor, Abraham's brother. *24* And his mistress (concubine), whose name was Reumah, she also bore Tebah, and Gaham, and Tahash, and Maacah.
   Reading 4 ends

Chapter 23
Sarah dies in Kiriath-arba and Abraham asks the Hittites for a burial site. He buys a cave and land from Ephron and buries Sarah there.
   Reading 5 begins
1 And the life of Sarah was 127 years; these were the years of the life of Sarah. *2* And Sarah died in Kiriatharba--the same is Hebron--in the land of Canaan; and Abraham came to mourn for Sarah, and to weep for her. *3* And Abraham rose up from before his dead, and spoke to the children of Heth, saying: *4* 'I am a stranger (a sojourner) and not a permanent resident with you: give me a possession of a burying-place with you, that I may bury my dead out of my sight.' *5* And the children of Heth answered Abraham, saying to him: *6* 'Hear us, my lord: you art a mighty prince among us; in the choice of our graves bury your dead; none of us shall withhold from you his burial place, but that you may bury your dead.' *7* And Abraham rose up, and bowed down to the people of the land, even to the children of Heth. *8* And he spoke with them, saying: 'If it be your mind that I should bury my dead out of my sight, hear me, and plead for me to Ephron the son of Zohar, *9* that he may give me the cave of Machpelah, which he has, which is in the end of his field; for the full price let him give it to me in the midst of you for a

possession of a burying-place.' *10* Now Ephron was sitting in the midst of the children of Heth; and Ephron the Hittite answered Abraham in the hearing of the children of Heth, even of all that went in at the gate of his city, saying:

11 'No, my lord, hear me: the field give I you, and the cave that is therein, I give it you; in the presence of the sons of my people I give it to you; bury your dead.' *12* And Abraham bowed down before the people of the land. *13* And he spoke to Ephron in the hearing of the people of the land, saying: 'But if you will, I pray you, hear me: I will give the price of the field; take it of me, and I will bury my dead there.' *14* And Ephron answered Abraham, saying to him: *15* 'My lord, hearken to me: a piece of land worth four hundred shekels of silver, what is that between me and you? bury therefore your dead.' *16* And Abraham hearkened to Ephron; and Abraham weighed to Ephron the silver, which he had named in the hearing of the children of Heth, four hundred shekels of silver, current money with the merchant. *17* So the field of Ephron, which was in Machpelah, which was before Mamre, the field, and the cave which was therein, and all the trees that were in the field, that were in all the border thereof round about, were made sure *18* to Abraham for a possession in the presence of the children of Heth, before all that went in at the gate of his city. *19* And after this, Abraham buried Sarah his wife in the cave of the field of Machpelah before Mamre--the same is Hebron--in the land of Canaan. *20* And the field, and the cave that is therein, were made sure to Abraham for a possession of a burying-place by the children of Heth.

Chapter 24

Abraham has his servant swear to go to Nahor to find a wife for Isaac. He meets Rebekah by the well and she agrees to go back with him to become Isaac's wife.

1 And Abraham was old, well stricken in age; and **YeHoVaH** had blessed Abraham in all things. *2* And Abraham said to his servant, the elder of his house that ruled over all that he had: 'Put, I pray you, your hand under my thigh. *3* And I will make you swear by **YeHoVaH**, the **Elohim** of heaven and the **Elohim** of the earth, that you shall not take a wife for my son of the daughters of the Canaanites, among whom I dwell. *4* But you shall go to my country, and to my family, and take a wife for my son Isaac.' *5* And the servant said to him: 'What if the woman will not be willing to follow me to this land; must I need bring your son back to the land from where you came?' *6* And Abraham said to him: 'Beware that you bring not my son back in that direction. *7* **YeHoVaH**, the **Elohim** of heaven, who took me from my father's house, and from the land of my birth, and who spoke to me, and who swore to me, saying: To your offspring will I give this land; He will send His angel before you, and you shall take a wife for my son from there. *8* And if the woman be not willing to follow you, then you shall be clear from this my oath; only you shall not bring my son back there.' *9* And the servant put his hand under the thigh of Abraham his master, and swore to him concerning this matter. *10* And the servant took ten camels of his master, and departed; having all goodly things of his master's in his hand; and he arose, and went to Aram-naharaim, to the city of Nahor.

11 And he made the camels to kneel down outside the city by the well of water at the time of evening, the time that women go out to draw water. *12* And he said: 'O **YeHoVaH**, the **Elohim** of my master Abraham, send me, I pray You, good speed this day, and show kindness to my master Abraham. *13* Behold, I stand by the fountain of water; and the daughters of the men of the city come out to draw water. *14* So let it come to pass, that the maiden (*damsel*) to whom I shall say: Let down your pitcher, I pray you, that I may drink; and she shall say: Drink, and I will give your camels drink also; let her be the one that You have appointed for Your servant Isaac; and thereby shall I know that You have shown kindness to my master.' *15* And it came to pass, before he had finished speaking, that, behold, Rebekah came out, who was born to Bethuel the son of Milcah, the wife of Nahor, *Abraham's brother*, with her pitcher upon her shoulder. *16* And the maiden was very fair to look upon, a virgin, neither had any man known (had relations with) her; and she went down to the fountain, and filled her pitcher, and came up. *17* And the servant ran to meet her, and said: 'Give me to drink, I pray you, a little water of your pitcher.' *18* And she said: 'Drink, my lord'; and she hastened, and let down her pitcher upon her hand, and gave him drink. *19* And when she had finished giving him drink, she said: 'I will draw for your camels also, until they are done drinking.' *20* And she hastened, and emptied her pitcher into the trough, and ran again to the well to draw, and drew for all his camels.

21 And the man looked firmly on her; holding his peace, to know whether **YeHoVaH** had made his journey prosperous or not. *22* And it came to pass, as the camels had finished drinking, that the man took a golden ring of half a **shekel** weight, and two bracelets for her hands of ten shekels weight of gold; *23* and said: 'Whose daughter are you? tell me, I pray you. Is there room in your father's house for us to lodge in?' *24* And she said to him: 'I am the daughter of Bethuel the son of Milcah, whom she bore to Nahor.' *25* She said to him: 'We have both enough straw and supplies, and room to lodge in.' *26* And the man bowed his head, and prostrated himself before **YeHoVaH**. *27* And he said: 'Blessed be **YeHoVaH**, the **Elohim** of my master Abraham, who has not abandoned His mercy and His truth toward my master; as for me, **YeHoVaH** has led me in the way to the house of my master's brethren.' *28* And the maiden ran, and told her mother's house according to these words. *29* And **Rebekah** had a brother, and his name was **Laban**; and Laban ran out to the man, to the fountain. *30* And it came to pass, when he saw the ring, and the bracelets upon his sister's hands, and when he heard the words of Rebekah his sister, saying: 'Thus spoke the man to me,' that he came to the man; and, behold, he stood by the camels at the fountain.

31 And he said: 'Come in, you blessed of **YeHoVaH**; why do you remain outside? for I have cleared the house, and made room for the camels.' *32* And the man came into the house, and he removed the harness from the camels; and he gave straw and food for the camels, and water to wash his feet and the feet of the men that were with him. *33* And there was set food before him to eat; but he said: 'I will not eat, until I have told my purpose.' And Laban said: 'Speak on.' *34* And he said: 'I am Abraham's servant. *35* And **YeHoVaH** has blessed my master greatly; and he has become great; and He has given him flocks and herds, and silver and gold, and men-servants and maidservants, and camels and donkeys. *36* And Sarah my master's wife bore a son to my master when she was old; and to him he has given all that he has. *37* And my master made me swear, saying: You shall not take a wife for my son of the daughters of the Canaanites, in whose land I dwell. *38* But you shall go to my father's house, and to my family, and take a wife for my son. *39* And I said to my master: What if the woman will not follow me. *40* And he said to me: **YeHoVaH**, before whom I walk, will send His angel with you, and prosper your way; and you shall take a wife for my son of my family, and of my father's house;

41 then shall you be clear from my oath, when you come to my family; and if they give her not to you, you shall be clear from my oath. *42* And I came this day to the fountain, and said: O **YeHoVaH**, the **Elohim** of my master Abraham, if now You do prosper the way which I go: *43* behold, I stand by the fountain of water; and let it come to pass, that the maiden that comes forth to draw, to whom I shall say: Give me, I pray you, a little water from your pitcher to drink; *44* and she shall say to me: Both drink, and I will also draw for your camels; let her be the woman whom **YeHoVaH** has appointed for my master's son. **45** And before I had finished speaking to my heart, behold, Rebekah came forth with her pitcher on her shoulder; and she went down to the fountain, and drew. And I said to her: Let me drink, I pray you. **46** And she made haste, and let down her pitcher from her shoulder, and said: Drink, and I will give your camels drink also. So I drank, and she made the camels drink also. **47** And I asked her, and said: Whose daughter are you? And she said: The daughter of Bethuel, Nahor's son, whom Milcah bore to him. And I put the ring upon her nose, and the bracelets upon her hands. **48** And I bowed my head, and prostrated myself before **YeHoVaH**, and blessed **YeHoVaH**, the **Elohim** of my master Abraham, who had led me in the right way to take my master's brother's daughter for his son. **49** And now if you will deal kindly and truly with my master, tell me; and if not, also tell me; that I may turn to the right hand, or to the left.' **50** Then Laban and Bethuel answered and said: 'The thing comes from **YeHoVaH**; we cannot speak to you bad or good.

51 Behold, **Rebekah** is before you, take her, and go, and let her be your master's son's wife, as **YeHoVaH** has spoken.' **52** And it came to pass, that, when Abraham's servant heard their words, he bowed himself down to the earth to **YeHoVaH**. **53** And the servant brought forth jewels of silver, and jewels of gold, and clothes, and gave them to Rebekah; he gave also to her brother and to her mother precious things. **54** And they did eat and drink, he and the men that were with him, and spent the night; and they rose up in the morning, and he said: 'Send me away to my master.' **55** And her brother and her mother said: 'Let the damsel abide with us a few days, at the least ten; after that she shall go.' **56** And he said to them: 'Delay me not, seeing **YeHoVaH** has prospered my way; send me away that I may go to my master.' **57** And they said: 'We will call the maiden, and see what she says.' **58** And they called Rebekah, and said to her: 'Will you go with this man?' And she said: 'I will go.' **59** And they sent Rebekah, their sister, away and her nurse, and Abraham's servant, and his men. **60** And they blessed Rebekah, and said to her: 'Our sister, be you the mother of thousands of tens of thousands, and let your offspring possess the gate of those that hate them.'

61 And Rebekah arose, and her maidens and they rode upon the camels, and followed the man. And the servant took Rebekah, and went his way. **62** And Isaac came from the way of Beer-lahai-roi; for he dwelt in the land of the South. **63** And Isaac went out to think in the field at the evening; and he lifted up his eyes, and saw, and, behold, there were camels coming. **64** And Rebekah lifted up her eyes, and when she saw Isaac, she quickly dismounted the camel. **65** And she said to the servant: 'What man is this that walks in the field to meet us?' And the servant said: 'It is my master.' And she took her veil, and covered herself. **66** And the servant told Isaac all the things that he had done. **67** And Isaac brought her into what had been his mother Sarah's tent, and took Rebekah, and she became his wife; and he loved her. And Isaac was comforted for his mother.

Chapter 25
Abraham dies and is buried with Sarah. Isaac and Rebekah have twins: Esau and Jacob. Esau sells his birthright to Jacob for food.

1 And Abraham took *another* wife, and her name was **Keturah**. **2** And she bore him Zimran, and Jokshan, and Medan, and Midian, and Ishbak, and Shuah. **3** And Jokshan fathered Sheba, and Dedan. And the sons of Dedan were Asshurim, and Letushim, and Leummim. **4** And the sons of Midian: Ephah, and Epher, and Hanoch, and Abida, and Eldaah. All these were the children of Keturah. **5** And Abraham *gave all that he had to Isaac*. **6** But to the sons of the mistresses, that Abraham had, Abraham gave gifts; and he sent them away from Isaac his son, while he yet lived, eastward, to the east country. *7* And these are the days of the years of Abraham's life that he lived, a 175 years. *8* And Abraham expired, and died in a good old age, an old man, and full of years; and was gathered to his people. *9* And Isaac and Ishmael his sons buried him in the cave of Machpelah, in the field of Ephron the son of Zohar the Hittite, which is before Mamre; *10* the field which Abraham purchased of the children of Heth; there was Abraham buried, and Sarah his wife.

11 And it came to pass after the death of Abraham, that **Elohim** blessed Isaac his son; and Isaac dwelt by Beer-lahai-roi. *12* Now these are the generations of Ishmael, Abraham's son, whom Hagar the Egyptian, Sarah's handmaid, bore to Abraham. *13* And these are the names of the sons of Ishmael, by their names, according to their generations: the first-born of Ishmael, Nebaioth; and Kedar, and Adbeel, and Mibsam, *14* and Mishma, and Dumah, and Massa; *15* Hadad, and Tema, Jetur, Naphish, and Kedem; *16* these are the sons of Ishmael, and these are their names, by their villages, and by their encampments; twelve princes according to their nations. *17* And these are the years of the life of Ishmael, 137; and he expired and died; and was gathered to his people. *18* And they dwelt from Havilah to Shur that is before Egypt, as you go toward Asshur: over against all his brethren he settled.
Reading 5 ends

Reading 6 begins
19 And these are the generations of Isaac, Abraham's son: Abraham fathered Isaac. *20* And Isaac was 40 years old when he took Rebekah, the daughter of Bethuel the Aramean, of Paddan-aram, the sister of Laban the Aramean, to be his wife.

21 And Isaac implored **YeHoVaH** for his wife, because she was barren; and **YeHoVaH** let Himself be implored of him, and Rebekah his wife conceived. *22* And the children struggled together *within* her; and she said: 'If it be so, where do I live?' And she went to inquire of **YeHoVaH**. *23* And **YeHoVaH** said to her: Two nations are in your womb, and two peoples shall be separated from your bowels; and the one people shall be stronger than the other people; and the elder shall serve the younger. *24* And when her days to deliver were fulfilled, behold, there were *twins* in her womb. *25* And the first came forth flushed, all over like a hairy blanket; and they called his name **Esau**. *26* And after that came forth his brother, and his hand had hold on Esau's heel; and his name was called **Jacob**. And Isaac was 60 years old when Rebekah bore them. *27* And the boys grew; and Esau was a cunning hunter, a man of the field; and Jacob was a quiet man, dwelling in tents. *28* Now Isaac loved Esau, because he did eat of his venison; and Rebekah loved Jacob. *29* And Jacob made stew; and Esau came in from the field, and he was faint. *30* And Esau said to Jacob: 'Let me eat, I pray you, some of this red stew; for I am faint.' Therefore his name was called Edom, meaning red (Esau).

31 And Jacob said: 'Sell me first your birthright.' *32* And Esau said: 'Behold, I am at the point to die; and what profit shall the birthright do for me?' *33* And Jacob said: 'Swear to me first'; and he swore to him; and *he sold his birthright to Jacob*. *34* And Jacob gave Esau bread and stew of lentils; and he did eat and drink, and rose up, and went his way. So Esau despised his birthright.

Chapter 26

In the town of Gerar Isaac lies about Rebekah. He grows so rich that Abimelech sends him away. He digs wells, and at Beersheba YeHoVaH blesses him.

1 And there was a famine in the land, beside the first famine that was in the days of Abraham. And Isaac went to Abimelech king of the Philistines to Gerar. **2** And **YeHoVaH** appeared to him, and said: 'Go not down to Egypt; dwell in the land that I shall tell you of. **3** Stay in this land, and I will be with you, and will bless you; for to you, and to your offspring, I will give all these lands, and I will establish the oath which I swore to Abraham your father; **4** and I will multiply your offspring as the stars of heaven, and will give to your offspring all these lands; and by your offspring shall all the nations of the earth bless themselves; **5** because Abraham listened to My voice, and kept My instructions, My commandments, My teachings, and My laws.' **6** And Isaac dwelt in Gerar. **7** And the men of the place asked him of his wife; and he said: 'She is my sister'; for he feared to say: 'My wife'; 'or else the men of the place should kill me for Rebekah, because she is fair to look upon.' **8** And it came to pass, when he had been there a long time, that Abimelech king of the Philistines looked out a window, and saw, and behold, Isaac was playing with Rebekah his wife. **9** And Abimelech called Isaac, and said: 'Behold, she is certainly your wife; and why do you say: She is my sister?' And Isaac said to him: 'Because I said: or else I die because of her.' **10** And Abimelech said: 'What is this you have done to us? one of the people might easily have laid with your wife, and you would have brought guilt upon us.'

11 And Abimelech charged all the people, saying: 'He that touches this man or his wife shall surely be put to death.' **12** And Isaac sowed in that land, and reaped crops in the same year a hundred-fold; and **YeHoVaH** blessed him. **13** And the man became great, and grew more and more until he became very great. **14** And he had possessions of flocks, and possessions of herds, and a great household; and the Philistines envied him. **15** Now all the wells that his father's servants had dug in the days of Abraham his father, the Philistines had stopped them, and filled them with earth. **16** And Abimelech said to Isaac: 'Go from us; for you are much mightier than we.' **17** And Isaac departed then, and camped in the valley of Gerar, and dwelt there. **18** And Isaac dug again the wells of water, which they had dug in the days of Abraham his father; for the Philistines had stopped them after the death of Abraham; and he called their names after the names by which his father had called them. **19** And Isaac's servants dug in the valley, and found a well of living water. **20** And the herdsmen of Gerar quarreled with Isaac's herdsmen, saying: 'The water is ours.' And he called the name of the well Esek; because they challenged him.

21 And they dug another well, and they fought for that also. And he called the name of it Sitnah. **22** And he moved from there, and dug another well; and for that they did not fight. And he called the name of it Rehoboth; and he said: 'For now **YeHoVaH** has made room for us, and we shall be fruitful in the land.' **23** And he went up from there to Beer-sheba. **24** And **YeHoVaH** appeared to him the same night, and said: 'I am the **Elohim** of Abraham your father. Fear not, for I am with you, and will bless you, and multiply your offspring for My servant Abraham's sake.' **25** And he built an altar there, and called upon the name of **YeHoVaH**, and pitched his tent there; and there Isaac's servants dug a well. **26** Then Abimelech went to him from Gerar, and Ahuzzath his friend, and Phicol the captain of his host. **27** And Isaac said to them: 'Why have you come to me, seeing you hate me, and have sent me away from you?' **28** And they said: 'We saw plainly that **YeHoVaH** was with you; and we said: Let there now be an oath between us and you, and let us make a covenant with you; **29** that you will do us no harm, as we have not touched you, and as we have done to you nothing but good, and have sent you away in peace; you are now the blessed of **YeHoVaH**.' *30* And he made them a feast, and they did eat and drink.

31 And they rose up early in the morning, and swore one to another; and Isaac sent them away, and they departed from him in peace. *32* And it came to pass the same day that Isaac's servants came, and told him concerning the well which they had dug, and said to him: 'We have found water.' *33* And he called it Shibah. Therefore the name of the city is Beer-sheba to this day. *34* And when Esau was 40 years old, he took to wife Judith the daughter of Beeri the Hittite, and Basemath the daughter of Elon the Hittite. *35* And they were a source of bitterness of spirit to Isaac and to Rebekah.

Chapter 27
Rebekah and Jacob trick Isaac into giving Jacob his blessing. Esau vows revenge so Rebekah tells Jacob to go to her brother Laban and stay until she sends for him.

1 And it came to pass, that when Isaac was old, and his eyes were dim, so that he could not see, he called Esau his elder son, and said to him: 'My son'; and he said to him: 'Here am I.' *2* And he said: 'Behold now, I am old, I know not the day of my death. *3* Now therefore take, I pray you, your weapons, your quiver and your bow, and go out to the field, and find me venison (deer); *4* and make me savory food, such as I love, and bring it to me, that I may eat; that my soul may bless you before I die.' *5* And Rebekah heard when Isaac spoke to Esau his son. And Esau went to the field to hunt for venison, and to bring it back. *6* And Rebekah spoke to Jacob her son, saying: 'Behold, I heard your father speak to Esau your brother, saying: *7* Bring me venison, and make me savory food, that I may eat, and bless you before **YeHoVaH** before my death. *8* Now therefore, my son, listen to my voice according to that which I command you. *9* Go now to the flock, and fetch me from there two good young goats; and I will make them savory food for your father, such as he loves; *10* and you shall bring it to your father, that he may eat, so that he may bless *you* before his death.'

11 And Jacob said to Rebekah his mother: 'Behold, Esau my brother is a hairy man, and I am a smooth man. *12* My father might feel me, and I shall seem to him as a mocker; and I shall bring a curse upon me, and not a blessing.' *13* And his mother said to him: 'Upon me be your curse, my son; only listen to my voice, and go fetch the goats.' *14* And he went, and fetched, and brought them to his mother; and his mother made savory food, such as his father loved. *15* And Rebekah took the choicest garments of Esau her elder son, which were with her in the house, and put them upon Jacob her younger son. *16* And she put the skins of the young goats upon his hands, and upon the smooth of his neck. *17* And she gave the savory food and the bread, which she had prepared, into the hand of her son Jacob. *18* And he came to his father, and said: 'My father'; and he said: 'Here am I; who art you, my son?' *19* And Jacob said to his father: 'I am Esau your first-born; I have done according as you told me. Arise, I pray you, sit and eat of my venison, that your soul may bless me.' *20* And Isaac said to his son: 'How is it that you have found it so quickly, my son?' And he said: 'Because **YeHoVaH** your **Elohim** sent me good speed.'

21 And Isaac said to Jacob: 'Come near, I pray you, that I may feel you, my son, whether you be my very son Esau or not.' *22* And Jacob went near to Isaac his father; and he felt him, and said: 'The voice is the voice of Jacob, but the hands are the hands of Esau.' *23* And he did not tell the difference, because his hands were hairy, as his brother Esau's hands; so he blessed him. **24** And he said: 'Are you my very son Esau?' And he said: 'I am.' **25** And he said: 'Bring it near to me, and I will eat of my son's venison, that my soul may bless you.' And he brought it near to him, and he did eat; and he brought him wine, and he drank. **26** And his father Isaac said to him: 'Come near now, and kiss me, my son.' **27** And he came near, and kissed him. And he smelled the smell of his clothes, and blessed him, and said: See, the smell of my son is as the smell of a field, which **YeHoVaH** has blessed. **28** So **Elohim** give you of the dew of heaven, and of the fat places of the earth, and plenty of corn and wine. **29** Let people serve you, and nations bow down to you. Be lord over your brethren, and let your mother's son's bow down to you. Cursed be every one that curses you, and blessed be every one that blesses you. **30** And it came to pass, as soon as Isaac had made an end of blessing Jacob, and Jacob was barely gone out from the presence of Isaac his father, that Esau his brother came in from his hunting.

31 And he also made savory food, and brought it to his father; and he said to his father: 'Let my father arise, and eat of his son's venison, that your soul may bless me.' **32** And Isaac his father said to him: 'Who are you?' And he said: 'I am your son, your first-born, Esau.' **33** And Isaac trembled very exceedingly, and said: 'Who then is he that has taken venison, and brought it to me, and I have eaten of all before you came, and have blessed him? yes, and he shall be blessed.' **34** When Esau heard the words of his father, he cried with an exceeding great and bitter cry, and said to his father: 'Bless me, even me also, O my father.' **35** And he said: 'Your brother came with cleverness, and has taken away your blessing.' **36** And he said: 'Is not he rightly named Jacob? for he has replaced me these two times: he took away my birthright; and, behold, now he has taken away my blessing.' And he said: 'Have you not reserved a blessing for me?' **37** And Isaac answered and said to Esau: 'Behold, I have made him your lord, and all his brethren have I given to him for servants; and with corn and wine have I sustained him; and what then shall I do for you, my son?' **38** And Esau said to his father: 'Have you only one blessing, my father? bless me, me also bless, O my father.' And Esau lifted up his voice, and wept. **39** And Isaac his father answered and said to him: Behold, of the fat places of the earth shall be your dwelling, and of the dew of heaven from above; **40** And by your sword shall you live, and you shall serve your brother; and it shall come to pass when you shall break loose, that you shall shake his yoke from off your neck.

41 And Esau hated Jacob because of the blessing that his father blessed him. And Esau said in his heart: 'Let the days of mourning for my father be at hand; then will I slay my brother Jacob.' **42** And the words of Esau her elder son were told to Rebekah; and she sent and called Jacob her younger son, and said to him: 'Behold, your brother Esau, does console himself, with purpose to kill you. **43** Now therefore, my son, listen to my voice; and arise, flee you to Laban my brother to Haran; **44** and stay with him a few days, until your brother's hatred turns away; **45** until your brother's anger turn away from you, and he forget that which you have done to him; then I will send, and fetch you from there; why should I be bereaved of you both in one day?' **46** And Rebekah said to Isaac: 'I am weary of my life because of the daughters of Heth. If Jacob take a wife of the daughters of Heth, such as these, of the daughters of the land, what good shall my life do me?'

Chapter 28
Isaac sends Jacob to marry one of Laban's daughters. In route Jacob dreams of a ladder reaching to heaven and YeHoVaH talks to him.

1 And Isaac called Jacob, and blessed him, and charged him, and said to him: 'You shall not take a wife of the daughters of Canaan. *2* Arise, go to Paddan-aram, to the house of Bethuel your mother's father; and take you a wife from there of the daughters of Laban your mother's brother. *3* And **YeHoVaH** Almighty bless you, and make you fruitful, and multiply you, that you may be a congregation of peoples; *4* and give you the blessing of Abraham, to you, and to your offspring with you; that you may inherit the land of your short stays (sojourning), which **Elohim** gave to Abraham.' *5* And Isaac sent away Jacob; and he went to Paddan-aram to Laban, son of Bethuel the Aramean, the brother of Rebekah, Jacob's and Esau's mother. *6* Now Esau saw that Isaac had blessed Jacob and sent him away to Paddan-aram, to take him a wife from there; and that as he blessed him he gave him instruction, saying: 'You shall not take a wife of the daughters of Canaan'; *7* and that Jacob listened to his father and his mother, and was gone to Paddan-aram; *8* and Esau saw that the daughters of Canaan pleased not Isaac his father; *9* so Esau went to Ishmael, and took to the wives that he had Mahalath the daughter of Ishmael Abraham's son, the sister of Nebaioth, to be his wife.

Reading 6 ends

Reading 7 begins
10 And Jacob went out from Beer-sheba, and went toward Haran.

11 And he arrived at the place, and stayed there all night, because the sun was set; and he took one of the stones and put it under his head, and lay down in that place to sleep. *12* And he dreamed, and behold a ladder set up on the earth, and the top of it reached to heaven; and behold the angels of **Elohim** ascending and descending on it. *13* And, behold, **YeHoVaH** stood beside him, and said: 'I am **YeHoVaH**, the **Elohim** of Abraham your father, and the **Elohim** of Isaac. The land whereon you lay, to you will I give it, and to your offspring. *14* And your offspring shall be as the dust of the earth, and you shall spread abroad to the west, and to the east, and to the north, and to the south. And in you and in your offspring shall all the families of the earth be blessed. *15* And, behold, I am with you, and will keep you wherever you go, and will bring you back into this land; for I will not leave you, until I have done that which I have spoken to you of.' *16* And Jacob awakened out of his sleep, and he said: 'Surely **YeHoVaH** is in this place; and I knew it not.' *17* And he was afraid, and said: 'How full of awe is this place! this is none other than the house of **Elohim**, and this is the gate of heaven.' *18* And Jacob rose up early in the morning, and took the stone that he had put under his head, and set it up for a pillar, and poured oil upon the top of it. *19* And he called the name of that place Beth-el, but the name of the city was Luz at the first. *20* And Jacob vowed a vow, saying: 'If **Elohim** will be with me, and will keep me in this way that I go, and will give me bread to eat, and clothes to put on,

21 so that I come back to my father's house in peace, then shall **YeHoVaH** be my **Elohim**, *22* and this stone, which I have set up for a pillar, shall be **Elohim**'s house; and of all that You shall give me I will surely give a tithe to You.'

Chapter 29
Jacob works for Laban seven years in order to marry Rachel, but Laban tricks him and gives him her sister Leah. He makes him work another seven years for Rachel. Leah gives birth to four sons.

1 Then Jacob went on his journey, and came to the land of the children of the east. *2* And he looked, and behold a well in the field, and, three flocks of sheep lying there by it. --For out of that well they watered the flocks. And the stone upon the well's mouth was great. *3* And there all the flocks gathered; and Jacob rolled the stone from the well's mouth, and watered the sheep, and put the stone back upon the well's mouth in its place. *4* And Jacob said to them: 'My brethren, where are you from?' And they said: 'We are of Haran' *5* And he said to them: 'Do you know Laban the son of Nahor?' And they said: 'We know him.' *6* And he said to them: 'Is it well with him?' And they said: 'It is well; and, behold, Rachel his daughter comes with the sheep.' *7* And he said: 'It is yet high noon, it is not time that the cattle should be gathered together; water your sheep, and go and feed them.' *8* And they said: 'We cannot, until all the flocks are gathered together, and they roll the stone from the well's mouth; then we can water the sheep.' *9* While he was yet speaking with them, Rachel came with her father's sheep; for she tended them. *10* And it came to pass, when Jacob saw Rachel the daughter of Laban his mother's brother, and the sheep of Laban that Jacob went near, and rolled the stone from the well's mouth, and watered the flock of Laban.

11 And Jacob kissed Rachel, and lifted up his voice, and wept. *12* And Jacob told Rachel that he was her father's relative and that he was Rebekah's son; and she ran and told her father. *13* And it came to pass, when Laban heard the tidings of Jacob his sister's son, that he ran to meet him, and embraced him, and kissed him, and brought him to his house. And he told Laban all these things. *14* And Laban said to him: 'Surely you are my bone and my flesh.' And he stayed with him for a month. *15* And Laban said to Jacob: 'Because you are my relative, shouldn't you therefore serve me for nothing? tell me, what shall your wages be?' *16* Now Laban had two daughters: the name of the elder was **Leah**, and the name of the younger was **Rachel**. *17* And Leah's eyes were weak; but Rachel was of beautiful form and fair to look upon. *18* And Jacob loved Rachel; and he said: 'I will serve you *seven years* for Rachel your younger daughter.' *19* And Laban said: 'It is better that I give her to you, than that I should give her to another man; abide with me.' *20* And Jacob served seven years for Rachel; and they seemed to him only a few days, for the love he had to her.

21 And Jacob said to Laban: 'Give me my wife, for my days are filled, that I may go in to her.' *22* And Laban gathered together all the men of the place, and made a feast. *23* And it came to pass in the evening, that he took *Leah* his daughter, and brought *her* to him; and he had relations (went in to her) with her. *24* And Laban gave Zilpah his handmaid to his daughter Leah for a handmaid. *25* And it came to pass in the morning that, behold, it was *Leah*; and he said to Laban: 'What is this you have done to me? did not I serve with you for Rachel? Then why have you tricked me?' *26* And Laban said: 'It is not done that way in our place, to give the younger before the first-born. *27* Fulfill the week with this one, and we will give you the other also for the service which you shall serve with me yet seven *more* years.' *28* And Jacob did so, and fulfilled her week; and he gave him Rachel his daughter to wife. *29* And Laban gave to his daughter Rachel, Bilhah his handmaid to be her handmaid. *30* And he had relations (went in to) also with Rachel, and he loved Rachel more than Leah, and served with Laban for seven more years.

31 And **YeHoVaH** saw that Leah was hated, and he opened her womb; but Rachel was barren. *32* And Leah conceived, and bore a son, and she called his name **Reuben**; for she said: 'Because **YeHoVaH** has looked upon my affliction; for now my husband will love me.' *33* And she conceived again, and bore a son; and said: 'Because **YeHoVaH** has heard that I am hated, He has therefore given me this son also.' And she called his name **Simeon**. *34* And she conceived again, and bore a son; and said: 'Now this time will my husband be joined to me, because I have borne him three sons.' Therefore was his name called **Levi**. *35* And she conceived again, and bore a son; and she said: 'This time will I praise **YeHoVaH**.' Therefore she called his name **Judah**; and she ceased bearing children.

Chapter 30

Rachel's maid has sons for Jacob, then Leah's maid, then Leah. Finally Rachel had a son. Laban gave Jacob flocks as wages to stay.

1 And when Rachel saw that she bore Jacob no children, Rachel envied her sister; and she said to Jacob: 'Give me children, or else I will die.' *2* And Jacob's anger was kindled against Rachel; and he said: 'Am I in *Elohim*'s place, who has withheld from you the fruit of the womb?' *3* And she said: 'Behold my maid Bilhah, go in to her; that she may bear upon my knees, and I also may be built up through her.' *4* And she gave him Bilhah her handmaid to wife; and Jacob had relations (went in to) with her. *5* And Bilhah conceived, and bore Jacob a son. *6* And Rachel said: *Elohim* has judged me, and has also heard my voice, and has given me a son.' Therefore she called his name **Dan**. *7* And Bilhah Rachel's handmaid conceived again, and bore Jacob a second son. *8* And Rachel said: 'With mighty contest, I waged with my sister, and have prevailed.' And she called his name **Naphtali**. *9* When Leah saw that she ceased bearing, she took Zilpah her handmaid, and gave her to Jacob to be his wife. *10* And Zilpah, Leah's handmaid bore Jacob a son.

11 And Leah said: 'Fortune has come!' And she called his name **Gad**. *12* And Zilpah Leah's handmaid bore Jacob a second son. *13* And Leah said: 'Happy am I! for the daughters will call me happy.' And she called his name **Asher**. *14* And Reuben went in the days of wheat harvest, and found *mandrakes* (a Mediterranean plant, with white or purple flowers and large yellow berries. It has a forked fleshy root that supposedly resembles the human form and was formerly widely used in medicine and magic. Also called a may apple.) in the field, and brought them to his mother Leah. Then Rachel said to Leah: 'Give me, I pray you, your son's mandrakes.' *15* And she said to her: 'Is it a small matter that you have taken away my husband? and would you take away my son's mandrakes also?' And Rachel said: 'Then Jacob shall lie with you tonight for your son's mandrakes.' *16* And Jacob came from the field in the evening, and Leah went out to meet him, and said: 'You must have relations with me; for I have surely hired you with my son's mandrakes.' And he lay with her that night. *17* And *Elohim* listened to Leah, and she conceived, and bore Jacob a fifth son. *18* And Leah said: ' *Elohim* has given me my hire, because I gave my handmaid to my husband. And she called his name **Issachar**. *19* And Leah conceived again, and bore a sixth son to Jacob. *20* And Leah said: *Elohim* has endowed me with a good dowry; now will my husband dwell with me, because I have borne him six sons.' And she called his name **Zebulun**.

21 And afterwards she bore a daughter, and called her name **Dinah**. *22* And *Elohim* remembered Rachel, and *Elohim* hearkened to her, and opened her womb. *23* And she conceived, and bore a son, and said: *Elohim* has taken away my reproach.' *24* And she called his name **Joseph**, saying: '*YeHoVaH* adds to me another son.' *25* And it came to pass, when Rachel had borne Joseph that Jacob said to Laban: 'Send me away that I may go to my own place, and to my country. *26* Give me my wives and my children for whom I have served you, and let me go; for you know my service that I have served you.' *27* And Laban said to him: 'If now I have found favor in your eyes--I have observed the signs, and *YeHoVaH* has blessed me for your sake.' *28* And he said: 'Appoint me your wages, and I will give it.' *29* And he said to him: 'You know how I have served you, and how your cattle have fared with me. *30* For it was little which you had before I came, and it has increased abundantly; and *YeHoVaH* has blessed you wherever I turned. And now when shall I provide for my own house?'

31 And he said: 'What shall I give you?' And Jacob said: 'You shall not *give* me anything; if you will do this thing for me, I will again feed your flock and keep it. *32* I will pass through all your flock today, removing from them every speckled and spotted one, and every dark one among the sheep, and the spotted and speckled among the goats; and of such shall be my hire. *33* So shall my righteousness witness against me forever, when you shall come to look over my work that is before you: every one that is not speckled and spotted among the goats, and dark among the sheep, that if found with me shall be counted stolen.' *34* And Laban said: 'Behold, it will be according to your word.' *35* And he removed that day the he-goats that were streaked and spotted, and all the she-goats that were speckled and spotted, every one that had white in it, and all the dark ones among the sheep, and gave them into the hand of his sons. *36* And he set three days' journey between himself and Jacob. And Jacob fed the rest of Laban's flocks. *37* And Jacob took rods of fresh poplar, and of the almond and of the plane tree; and peeled white streaks in them, making the white appear which was in the rods. *38* And he set the rods that he had peeled over against the flocks in the gutters in the watering-troughs where the flocks came to drink; and they conceived when they came to drink. *39* And the flocks conceived at the sight of the rods, and the flocks brought forth streaked, speckled, and spotted. *40* And Jacob separated the lambs--he also set the faces of the flocks toward the streaked and all the dark in the flock of Laban-- and put his own droves apart, and did not put them into Laban's flock.

41 And it came to pass, whenever the stronger of the flock did conceive, that Jacob laid the rods before the eyes of the flock in the gutters, that they might conceive among the rods; *42* but when the flock were feeble, he did not put them in; so the feebler were Laban's, and the stronger Jacob's. *43* And the man increased exceedingly, and had large flocks, and maidservants and men-servants, and camels and donkeys.

CHAPTERS 31- 40

Chapter 31

YeHoVaH talks to Jacob and tells him to return home. Jacob leaves secretly and Rachel takes Laban's idols. Laban finds out and follows Jacob but YeHoVaH warns him in a dream not to harm Jacob.

1 And Laban's sons told him, saying: 'Jacob has taken away all that was our father's; and of that which was our father's has he earned all this wealth.' *2* And Laban's opinion of Jacob changed, and, behold, it was not toward him as before. *3* And **YeHoVaH** said to Jacob: 'Return to the land of your fathers, and to your kindred; and I will be with you.' *4* And Jacob sent and called Rachel and Leah to the field to his flock, *5* and said to them: 'I see in your father's face, that it is not toward me as before; but the **Elohim** of my father has been with me. *6* And you know that with all my power I have served your father. *7* And your father has mocked me, and changed my wages ten times; but **Elohim** warned him not to hurt me. *8* If he said thus: The speckled shall be your wages; then all the flock bore speckled; and if he said thus: The streaked shall be your wages; then bore all the flock streaked. *9* Thus **Elohim** has taken away the flocks of your father, and given them to me. *10* And it came to pass at the time that the flock conceived, that I lifted up my eyes, and saw in a dream, and, behold, the he-goats which leaped upon the flock were streaked, speckled, and grizzled.

11 And the angel of **Elohim** said to me in the dream: Jacob; and I said: Here am I. *12* And he said: Lift up now your eyes, and see, all the he-goats which leap upon the flock are streaked, speckled, and grizzled; for I have seen all that Laban does to you. *13* I am the **Elohim** of Beth-el, where you did anoint a stone pillar, where you did vow a vow to Me. Now arise, get you out from this land, and return to the land of your birth.' *14* And Rachel and Leah answered and said to him: 'Is there yet any portion or inheritance for us in our father's house? *15* Are we not counted by him as strangers? for he has sold us, and has also quite devoured our money. *16* For all the riches that **Elohim** has taken away from our father that is ours and our children's. Now then, whatever **Elohim** has said to you, do.' *17* Then Jacob rose up, and set his sons and his wives upon the camels; *18* and he carried away all his cattle, and all his materials which he had gathered, the cattle of his getting, which he had gathered in Paddan-aram, to go to Isaac his father to the land of Canaan. *19* Now Laban was gone to shear his sheep. And Rachel stole the idols (teraphim) that were her father's. *20* And Jacob outwitted Laban the Aramean, in that he did not tell him that he was leaving.

21 So he fled with all that he had; and he rose up, and passed over the River, and set his face toward the mountain of Gilead. *22* And it was told Laban on the third day that Jacob had fled. *23* And he took his brethren with him, and pursued after him seven days' journey; and he overtook him in the mountain of Gilead. *24* And **Elohim** came to Laban the Aramean in a dream of the night, and said to him: 'Take heed to yourself that you speak not to Jacob either good or bad.' *25* And Laban caught up with Jacob. Now Jacob had pitched his tent in the mountain; and Laban with his brethren pitched in the mountain of Gilead. *26* And Laban said to Jacob: 'What have you done, that you have outwitted me, and carried away my daughters as captives of the sword? *27* Wherefore did you flee secretly, and outwit me; and did not tell me, that I might have sent you away with gladness (mirth**)** and with songs, with drums (*tabret*) and with harp; *28* and did not allow me to kiss my sons and my daughters? now have you done foolishly. *29* It is in the power of my hand to do you harm; but the **Elohim** of your father spoke to me last night, saying: Take heed to yourself that you speak not to Jacob either good or bad. *30* And now that you are surely gone, because you longed after your father's house, why have you stolen my gods?'

31 And Jacob answered and said to Laban: 'Because I was afraid; for I said: If you should take your daughters from me by force. *32* With whomever you find your gods, he shall not live; before our brethren discern you what is yours with me, and take it to you.' For Jacob knew not that Rachel had stolen them. *33* And Laban went into Jacob's tent, and into Leah's tent, and into the tent of the two maidservants; but he found nothing. And he went out of Leah's tent, and entered into Rachel's tent. *34* Now Rachel had taken the idols/gods, and put them in the saddle of the camel, and sat upon them. And Laban felt about the entire tent, but found no idols. *35* And she said to her father: 'Let not my lord be angry that I cannot rise up before you; for the manner of women (her minstrel period) is upon me.' And he searched, but found not the gods. *36* And Jacob was angry, and strove with Laban. And Jacob answered and said to Laban: 'What is my trespass? what is my sin that you have hotly pursued after me? *37* Whereas you have felt about all my things, what have you found of all your household possessions? Set it here before my brethren and your brethren, that they may judge between us two. *38* These 20 years have I been with you; your ewes and your she-goats have not cast their young, and the rams of your flocks have I not eaten. *39* That which was torn of beasts I brought not to you; I bore the loss of it; of my hand did you require it, whether stolen by day or stolen by night. *40* Thus I was: in the day the drought consumed me, and the frost by night; and my sleep fled from my eyes.

41 These twenty years have I been in your house: I served you 14 years for your two daughters, and six years for your flock; and you have changed my wages ten times. *42* Except the **Elohim** of my father, the **Elohim** of Abraham, and the Fear of Isaac, had been on my side, surely now have you sent me away empty. **YeHoVaH** has seen my affliction and the labor of my hands, and gave judgment last night.' *43* And Laban answered and said to Jacob: 'The daughters are my daughters, and the children are my children, and the flocks are my flocks, and all that you see is mine; and what can I do this day for these my daughters, or for their children whom they have borne? *44* And now come, let us make a covenant, I and you; and let it be for a witness between me and you.' *45* And Jacob took a stone, and set it up for a pillar. *46* And Jacob said to his brethren: 'Gather stones'; and they took stones, and made a pile. And they did eat there by the pile. *47* And Laban called it Jegar-sahadutha; but Jacob called it Galeed. *48* And Laban said: 'This stone pile is witness between me and you this day.' Therefore was the name of it called Galeed; *49* and Mizpah, for he said: '**YeHoVaH** watch between me and you, when we are absent from one another. *50* If you shall afflict my daughters, and if you shall take wives beside my daughters, no man being with us; see, **Elohim** is witness between me and you.'

51 And Laban said to Jacob: 'Behold this pile, and behold the pillar, which I have set up between me and you. *52* This pillar is witness, that I will not pass over these stones to you, and that you shall not pass over these stones and this pillar to me, for harm. *53* The **Elohim** of Abraham, and the **Elohim** of Nahor, the **Elohim** of their father, judge between us.' And Jacob swore by the fear of his father Isaac. *54* And Jacob offered a sacrifice in the mountain, and called his brethren to eat bread; and they did eat bread, and stayed all night in the mountain.

Chapter 32
Jacob is told that Esau is coming to meet him. He is afraid and sends gifts ahead to Esau. That night Jacob wrestles with a man who changes his name to Israel.

1 And early in the morning Laban rose up, and kissed his sons and his daughters, and blessed them. And Laban departed, and returned to his place. *2* And Jacob went on his way, and the angels of **Elohim** met him.
   Reading 7 ends

   Reading 8 begins
3 And Jacob said when he saw them: 'This is **Elohim**'s camp.' And he called the name of that place Mahanaim. *4* And Jacob sent messengers before him to Esau his brother to the land of Seir, the field of Edom. *5* And he commanded them, saying: 'Thus shall you say to my lord Esau: Thus says your servant Jacob: I have stayed with Laban, and stayed until now. *6* And I have oxen, and donkeys and flocks, and men-servants and maid-servants; and I have sent to tell my lord, that I may find favor in your sight.' *7* And the messengers returned to Jacob, saying: 'We came to your brother Esau, and moreover he comes to meet you, and four hundred men with him.' *8* Then Jacob was greatly afraid and was distressed. And he divided the people that were with him, and the flocks, and the herds, and the camels, into two camps. *9* And he said: 'If Esau comes to the one camp, and destroy it, then the camp which is left shall escape.' *10* And Jacob said: 'O **Elohim** of my father Abraham, and **Elohim** of my father Isaac, O **YeHoVaH**, who says to me: Return to your country, and to your kindred, and I will do you good;

11 I am not worthy of all the mercies, and of all the truth, which You have shown to Your servant; for with my staff I passed over this Jordan; and now I have become two camps. *12* Deliver me, I pray You, from the hand of my brother, from the hand of Esau; for I fear him, lest he come and kill me, the mother with the children. *13* And You said: I will surely do you good, and make your offspring as the sand of the sea, which cannot be numbered for multitude.' *14* And he lodged there that night; and took of that which he had with him a present for Esau his brother: *15* two hundred she-goats and twenty he-goats, two hundred ewes and twenty rams, *16* thirty camels and their colts, forty cows and ten bulls, twenty she-donkeys and ten foals. *17* And he delivered them into the hand of his servants, every drove by itself; and said to his servants: 'Pass over before me, and put a space between drove and drove.' *18* And he commanded the foremost, saying: 'When Esau my brother meets you, and asks you, saying: Whose are you? and where you go? and whose are these before you? *19* then you shall say: They are your servant's Jacob; it is a present sent to my lord, to Esau; and, behold, he also is behind us.' *20* And he commanded also the second, and the third, and all that followed the droves, saying: 'In this manner shall you speak to Esau, when you find him;

21 and you shall say: Moreover, behold, your servant Jacob is behind us.' For he said: 'I will appease him with the present that goes before me, and afterward I will see his face; if he will accept me.' *22* So the present passed over before him and he himself lodged that night in the camp. *23* And he rose up that night, and took his two wives, and his two handmaids, and his eleven children, and passed over the waters of the Jabbok. *24* And he took them, and sent them over the stream, and sent over that which he had. *25* And Jacob was left alone; and there a man wrestled with him until the breaking of the day. *26* And when he saw that he prevailed not against him, he touched the hollow of his thigh; and the hollow of Jacob's thigh was strained, as he wrestled with him. *27* And he said: 'Let me go, for the day dawns.' And he said: 'I will not let you go, unless you bless me.' *28* And he said to him: 'What is your name?' And he said: 'Jacob.' *29* And he said: 'Your name shall no longer be called Jacob, but **Israel**; for you have struggled with **YeHoVaH** and with men, and have prevailed.' *30* And Jacob asked him, and said: 'Tell me, I pray you, your name.' And he said: 'Why is it that you ask after my name?' And he blessed him there.

31 And Jacob called the name of the place Peniel: 'for I have seen a divine being *face to face*, and my life is preserved.' *32* And the sun rose upon him as he passed over Peniel, and he limped upon his thigh. *33* Therefore the children of Israel do not eat the tendon of the thigh-vein that is upon the hollow of the thigh, to this day; because he touched the hollow of Jacob's thigh, even in the tendon of the thigh-vein.

Chapter 33

When Esau and his men arrive Jacob bows down but Esau runs to embrace him. They go their separate ways Jacob settles near Shechem and builds an altar.

1 And Jacob lifted up his eyes and looked, and, behold, Esau came, and with him four hundred men. And he divided the children to Leah, and to Rachel, and to the two handmaids. *2* And he put the handmaids and their children foremost, and Leah and her children after, and Rachel and Joseph further behind. *3* And he himself passed over before them, and bowed himself to the ground seven times, until he came near to his brother. *4* And Esau ran to meet him, and embraced him, and fell on his neck, and kissed him; and they wept. *5* And he lifted up his eyes, and saw the women and the children; and said: 'Who are these with you?' And he said: 'The children whom **Elohim** has graciously given your servant.' *6* Then the handmaids came near, they and their children, and they bowed down. *7* And Leah also and her children came near, and bowed down; and after came Joseph near and Rachel, and they bowed down. *8* And he said: 'What do you mean by all this camp which I met?' And he said: 'To find favor in the sight of my lord.' *9* And Esau said: 'I have enough; my brother, let that which you have be yours.' *10* And Jacob said: 'No, I pray you, if now I have found favor in your sight, then receive my gift at my hand; forasmuch as I have seen your face, as one sees the face of **Elohim**, and you were pleased with me.

11 Take, I pray you, my gift that is brought to you; because **Elohim** has dealt graciously with me, and because I have enough.' And he urged him, and he took it. *12* And he said: 'Let us take our journey, and let us go, and I will go before you.' *13* And he said to him: 'My lord knows that the children are tender, and that the flocks and herds giving milk are a care to me; and if they overdrive them one day, all the flocks will die. *14* Let my lord, I pray you, pass over before his servant; and I will journey on gently, according to the pace of the cattle that are before me and according to the pace of the children, until I come to my lord to Seir.' *15* And Esau said: 'Let me now leave with you some of the people that are with me.' And he said: 'What do I need? let me find favor in the sight of my lord.' *16* So Esau returned that day on his way to Seir. *17* And Jacob journeyed to Succoth, and built a house, and made **booths** for his cattle. Therefore the name of the place is called **Succoth**. *18* And Jacob came in peace to the city of Shechem, which is in the land of Canaan, when he came from Paddan-aram; and camped before the city. *19* And he bought the parcel of ground, where he had spread his tent, at the hand of the children of Hamor, Shechem's father, for a hundred pieces of money. *20* And he erected there an altar, and called it El-elohe-Israel. (Booths are the custom at the holiday of Sukkot)

Chapter 34
Shechem rapes Jacob's daughter Dinah then asks if he can marry her. Jacob's sons tell him to circumcise his men, then Simeon and Levi kill them all.

1 And Dinah the daughter of Leah, whom she had borne to Jacob, went out to see the daughters of the land. *2* And Shechem the son of Hamor the Hivite, the prince of the land, saw her; and he took her, and lay with her, and humbled her. *3* And his soul did cleave to Dinah the daughter of Jacob, and he loved the maiden, and spoke comfortingly to her. *4* And Shechem spoke to his father Hamor, saying: 'Get me this maiden as my wife.' *5* Now Jacob heard that he had defiled Dinah his daughter; and his sons were with his cattle in the field; and Jacob held his peace until they came. *6* And Hamor the father of Shechem went out to Jacob to speak with him. *7* And the sons of Jacob came in from the field when they heard it; and the men were grieved, and they were very angry, because he had brought a vile deed in Israel in lying with Jacob's daughter; which should not had been done. *8* And Hamor spoke with them, saying 'The soul of my son Shechem longs for your daughter. I pray you give her to him to be his wife. *9* And make you marriages with us; give your daughters to us, and take our daughters to you. *10* And you shall dwell with us; and the land shall be before you; dwell and trade here therein, and get you possessions here.'

11 And Shechem said to her father and to her brethren: 'Let me find favor in your eyes, and what you shall say to me I will give.*12* Ask me never so much money and gift, and I will give according as you shall say to me; but give me the maiden for his wife.' *13* And the sons of Jacob answered Shechem and Hamor his father with guile, and spoke, because he had defiled

Dinah their sister, *14* and said to them: 'We cannot do this thing, to give our sister to one that is *uncircumcised*; for that is a reproach to us. *15* Only on this condition will we consent to you: if you will be as we are, that every male of you be circumcised; *16* then will we give our daughters to you, and we will take your daughters to us, and we will dwell with you, and we will become one people. *17* But if you will not listen to us, to be circumcised; then will we take our daughter, and we will be gone.' *18* And their words pleased Hamor, and Shechem Hamor's son. *19* And the young man agreed to do the thing, because he had delight in Jacob's daughter. And he was honored above all the house of his father. *20* And Hamor and Shechem his son came to the gate of their city, and spoke with the men of their city, saying:

21 'These men are peaceable with us; therefore let them dwell in the land, and trade therein; for, behold, the land is large enough for them; let us take their daughters to us for wives, and let us give them our daughters. *22* Only on this condition will the men consent to us to dwell with us, to become one people, if every male among us be circumcised, as they are circumcised. *23* Shall not their cattle and their belongings and all their beasts be ours? only let us give consent to them, and they will dwell with us.' *24* And to Hamor and to Shechem his son hearkened all that went out of the gate of his city; and every male was circumcised, all that went out of the gate of his city. *25* And it came to pass on the *third* day, when they *were in pain*, that two of the sons of Jacob, Simeon and Levi, Dinah's brothers, took each man his sword, and came upon the city silently, and slew all the males. *26* And they slew Hamor and Shechem his son with the edge of the sword, and took Dinah out of Shechem's house, and went forth. *27* The sons of Jacob came upon the slain, and destroyed the city, because they had defiled their sister. *28* They took their flocks and their herds and their donkeys, and that which was in the city and that which was in the field; *29* and all their wealth, and all their little ones and their wives, they took captive and all the goods, even all that was in the house. *30* And when Jacob found out, he said to Simeon and Levi: 'You have troubled me, to make me detestable to the inhabitants of the land, even to the Canaanites and the Perizzites; and, I being few in number, they will gather themselves together against me and kill me; and I shall be destroyed, I and my house.'

31 And they said: 'Should one deal with our sister as with a harlot?'

Chapter 35
Jacob goes to Bethel and YeHoVaH renames him Israel. They journeyed on. Rachel dies having Israel's (Jacob's) twelfth son, Benjamin. Isaac dies in Hebron.

1 And **Elohim** said to Jacob: 'Arise, go up to Beth-el, and dwell there; and make there an altar to Me, who appeared to you when you did flee from the face of Esau your brother.' *2* Then Jacob said to his household, and to all that were with him: 'Put away the strange gods that are among you, and purify yourselves, and change your garments; *3* and let us arise, and go up to Beth-el; and I will make there an altar to **Elohim**, who answered me in the day of my distress, and was with me in the way which I went.' *4* And they gave to Jacob all the foreign gods that were in their hand, and the rings which were in their ears; and Jacob hid them under the cashew tree which was by Shechem. *5* And they journeyed; and a terror of **Elohim** was upon the cities that were around them, and no one pursued after the sons of Jacob. *6* So Jacob came to Luz, which is in the land of Canaan--the same is Beth-el--he and all the people that were with him. *7* And he built there an altar, and called the place El-beth-el, because there, **Elohim** was revealed to him, when he fled from the face of his brother. *8* And Deborah,

Rebekah's nurse died, and she was buried below Beth-el under the oak; and the name of it was called Allon-bacuth. *9* And **Elohim** appeared to Jacob again, when he came from Paddan-aram, and blessed him. *10* And **Elohim** said to him: 'Your name is Jacob: your name shall not be called any more Jacob, but **Israel** shall be your name'; and He called his name **Israel**.

11 And **Elohim** said to him: 'I am **El Shaddai** (God Almighty): be fruitful and multiply; a nation and a company of nations shall be of you, and kings shall come out of your loins; *12* and the land which I gave to Abraham and Isaac, to you I will give it, and to your offspring after you will I give the land.' *13* And **Elohim** went up from him in the place where He spoke with him. *14* And Jacob (Israel) set up a pillar in the place where He spoke with him, a pillar of stone, and he offered a drink on it and poured oil on it. *15* And Jacob called the name of the place where **Elohim** spoke with him, Beth-el. *16* And they journeyed from Beth-el; and there was still some way to come to Ephrath; and Rachel was in pain with labor. *17* And it came to pass, when she was in hard labor that the mid-wife said to her: 'Fear not; for this also is a son for you.' *18* And it came to pass, as her soul was in departing--for she died--that she called his name Ben-oni; but his father called him **Benjamin**. *19* And Rachel died, and was buried in the way to Ephrath--the same is Beth-lehem. *20* And Jacob set up a pillar upon her grave; the same is the pillar of Rachel's grave to this day.

21 And Israel (Jacob) journeyed, and spread his tent beyond Migdal-eder. *22* And it came to pass, while Israel dwelt in that land that Reuben went and laid with Bilhah his father's concubine; and Israel heard of it. Now the sons of Jacob were *twelve*: *23* the sons of Leah: Reuben, Jacob's first-born, and Simeon, and Levi, and Judah, and Issachar, and Zebulun; *24* the sons of Rachel: Joseph and Benjamin; *25* and the sons of Bilhah, Rachel's handmaid: Dan and Naphtali; *26* and the sons of Zilpah, Leah's handmaid: Gad and Asher. These are the sons of Jacob that were born to him in Paddan-aram. *27* And Jacob came to Isaac his father to Mamre, to Kiriatharba--the same is Hebron--where Abraham and Isaac sojourned. *28* And the days of Isaac were 180 years. *29* And *Isaac died*, and was gathered to his people, old and full of days; and Esau and Jacob his sons buried him.

Chapter 36
Esau has sons named Eliphaz, Reuel, Jeush, Jalam and Korah. He and his family move away to Seir and become the Edomites.

1 Now these are the generations of Esau (Edom). *2* Esau took his wives of the daughters of Canaan; Adah the daughter of Elon the Hittite, and Oholibamah the daughter of Anah, the daughter of Zibeon the Hivite, *3* and Basemath Ishmael's daughter, sister of Nebaioth. *4* And Adah bore to Esau Eliphaz; and Basemath bore Reuel; *5* and Oholibamah bore Jeush, and Jalam, and Korah. These are the sons of Esau, that were born to him in the land of Canaan. *6* And Esau took his wives, and his sons, and his daughters, and all the members of his house, and his cattle, and all his animals, and all his possessions, which he had gathered in the land of Canaan; and went into a land away from his brother Jacob. *7* For their possessions were too great for them to dwell together; and the land they were living could not bear them because of their cattle. *8* And Esau dwelt in the mountain-land of Seir--Esau is Edom. *9* And these are the generations of Esau the father of the Edomites in the mountain-land of Seir. *10* These are the names of Esau's sons: Eliphaz the son of Adah the wife of Esau, Reuel the son of Basemath the wife of Esau.

11 And the sons of Eliphaz were Teman, Omar, Zepho, and Gatam, and Kenaz. *12* And Timna was mistress to Eliphaz Esau's son; and she bore to Eliphaz Amalek. These are the sons of Adah Esau's wife. *13* And these are the sons of Reuel: Nahath, and Zerah, Shammah, and Mizzah. These were the sons of Basemath Esau's wife. *14* And these were the sons of Oholibamah the daughter of Anah, the daughter of Zibeon, Esau's wife; and she bore to Esau Jeush, and Jalam, and Korah. *15* These are the chiefs of the sons of Esau: the sons of Eliphaz the first-born of Esau: the chief of Teman, the chief of Omar, the chief of Zepho, the chief of Kenaz, *16* the chief of Korah, the chief of Gatam, the chief of Amalek. These are the chiefs that came of Eliphaz in the land of Edom. These are the sons of Adah. *17* And these are the sons of Reuel Esau's son: the chief of Nahath, the chief of Zerah, the chief of Shammah, the chief of Mizzah. These are the chiefs that came of Reuel in the land of Edom. These are the sons of Basemath Esau's wife. *18* And these are the sons of Oholibamah Esau's wife: the chief of Jeush, the chief of Jalam, the chief of Korah. These are the chiefs that came of Oholibamah the daughter of Anah, Esau's wife. *19* These are the sons of Esau, and these are their chiefs; the same is Edom. *20* These are the sons of Seir the Horite, the inhabitants of the land: Lotan and Shobal and Zibeon and Anah,

21 and Dishon and Ezer and Dishan. These are the chiefs that came of the Horites, the children of Seir in the land of Edom. *22* And the children of Lotan were Hori and Hemam; and Lotan's sister was Timna. *23* And these are the children of Shobal: Alvan and Manahath and Ebal, Shepho and Onam. *24* And these are the children of Zibeon: Aiah and Anah--this is Anah who found the hot springs in the wilderness, as he fed the donkeys of Zibeon his father. *25* And these are the children of Anah: Dishon and Oholibamah the daughter of Anah. *26* And these are the children of Dishon: Hemdan and Eshban and Ithran and Cheran. *27* These are the children of Ezer: Bilhan and Zaavan and Akan. *28* These are the children of Dishan: Uz and Aran. *29* These are the chiefs that came of the Horites: the chief of Lotan, the chief of Shobal, the chief of Zibeon, the chief of Anah, *30* the chief of Dishon, the chief of Ezer, the chief of Dishan. These are the chiefs that came of the Horites, according to their chiefs in the land of Seir.

31 And these are the kings that reigned in the land of Edom, before there reined any king over the children of Israel. *32* And Bela the son of Beor reigned in Edom; and the name of his city was Dinhabah. *33* And Bela died, and Jobab the son of Zerah of Bozrah reigned in his place. *34* And Jobab died, and Husham of the land of the Temanites reigned in his place. *35* And Husham died, and Hadad the son of Bedad, who destroyed Midian in the field of Moab, reined in his stead; and the name of his city was Avith. *36* And Hadad died, and Samlah of Masrekah reigned in his stead. *37* And Samlah died, and Shaul of Rehoboth by the River reigned in his stead. *35* And Shaul died, and Baal-hanan the son of Achbor reigned in his stead. *38* And at the death of Shaul, Baal-hanan, son of Achbor, became king. *39* And Baal-hanan the son of Achbor died, and Hadar reigned in his stead; and the name of the city was Pau; and his wife's name was Mehetabel, the daughter of Matred, the daughter of Me-zahab. *40* And these are the names of the chiefs that came of Esau, according to their families, after their places, by their names: the chief of Timna, the chief of Alvah, the chief of Jetheth;

41 the chief of Oholibamah, the chief of Elah, the chief of Pinon; *42* the chief of Kenaz, the chief of Teman, the chief of Mibzar; *43* the chief of Magdiel, the chief of Iram. These are the chiefs of Edom, according to their place of residence in the land of their possession. This is Esau the father of the Edomites.

Reading 8 ends

GENESIS

Chapter 37

Joseph, who is Israel's (Jacob's) favorite son, has dreams and his brothers are jealous so they sell him to the Ishmaelites for twenty shekels of silver. The Ishmaelites sell him to Potiphar, an officer of Pharaoh's, who was the captain of the guard in Egypt.

Reading 9 begins

1 And Jacob dwelt in the land where his father had once lived, in the land of Canaan. *2* These are the generations of **Jacob**. **Joseph**, being seventeen years old, was feeding the flock with his brethren, being still young and with the sons of Zilpah, his father's wives; and Joseph brought evil report of them to their father. *3* Now Israel loved Joseph *more* than all his children, because he was the son of his old age; and he made him a *coat of many colors*. *4* And when his brothers saw that their father loved him more than all his brethren, they *hated* him, and could not speak peaceably to him. *5* One night Joseph dreamed a dream, and he told it to his brothers; and they hated him all the more. *6* And he said to them: 'Hear, I pray you, this dream which I have dreamed: *7* for, behold, we were binding sheaves in the field, and, my sheaf arose, and also stood upright; and, behold, your sheaves came round about, and bowed down to my sheaf.' *8* And his brethren said to him: 'Shall you indeed reign over us? or shall you indeed have dominion over us?' And they hated him even *more* for his dreams, and for his words. *9* And he dreamed yet another dream, and told it to his brothers, and said: 'Behold, I have dreamed yet another dream: and, behold, the sun and the moon and eleven stars bowed down to me.' *10* And he told it to his father, and to his brothers; and his father reprimanded (rebuked) him, and said to him: 'What is this dream that you have dreamed? Shall I and your mother and your brothers indeed come to bow down to you to the earth?'

11 And his brothers envied him; but his father kept the dream in his mind. *12* And his brothers went to feed their father's flock in Shechem. *13* And Israel (Jacob) said to Joseph: 'Do not your brothers feed the flock in Shechem? come, and I will send you to them.' And he said to him: 'Here am I.' *14* And he said to him: 'Go now, see whether it is well with your brothers, and well with the flock; and bring me back word.' So he sent him out of the valley of Hebron, and he came to Shechem. *15* And a certain man found him, and, behold, he was wandering in the field. And the man asked him, saying: 'What are you seeking?' *16* And Joseph said: 'I seek my brethren. Tell me, I pray you, where they are feeding the flock.' *17* And the man said: 'They departed that way; for I heard them say: Let us go to Dothan.' And Joseph went after his brothers, and found them in Dothan. *18* And they saw him far off, and before he came near to them, they conspired against him to slay him. *19* And they said one to another: 'Behold, this dreamer comes. *20* Come now therefore, and let us slay him, and cast him into one of the pits, and we will say: An evil beast devoured him; and we shall see what will become of his dreams.'

21 And Reuben heard it, and delivered him out of their hand; and said: 'Let us not take his life.' *22* And Reuben said to them: 'Shed no blood; cast him into this pit that is in the wilderness, but lay no hand upon him'. Reuben wanted to deliver him out of their hand, to restore him to his father. *23* And it came to pass, when Joseph came to his brothers, that they stripped Joseph of his coat, the coat of many colors that was on him; *24* and they took him, and cast him into the pit--and the pit was empty, there was no water in it. *25* And they sat down to eat bread; and they lifted up their eyes and looked, and, behold, a caravan of Ishmaelites came from Gilead, with their camels bearing spics and balm and perfume (*ladanum*), going to carry it down to Egypt. *26* And *Judah* said to his brothers: 'What profit is it if we slay our brother and conceal his blood? *27* Come, and let us sell him to the Ishmaelites, and let not our hand be upon him; for he is our brother, our flesh.' And his brethren listened to him. *28* And there passed by Midianites, merchantmen; and they drew and lifted up Joseph out of the pit, and sold Joseph to the Ishmaelites for twenty shekels of silver. And the Ishmaelites brought Joseph into Egypt. *29* And Reuben returned to the pit; and, behold, Joseph was not in the pit; and he tore (*rent*) *his clothes.* *30* And he returned to his brothers, and said: 'Joseph is not there; and as for me, where shall I go?'

31 And they took Joseph's coat, and killed a he-goat, and dipped the coat in the blood; *32* and they sent the coat of many colors, and they brought it to their father; and said: 'This we have found. Know now whether it is your son's coat or not.' *33* And he knew it, and said: 'It is my son's coat; an evil beast has devoured him; Joseph is without doubt torn in pieces.' *34* And Jacob *tore (rent) his garments*, and put sackcloth upon his loins, and mourned for his son many days. *35* And all his sons and all his daughters rose up to comfort him; but he refused to be comforted; and he said: 'I will go down to the grave to my son mourning.' And his father wept for him. *36* And the Midianites sold him into Egypt to **Potiphar**, an officer of Pharaoh's, the captain of the guard.

Chapter 38
YeHoVaH kills Judah's sons Er and Onan because they were evil, leaving Tamar a widow. Judah sends her away but years later she put on a veil and he (Judah) has relations with her and she has twins.

1 And it came to pass at that time that Judah went down from his brothers, and turned to a certain Adullamite, whose name was Hirah. *2* And Judah saw there a daughter of a Canaanite whose name was Shua; and he took her, and had relations (went in to) with her. *3* And she conceived, and bore a son; and he called his name Er. *4* And she conceived again, and bore a son; and she called his name Onan. *5* And she conceived again bore a son, and called his name Shelah; and he was at Chezib, when she bore him. *6* And Judah took a wife for Er his first-born, and her name was **Tamar**. *7* And Er, Judah's first-born, was wicked in the sight of **YeHoVaH**; and **YeHoVaH** killed (slew) him. *8* And Judah said to Onan: 'Have relations (go in to) your brother's wife, and *perform the duty of a husband's brother* to her, and raise up offspring to your brother.' *9* And Onan knew that the *offspring would not be his; and it came to pass when he went in to his brother's wife, that he spilled his seed on the ground*, so he would not give offspring to his brother. *10* And the thing that he did was evil in the sight of **YeHoVaH**; and He slew him also.

11 Then Judah said to Tamar his daughter-in-law: 'Remain a widow in your father's house, till Shelah my son grows of age'; for he said: 'Or he will also die, like his brother.' And Tamar went and dwelt in her father's house. *12* And after some time Shua's daughter, the wife of Judah, died; and Judah was comforted, and went up to his sheep-shearers to Timnah, he and his friend Hirah the Adullamite. *13* And it was told Tamar, saying: 'Behold, your father-in-law goes up to Timnah to shear his sheep.' *14* And she put took off the garments of her widowhood, and covered herself with her veil, and wrapped herself, and sat in the entrance of Enaim, which is by the way to Timnah; for she saw that Shelah was grown up, and she was not given to him for a wife as was custom. *15* When Judah saw her, he thought she was a harlot; for she had covered her face. *16* And he turned to her by the way, and said: 'Come, I pray you, let me have relations with (come in to) you'; for he didn't know that she was his daughter-in-law. And she said: 'What will you give me, that you may come in to me?' *17* And he said: 'I will send you a goat from the flock.' And she said: 'Will you give me a pledge, till you send it?' *18* And he said:

'What pledge shall I give you?' And she said: 'Your ring (*signet*) and your cord, and your staff that is in your hand.' And he gave them to her, and came in to her, and she conceived by him. *19* And she arose, and went away, and put off her veil from her, and put on the garments of her widowhood. *20* And Judah sent the young goat by the hand of his friend the Adullamite, to receive the pledge from the woman's hand; but he could not find her.

21 Then he asked the men where she was, saying: 'Where is the harlot that was at Enaim by the wayside?' And they said: 'There has been no harlot here.' *22* And he returned to Judah, and said: 'I have not found her; and also the men of the place said: There has been no harlot here.' *23* And Judah said: 'Let her take it, lest we be put to shame; behold, I sent this goat, and you have not found her.' *24* And it came to pass about three months later, that it was told Judah, saying: 'Tamar your daughter-in-law has played the harlot; and moreover, behold, she is with child by harlotry (prostitution).' And Judah said: 'Bring her forth, and let her be burnt.' *25* When she was brought forth, she sent to her father-in-law, saying: 'By the man, whose these are, I am with child'; and she said: 'Decide, I pray you, whose are these, the signet, and the cords, and the staff.' *26* And Judah acknowledged them, and said: 'She is more righteous than I; forasmuch as I gave her not to Shelah my son.' And he knew her again no more. *27* And it came to pass in the time of her troubles, that, behold, twins were in her womb. *28* And it came to pass, when she was in labor, that one put out a hand; and the midwife took and bound upon his hand a scarlet thread, saying: 'This one came out first.' *29* And it came to pass, as he drew back his hand, that, behold his brother came out; and she said: 'Why have you made a breach for yourself?' Therefore his name was called **Perez**. *30* And afterward came out his brother, that had the scarlet thread upon his hand; and his name was called **Zerah**.

Chapter 39
Potiphar, the captain of the guard puts Joseph in charge of his house. His wife tries to seduce Joseph, and then lies about it, so Potiphar throws Joseph in prison.

1 And Joseph was brought down to Egypt; and Potiphar, an officer of Pharaoh's, the captain of the guard, an Egyptian, bought him from the hand of the Ishmaelites, that had brought him there. *2* And **YeHoVaH** was with Joseph, and he was a prosperous man; and he was in the house of his master the Egyptian. *3* And his master saw that **YeHoVaH** was with him, and that **YeHoVaH** made all that he did to prosper in his hand. *4* And Joseph found favor in his sight, and he ministered to him. And he appointed him overseer over his house, and all that he had he put into his hand. And it came to pass from the time that he appointed him overseer in his house and over all that he had, that **YeHoVaH** blessed the Egyptian's house for Joseph's sake; and the blessing of **YeHoVaH** was upon all that he had, in the house and in the field. *6* And he left all that he had in Joseph's hand; and, having him, he knew nothing about the bread that he did eat. And Joseph was of handsome form, and fair to look upon. *7* And it came to pass after these things that his master's wife cast her eyes upon Joseph; and she said: 'Lie with me.' *8* But he refused, and said to his master's wife: 'Behold, my master, knows not what is in the house, and he has put all that he has into my hand; *9* he is not greater in this house than I; neither has he kept back anything from me but you, because you are his wife. How then can I do this great wickedness, and sin against **Elohim**?' *10* And it came to pass, as she spoke to Joseph day by day, that he did not listen to her, or lie by her, or be with her.

11 And it came to pass one day, when he went into the house to do his work, and there was none of the men of the house there, *12* that she caught him by his garment, saying: 'Lie with me.' And he fled and left his garment in her hand, and got out. *13* And it came to pass, when she saw that he had left his garment in her hand, and had fled, *14* that she called to the men of her house, and spoke to them, saying: 'See, he has brought in a *Hebrew* to us to mock us; he came in to me to lie with me, and I cried with a loud voice. *15* And when he heard that I lifted up my voice and cried, he left his garment by me, and fled, and got out.' *16* And she laid up his garment by her, until his master came home. *17* And she spoke to him according to these words, saying: 'The Hebrew servant, whom you have brought to us, came in to me to mock me. *18* And it came to pass, as I lifted up my voice and cried, that he left his garment by me, and fled out.' *19* And it came to pass, when his master heard the words of his wife, which she spoke to him, saying: 'This is what your servant did to me'; that his anger was sparked. *20* And Joseph's master took him, and put him into the prison, the place where the king's prisoners were bound; and he remained there in the prison.

21 But **YeHoVaH** was with Joseph, and showed kindness to him, and gave him favor in the sight of the keeper of the prison. *22* And the keeper of the prison assigned to Joseph's hand all the prisoners that were in the prison; and whatever they did there, he was responsible for it. *23* The keeper of the prison did not have to follow up on anything that was under his hand, because **YeHoVaH** was with him; and that which he did, **YeHoVaH** made it to prosper.

Chapter 40

The cupbearer and baker of Pharaoh are put in prison. While there Joseph interprets their dreams. Joseph's interpretations come true as the cupbearer is restored but the baker is hanged.

1 And it came to pass after these things, that the butler of the king of Egypt and his baker offended their lord the king of Egypt. *2* And Pharaoh was wroth against his two officers, against the chief of the butlers, and against the chief of the bakers. *3* And he put them in ward in the house of the captain of the guard, into the prison, the place where Joseph was kept. *4* And the captain of the guard charged Joseph to be with them, and he ministered to them; and they were in confinement for some time. *5* And they dreamed a dream, both of them, each man his dream, in the same night, each man according to the interpretation of his dream, the butler and the baker of the king of Egypt, who were bound in the prison. *6* And Joseph came to them in the morning, and saw them, and, behold, they were sad. *7* And he asked Pharaoh's officers that were with him in the ward of his master's house, saying: 'Why do you look so sad today?' *8* And they said to him: 'We have dreamed a dream, and there is no one that can interpret it.' And Joseph said to them: 'Do not interpretations belong to **Elohim**? Tell me the dream, I pray you.' *9* And the chief butler told his dream to Joseph, and said to him: 'In my dream, behold, a vine was before me; *10* and in the vine were three branches; and as it was budding, its blossoms shot forth, and the clusters thereof brought forth ripe grapes,

11 and Pharaoh's cup was in my hand; and I took the grapes, and pressed them into Pharaoh's cup, and I gave the cup into Pharaoh's hand.' *12* And Joseph said to him: 'This is the interpretation of it: the three branches are three days; *13* within you three days shall Pharaoh lift up your head, and restore you to your office; and you shall give Pharaoh's cup into his hand, after the former manner when you were his butler. *14* But keep me in your memory when it shall be well with you, and show kindness, I pray you, to me, and make mention of me to Pharaoh, and bring me out of this prison. *15* For indeed I was stolen away out of the land of the Hebrews; and here have I done nothing that they should put me into the dungeon.' *16* When the chief baker saw that the interpretation was good, he said to Joseph: 'I also saw in my dream, and, behold, three baskets of white bread were on my head; *17* and in the top basket there was all manner of baked food for Pharaoh; and the birds did eat them out of the basket upon my head.' *18* And Joseph answered and said: 'This is the interpretation: the three baskets are three days; *19* within yet three days shall Pharaoh lift up your head from off you, and shall hang you on a tree; and the birds shall eat your flesh from off you.' *20* And it came to pass the third day, which was Pharaoh's birthday that he made a feast to all his servants; and he lifted up the head of the chief butler and the head of the chief baker among his servants.

21 And he restored the chief butler back to his duties; and he gave the cup into Pharaoh's hand. *22* But he hanged the chief baker, as Joseph had interpreted to them. *23* But the chief butler did not remember Joseph, but forgot him.
Reading 9 ends

CHAPTERS 41- 50

Chapter 41
Pharaoh has a disturbing dream and asks Joseph to interpret it. Joseph is rewarded for his interpretation. The great famine begins in Egypt.
Reading 10 begins

1 And it came to pass at the end of two full years that Pharaoh dreamed: and, behold, he stood by the river. *2* And, behold, there came up out of the river seven cows, well favored and fat; and they fed in the reed-grass. *3* And, behold, seven other cows came up after them out of the river, ill-favored and thin; and stood by the other cows upon the bank of the river. *4* And the ill-favored and thin cows ate up the seven well-favored and fat cows. So Pharaoh awoke. *5* And he slept and dreamed a second time: and, behold, seven ears of corn came up upon one stalk, full and good. *6* And, behold, seven ears, thin and blasted with the east wind, sprung up after them. *7* And the thin ears swallowed up the seven good and full ears. And Pharaoh awoke, and, behold, it was a dream. *8* And it came to pass in the morning that his spirit was troubled; and he sent and called for all the magicians of Egypt, and all the wise men; and Pharaoh told them his dream; but there was none that could interpret them to Pharaoh. *9* Then the chief butler spoke to Pharaoh, saying: 'I remember my faults this day: *10* when Pharaoh was angry with his servants, and put me in the prison of the house of the captain of the guard, the chief baker and me.

11 And we both dreamed a dream in one night, we dreamed each man according to the interpretation of his dream. *12* And there was with us there a young man, a Hebrew, servant to the captain of the guard; and we told him, and he interpreted each of our dreams; *13* And it came to pass, as he interpreted to us, so it was: I was restored to my office, and he was hanged.' *14* Then Pharaoh sent and called Joseph, and they brought him hurriedly out of the dungeon. And he shaved himself, and changed his clothes, and came in to Pharaoh. *15* And Pharaoh said to Joseph: 'I have dreamed a dream, and there is no one that can interpret it; and I have heard say of you, that when you hear a dream you can interpret it.' *16* And Joseph answered Pharaoh, saying: 'It is not in me; *Elohim* will give Pharaoh an answer of peace.' *17* And Pharaoh spoke to Joseph: 'In my dream, behold, I stood upon the brink of the river. *18* And, behold, there came up out of the river seven cows, fat and well-favored; and they fed in the reed grass. *19* And, behold, seven other cows came up after them, poor and very ill-favored and thin, such as I never saw in all the land of Egypt for badness. *20* And the thin and ill-favored cows ate up the first seven fat cows.

21 And when they had eaten them up, it could not be known that they had eaten them; but they were still ill-favored as in the beginning. So I awoke. *22* And I saw in my dream, and, behold, seven ears came up upon one stalk, full and good. *23* And, behold, seven ears, withered, thin, and blasted with the east wind, sprung up after them. *24* And the thin ears swallowed up the seven good ears. And I told it to the magicians; but there was no one that could interpret it to me.' *25* And Joseph said to Pharaoh: 'The dream of Pharaoh is one; what **Elohim** is about to do He has declared to Pharaoh. *26* The seven good cows are seven years; and the seven good ears are seven years: the dream is one. *27* And the seven lean and ill-favored cows that came up after them are seven years, and also the seven empty ears blasted with the east wind; they shall be seven years of famine. *28* That is the thing which Joseph spoke to Pharaoh: what **Elohim** is about to do He has shown to Pharaoh. *29* Behold, there comes seven years of great plenty throughout all the land of Egypt. *30* And there shall arise after them seven years of famine; and all the plenty shall be forgotten in the land of Egypt; and the famine shall consume the land;

31 and the plenty shall not be known in the land by reason of that famine which follows; for it shall be very grave. *32* And for that the dream was doubled to Pharaoh twice, it is because the thing is established by **Elohim**, and **Elohim** will shortly bring it to pass. *33* Now therefore let Pharaoh seek out a man discreet and wise, and set him over the land of Egypt. *34* Let Pharaoh do this, and let him appoint overseers over the land, and take up the fifth part of the land of Egypt in the seven years of plenty. *35* And let them gather all the food of these good years that come, and lay up corn under the hand of Pharaoh for food in the cities, and let them keep it. *36* And the food shall be for a store to the land against the seven years of famine, which shall be in the land of Egypt; that the land perish not through the famine.' *37* And the thing was good in the eyes of Pharaoh, and in the eyes of all his servants. *38* And Pharaoh said to his servants: 'Can we find such a one as this, a man in whom the spirit of **Elohim** resides?' *39* And Pharaoh said to Joseph: 'Forasmuch as **Elohim** has shown you all this, there is none as discreet and wise as you. *40* You shall be over my house, and according to your word shall all my people be ruled; only in the throne will I be greater than you.'

41 And Pharaoh said to Joseph: 'See, I have set you over all the land of Egypt.' *42* And Pharaoh took off his signet ring from his hand, and put it upon Joseph's hand, and dressed him in garments of fine linen, and put a gold chain about his neck. *43* And he made him to ride in the second chariot that he had; and they cried before him: **'Abrech'**; and he set him over all the land of Egypt. *44* And Pharaoh said to Joseph: 'I am Pharaoh, and without you shall no man lift up his hand or his foot in all the land of Egypt.' *45* And Pharaoh called Joseph's name Zaphenath-paneah; and he gave him to wife **Asenath** the daughter of Poti-phera priest of On. And Joseph went out over the land of Egypt. *46* And Joseph was 30 years old when he stood before Pharaoh King of Egypt. --And Joseph went out from the presence of Pharaoh, and went throughout all the land of Egypt. *47* And in the seven years of plenty the earth brought forth in heaps. *48* And he gathered up one fifth of all the food of the seven years which were in the land of Egypt, and laid up the food in the cities; the food of the field, which was around every city, he stored the grain. *49* And Joseph laid up corn as the sand of the sea, very much, until they left off numbering; for it was without number. *50* And to Joseph were born two sons before the year of famine came, whom Asenath the daughter of Poti-phera priest of On bore to him.

51 And Joseph called the name of the first-born **Manasseh**: 'for *Elohim* has made me forget all my toil, and all my father's house.' *52* And the name of the second he called **Ephraim**: 'for *Elohim* has made me fruitful in the land of my affliction.' *53* And the seven years of plenty, that was in the land of Egypt, came to an end. *54* And the seven years of famine began to come, according to what Joseph had said; and there was famine in all lands; but in all the land of Egypt there was bread. *55* And when all the land of Egypt was famished, the people cried to Pharaoh for bread; and Pharaoh said to all the Egyptians: 'Go to Joseph; what he says to you, do.' *56* And the famine was over all the face of the earth; and Joseph opened all the storehouses, and sold to the Egyptians; and the famine was grave in the land of Egypt. *57* And all countries came into Egypt to Joseph to buy corn; because the famine was great in all the lands.

Chapter 42

Joseph's brothers come to Egypt to buy food and meet their brother Joseph who they do not recognize.

1 Now Jacob (Israel) saw that there was corn in Egypt, and Jacob said to his sons: 'Why do you look one upon another?' *2* And he said: 'Behold, I have heard that there is corn in Egypt. Go there, and buy for us from there; that we may live, and not die.' *3* And Joseph's ten brethren went down to buy corn from Egypt. *4* But Benjamin, Joseph's brother, Jacob did not send with his brothers; for he said: 'Lest harm befall him.' *5* And the sons of Israel came to buy among all the others that came; for the famine was in the land of Canaan. *6* And Joseph was the governor over the land; he was the one that sold to all the people of the land. And Joseph's brothers came, and bowed down to him with their faces to the earth. *7* And Joseph saw his brothers, and he knew them, but pretended not to recognize them, and spoke roughly with them; and he said to them: 'Where do you come from?' And they said: 'From the land of Canaan to buy food.' *8* And Joseph knew his brothers, but they knew him not. *9* And Joseph remembered the dreams that he dreamed of them, and said to them: 'You are spies; to see the secretes of the land you have come.' *10* And they said to him: 'No, my lord, but to buy food have your servants come.

11 We are all one man's sons; we are upright men, your servants are not spies.' *12* And he said to them: 'No, but to see the value of the land you have come.' *13* And they said: 'We your servants are twelve brothers, the sons of one man in the land of Canaan; and, behold, the youngest is this day with our father, and one is not.' *14* And Joseph said to them: 'That is it that I spoke to you, saying: You are spies. *15* Hereby you shall prove it, as Pharaoh lives, you shall not go further, unless your youngest brother come here. *16* Send one of you, and let him fetch your brother, and you shall be bound, that your words may be proved, whether there be truth in you; or else, as Pharaoh lives, surely you are spies.' *17* And he put them all together into prison three days. *18* And Joseph said to them the third day. 'Do this and live; for I fear *Elohim*: *19* if you are upright men, let one of your brothers be bound in your prison-house; but go you, carry corn for the famine of your houses; *20* and bring your youngest brother to me; so shall your words be verified, and you shall not die.' And they did so.

21 And they said one to another: 'We are surely guilty concerning our brother, in that we saw the distress of his soul, when he sought us, and we would not hear; therefore is this distress come upon us.' *22* And Reuben answered them, saying: 'Didn't I speak to you, saying: Do not sin against the child; and you would not listen? therefore, behold, his blood is required.' *23* And they knew not that Joseph understood them; for the interpreter was between them. *24* And he turned himself from them, and wept; and he returned to them, and spoke to them, and took Simeon from among them, and bound him before their eyes. *25* Then Joseph commanded to fill their vessels with corn, and to restore every man's money into his sack, and to give them provision for the way; and thus was it done to them. *26* And they loaded their donkeys with their corn, and departed. *27* And as one of them opened his sack to give his donkey food in the lodging-place, he saw his money; and, behold, it was in the mouth of his sack. *28* And he said to his brothers: 'My money is restored; and, behold, it is even in my sack.' And their heart failed them, and they turned trembling one to another, saying: 'What is this that **Elohim** has done to us?' *29* And they returned to Jacob their father to the land of Canaan, and told him all that had happened to them, saying: *30* 'The man, the lord of the land, spoke roughly with us, and took us for spies of the country.

31 And we said to him: We are upright men; we are not spies. *32* We are twelve brothers, sons of our father; one is no longer (Joseph), and the youngest is this day with our father in the land of Canaan. *33* And the man, the lord of the land, said to us: Hereby shall I know that you are upright men: leave one of your brothers with me, and take corn for the famine of your houses, and go your way. *34* And bring your youngest brother to me; then shall I know that you are not spies, but that you are upright men; so will I deliver you your brother, and you shall travel in the land.' *35* And it came to pass as they emptied their sacks, that, behold, every man's bundle of money was in his sack; and when they and their father saw their bundles of money, they were afraid. *36* And Jacob their father said to them: 'Of me have you bereaved of my children: Joseph is no longer, and Simeon is there, and you want to take Benjamin away; upon me are all these things come.' *37* And Reuben spoke to his father, saying: 'You shall slay my two sons, if I don't bring him back to you; deliver him into my hand, and I will bring him back to you.' *38* And he said: 'My son shall not go down with you; for his brother is dead, and he only is left; if harm befall him by the way in which you go, then will you bring down my gray hairs with sorrow to the grave.

Chapter 43
Joseph's brothers return to Egypt for food and to retrieve their brother Simeon.

1 And the famine was great in the land. *2* And it came to pass, when they had eaten all the corn which they had brought out of Egypt, their father said to them: 'Go again, buy us a little food.' *3* And Judah spoke to him, saying: 'The man did seriously warn us, saying: You shall not see my face, unless your brother be with you. *4* If you will send our brother with us, we will go down and buy you food; 5 but if you will not send him, we will not go down, for the man said to us: You shall not see my face, unless your brother is with you.' *6* And Israel (Jacob) said: 'Why did you deal ill with me, as to tell the man that you had yet a brother?' *7* And they said: 'The man asked outright concerning ourselves, and concerning our kindred, saying: Is your father yet alive? have you another brother? and we told him according to the meaning of these words; could we in any way know that he would say: Bring your brother down?' *8* And Judah said to Israel his father: 'Send the lad with me, and we will arise and go, that we may live, and not die, both we, and you, and also our little ones. *9* I will be ransom for him; of my hand shall you require him; if I don't bring him to you, and set him before you, then let me bear the blame forever. *10* For if we had not lingered this long, surely we have already returned a second time by now.'

11 And their father Israel said to them: 'If it be so now, do this: take of the choice fruits of the land in your vessels, and carry down the man a present, a little balm, and a little honey, spice and perfume, nuts, and almonds; *12* and take double money in your hand; and the money that was returned in the mouth of your sacks carry back in your hand; in case it was an oversight; *13* take also your brother, and arise, go again to the man; *14* and **El Shaddai** Almighty give you mercy before the man, that he may release to you your other brother and Benjamin. And as for me, if I be deprived of my children, I am deprived.' *15* And the men took that present, and they took double money in their hand, and Benjamin; and rose up, and went down to Egypt, and stood before Joseph. *16* And when Joseph saw Benjamin with them, he said to the steward of his house: 'Bring the men into the house, and kill animals, and prepare an animal; for the men shall dine with me at noon.' *17* And the man did as Joseph instructed: and the man brought the men into Joseph's house. *18* And the men were afraid, because they were brought into Joseph's house; and they said: 'Because of the money that was returned in our sacks at the first time are we brought in; that he may seek harm against us, and fall upon us, and take us for bondmen, and our donkeys.' *19* And they came near to the steward of Joseph's house, and they spoke to him at the door of the house, *20* and said: 'Oh my lord, we came indeed down the first time to buy food.

21 And it came to pass, when we came to the lodging-place, that we opened our sacks, and, behold, every man's money was in the mouth of his sack, our money in full weight; and we have brought it back in our hand. *22* And other money have we brought down in our hand to buy food. We know not who put our money in our sacks.' *23* And he said: 'Peace be to you, fear not; your **YeHoVaH**, and the **Elohim** of your father, has given you treasure in your sacks; I had your money.' And he brought Simeon out to them. *24* And the man brought the men into Joseph's house, and gave them water, and they washed their feet; and he gave their donkeys food. *25* And they made ready their presents for Joseph's coming at noon; for they heard that they should eat bread there. *26* And when Joseph came home, they brought him the present that was in their hand into the house, and bowed down to him to the earth. *27* And he asked them of their welfare, and said: 'Is your father well, the old man of whom you spoke? Is he alive?' *28* And they said: 'Your servant our father is well, he is still alive.' And they bowed their heads, and showed respect. *29* And he lifted up his eyes, and saw Benjamin his brother, his mother's son, and said: 'Is this your youngest brother of whom you spoke to me?' And he said: '**Elohim** be gracious to you, my son.' *30* And Joseph hurried; for his heart yearned toward his brother; and he sought where to weep; and he entered into his chamber, and wept there.

31 And he washed his face, and came out; and he refrained himself, and said: 'Set on bread.' *32* And they set on for him by himself, and for them by themselves, and for the Egyptians, that did eat with him, by themselves; *because the Egyptians might not eat bread with the Hebrews*; for that is a disgrace to the Egyptians. *33* And they sat before him, the firstborn according to his birthright, and the youngest according to his youth; and the men marveled with one another. *34* And portions were taken to them from before him; but Benjamin's portion was five times so much as any of theirs. And they drank, and were merry with him.

Chapter 44
Joseph hides his cup in Benjamin's sack, and then sends a steward to overtake his brothers. Judah offers himself as a slave in place of Benjamin.

1 And Joseph commanded the steward of his house, saying: 'Fill the men's sacks with food, as much as they can carry, and put every man's money in his sack's mouth. *2* And put my goblet, the silver goblet, in the sack's mouth of the youngest, and his corn money.' And the steward did according to the word that Joseph had spoken. *3* As soon as the morning was light, the men were sent away, they and their donkeys. *4* And when they were gone out of the city, and were yet not far off, Joseph said to his steward: 'Go up, follow after the men; and when you do overtake them, say to them: Why have you rewarded evil for good? *5* Is not this in which my lord drinks, and whereby he indeed rules? you have done evil in so doing.' *6* And he overtook them, and he spoke to them these words. *7* And they said to him: 'Why does my lord speak such words as these? Far be it from your servants that they should do such a thing. *8* Behold, the money, which we found in our sacks' mouths, we brought back to you out of the land of Canaan; how then should we steal out of your lord's house silver or gold? *9* With whomever of your servants it be found, let him die, and we also will be my lord's bondmen.' *10* And he said: 'Now also let it be according to your words: he with whom it is found shall be my bondman; and you shall be blameless.'

11 Then they hurried, and took down every man's sack to the ground, and opened everyone. *12* And he searched, beginning at the eldest, and leaving off at the youngest; and the goblet was found in Benjamin's sack. *13* And they tore their clothes, and loaded every man his donkey, and returned to the city. *14* And Judah and his brothers came to Joseph's house, and he was out there; and they fell before him on the ground. *15* And Joseph said to them: 'What deed is this that you have done? Don't you know that such a man as I will know your intent?' *16* And Judah said: 'What shall we say to my lord? what shall we speak? or how shall we clear ourselves? **Elohim** has found out the iniquity of your servants; behold, we are my lord's bondmen, both we, and he also in whose hand the cup was found.' *17* And he said: 'Far be it from me that I should do so; the man in whose hand the goblet is found, he shall be my bondman; but as for you, get you up in peace to your father.'

Reading 10 ends

Reading 11 begins

18 Then Judah came near to him, and said: 'Oh my lord, let your servant, I pray you, speak a word in my lord's ears, and let not your anger burn against your servant; for you are even as Pharaoh. *19* My lord asked his servants, saying: Have you a father, or a brother? *20* And we said to my lord: We have a father, an old man, and a child of his old age, a little one; and his brother is dead, and he alone is left of his mother, and his father loves him.

21 And you said to your servants: Bring him down to me, that I may set mine eyes upon him. *22* And we said to my lord: The boy cannot leave his father; for if he should leave his father, his father would die. *23* And you said to your servants: Unless your youngest brother comes down with you, you shall see my face no more. *24* And it came to pass when we came up to your servant my father; we told him the words of my lord. *25* And our father said: Go again and buy us a little food. *26* And we said: We cannot go down; if our youngest brother is not with us, then will we go down; for we may not see the man's face, unless our youngest brother be with us. *27* And your servant my father said to us: You know that my wife bore me two sons; *28* and the one went out from me, and I said: Surely he is torn in pieces by wild animals; and I have not seen him since; *29* and if you take this one also from me, and harm befall him, you will bring down my gray hairs with sorrow to the grave. *30* Now therefore when I come to your servant my father, and the boy is not with us; seeing that his soul is bound up with the boy's soul;

31 it will come to pass, when he sees that the boy is not with us, that he will die; and your servants will bring down the gray hairs of your servant our father with sorrow to the grave. **32** For your servant became insurance for the boy to my father, saying: If I bring him not to you, then shall I bear the blame to my father forever. **33** Now therefore, let your servant, I pray you, stay instead of the boy a bondman to my lord; and let the boy go up with his brothers. **34** For how shall I go up to my father, if the boy is not with me? Or I look upon the evil that shall come on my father.'

Chapter 45
Joseph reveals himself to his brothers.

1 Then Joseph could not refrain himself before all those that stood by him; and he cried: 'Have every man to go out from me.' And there stood no man with him, while Joseph made himself known to his brothers. **2** And he wept aloud; and the Egyptians heard, and the house of Pharaoh heard. **3** And Joseph said to his brothers: 'I am Joseph; does my father still live?' And his brothers could not answer him for they were afraid at his presence. **4** And Joseph said to his brothers: 'Come near to me, I pray you.' And they came near. And he said: 'I am Joseph your brother, whom you sold into Egypt. **5** And now be not grieved, nor angry with yourselves, that you sold me there; for *Elohim* sent me before you to preserve life. **6** For these two years has the famine been in the land; and there are five more years, in which there shall be neither plowing nor harvest. **7** And *YeHoVaH* sent me before you to give you a remnant on the earth and to save you alive for a great deliverance. **8** So now it was not you that sent me there, but *Elohim*; and He has made me a father to Pharaoh and lord of all his house, and ruler over all the land of Egypt. **9** Hurry now, and go up to my father, and say to him: Thus says your son Joseph: *Elohim* has made me lord of all Egypt; come down to me without delay. **10** And you shall dwell in the land of Goshen, and you shall be near to me, you, and your children, and your children's children, and your flocks, and your herds, and all that you have;

11 and there will I sustain you; for there are five more years of famine; to keep you from poverty, you, and your household, and all that you have. **12** And, behold, your eyes see, and the eyes of my brother Benjamin, that it is my mouth that speaks to you. **13** And you shall tell my father of all my glory in Egypt, and of all that you have seen; and you shall hurry and bring my father here.' **14** And he fell upon his brother Benjamin's neck, and wept; and Benjamin wept upon his neck. **15** And he kissed all his brothers, and wept upon them; and after that his brothers talked with him. **16** And the report was heard in Pharaoh's house, saying: 'Joseph's brothers are here; and it pleased Pharaoh well, and his servants. **17** And Pharaoh said to Joseph: 'Say to your brothers: This do you: cover your beasts, and go, get you to the land of Canaan; **18** and take your father and your households, and come to me; and I will give you the good of the land of Egypt, and you shall eat the fat of the land. **19** Now you are commanded, to do this: take you wagons out of the land of Egypt for your little ones, and for your wives, and bring your father, and come. **20** Also do not be concerned about your goods; for the good things of all the land of Egypt are yours.'

21 And the sons of Israel (Jacob) did so; and Joseph gave them wagons, according to the commandment of Pharaoh, and gave them provisions for the way. **22** To all of them he gave each man changes of garments; but to Benjamin he gave 300 shekels of silver, and five changes of garments. **23** And to his father he sent in like manner 10 donkeys laden with the good things of Egypt, and ten she-donkeys laden with corn and bread and grain for his father.

24 So he sent his brothers away, and they departed; and he said to them: 'See that you do not quarrel along the way.' **25** And they went up out of Egypt, and came into the land of Canaan to Jacob their father. **26** And they told him, saying: 'Joseph is still alive, and he is ruler over all the land of Egypt.' And Jacob's heart fainted, for he believed them not. **27** And they told him all the words of Joseph, which he had said to them; and when he saw the wagons that Joseph had sent to carry him, the spirit of Jacob (Israel) their father revived. **28** And Jacob said: 'It is enough; Joseph my son is still alive; I will go and see him before I die.'

Chapter 46
Joseph's father (Jacob) and brothers and their families travel to Egypt to live.

1 And Israel (Jacob) took his journey with all that he had, and came to Beer-sheba, and offered sacrifices to the **Elohim** of his father Isaac. **2** And **YeHoVaH** spoke to Israel in the visions of the night, and said: 'Jacob, Jacob.' And he said: 'Here am I.' **3** And He said: 'I am **YeHoVaH**, the **Elohim** of your father; fear not to go down into Egypt; for I will there make of you a great nation. **4** I will go down with you to Egypt; and I will also surely bring you up again; and Joseph shall put his hand upon your eyes.' **5** And Jacob rose up from Beer-sheba; and the sons of Israel carried Jacob their father, and their little ones, and their wives, in the wagons that Pharaoh had sent to carry him. **6** And they took their cattle, and their goods, which they had gotten in the land of Canaan, and came into Egypt, Jacob, and all his offspring with him; **7** his sons, and his sons' sons with him, his daughters, and his sons' daughters, and all his offspring brought he with him into Egypt. **8** And these are the names of the children of Israel, who came into Egypt, Jacob and his sons: Reuben, Jacob's first-born. **9** And the sons of Reuben: Hanoch, and Pallu, and Hezron, and Carmi. **10** And the sons of Simeon: Jemuel, and Jamin, and Ohad, and Jachin, and Zohar, and Shaul the son of a Canaanitish woman.

11 And the sons of Levi: Gershon, Kohath, and Merari. **12** And the sons of Judah: Er, and Onan, and Shelah, and Perez, and Zerah; but Er and Onan died in the land of Canaan. And the sons of Perez were Hezron and Hamul. **13** And the sons of Issachar: Tola, and Puvah, and Iob, and Shimron. **14** And the sons of Zebulun: Sered, and Elon, and Jahleel. **15** These are the sons of Leah, whom she bore to Jacob in Paddan-aram, with his daughter Dinah; all the souls of his sons and his daughters were 33. **16** And the sons of Gad: Ziphion, and Haggi, Shuni, and Ezbon, Eri, and Arodi, and Areli. **17** And the sons of Asher: Imnah, and Ishvah, and Ishvi, and Beriah, and Serah their sister; and the sons of Beriah: Heber, and Malchiel. **18** These are the sons of Zilpah, whom Laban gave to Leah his daughter, and these she bore to Jacob, even 16 children. **19** The sons of Rachel Jacob's wife: Joseph and Benjamin. **20** And to Joseph in the land of Egypt were born Manasseh and Ephraim, whom Asenath the daughter of Poti-phera priest of On bore to him.

21 And the sons of Benjamin: Bela, and Becher, and Ashbel, Gera, and Naaman, Ehi, and Rosh, Muppim, and Huppim, and Ard. **22** These are the sons of Rachel, who were born to Jacob; all the souls were 14. **23** And the sons of Dan: Hushim. **24** And the sons of Naphtali: Jahzeel, and Guni, and Jezer, and Shillem. **25** These are the sons of Bilhah, whom Laban gave to Rachel his daughter, and these she bore to Jacob; all the offspring were seven. **26** All the children belonging to Jacob that came into Egypt, that came out of his loins, besides Jacob's sons' wives, all the children, were 66. **27** And the sons of Joseph, who were born to him in Egypt, were two; all the children of the house of Jacob that came into Egypt, were 70. **28** And he sent Judah before him to Joseph, to show the way before him to Goshen; and they came into the land of Goshen. *29* And Joseph made ready his chariot, and went up to meet Israel his father, to Goshen; and he presented himself to him, and fell on his neck, and wept on his neck a good while. *30* And Israel said to Joseph: 'Now let me die, since I have seen your face, that you are still alive.'

31 And Joseph said to his brothers, and to his father's house: 'I will go up, and tell Pharaoh, and will say to him: My brothers, and my father's house, who were in the land of Canaan, have come to me; *32* and the men are shepherds, for they have been keepers of cattle; and they have brought their flocks, and their herds, and all that they have. *33* And it shall come to pass, when Pharaoh shall call you, and shall say: What is your occupation? *34* that you shall say: Your servants have been keepers of cattle* from our youth even until now, both we, and our fathers; that you may dwell in the land of Goshen; for every shepherd is a disgrace (abomination) to the Egyptians.' (*cattle, as used in the bible are all beasts of burden greater and less, in both the flock and the herd, and also camels, horses, mules, and asses.

Chapter 47
Pharaoh give Joseph's family land and all the food needed to feed their families to eat. The famine continues and all of Egypt surrenders they money, land, livestock and then their selves to Pharaoh for food to stay alive.

1 Then Joseph went in and told Pharaoh, and said: 'My father and my brothers, and their flocks, and their herds, and all that they have, have come out of the land of Canaan; and, behold, they are in the land of Goshen.' *2* And from among his brothers he took five men, and presented them to Pharaoh. *3* And Pharaoh said to his brothers: 'What is your occupation?' And they said to Pharaoh: 'Your servants are shepherds, both we, and our fathers.' *4* And they said to Pharaoh: 'To stay in the land where we have come; for there is no pasture for your servants' flocks; for the famine is sore in the land of Canaan. Now therefore, we pray you, let your servants dwell in the land of Goshen.' *5* And Pharaoh spoke to Joseph, saying: 'Your father and your brothers have come to you; *6* the land of Egypt is before you; in the best of the land make your father and your brothers to dwell; in the land of Goshen let them dwell. And if you know any able men among them, then make them rulers over my cattle.' *7* And Joseph brought in Jacob his father, and set him before Pharaoh. And Jacob blessed Pharaoh. *8* And Pharaoh said to Jacob: 'How many are the days of your life?' *9* And Jacob said to Pharaoh: 'The days of my travels are 130 years; few and evil have been the days of the years of my life, and they have not attained to the days of the years of the life of my fathers in the days of their travels.' *10* And Jacob blessed Pharaoh, and went out from the presence of Pharaoh.

11 And Joseph placed his father and his brothers, and gave them a possession in the land of Egypt, in the best of the land, in the land of Rameses, as Pharaoh had commanded. *12* And Joseph took care of his father, and his brothers, and all his father's household, with bread, according to the want of their little ones. *13* And there was no bread in all the land; for the famine was very sore, so that the land of Egypt and the land of Canaan languished by reason of the famine. *14* And Joseph gathered up all the money that was found in the land of Egypt, and in the land of Canaan, for the corn that they bought; and Joseph brought the money into Pharaoh's house. *15* And when the money was all collected in the land of Egypt, and in the land of Canaan, all the Egyptians came to Joseph, and said: 'Give us bread; for why should we die in your presence? for our money is gone.' *16* And Joseph said: Bring your cattle, and I will give you bread in exchange for your cattle, if you have no money.' *17* And they brought their cattle to

Joseph. And Joseph gave them bread in exchange for the horses, and for the flocks, and for the herds, and for the donkeys; and he fed them with bread in exchange for all their cattle for that year. *18* And when that year was ended, they came to him the second year, and said to him: 'We will not hide from my lord, how that our money is all spent; and the herds of cattle are my lord's; there is nothing left in the sight of my lord, but our bodies, and our lands. *19* Why should we die before your eyes, both we and our land? buy us and our land for bread, and we and our land will be indebted to Pharaoh; and give us offspring, that we may live, and not die, and that the land be not desolate.' *20* So Joseph bought all the land of Egypt for Pharaoh; for the Egyptians sold every man his field, because the famine was hard upon them; and the land became Pharaoh's.

21 And as for the people, he removed them city by city, from one end of the border of Egypt even to the other end thereof. *22* Only the land of the priests did he not buy, for the priests had a portion from Pharaoh, and ate their portion that Pharaoh gave them; because they sold not their land. *23* Then Joseph said to the people: 'Behold, I have bought you this day and your land for Pharaoh. Here is offspring for you, and you shall sow the land. *24* And it shall come to pass at the harvest, that you shall give a fifth to Pharaoh, and four parts shall be your own, for offspring of the field, and for your food, and for them of your households, and for food for your little ones.' *25* And they said: 'You have saved our lives. Let us find favor in the sight of my lord, and we will be Pharaoh's slave.' *26* And Joseph made it a statute concerning the land of Egypt to this day, that Pharaoh should have the fifth; only the land of the priests alone did not become Pharaoh's. *27* And Israel dwelt in the land of Egypt, in the land of Goshen; and they got their possessions there, and were fruitful, and multiplied exceedingly.

Reading 11 ends

Reading 12 begins

28 And Jacob lived in the land of Egypt 17 years; so the days of Jacob, the years of his life, were 147. *29* And the time drew near that Israel must die; and he called his son Joseph, and said to him: 'If now I have found favor in your sight, I pray you, put your hand under my thigh, and deal kindly and truly with me; do not bury me, I pray you, in Egypt. *30* But when I sleep with my fathers, you shall carry me out of Egypt, and bury me in their burying-place.' And he said: 'I will do as you have said.'

31 And he said: 'Swear to me.' And Joseph swore to him. And Israel bowed down upon the bed's head.

Chapter 48

Jacob's life is ending. He blesses Joseph's sons but not the way Joseph expects.

1 And it came to pass after these things, that they said to Joseph: 'Behold, your father is sick.' And Joseph took with him his two sons, Manasseh and Ephraim. *2* And they told Jacob, and said: 'Behold, your son Joseph comes to see you.' And Israel (Jacob) strengthened himself, and sat upon the bed. *3* And Jacob said to Joseph: '**YeHoVaH** Almighty appeared to me at Luz in the land of Canaan, and blessed me, *4* and said to me: Behold, I will make you fruitful, and multiply you, and I will make of you a company of nations; and will give this land to your offspring after you for an everlasting possession. *5* And now your two sons, who were born to you in the land of Egypt before I came to you in Egypt, are *mine*; Ephraim and Manasseh, even as Reuben and Simeon, shall be mine. *6* And your offspring, that you bring forth after them, shall be yours; they shall be called after the name of their brothers in their inheritance. **7** And as for me, when I came from Paddan, Rachel died to me in the land of Canaan in the way, when there was still some way to go to Ephrath; and I buried her there in the way to Ephrath—which is Beth-lehem.' **8** And Israel beheld Joseph's sons, and said: 'Who are these?' **9** And Joseph said to his father: 'They are my sons, whom **YeHoVaH** has given me here.' And he said: 'Bring them, I pray you, to me, and I will bless them.' **10** Now the eyes of Israel were dim from age, so that he could not see. And he brought them near to him; and he kissed them, and embraced them.

11 And Israel said to Joseph: 'I had not thought to see your face; and, yet, **Elohim** has let me see your offspring also.' **12** And Joseph brought them out from between his knees; and he fell down on his face to the earth. **13** And Joseph took them both, Ephraim in his right hand toward Israel's left hand, and Manasseh in his left hand toward Israel's right hand, and brought them near to him. **14** And Israel stretched out his right hand, and laid it upon Ephraim's head, who was the younger, and his left hand upon Manasseh's head, guiding his hands purposely; for Manasseh was the first-born. **15** And he blessed Joseph, and said: 'The **Elohim**, before whom my fathers Abraham and Isaac did walk, the **Elohim** who has been my shepherd all my life long to this day, **16** the angel who has redeemed me from all evil, bless the lads; and let my name be named in them, and the name of my fathers Abraham and Isaac; and let them grow into a multitude in the midst of the earth.' **17** And when Joseph saw that his father was laying his right hand upon the head of Ephraim, it displeased him, and he held up his father's hand, to remove it from Ephraim's head to Manasseh's head. **18** And Joseph said to his father: 'Not so, my father, for this is the first-born; put your right hand upon his head.' **19** And his father refused, and said: 'I know it, my son, I know it; he also shall become a people, and he also shall be great; and his younger brother shall be greater than he, and his offspring shall become a multitude of nations.' **20** And he blessed them that day, saying: 'By you shall Israel bless, saying: **Elohim** make you as Ephraim and as Manasseh.' And he set Ephraim before Manasseh.

21 And Israel said to Joseph: 'Behold, I die; but **YeHoVaH** will be with you, and bring you back to the land of your fathers. **22** Moreover I have given to you *one portion more than* your brothers, which I took out of the hand of the Amorite with my sword and with my bow.'

Chapter 49
Jacob tells his sons their future before he dies. The twelve tribes of Israel are named.

1 And Jacob called to his sons, and said: 'Gather yourselves together, that I may tell you that which shall befall you in the end of days. **2** Assemble yourselves, and hear, you sons of Jacob; and listen to Israel your father. **3 Reuben**, you are my first-born, my might, and the first-fruits of my strength; the excellency of dignity, and the excellency of power. **4** Unstable as water, you do not excel; because you went up to your father's bed; then defiled it--he went up onto my mistress's bed. **5 Simeon** and Levi are brothers; weapons of violence their kinship. **6** Let my soul not come into their council; to their assembly let my glory not be united; for in their anger they killed men, and in their self-will they lamed an oxen in pleasure. **7** Cursed be their anger, for it was fierce, and their wrath, for it was cruel; I will divide them in Jacob, and scatter them in Israel. **8 Judah**, you shall praise your brothers; your hand shall be on the neck of your enemies; your father's sons shall bow down before you. **9** Judah is a lion's cub; from the prey, my son, you have gone up. He bowed down, he crouched as a lion, and as a lioness; who shall awaken him? *10* The scepter shall not depart from Judah, nor the ruler's staff from between his feet, as long as men come to Shiloh; and to him shall the obedience of the peoples be.

11 Binding his donkey to the vine, and his donkey's colt to the choice vine; he washes his garments in wine, and his vesture in the blood of grapes; *12* His eyes shall be red with wine, and his teeth white with milk. *13 Zebulun* shall dwell at the shore of the sea, and he shall be a shore for ships, and his flank shall be upon Zidon. *14 Issachar* is a strong donkey, crouching down between the sheep pens. *15* For he saw a resting-place that it was good, and the land that it was pleasant; and he bowed his shoulder to bear, and became a servant under forced labor. *16 Dan* shall judge his people, as one of the tribes of Israel. *17* Dan shall be a serpent in the way, a horned snake in the path that bites the horse's heels, so that his rider falls backward. *18* I wait for Your salvation, O **YeHoVaH**. *19 Gad*, a raider shall raid upon him; but he shall raid upon their heel. *20* As for **Asher**, his bread shall be rich, and he shall yield royal dainties.

21 Naphtali is a doe set free: which yields lovely fawns. *22 Joseph* (2 portions) is a fruitful vine, a fruitful vine by a fountain; its branches run over the wall. *23* The archers have dealt bitterly with him, and shot at him, and hated him; *24* But his bow stayed firm, and the arms of his hands were made strong, by the hands of the Mighty One of Jacob, from there is the Shepherd, the Stone of Israel, *25* Even by the **Elohim** of your father, who shall help you, and by the Almighty, who shall bless you, with blessings of heaven above, blessings of the deep that lies beneath, blessings of the breasts, and of the womb. *26* The blessings of your father are mighty beyond the blessings of my ancestors to the utmost bound of the everlasting hills; they shall be on the head of Joseph, and on the crown of the head of the prince among his brothers. *27 Benjamin* is a wolf that tears; in the morning he devours the prey, and at evening he divides the spoil.' *28* All these are the **twelve tribes of Israel** (Jacob), and this is what their father spoke to them and blessed them; every one according to his blessing he blessed them. *29* And he charged them, and said to them: 'I am to be gathered to my people; bury me with my fathers in the cave that is in the field of Ephron the Hittite, *30* in the cave that is in the field of Machpelah, which is before Mamre, in the land of Canaan, which Abraham bought with the field from Ephron the Hittite for a possession of a burying-place.

31 There they buried *Abraham and Sarah* his wife; there they buried *Isaac and Rebekah* his wife; and there I buried *Leah*. *32* The field and the cave that is therein, which was purchased from the children of Heth.' *33* And when Jacob finished instructing his sons, he gathered up his feet into the bed, and died, and was gathered to his people.

Chapter 50
Jacob's (Israel) passing is mourned by all Egypt and he is buried in the cave of the field of Machpelah with Leah, as he requested. Joseph forgives his brothers for the wrong they did him because it was the will of YeHoVaH. Joseph dies and is buried in Egypt.

1 And Joseph fell upon his father's face, and wept upon him, and kissed him. *2* And Joseph commanded his servants the physicians to embalm his father. And the physicians embalmed Israel. *3* And 40 days were fulfilled for him; for so are fulfilled the days of embalming. And the Egyptians wept for him 70 days. *4* And when the days of weeping for him were past, Joseph spoke to the house of Pharaoh, saying: 'If now I have found favor in your eyes, speak, I pray you, in the ears of Pharaoh, saying: *5* My father made me swear, saying: I am dyeing, in my grave which I have dug for me in the land of Canaan, there shall you bury me. Now therefore let me go up, I pray you, and bury my father, and I will come back.' *6* And Pharaoh said: 'Go up, and bury your father, according as he made you swear.' *7* And Joseph went up to bury his father; and with him went up all the servants of Pharaoh, the elders of his house, and all the elders of the land of Egypt, *8* and all the house of Joseph, and his brothers, and his father's house; only their little ones, and their flocks, and their herds, they left in the land of Goshen. *9* And they went up with him with chariots and horsemen; and it was a very great company. *10* And they came to the threshing-floor of Atad, which is beyond the Jordan, and there they cried with a very great and sad cry; and he mourned for his father seven days.

11 And when the inhabitants of the land, the Canaanites, saw the mourning in the floor of Atad, they said: 'This is a grievous mourning to the Egyptians.' That is why the name of it was called Abel-mizraim, which is beyond the Jordan. *12* And his sons did to Jacob according as he commanded them. *13* For his sons carried him into the land of Canaan, and buried him in the cave of the field of Machpelah, which Abraham bought with the field, for a possession of a burying-place, of Ephron the Hittite, in front of Mamre. *14* And Joseph returned to Egypt, he, and his brothers, and all that went up with him to bury his father, after he had buried his father. *15* And when Joseph's brothers saw that their father was dead, they said: 'It may be that Joseph will hate us, and will fully repay us all the evil which we did to him.' *16* And they sent a message to Joseph, saying: 'Your father did command before he died, saying: *17* So shall you say to Joseph: Forgive, I pray you now, the wrongdoing of your brothers, and their sin, for that they did to you evil. And now, we pray you, forgive the wrongdoing of the servants of the **Elohim** of your father.' And Joseph wept when they spoke to him. *18* And his brothers also went and fell down before his face; and they said: 'Behold, we are your servants.' *19* And Joseph said to them: 'Fear not; for am I in the place of **YeHoVaH**? *20* And as for you, you meant evil against me; but **YeHoVaH** meant it for good, in order to do it as it is this day, to keep a great many people alive.

21 Now therefore do not fear; I will sustain you, and your little ones.' And he comforted them, and spoke kindly to them. *22* And Joseph dwelt in Egypt, he, and his father's house; and Joseph lived 110 years. And Joseph saw Ephraim's children of the third generation; the children also of Machir the son of Manasseh were born upon Joseph's knees. *24* And Joseph said to his brothers; but **YeHoVaH** will surely remember you, and bring you up out of this land to the land which He swore to Abraham, to Isaac, and to Jacob.' *25* And Joseph took an oath of the children of Israel, saying: **YeHoVaH** will surely remember you, and you shall carry up my bones from here' *26* So Joseph died, being 110 years old. And they embalmed him, and he was put in a coffin in Egypt.
   Reading 12 ends

Thus Ends the Book Of Genesis   Praise **YeHoVaH**

~EXODUS~

Genesis, Exodus, Leviticus, Numbers, Deuteronomy

The 2nd Book of Moses

Exodus in Hebrew is Shemot (sh-MOTE), meaning "Names," refers to the names of the Jews who entered Egypt with Jacob. It deals with their exile, slavery and suffering; the life of Moses, and his initial prophecies; the Ten Plagues and the Exodus. It also describes the Revelation at Mt. Sinai, where the Jewish people received the Ten Commandments, and the Torah. Exodus closes with the building of the Tabernacle (Mishkan), a portable Temple that housed the Holy Ark containing the two Tablets of instruction.

READINGS FOR EXODUS

The name in (parentheses) is the Hebrew name for that week. For example: Week 13 'Names' in Hebrew is 'Shemot'.

Reading 13 "*Names*" (Shemot) Exodus **1:1 - 6:1**
The new Pharaoh does not remember Joseph, and makes the Israelites his slaves. Pharaoh then demands that all Israelite baby boys be killed at birth. Moses' mother puts her son in a basket in the river, and he is saved by Pharaoh's daughter. As an adult, Moses kills an Egyptian taskmaster who was beating an Israelite slave. Moses flees to Midian and marries Zipporah. *YeHoVaH* appears before Moses in a burning bush and tells him to free the Israelites from slavery. An apprehensive Moses returns to Egypt, where he and his brother Aaron demand that Pharaoh free the Israelite slaves. Pharaoh refuses and *YeHoVaH* promises to punish him.

Reading 14 "*And I Appeared*" (Vaera) Exodus **6:2 - 9:35**
YeHoVaH tells Moses and Aaron to go to Pharaoh to demand freedom for the Israelites. Pharaoh refuses, and *YeHoVaH* unleashes plagues on the Egyptians. Pharaoh promises to free the Israelites, but *YeHoVaH* hardens Pharaoh's heart. The portion ends with the plague of hail stopping and Pharaoh changing his mind once again.

Reading 15 "*Come*" (Bo) Exodus **10:1 - 13:16**
YeHoVaH sends the eighth and ninth plagues, locusts and darkness, but Pharaoh still refuses to free the Israelite slaves. *YeHoVaH* tells Moses that the 10th plague will be killing all the firstborn Egyptians. *YeHoVaH* commands each Israelite home to slaughter a lamb and spread the blood on their doorposts, in order to protect their firstborns. After the death of the firstborns, Pharaoh demands that the Israelites leave.

Reading 16 "*When He Let Go*" (Beshalach) Exodus **13:17 - 17:16**
YeHoVaH tells Moses to have the Israelites set up camp at the Sea of Reeds, but then Pharaoh changes his mind about freeing the Israelites and chases his former slaves. With the Egyptians on the Israelites' tail, *YeHoVaH* splits the sea and Moses leads the Israelites through it. When the Egyptians enter, *YeHoVaH* closes the waters, and the Egyptians drown. Miriam leads all the Israelite women in song and dance to celebrate. Soon after, the Israelites begin to complain about life in the desert. *YeHoVaH* provides quail and manna to feed them. The Israelites battle the Amalekites and win.

Reading 17 "*Jethro*" (Yitro) Exodus **18:1 - 20:23**
Moses tells his father-in-law, Jethro, about the miracle of the exodus. Jethro proclaims that the Israelite *Elohim* is greater than all other gods, and he makes a sacrifice. Jethro then advises Moses to delegate leadership roles in order not to tire himself out. The Israelites camp at the bottom of Mount Sinai. After three days, the mountain fills with smoke, and *Elohim* delivers the Ten Commandments to His people.

Reading 18 "*Instructions*" (Mishpatim) Exodus **21:1 - 24:18**
Moses details many of *YeHoVaH*'s instructions to the Israelites. These include instructions about worshiping other gods, kashrut, business ethics and treatment of animals. *YeHoVaH* outlines the details of three holidays: Passover, Shavuot and Sukkot. *YeHoVaH* provides an angel to protect the Israelites from their enemies and warns the Israelites not to worship other gods. Moses ascends Mount Sinai to meet with *YeHoVaH* for 40 days and 40 nights, leaving Aaron and Hur in charge.

Reading 19 "*Donation*" (Terumah) Exodus **25:1 - 27:19**
Moses receives *YeHoVaH*'s commandments on stone tablets. *YeHoVaH* tells Moses to create a dwelling place for *YeHoVaH*, where the Israelites can bring *YeHoVaH* gifts. *YeHoVaH* details what this Mishkan

(Tabernacle) will look like and how it should be made. The Tabernacle includes an ark, two cherubs, curtains and a menorah.

Reading 20 "**You Shall Command**" (Tetzaveh) Exodus **27:20 - 30:10**
YeHoVaH appoints Aaron and his sons as priests. *YeHoVaH* describes the priestly clothing and explains how to properly sanctify the priests. Aaron is commanded to make incense offerings to *YeHoVaH* every morning on an altar. *YeHoVaH* explains that once a year Aaron will make an offering on that altar to atone for all of the Israelites' sins.

Reading 21 "**When You Elevate**" (Ki Tisa) Exodus **30:11 - 34:35**
Moses stays with *YeHoVaH* on Mount Sinai for 40 days and 40 nights. There, he is given the 10 Commandments on stone tablets. Fearing Moses will never return, the Israelites turn to Aaron, who demands that everyone bring him their gold, so he can make a golden calf. When Moses comes down the mountain and sees the people dancing around this idol, he smashes the tablets on the ground. *YeHoVaH* punishes with a plague all the Israelites who were involved. Moses builds a tent to be his meeting place with *YeHoVaH*.

Reading 22 "**And He Assembled**" (Vayakhel) Exodus **35:1 - 38:20**
YeHoVaH commands the Israelites not to do any work in the sanctuary on Shabbat. The Israelites gather gifts for *YeHoVaH*, gathering so many that they are restrained from searching for more. Moses says that Ohaliab and Bezalel, who are filled with the spirit of *YeHoVaH*, should take the gifts of the Israelites and build *Elohim's* Sanctuary.
And . . . (two readings this week)

Reading 23 "**Accountings Of**" (Pekudei) Exodus **38:21 - 40:38**
Aaron and the priests are given their clothing for work in the Sanctuary. This marks the completion of the Tabernacle construction. Moses anoints Aaron and his sons to make their priestly positions official. A cloud descends upon the Tent of Meeting, and *Elohim's* presence fills the Tabernacle.

-End Torah Potions for Exodus

CHAPTERS 1- 10

Chapter 1

Even though the Israelites prospered in Egypt, a new king arose and forced them into hard labor because he feared them. He ordered that all males born to the Hebrew women were to be killed.

Reading 13 begins

1 Now these are the names of the children of Israel (Jacob), which came into Egypt; every man and his household came with Jacob (Israel). *2* Reuben, Simeon, Levi, and Judah, *3* Issachar, Zebulun, and Benjamin, *4* Dan, and Naphtali, Gad, and Asher. *5* And all the people that came out of the loins of Jacob were 70 souls: for Joseph was in Egypt already. *6* And Joseph died, and all his brethren, and all that generation. *7* And the children of Israel were fruitful, and increased abundantly, and multiplied, and became exceedingly mighty; and the land was filled with them. *8* Now there arose a new king over Egypt, which knew not Joseph. *9* And he said to his people, Behold, the people of the children of Israel are more and mightier than we: *10* Come, let us deal wisely with them; or they multiply, and it come to pass, that, when there is any war, they join to our enemies, and fight against us, and so get them up out of the land.

11 Therefore they did set over them taskmasters to anguish them with their burdens. And they built for Pharaoh treasure cities, Pithom and Raamses. *12* But the more they distressed them, the more they multiplied and grew. And they were grieved because of the children of Israel. *13* And the Egyptians made the children of Israel to serve with harshness: *14* And they made their lives bitter with hard bondage, in mortar, and in brick, and in all manner of service in the field: all their service, wherein they made them serve, was with harshness. *15* And the king of Egypt spoke to the Hebrew midwives, of which the name of the one was Shiphrah, and the name of the other Puah: *16* And he said, When you do the duty of a midwife to the Hebrew women, and see them upon the stools; if it be a son, then you shall kill him: but if it be a daughter, then she shall live. *17* But the midwives feared **YeHoVaH**, and did not as the king of Egypt commanded them, but saved the male children. *18* And the king of Egypt called for the midwives, and said to them, Why have you done this thing, and saved the male children alive? *19* And the midwives said to Pharaoh, because the Hebrew women are not as the Egyptian women; for they are lively, and they deliver before the midwives come to them. *20* Therefore **Elohim** dealt well with the midwives: and the people multiplied, and became very mighty.

21 And it came to pass, because the midwives feared **Elohim**, that he made them households. *22* And Pharaoh charged all his people, saying, every son that is born you shall cast into the river, and every daughter you shall save alive.

Chapter 2

Pharaoh's daughter finds a Hebrew baby by the river and names him Moses. When he grows up, Moses kills an Egyptian and flees to Midian.

1 And there went a man of the house of Levi, and took for his wife a daughter of Levi. *2* And the woman conceived, and bore a son: and when she saw that he was a goodly child, she kept him hid for three months. *3* And when she was no longer able to keep him secret, she made a basket out of the stems of water-plants, pasting tree pitch over it to keep the water out; and placing the baby in it she put it among the plants by the edge of the Nile.. *4* And his sister stood afar off, to see what would be done to him. *5* And the daughter of Pharaoh came down to wash herself at the river; and her maidens walked along by the river's side; and when she saw the basket among the reeds, she sent her maid to fetch it. *6* And when she had opened it, she saw the child: and, behold, the babe wept. And she had compassion on him, and said, This is one of the Hebrews' children. *7* Then said his sister to Pharaoh's daughter, Shall I go and call to you a nurse of the Hebrew women, that she may nurse the child for you? *8* And Pharaoh's daughter said to her, Go. And the maid went and called the child's mother. *9* And Pharaoh's daughter said to her, Take this child away, and nurse it for me, and I will give you your wages. And the women took the child, and nursed it. *10* And the child grew, and she brought him to Pharaoh's daughter, and he became her son. And she called his name **Moses**: and she said, because I drew him out of the water.

11 And it came to pass in those days, when Moses was grown, that he went out to his brethren, and looked on their hardships: and he spied an Egyptian beating a Hebrew, one of his brethren. *12* And he looked both ways, and when he saw that there was no man, he killed the Egyptian, and hid him in the sand. *13* And when he went out the second day, behold, two men of the Hebrews fought together: and he said to him that did the wrong, Why kill you your fellow? *14* And he said, Who made you a prince and a judge over us? Do you intend to kill me, as you killed the Egyptian? And Moses feared, and said, Surely this matter is known. *15* Now when Pharaoh heard this matter, he sought to slay Moses. But Moses fled from the face of Pharaoh, and dwelt in the land of Midian: and he sat down by a well. *16* Now the priest of Midian had seven daughters: and they came and drew water, and filled the troughs to water their father's flock. *17* And the shepherds came and drove them away: but Moses stood up and helped them, and watered their flock. *18* And when they came to Reuel their father, he said, How is it that you have come so soon today? *19* And they said, An Egyptian delivered us out of the hand of the shepherds, and also drew water for us, and watered the flock. *20* And he said to his daughters, And where is he? why is it that you have left the man? call him, that he may eat bread with us.

21 And Moses was content to dwell with the man: and he gave Moses **Zipporah** his daughter. *22* And she bore him a son, and he called his name Gershom: for he said, I have been a stranger in a strange land. *23* And it came to pass in time, that the king of Egypt died: and the children of Israel sighed by reason of the bondage, and they cried, and their cry came up to **Elohim**. *24* And **YeHoVaH** heard their groaning, and **Elohim** remembered his covenant with Abraham, with Isaac, and with Jacob. *25* And **Elohim** looked upon the children of Israel, and He knew.

Chapter 3

A burning bush appears to Moses. YeHoVaH tells him to lead the Israelites out of Egypt. Moses asks YeHoVaH his name and YeHoVaH says, "I am who I am."

1 Now Moses kept the flock of Jethro his father-in-law the priest of Midian: and he led the flock to the backside of the desert, and came to the mountain of **Elohim**, Horeb. *2* And the angel of **YeHoVaH** appeared to him in a flame of fire out of the midst of a bush: and he looked, and, behold, the bush burned with fire, and the bush was not consumed. *3* And Moses said, I will now turn aside, and see this great sight, why the bush is not burnt. *4* And when **YeHoVaH** saw that he turned aside to see, **Elohim** called to him out of the midst of the bush, and said, Moses, Moses. And he said, Here am I. *5* And he said, do not draw near: put off your shoes from your feet, for the place where you stand is holy ground. *6* Moreover he said, I am the **Elohim** of your father, the **Elohim** of Abraham, the **Elohim** of Isaac, and the **Elohim** of Jacob. And Moses hid his face; for he was afraid to look upon **Elohim**. *7* And **YeHoVaH** said, I have surely seen the affliction of my people which are in Egypt, and have heard their cry by reason of their taskmasters; for I know their sorrows; *8* And I have come down to deliver them out of the hand of the Egyptians, and to bring them up out of that land into a good and spacious land, to a land flowing with milk and honey; to the place of the Canaanites, and the Hittites, and the Amorites, and the Perizzites, and the Hivites, and the Jebusites. *9* Now therefore, behold, the cry of the children of Israel comes to me: and I have also seen the oppression that the Egyptians oppress them. *10* Come now, and I will send you to Pharaoh, that you may bring forth my people, the children of Israel out of Egypt.

11 And Moses said to **Elohim**, Who am I, that I should go to Pharaoh, and that I should bring forth the children of Israel out of Egypt? *12* And he said, Certainly I will be with you; and this shall be a token to you, that I have sent you: When you have brought forth the people out of Egypt, you shall serve Me upon this mountain. *13* And Moses said to **Elohim**, Behold, when I come to the children of Israel, and say to them, The **Elohim** of your fathers has sent me to you; and they shall say to me, What is his name? what shall I say to them? *14* And **Elohim** said to Moses, "I AM THAT I AM" (**YeHoVaH**): (See Introduction to His Name) and he said, Thus shall you say to the children of Israel, I AM has sent me to you. *15* And **YeHoVaH** said to Moses, Thus shall you say to the children of Israel, the **Elohim** of your fathers, the **Elohim** of Abraham, the **Elohim** of Isaac, and the **Elohim** of Jacob, has sent me to you: *this is my name forever (le-olam), and this is my memorial to **all generations**.* *16* Go, and gather the elders of Israel together, and say to them, The **Elohim** of your fathers, the **Elohim** of Abraham, of Isaac, and of Jacob, appeared to me, saying, I have surely visited you, and seen that which is done to you in Egypt: *17* And I have said, I will bring you up out of the affliction of Egypt to the land of the Canaanites, and the Hittites, and the Amorites, and the Perizzites, and the Hivites, and the Jebusites, to a land flowing with milk and honey. *18* And they shall hearken to your voice: and you shall come, you and the elders of Israel, to the king of Egypt, and you shall say to him, **YeHoVaH, Elohim** of the Hebrews has met with us: and now let us go, we beseech you, three days' journey into the wilderness, that we may sacrifice to **YeHoVaH** our **Elohim**. *19* And I am sure that the king of Egypt will not let you go, no, not by a mighty hand. *20* And I will stretch out my hand, and plague Egypt with all my wonders that I will do in the midst there: and after that he will let you go.

21 And I will give this people favor in the sight of the Egyptians: and it shall come to pass, that, when you go, you shall not go empty. *22* But every woman shall borrow of her neighbor, and of her that lives in her house, jewels of silver, and jewels of gold, and raiment: and you shall put them upon your sons, and upon your daughters; and you shall spoil the Egyptians.

Chapter 4

YeHoVaH gives Moses signs so that the people would listen. Moses was afraid, so YeHoVaH sends his brother Aaron to speak for him.

1 And Moses answered and said, But, behold, they will not believe me, nor listen to my voice: for they will say, **YeHoVaH** has not appeared to you. *2* And **YeHoVaH** said to him, What is that in your hand? And he said, a rod. *3* And he said, Cast it on the ground. And he cast it on the ground, and it became a serpent; and Moses fled from before it. *4* And **YeHoVaH** said to

Moses, Put forth your hand, and take it by the tail. And he put forth his hand, and caught it, and it became a rod in his hand: **5** That they may believe that the **Elohim** of their fathers, the **Elohim** of Abraham, the **Elohim** of Isaac, and the **Elohim** of Jacob, has indeed appeared to you. **6** And **YeHoVaH** said furthermore to him, Put your hand into your bosom. And he put his hand into his bosom: and when he took it out, behold, his hand was leprous as snow. **7** And he said, Put your hand into your bosom again. And he put his hand into his bosom again; and removed it out of his bosom, and, behold, it was turned again as his other flesh. **8** And it shall come to pass, if they will not believe you, neither listen to the voice of the first sign, that they will believe the voice of the last sign. **9** And it shall come to pass, if they will not believe also these two signs, neither listen to your voice, that you shall take of the water of the river, and pour it upon the dry land: and the water which you take out of the river shall become blood upon the dry land. **10** And Moses said to **YeHoVaH**, O my Lord, I am not eloquent, nor since you have spoken to me your servant: but I am slow of speech, and of a slow tongue.

11 And **YeHoVaH** said to him, Who has made man's mouth? or who makes the dumb, or deaf, or the seeing, or the blind? Was it not me? **12** Now therefore go, and I will be with your mouth, and teach you what you shall say. **13** And he said, O **YeHoVaH**, send, I pray you, by the hand of him whom you will send. **14** And the anger of **YeHoVaH** was kindled against Moses, and he said, Is not Aaron the Levite your brother? I know that he can speak well. And also, behold, he comes forth to meet you: and when he sees you, he will be glad in his heart. **15** And you shall speak to him, and put words in his mouth: and I will be with your words, and with his words, and will teach you what you shall do. **16** And he shall be your spokesman to the people: and he shall be, even he shall be to you instead of a mouth, and you shall be to him instead of **Elohim**. **17** And you shall take this rod in your hand, and you shall do signs. **18** And Moses went and returned to Jethro his father-in-law, and said to him, Let me go, I pray you, and return to my brethren who are in Egypt, and see whether they are yet alive. And Jethro said to Moses, Go in peace. **19** And **YeHoVaH** said to Moses in Midian, Go, return to Egypt: for all the men are dead which sought your life. **20** And Moses took his wife and his sons, and set them upon a donkey, and he returned to the land of Egypt: and Moses took the rod of **YeHoVaH** in his hand.

21 And **YeHoVaH** said to Moses, When you go to return to Egypt, see that you do all those wonders before Pharaoh, which I have put in your hand: but I will harden his heart, that he shall not let the people go. **22** And you shall say to Pharaoh, Thus says **YeHoVaH**, *Israel is my son, even my firstborn*: **23** And I say to you, Let my son go, that he may serve me: and if you refuse to let him go, behold, I will slay your son, even your firstborn. **24** And it came to pass by the way in the inn, that **YeHoVaH** met him, and sought to kill him. **25** Then Zipporah took a sharp stone, and cut off the foreskin of her son, and cast it at his feet, and said, Surely a bloody husband are you to me. **26** So he let him go: then she said, A bloody husband you are, because of the circumcision. **27** And **YeHoVaH** said to Aaron, Go into the wilderness to meet Moses. And he went, and met him in the mount of **Elohim** , and kissed him. **28** And Moses told Aaron all the words of **YeHoVaH** who had sent him, and all the signs that he had commanded him. **29** And Moses and Aaron went and gathered together all the elders of the children of Israel: **30** And Aaron spoke all the words that **YeHoVaH** had spoken to Moses, and did the signs in the sight of the people.

31 And the people believed: and when they heard that **YeHoVaH** had visited the children of Israel, and that he had looked upon their affliction, then they bowed their heads and worshipped.

EXODUS

Chapter 5

Moses and Aaron go to Pharaoh and tell him to let the Israelites go into the desert to worship but Pharaoh refuses and increases their workload instead.

1 And afterward Moses and Aaron went in, and told Pharaoh, Thus says **YeHoVaH Elohim** of Israel, Let my people go, that they may hold a feast to me in the wilderness. *2* And Pharaoh said, who is the Lord that I should obey his voice to let Israel go? I know not the Lord, neither will I let Israel go. *3* And they said, The **Elohim** of the Hebrews has met with us: let us go, we pray you, three days' journey into the desert, and sacrifice to **YeHoVaH** our **Elohim**; for fear that he fall upon us with pestilence, or with the sword. *4* And the king of Egypt said to them, Why do you, Moses and Aaron, let the people from their work? get you to your labor. *5* And Pharaoh said, Behold, the people of the land now are many, and you make them rest from their labors. *6* And Pharaoh commanded the same day the taskmasters of the people, and their officers, saying, *7* You shall no more give the people straw to make brick, as before: let them go and gather straw for themselves. *8* But see that they make the same number of bricks as before, and no less: for they have no love for work; and so they are crying out and saying, Let us go and make an offering to our **Elohim**. *9* Give the men harder work, and see that they do it; let them not give attention to false words. *10* And the taskmasters of the people went out, and their officers, and they spoke to the people, saying, thus says Pharaoh; I will not give you straw.

11 Go you, get you straw where you can find it: yet no thought of your work be diminished. *12* So the people were scattered abroad throughout all the land of Egypt to gather stubble instead of straw. *13* And the taskmasters hurried them, saying, Fulfill your work, your daily tasks, as when there was straw. *14* And the officers of the children of Israel, which Pharaoh's taskmasters had set over them, were beaten, and demanded, Wherefore have you not fulfilled your task in making brick both yesterday and today, as before? *15* Then the officers of the children of Israel came and cried to Pharaoh, saying, Why deal you with your servants? *16* There is no straw given to your servants, and they say to us, Make brick: and, behold, your servants are beaten; but the fault is in your own people. *17* But he said, You are idle, you are idle: therefore you say, Let us go and do sacrifice to your **Elohim**. *18* Go therefore now, and work; for there shall be no straw given to you, yet shall you deliver the tale of bricks. *19* Then the responsible men of the children of Israel saw that they were purposing evil when they said, The number of bricks which you have to make every day will be no less than before. *20* And they met Moses and Aaron, who stood in the way, as they came forth from Pharaoh:

21 And they said to them, May **YeHoVaH** take note of you and be your judge; for you have given Pharaoh and his servants a bad opinion of us, putting a sword in their hands for our destruction. *22* And Moses returned to **YeHoVaH**, and said, why have you so evil implored this people? why is it that you have sent me? *23* For since I came to Pharaoh to speak in your name, he has done evil to this people; neither have you delivered your people at all.

Reading 13 ends

Chapter 6

YeHoVaH tells Moses that he will lead the Israelites out of Egypt to the Promised Land. Aaron and Moses are both from the tribe of Levi.

Reading 14 begins

1 Then **YeHoVaH** said to Moses, Now shall you see what I will do to Pharaoh: for with a strong hand shall he let them go, and with a strong hand shall he drive them out of his land. *2* And **Elohim** spoke to Moses, and said to him, I am **YeHoVaH**: *3* And I appeared to Abraham, and to Isaac, and to Jacob, by the name of **El Shaddai** Almighty, but by my name **YeHoVaH** was I not known to them. *4* And I have also established my covenant with them, to give them the land of Canaan, the land of their pilgrimage, wherein they were strangers. *5* And I have also heard the groaning of the children of Israel, whom the Egyptians keep in bondage; and I have remembered my covenant. *6* Therefore say to the children of Israel, I am **YeHoVaH**, and I will bring you out from under the burdens of the Egyptians, and I will rid you out of their bondage, and I will redeem you with a stretched out arm, and with great judgments: *7* And I will take you to me for a people, and I will be to you your **Elohim**: and you shall know that I am **YeHoVaH** your **Elohim**, which brings you out from under the burdens of the Egyptians. *8* And I will bring you in to the land, concerning that which I did swear to give to Abraham, to Isaac, and to Jacob; and I will give it to you for a heritage: I am **YeHoVaH**. *9* And Moses spoke so to the children of Israel: but they listened not to Moses for anguish of spirit, and for cruel bondage. *10* And **YeHoVaH** spoke to Moses, saying,

11 Go in, speak to Pharaoh King of Egypt, that he let the children of Israel go out of his land. *12* And Moses spoke before **YeHoVaH**, saying, Behold, the children of Israel have not listened to me; how then shall Pharaoh hear me, who am of uncircumcised lips? *13* And **YeHoVaH** spoke to Moses and to Aaron, and gave them a charge to the children of Israel, and to Pharaoh king of Egypt, to bring the children of Israel out of the land of Egypt. *14* These be the heads of their fathers' houses: The sons of Reuben the firstborn of Israel; Hanoch, and Pallu, Hezron, and Carmi: these be the families of Reuben. *15* And the sons of Simeon; Jemuel, and Jamin, and Ohad, and Jachin, and Zohar, and Shaul the son of a Canaanitish woman: these are the families of Simeon. *16* And these are the names of the sons of Levi according to their generations; Gershon, and Kohath, and Merari: and the years of the life of Levi were 137 years. *17* The sons of Gershon; Libni, and Shimi, according to their families. *18* And the sons of Kohath; Amram, and Izhar, and Hebron, and Uzziel: and the years of the life of Kohath were 133 years. *19* And the sons of Merari; Mahali and Mushi: these are the families of Levi according to their generations. *20* And Amram took him Jochebed his father's sister to wife; and she bare him Aaron and Moses: and the years of the life of Amram were 137 years.

21 And the sons of Izhar; Korah, and Nepheg, and Zichri. *22* And the sons of Uzziel; Mishael, and Elzaphan, and Zithri. *23* And Aaron took him Elisheba, daughter of Amminadab, sister of Naashon, to wife; and she bore him Nadab, and Abihu, Eleazar, and Ithamar. *24* And the sons of Korah; Assir, and Elkanah, and Abiasaph: these are the families of the Korhites. *25* And Eleazar Aaron's son took him one of the daughters of Putiel to wife; and she bare him Phinehas: these are the heads of the fathers of the Levites according to their families. *26* These are that Aaron and Moses, to whom **YeHoVaH** said, Bring out the children of Israel from the land of Egypt according to their armies. *27* These are they which spoke to Pharaoh king of Egypt, to bring out the children of Israel from Egypt: these are that Moses and Aaron. *28* And it came to pass on the day when **YeHoVaH** spoke to Moses in the land of Egypt, *29* That **YeHoVaH** spoke to Moses, saying, I am **YeHoVaH**: speak to Pharaoh king of Egypt all that I say to you. *30* And Moses said before **YeHoVaH**, Behold, I am of uncircumcised lips, and how shall Pharaoh listen to me?

Chapter 7

Moses and Aaron go to Pharaoh. The ten plagues begin but Pharaoh's heart remains hardened and he will not listen.

1 And **YeHoVaH** said to Moses, See, I have made you a god to Pharaoh: and Aaron your brother shall be your prophet. *2* You shall speak all that I command you: and Aaron your brother shall speak to Pharaoh, that he send the children of Israel out of his land. *3* And I will harden Pharaoh's heart, and multiply my signs and my wonders in the land of Egypt. *4* But Pharaoh shall not listen to you, that I may lay my hand upon Egypt, and bring forth my armies, and my people the children of Israel, out of the land of Egypt by great judgments. *5* And the Egyptians shall know that I am **YeHoVaH**, when I stretch forth my hand upon Egypt, and bring out the children of Israel from among them. *6* And Moses and Aaron did as **YeHoVaH** commanded them. *7* And Moses was 80 years old, and Aaron 83 years old, when they spoke to Pharaoh. *8* And **YeHoVaH** spoke to Moses and to Aaron, saying, *9* When Pharaoh speaks to you, saying, Show a miracle for you: then you shall say to Aaron, Take your rod, and cast it before Pharaoh, and it shall become a serpent. *10* And Moses and Aaron went to Pharaoh, and they did as **YeHoVaH** had commanded: and Aaron cast down his rod before Pharaoh, and before his servants, and it became a serpent.

11 Then Pharaoh also called the wise men and the sorcerers and the magicians of Egypt, they also did in like manner with their secret arts. *12* For they cast down every man his rod, and they became serpents: but Aaron's rod swallowed up their rods. *13* And he hardened Pharaoh's heart that he listened not to them; as **YeHoVaH** had said. *14* And **YeHoVaH** said to Moses, Pharaoh's heart is hardened, he refuses to let the people go. *15* Go to Pharaoh in the morning; when he goes out into the water; and you shall stand by the river's brink where he is; and the rod which was turned to a serpent shall you take in your hand. *16* And you shall say to him, **YeHoVaH Elohim** of the Hebrews has sent me to you, saying, Let my people go, that they may serve me in the wilderness: and, behold, so far you would not hear. *17* Thus says **YeHoVaH**, In this you shall know that I am **YeHoVaH**: behold, I will cut with the rod that is in my hand upon the waters which are in the river, and they shall be turned to blood. *18* And the fish that are in the river shall die, and the river shall smell; and the Egyptians shall hate to drink of the water of the river. *19* And **YeHoVaH** spoke to Moses, Say to Aaron, Take your rod, and stretch out your hand upon the waters of Egypt, upon their streams, upon their rivers, and upon their ponds, and upon all their pools of water, that they may become blood; and that there may be blood throughout all the land of Egypt, both in vessels of wood, and in vessels of stone. *20* And Moses and Aaron did so, as **YeHoVaH** commanded; and he lifted up the rod, and poisoned the waters that were in the river, in the sight of Pharaoh, and in the sight of his servants; and all the waters that were in the river were turned to blood.

21 And the fish that were in the river died; and the river smelled, and the Egyptians could not drink of the water of the river; and there was blood throughout all the land of Egypt. *22* And the magicians of Egypt also did so with their enchantments: and Pharaoh's heart was hardened, neither did he listen to them; as **YeHoVaH** had said. *23* And Pharaoh turned and went into his house; neither did he set his heart to this also. *24* And all the Egyptians dug round about the river for water to drink; for they could not drink of the water of the river. *25* And seven days were fulfilled, after **YeHoVaH** had poisoned the river. *26* And **YeHoVaH** spoke unto Moses: 'Go in unto Pharaoh, and say unto him: Thus saith **YeHoVaH**: Let My people go, that they may serve Me. *27* And if thou refuse to let them go, behold, I will smite all thy borders with frogs. *28* And the river shall swarm with frogs, which shall go up and come into thy house, and into thy bed-chamber, and upon thy bed, and into the house of thy servants, and upon thy people, and into thine ovens, and into thy kneading-troughs. **29** And the frogs shall come up both upon thee, and upon thy people, and upon all thy servants.'

Chapter 8

YeHoVaH sends a plague of frogs in to Egypt. Pharaoh begs for relief but then hardens his heart again. YeHoVaH sends gnats and then flies.

1 And **YeHoVaH** spoke to Moses, Say to Aaron, Stretch forth your hand with your rod over the streams, over the rivers, and over the ponds, and cause frogs to come up upon the land of Egypt. *2* And Aaron stretched out his hand over the waters of Egypt; and the frogs came up, and covered the land of Egypt. *3* And the magicians could also do with their magical arts, and brought up frogs upon the land of Egypt. *4* Then Pharaoh called for Moses and Aaron, and said, Pray to **YeHoVaH**, that he may take away the frogs from me, and from my people; and I will let the people go, that they may do sacrifice to their god. *5* And Moses said to Pharaoh, Glory over me: when shall I pray for you, and for your servants, and for your people, to destroy the frogs from you and your houses, that they may remain in the river only? *6* And he said, tomorrow. And he said, Be it according to your word: that you may know that there is none like **YeHoVaH** our **Elohim**. *7* And the frogs shall depart from you, and from your houses, and from your servants, and from your people; they shall remain in the river only. *8* And Moses and Aaron went out from Pharaoh: and Moses cried to **YeHoVaH** because of the frogs that he had brought against Pharaoh. *9* And **YeHoVaH** did according to the word of Moses; and the frogs died out of the houses, out of the villages, and out of the fields. *10* And they gathered them together upon heaps: and the land smelled.

11 But when Pharaoh saw that there was relief, he hardened his heart again, and listened not to them; as **YeHoVaH** had said. *12* And **YeHoVaH** said to Moses, Say to Aaron, Stretch out your rod, and change the dust of the land, that it may become lice throughout all the land of Egypt. *13* And they did so; for Aaron stretched out his hand with his rod, and changed the dust of the earth, and it became lice in man, and in beast; all the dust of the land became lice throughout all the land of Egypt. *14* But the magicians with their secret arts, attempting to make insects, were unable to do so: and there were insects on man and on beast. *15* Then the magicians said to Pharaoh, This is the finger of **Elohim**: and Pharaoh's heart was hardened, and he listened not to them; as **YeHoVaH** had said. *16* And **YeHoVaH** said to Moses, Rise up early in the morning, and stand before Pharaoh; when he comes forth to the water; and say to him, Thus says **YeHoVaH**, "Let my people go, that they may serve me". *17* Or else, if you will not let my people go, behold, I will send swarms of flies upon you, and upon your servants, and upon your people, and into your houses: and the houses of the Egyptians shall be full of swarms of flies, and also the ground where they are. *18* And I will separate in that day the land of Goshen, in which my people dwell, that no swarms of flies shall be there; to the end you may know that I am **YeHoVaH** in the midst of the earth. *19* And I will put a division between my people and your people: tomorrow shall this sign be. *20* And **YeHoVaH** did so; and there came a severe swarm of flies into the house of Pharaoh, and into his servants' houses, and into all the land of Egypt: the land was corrupted by the swarm of flies.

21 And Pharaoh called for Moses and for Aaron, and said, Go you, sacrifice to your **Elohim** in the land. *22* And Moses said, It is not meant so to do; for we shall sacrifice the abomination of the Egyptians to **YeHoVaH** our **Elohim**: and shall we sacrifice the abomination of the Egyptians before their eyes, and will they not stone us? *23* We will go three days' journey into the wilderness, and sacrifice to **YeHoVaH** our **Elohim**, as he shall command us. *24* And Pharaoh said, I will let you go, that you may sacrifice to your **Elohim** in the wilderness; only you shall not go very far away: pray for me. *25* And Moses said, Behold, I go out from you, and I will pray to **YeHoVaH** that the swarms of flies may depart from Pharaoh, from his servants, and from his people, tomorrow: but let not Pharaoh deal deceitfully any more in not letting the people go to sacrifice to **YeHoVaH**. *26* And Moses went out from Pharaoh, and prayed to **YeHoVaH**. *27* And **YeHoVaH** did according to the word of Moses; and he removed the swarms of flies from Pharaoh, from his servants, and from his people; there remained not one. *28* And Pharaoh hardened his heart once *again*, and would not let the people go.

Chapter 9

YeHoVaH sends a plague on all the livestock of Egypt, then boils and then hail. Pharaoh again begs for relief but again his heart is hardened.

1 Then **YeHoVaH** said to Moses, Go to Pharaoh, and tell him, Thus says **YeHoVaH Elohim** of the Hebrews, Let my people go, that they may serve me. *2* For if you refuse to let them go, and will hold them still, *3* Behold, the hand of **YeHoVaH** is upon your cattle which is in the field, upon the horses, upon the donkeys, upon the camels, upon the oxen, and upon the sheep: there shall be a very severe infection. *4* And infectious diseases shall separate between the cattle of Israel and the cattle of Egypt: and there shall nothing die of all that is the children's of Israel. *5* And **YeHoVaH** appointed a set time, saying, Tomorrow **YeHoVaH** shall do this in the land. *6* And **YeHoVaH** did as He said the next day, and all the cattle of Egypt died: but of the cattle of the children of Israel died not one. *7* And Pharaoh sent, and, behold, there was not one of the cattle of the Israelites dead. And the heart of Pharaoh was hardened, and he did not let the people go. *8* And **YeHoVaH** said to Moses and to Aaron, Take to you handfuls of ashes of the furnace, and let Moses sprinkle it toward the heaven in the sight of Pharaoh. *9* And it shall become small dust in all the land of Egypt, and shall be a boil breaking forth with sores upon man, and upon beast, throughout all the land of Egypt. *10* And they took ashes of the furnace, and stood before Pharaoh; and Moses sprinkled it up toward heaven; and it became a boil breaking forth with sores upon man, and upon beast.

11 And the magicians could not stand before Moses because of the boils; for the boil was upon the magicians, and upon all the Egyptians. *12* And **YeHoVaH** hardened the heart of Pharaoh, and he listened not to them; as **YeHoVaH** had spoken to Moses. *13* And **YeHoVaH** said to Moses, Rise up early in the morning, and stand before Pharaoh, and say to him, Thus says **YeHoVaH Elohim** of the Hebrews, Let my people go, that they may serve me. *14* For I will at this time send all my plagues upon your heart, and upon your servants, and upon your people; that you may know that there is none like me in all the earth. *15* For now I will stretch out my hand that I may strike you and your people with pestilence; and you shall be cut off from the earth. *16* And for this reason have I raised you up, for to show you my power; and that my name may be declared throughout all the earth. *17* As yet exalts you yourself against my people that you will not let them go? *18* Behold, tomorrow about this time I will cause it to rain a very severe hail, such as has not been in Egypt since the foundation thereof even until now. *19* Send therefore now, and gather your cattle, and all that you have in the field; for upon every man and beast which shall be found in the field, and shall not be brought home, the hail shall come down upon them, and they shall die. *20* He that feared the word of **YeHoVaH** among the servants of Pharaoh made his servants and his cattle flee into the houses:

21 And he that did not regard the word of **YeHoVaH** left his servants and his cattle in the field. *22* And **YeHoVaH** said to Moses, Stretch forth your hand toward heaven, that there may be hail in all the land of Egypt, upon man, and upon beast, and upon every plant of the field, throughout the land of Egypt. *23* And Moses stretched forth his rod toward heaven: and **YeHoVaH** sent thunder and hail, and the fire ran along upon the ground; and **YeHoVaH** rained hail upon the land of Egypt. *24* So there was hail, and fire mingled with the hail, very severe, such as there was none like it in all the land of Egypt since it became a nation. *25* And the hail destroyed throughout all the land of Egypt all that was in the field, both man and beast; and the hail destroyed every plant of the field, and broke every tree of the field. *26* Only in the land of Goshen, where the children of Israel were, was there no hail. *27* And Pharaoh sent, and called for Moses and Aaron, and said to them, I have sinned this time: **YeHoVaH** is righteous, and I and my people are wicked. *28* Make prayer to **YeHoVaH**; for there has been enough of this thunder and ice-storms; and I will let you go and will keep you no longer. *29* And Moses said to him, As soon as I am gone out of the city, I will spread abroad my hands to **YeHoVaH**; and the thunder shall cease, neither shall there be any more hail; that you may know how that the earth is **YeHoVaH's**. *30* But as for you and your servants, I know that you still do not yet fear **YeHoVaH Elohim**.

31 And the flax and the barley were destroyed: for the barley was in the ear, and the flax was ready to harvest. *32* But the wheat and the rye were not destroyed: for they were not fully-grown. *33* And Moses went out of the city from Pharaoh, and spread wide his hands to **YeHoVaH**: and the thunder and hail ceased, and the rain was no longer poured upon the earth. *34* And when Pharaoh saw that the rain and the hail and the thunders had ceased, he sinned yet more, and hardened his heart, he and his servants. *35* And the heart of Pharaoh was hardened, neither would he let the children of Israel go; as **YeHoVaH** had spoken by Moses.
   Reading 14 ends

Chapter 10

YeHoVaH sends a plague of locusts but Pharaoh's heart remains hardened so YeHoVaH sends darkness for three days.
   Reading 15 begins
1 And **YeHoVaH** said to Moses, Go to Pharaoh: for I have hardened his heart, and the heart of his servants, that I might show these my signs before him: *2* And that you may tell in the ears of your son, and of your son's son, what things I have brought in Egypt, and my signs which I have done among them; that you may know how that I am **YeHoVaH**. *3* And Moses and Aaron came in to Pharaoh, and said to him, Thus says **YeHoVaH Elohim** of the Hebrews, How long will you refuse to humble yourself before me? let my people go, that they may serve me. *4* Or else, if you refuse to let my people go, behold, tomorrow will I bring the locusts into your land: *5* And they shall cover the face of the earth, that one cannot be able to see the earth: and they shall eat everything that remains to you from the hail, and shall eat every tree which grows for you out of the field: *6* And they shall fill your houses, and the houses of all your servants, and the houses of all the Egyptians; which neither your fathers, nor your fathers' fathers have seen, since the day that they were upon the earth to this day. And he turned himself, and went out from Pharaoh. *7* And Pharaoh's servants said to him, How long shall this man be a snare to us? let the men go, that they may serve their Lord their **Elohim**: know you not yet that Egypt is

destroyed? *8* And Moses and Aaron were brought again to Pharaoh: and he said to them, Go, serve the Lord your god: but who are they that shall go? *9* And Moses said, We will go with our young and with our old, with our sons and with our daughters, with our flocks and with our herds will we go; for we must hold a feast to **YeHoVaH**. *10* And he said to them, May the Lord be with you, if I will let you and your little ones go! take care, for your purpose clearly is evil.

11 Not so: go now you that are men, and serve your Lord; for that you did desire. And they were driven out from Pharaoh's presence. *12* And **YeHoVaH** said to Moses, Stretch out your hand over the land of Egypt for the locusts, that they might come up upon the land of Egypt, and eat every plant of the land, even all that the hail has left. *13* And Moses stretched forth his rod over the land of Egypt, and **YeHoVaH** brought an east wind upon the land all that day, and all that night; and when it was morning, the east wind brought the locusts. *14* And the locusts went up over all the land of Egypt, resting on every part of the land, in very great numbers; such an army of locusts had never been seen before, and never will be again. *15* For they covered the face of the whole earth, so that the land was darkened; and they did eat every plant of the land, and all the fruit of the trees which the hail had left: and there remained not any green thing in the trees, or in the plants of the field, through all the land of Egypt. *16* Then Pharaoh called for Moses and Aaron in haste; and he said, I have sinned against Adonai your **Elohim**, and against you. *17* Now therefore forgive, I pray you, my sin only this once, and pray to the Lord your god, that he may take away from me this death only. *18* And he went out from Pharaoh, and prayed to **YeHoVaH**. *19* And **YeHoVaH** turned a mighty strong west wind, which took away the locusts, and cast them into the Red sea; there remained not one locust in all the coasts of Egypt. *20* But **YeHoVaH** hardened Pharaoh's heart, so that he would not let the children of Israel go.

21 And **YeHoVaH** said to Moses, Stretch out your hand toward heaven, that there may be darkness over the land of Egypt, even darkness that may be felt. *22* And Moses stretched forth his hand toward heaven; and there was a thick darkness in all the land of Egypt three days: *23* They saw not one another, neither rose any from his place for three days: but all the *children of Israel* had light in their dwellings. *24* And Pharaoh called to Moses, and said, Go you, serve your Lord; only let your flocks and your herds stay: let your little ones also go with you. *25* And Moses said, You must give us also sacrifices and burnt offerings, that we may sacrifice to **YeHoVaH** our **Elohim**. *26* Our cattle also shall go with us; there shall not one hoof be left behind; for thereof must we take to serve **YeHoVaH** our **Elohim**; and we know not with what we must serve **YeHoVaH**, until we come there. *27* But **YeHoVaH** hardened Pharaoh's heart, and he would not let them go. *28* And Pharaoh said to him, Get you from me, take heed to yourself, see my face no more; for in the day you see my face you shall die. *29* And Moses said, You have spoken clearly, I will see your face again no more.

CHAPTERS 11- 20

Chapter 11

YeHoVaH says that He will send one more plague: all the firstborn Egyptians will die, including Pharaoh's son. Then Pharaoh will finally let the Israelites go.

1 And **YeHoVaH** said to Moses, Yet will I bring one more plague upon Pharaoh, and upon Egypt; after that he will let you go: when he shall let you go, he shall surely thrust you out altogether. *2* Speak now in the ears of the people, and let every man borrow of his neighbor, and every woman of her neighbor, jewels of silver and jewels of gold. *3* And **YeHoVaH** gave the people favor in the sight of the Egyptians. Moreover the man Moses was very great in the land of Egypt, in the sight of Pharaoh's servants, and in the sight of the people. *4* And Moses said, Thus says **YeHoVaH**, About midnight will I go out into the midst of Egypt: *5* And all the firstborn in the land of Egypt shall die, from the first born of Pharaoh that sits upon his throne, even to the firstborn of the maidservant that is behind the mill; and all the firstborn of animals. *6* And there shall be a great cry throughout all the land of Egypt, like never before, nor shall be like it again. *7* But against any of the children of Israel shall not a dog move his tongue, against man or animal: that you may know how **YeHoVaH** does put a difference between the Egyptians and Israel. *8* And all these, your servants shall come down to me, and bow down to me, saying, Get you out, and all the people that follow you: and after that I will go out. And he went out from Pharaoh in a great anger. *9* And **YeHoVaH** said to Moses, Pharaoh shall not listen to you; that my wonders may be multiplied in the land of Egypt. *10* And Moses and Aaron did all these wonders before Pharaoh: and **YeHoVaH** hardened Pharaoh's heart, so that he would not let the children of Israel go out of his land.

Chapter 12

YeHoVaH tells the Israelites to prepare for the Passover. That night all the firstborn Egyptians were killed. Pharaoh, in great sorrow over his son's death tells the Israelites to go.

1 And **YeHoVaH** spoke to Moses and Aaron in the land of Egypt saying, *2* This month shall be to you the beginning of months: it shall be the *first month of the year to you*. *3* Speak to all the congregation of Israel, saying, In the tenth day of this month they shall take to them every man a lamb, according to the house of their fathers, a lamb for each house: *4* And if the household be too little for the lamb, let him and his neighbor next to his house take it according to the number of the people; every man according to his eating shall make your count for the lamb. *5* Your lamb shall be without blemish, a male of the first year: you shall take it out from the sheep, *or from the goats*: *6* And you shall keep it up until the fourteenth day of the same month: and the whole assembly of the congregation of Israel shall kill it in the evening. *7* And they shall take of the blood, and put it on the two side posts and on the upper doorpost of the houses, wherein they shall eat it. *8* And they shall eat the flesh in that night, roast with fire, and unleavened bread; and with bitter herbs they shall eat it. *9* Eat not of it raw, nor soak at all with water, but roast with fire; his head with his legs, and with the internal organs. *10* And you shall let nothing of it remain until the morning; and that which remains of it until the morning you shall burn with fire.

11 And thus shall you eat it; with your loins girded, your shoes on your feet, and your staff in your hand; and you shall eat it in haste: it is **YeHoVaH** 's Passover. *12* For I will pass through the land of Egypt this night, and will kill all the firstborn in the land of Egypt, both man and animal; and against all the gods of Egypt I will execute judgment: I am **YeHoVaH**. *13* And the blood shall be to you for a token upon the houses where you are: and when I see the blood, I will pass over you, and the plague shall not be upon you to destroy you, when I destroy the land of Egypt. *14* And this day shall be to you for a memorial; and you shall keep it a feast to **YeHoVaH** *throughout your generations*; you shall keep it a feast by an instruction **forever**. *15* Seven days shall you eat unleavened bread; even the first day you shall put away leaven out of your houses: for whosoever eats leavened bread from the first day until the seventh day, that soul shall be cut off from Israel. *16* And in the first day there shall be a holy gathering, and in the seventh day there shall be a holy gathering to you; no manner of work shall be done in them, **except** *that which every man must eat*, that only may be done of you. *17* And you shall observe the feast of unleavened bread; for in this same day have I brought your armies out of the land of Egypt: therefore shall you observe this day in your generations by an ordinance forever. *18* In the first month, on the fourteenth day of the month at evening, you shall eat unleavened bread, until the one and twentieth day of the month at evening. *19* Seven days shall there be no leaven found in your houses: for whosoever eats that which is leavened, even that soul shall be cut off from the congregation of Israel, whether he be a stranger, or born in the land. *20* You shall eat nothing leavened; in all your habitations shall you eat unleavened bread.

21 Then Moses called for all the elders of Israel, and said to them, Draw out and take you a lamb according to your families, and kill the Passover lamb. *22* And you shall take a bunch of hyssop, and dip it in the blood that is in the pan, and strike the lintel and the two side posts with the blood that is in the pan; and none of you shall go out at the door of his house until the morning. *23* For **YeHoVaH** will pass through to kill the Egyptians; and when he sees the blood upon the lintel, and on the two side posts, **YeHoVaH** will pass over the door, and will not suffer the destroyer to come in to your houses to kill you. *24* And you shall observe this thing for a command to you and to your sons **forever**. *25* And it shall come to pass, when you come to the land that **YeHoVaH** will give you, according as he has promised, that you shall keep this service. *26* And it shall come to pass, when your children shall say to you, What does this service mean? *27* That you shall say, It is the sacrifice of **YeHoVaH's** Passover, who passed over the houses of the children of Israel in Egypt, when he killed the Egyptians, and delivered our houses. And the people bowed the head and worshipped. *28* And the children of Israel went away, and did as **YeHoVaH** had commanded Moses and Aaron. *29* And it came to pass, that at midnight **YeHoVaH** killed all the firstborn in the land of Egypt, from the firstborn of Pharaoh that sat on his throne to the firstborn of the captive that was in the dungeon; and all the firstborn of animals. *30* And Pharaoh rose up in the night, he, and all his servants, and all the Egyptians; and there was a great cry in Egypt; for there was not a house where there was not one dead.

31 And he called for Moses and Aaron by night, and said, Rise up, from among my people, both you and the children of Israel; and go, serve your Lord, as you have said. *32* Also take your flocks and your herds, as you have said, and be gone; and bless me also. *33* And the Egyptians were urgent upon the people, that they might send them out of the land in haste; for they said, We will all be dead men. *34* And the people took their dough before it was leavened, their kneading troughs being bound up in their clothes upon their shoulders. *35* And the children of Israel did according to the word of Moses; and they borrowed of the Egyptians jewels of silver, and jewels of gold, and clothing: *36* And **YeHoVaH** gave the people favor in the sight of the Egyptians, so that they lent to them such things as they required. And they plundered the Egyptians. *37* And the children of Israel journeyed from Rameses to Succoth, about six hundred thousand on foot that were men, beside children. *38* And a *mixed multitude went up also with them*; and flocks, and herds, even very much cattle. *39* And they baked unleavened cakes of the dough which they brought forth out of Egypt, for it was not leavened; because they were thrust out of Egypt, and could not delay, neither had they prepared for themselves any food. *40* Now the traveling of the children of Israel, who dwelt in Egypt, was 430 years.

41 And it came to pass at the end of the **430** years, even the same day it came to pass, that all the hosts of **YeHoVaH** went out from the land of Egypt. *42* It is a night to be much observed to

YeHoVaH for bringing them out from the land of Egypt: this is that night of *YeHoVaH* to be observed of all the children of Israel in their generations. *43* And *YeHoVaH* said to Moses and Aaron, This is the command of the Passover: *There shall be no stranger eat thereof.* *44* But every man's servant that is bought for money, when you have *circumcised* him, then shall he eat thereof. *45 A foreigner and a hired servant shall not eat thereof.* *46* In one house shall it be eaten; you shall not carry forth any of the flesh outside of the house; neither shall you break a bone thereof. *47* All the congregation of Israel shall keep it. *48* And when a stranger shall travel with you, and will keep the Passover to *YeHoVaH*, let all his males be *circumcised*, and then let him come near and keep it; and he shall be as one that is born in the land: for *no uncircumcised person shall eat thereof.* *49* **One** *instruction (law)* shall be to him that is home born, **and** to the **stranger** that travels among you. *50* Thus did all the children of Israel; as *YeHoVaH* commanded Moses and Aaron.

51 And it came to pass the same day that *YeHoVaH* did bring the children of Israel out of the land of Egypt by their armies.

Chapter 13

YeHoVaH tells the Israelites to dedicate their firstborns to Him. He guides them with a pillar of clouds by day and by fire by night.

1 And *YeHoVaH* spoke to Moses, saying, *2* Sanctify to me all the firstborn, whatsoever opens the womb among the children of Israel, both of man and of animal: it is mine. *3* And Moses said to the people, Remember this day, in which you came out from Egypt, out of the house of bondage; for by strength of hand *YeHoVaH* brought you out from this place: there shall no leavened bread be eaten. *4* This day you came out in the month Abib. *5* And it shall be when *YeHoVaH* shall bring you into the land of the Canaanites, and the Hittites, and the Amorites, and the Hivites, and the Jebusites, which he swore to your fathers to give you, a land flowing with milk and honey, that you shall keep this service in this month. *6* Seven days you shall eat unleavened bread, and in the seventh day shall be a feast to *YeHoVaH*. *7* Unleavened bread shall be eaten seven days; and there shall **no** leavened bread be seen with you, neither shall there be leaven seen with you in all your quarters. *8* And you shall show your son in that day, saying, This is done because of that which *YeHoVaH* did to me when I came forth out of Egypt. *9* And it shall be for a sign to you upon your hand, and for a memorial between your eyes, that *YeHoVaH's* instruction may be in your mouth: for with a strong hand has *YeHoVaH* brought you out of Egypt. *10* You shall therefore keep this ordinance in his season *from year to year*.

11 And it shall be when *YeHoVaH* shall bring you into the land of the Canaanites, as he swore to you and to your fathers, and shall give it to you, *12* You are to put on one side for *YeHoVaH* every mother's first **male** child, the first-fruit of her body, and the first young one of every animal; every male is holy to *YeHoVaH*. *13* And every firstling of a donkey you shall redeem with a lamb; and if you will not redeem it, then you shall break his neck: and all the firstborn of man among your children shall you redeem. *14* And it shall be when your son asks you in time to come, saying, What is this? that you shall say to him, By strength of hand *YeHoVaH* brought us out from Egypt, from the house of bondage: *15* And it came to pass, when Pharaoh would not let us go, that *YeHoVaH* slew all the firstborn in the land of Egypt, both the firstborn of man, and the firstborn of animal: therefore I sacrifice to *YeHoVaH* all that opens the womb, being *males*; but all the firstborn of my children I redeem. *16* And this will be for a sign on your hand

and for a mark on your brow: for by the strength of his hand **YeHoVaH** took us out of Egypt.
Reading 15 ends

Reading 16 begins
17 And it came to pass, when Pharaoh had let the people go, that **Elohim** led them not through the way of the land of the Philistines, although that was near; for **Elohim** said, For fear that by chance the people repent when they see war, and they return to Egypt: **18** But **Elohim** led the people about, through the way of the wilderness of the Red sea: and the children of Israel went up together out of the land of Egypt. **19** And *Moses took the bones of Joseph* with him: for he had sworn the children of Israel, saying, **Elohim** will surely visit you; and you shall carry up my bones away then with you. **20** And they took their journey from Succoth, and encamped in Etham, in the edge of the wilderness.

21 And **YeHoVaH** went before them by day in a pillar of a cloud, to lead them the way; and by night in a pillar of fire, to give them light; to go by day and night: **22** He took not away the pillar of the cloud by day, nor the pillar of fire by night, from before the people.

Chapter 14

Pharaoh sends his army to catch the Israelites by the sea. YeHoVaH parts the waters so the Israelites can cross. He then drowns the Egyptian army by closing the waters.

1 And **YeHoVaH** spoke to Moses, saying, **2** Speak to the children of Israel, that they turn and camp before Pharaoh, between Migdol and the sea, over against Baalzephon: before it shall you camp by the sea. **3** For Pharaoh will say of the children of Israel, They are entangled in the land, the wilderness has shut them in. **4** And I will harden Pharaoh's heart, that he shall follow after them; and I will be honored upon Pharaoh, and upon all his host; that the Egyptians may know that I am **YeHoVaH**. And they did so. **5** And it was told the king of Egypt that the people fled: and the heart of Pharaoh and of his servants was turned against the people, and they said, Why have we done this, that we have let Israel go from serving us? **6** And he made ready his chariot, and took his people with him: **7** And he took **600** chosen chariots, and all the chariots of Egypt, and captains over every one of them. **8** And **YeHoVaH** hardened the heart of Pharaoh king of Egypt, and he pursued after the children of Israel: and the children of Israel went out with a high hand. **9** But the Egyptians pursued after them, all the horses and chariots of Pharaoh, and his horsemen, and his army, and saw them camping by the sea, beside Pihahiroth, before Baalzephon. **10** And when Pharaoh drew near, the children of Israel lifted up their eyes, and, behold, the Egyptians marched after them; and they were very afraid: and the children of Israel cried out to **YeHoVaH**.

11 And they said to Moses, Because there were no graves in Egypt, have you taken us away to die in the wilderness? why have you dealt thus with us, to carry us forth out of Egypt? **12** Is not this the word that we did tell you in Egypt, saying, Let us alone, that we may serve the Egyptians? For it had been better for us to serve the Egyptians, than that we should die in the wilderness. **13** And Moses said to the people, Fear you not, stand still, and see the salvation of **YeHoVaH**, which he will show to you today: for the Egyptians whom you have seen today, you shall see them again no more forever. **14** **YeHoVaH** shall fight for you, and you shall hold your peace. **15** And **YeHoVaH** said to Moses, Why do you cry to me? speak to the children of Israel, that they go forward **16** But lift you up your rod, and stretch out your hand over the sea, and divide it: and the children of Israel shall go on dry ground through the midst of the sea. **17** And I, behold, I will harden the hearts of the Egyptians, and they shall follow them: and I will get honor upon Pharaoh, and upon all his host, upon his chariots, and upon his horsemen. *18* And the Egyptians shall know that I am **YeHoVaH**, when I have gotten my honor upon Pharaoh, upon his chariots, and upon his horsemen. *19* And the angel of **YeHoVaH**, which went before the camp of Israel, removed and went behind them; and the pillar of the cloud went from before their face, and stood behind them: *20* And it came between the camp of the Egyptians and the camp of Israel; and it was a cloud and darkness to them, but it gave light by night to these: so that the one came not near the other all the night.

21 And Moses stretched out his hand over the sea; and **YeHoVaH** caused the sea to go back by a strong east wind all that night, and made the sea dry land, and the waters were divided. *22* And the children of Israel went into the midst of the sea upon the dry ground: and the waters were a wall to them on their right hand, and on their left. *23* And the Egyptians pursued, and went in after them to the midst of the sea, even all Pharaoh's horses, his chariots, and his horsemen. *24* And it came to pass, that in the morning watch **YeHoVaH** looked to the host of the Egyptians through the pillar of fire and of the cloud, and troubled the host of the Egyptians, *25* And took off their chariot wheels, that they drove them heavily: so that the Egyptians said, Let us flee from the face of Israel; for **YeHoVaH** fights for them against the Egyptians. *26* And **YeHoVaH** said to Moses, Stretch out your hand over the sea, that the waters may come again upon the Egyptians, upon their chariots, and upon their horsemen. *27* And Moses stretched forth his hand over the sea, and the sea returned to its strength when the morning appeared; and the Egyptians fled against it; and **YeHoVaH** overthrew the Egyptians in the midst of the sea. *28* And the waters returned, and covered the chariots, and the horsemen, and all the host of Pharaoh that came into the sea after them; there remained not so much as one of them. *29* But the children of Israel walked upon dry land in the midst of the sea; and the waters were a wall to them on their right hand, and on their left. *30* Thus **YeHoVaH** saved Israel that day out of the hand of the Egyptians; and Israel saw the Egyptians dead upon the seashore. *31* And Israel saw that great work which **YeHoVaH** did upon the Egyptians: and the people feared **YeHoVaH**, and believed **YeHoVaH**, and his servant Moses.

Chapter 15

Moses and the Israelites sing: "I will sing to YeHoVaH, for he has triumphed; horse and rider he has thrown into the sea." They then camp at Elim.

1 Then sang Moses and the children of Israel this song to **YeHoVaH** and spoke, saying, I will sing to **YeHoVaH**, for he has triumphed gloriously: the horse and his rider has he thrown into the sea. *2* **YeHoVaH** is my strength and song, and He has become my salvation: He is my **Elohim**, and I will prepare Him an environment; my father's **Elohim**, and I will exalt Him. *3* **YeHoVaH** is a man of war: **YeHoVaH** is His name. *4* Pharaoh's chariots and his host has he cast into the sea: his chosen captains also are drowned in the Red sea. *5* The depths have covered them: they sank into the bottom like a stone. *6* Your right hand, O **YeHoVaH**, has become glorious in power: Your right hand, O **YeHoVaH**, has dashed in pieces the enemy. *7* And in the greatness of Your excellency You have overthrown them that rose up against You: You sent forth Your wrath, which consumed them as stubble. *8* And with the blast of Your nostrils the waters were gathered together, the floods stood upright as a heap, and the depths were firm in the heart of the sea. *9* The enemy said, I will pursue, I will overtake, I will divide the spoil; my lust shall be satisfied upon them; I will draw my sword, my hand shall destroy them. *10* You did blow with your wind, the sea covered them: they sank as lead in the mighty waters.

11 Who is like to You, O **YeHoVaH**, among the gods? who is like You, glorious in holiness, fearful in praises, doing wonders? *12* You stretched out Your right hand, the earth swallowed them. *13* You in Your mercy has led forth the people that You have redeemed: You have guided them in Your strength to Your holy environment. *14* The people shall hear, and be afraid: sorrow shall take hold on the inhabitants of Palestina. *15* Then the dukes of Edom shall be amazed; the mighty men of Moab, trembling shall take hold upon them; all the inhabitants of Canaan shall melt away. *16* Fear and dread shall fall upon them; by the greatness of Your arm they shall be as still as a stone; till Your people pass over, O **YeHoVaH**, till the people pass over, which You have purchased. *17* You shall bring them in, and plant them in the mountain of Your inheritance, in the place, O **YeHoVaH**, which You have made for You to dwell in, in the Sanctuary, O **YeHoVaH**, which Your hands have established. *18* **YeHoVaH** shall reign forever and ever. *19* For the horse of Pharaoh went in with his chariots and with his horsemen into the sea, and **YeHoVaH** brought again the waters of the sea upon them; but the children of Israel went on dry land in the midst of the sea. *20* And Miriam the prophetess, the sister of Aaron, took a timbrel (tambourine) in her hand; and all the women went out after her with timbrels and with dances.

21 And Miriam answered them, Sing you to **YeHoVaH**, for He has triumphed gloriously; the horse and his rider has He thrown into the sea. *22* So Moses brought Israel from the Red sea, and they went out into the wilderness of Shur; and they went three days in the wilderness, and found no water. *23* And when they came to Marah, they could not drink of the waters of Marah, for they were bitter: therefore the name of it was called Marah. *24* And the people murmured against Moses, saying, What shall we drink? *25* And he cried to **YeHoVaH**; and the **YeHoVaH** showed him a tree, which when he had cast into the waters, the waters were made sweet: there he made for them a statute and an instruction, and there he proved them, *26* And said, If you will diligently listen to the voice of **YeHoVaH** your **Elohim**, and will do that which is right in His sight, and will give ear to His commandments, and keep all His statutes, I will put none of these diseases upon you, which I have brought upon the Egyptians: for I am **YeHoVaH** that heals you. *27* And they came to Elim, where twelve wells of water were, and 70 palm trees: and they camped there by the waters.

Chapter 16

The Israelites complained to Moses that they had no food, so he prays to YeHoVaH. YeHoVaH is not pleased with their complaining but provides quails and manna. YeHoVaH tells Moses to rest on the Sabbath.

1 And they took their journey from Elim, and all the congregation of the children of Israel came to the wilderness of Sin, which is between Elim and Sinai, on the fifteenth day of the second month after their departing out of the land of Egypt. *2* And the whole congregation of the children of Israel complained against Moses and Aaron in the wilderness: *3* And the children of Israel said to them, It would have been better for **YeHoVaH** to have put us to death in the land of Egypt, where we were seated by the flesh-pots and had bread enough for our needs; for you have taken us out to this waste of sand, to put all this people to death through need of food. *4* Then said **YeHoVaH** to Moses, Behold, I will rain bread from heaven for you; and the people shall go out and gather a certain amount every day, that I may test them, whether they will walk in my instruction, or not. *5* And it shall come to pass, that on the *sixth* day they shall prepare that which they bring in; and it shall be twice as much as they gather daily. *6* And Moses and

Aaron said to all the children of Israel, At evening, then you shall know that **YeHoVaH** has brought you out from the land of Egypt: **7** And in the morning, then you shall see the glory of **YeHoVaH**; for that he hears your moaning against Him: and what are we, that you murmur against us? **8** And Moses said, This shall be, when **YeHoVaH** shall give you in the evening flesh to eat, and in the morning bread to the full; for that **YeHoVaH** hears your complaints which you murmur against him: and what are we? your complaints are not against us, but against **YeHoVaH**. **9** And Moses spoke to Aaron, Say to all the congregation of the children of Israel, Come near before **YeHoVaH**: for he has heard your complaints. **10** And it came to pass, as Aaron spoke to the whole congregation of the children of Israel, that they looked toward the wilderness, and, behold, the glory of **YeHoVaH** appeared in the cloud.

11 And **YeHoVaH** spoke to Moses, saying, **12** I have heard the murmurings of the children of Israel: speak to them, saying, At evening you shall eat flesh, and in the morning you shall be filled with bread; and you shall know that I am **YeHoVaH** your **Elohim**. **13** And it came to pass, that at evening the quails came up, and covered the camp: and in the morning the dew lay round about the host. **14** And when the dew was gone, on the face of the earth there were small round disks, like small drops of ice on the earth. **15** And when the children of Israel saw it, they said to one another, What is it? for they had no idea what it was. And Moses said to them, it is the bread that **YeHoVaH** has given you for your food. **16** This is the thing which **YeHoVaH** has commanded, Gather of it every man according to his eating, an omer (A measure of capacity among the Hebrews; the tenth part of an ephah; a little more than five pints.) for every man, according to the number of your family; take every man for them which are in his tents. **17** And the children of Israel did so, and gathered, some more, some less. **18** And when they did measure it with an omer, he that gathered much had nothing left over, and he that gathered little had no lack of need; they gathered every man according to his eating. **19** And Moses said, Let no man leave any of it until the morning. **20** But they did not listen to Moses; but some of them left of it until the morning, and it filled with worms, and smelled badly: and Moses was angry with them.

21 And they gathered it every morning, every man according to his eating: and when the sun shown hot, it melted. **22** And it came to pass, that on the sixth day they gathered twice as much bread, two omers for one man: and all the rulers of the congregation came and told Moses. **23** And he said to them, This is what **YeHoVaH** *has* said, Tomorrow is the rest of the holy Sabbath to **YeHoVaH**: bake that which you will bake today, and see that you will see; and that which remains over lay up for you to be kept until the morning. **24** And they laid it up till the morning, as Moses instructed: and it did not spoil and smell, neither was there any worm in it. **25** And Moses said, Eat that today; for today is a Sabbath to **YeHoVaH**: today you shall not find it in the field. **26** Six days you shall gather it; on the seventh day, the Sabbath, there will be none." **27** And it came to pass, that there went out some of the people on the seventh day to gather, and they found none. **28** And **YeHoVaH** said to Moses, How long do they refuse to keep my Torah (instructions)? **29** See, for that **YeHoVaH** has given you the Sabbath, therefore he gives you on the sixth day the bread of two days; abide you every man in his place, let no man go out of his place on the seventh day. **30** So the people rested on the *seventh* day.

31 And the house of Israel called the name Manna: and it was like coriander seed, white; and the taste of it was like wafers made with honey. **32** And Moses said, This is that which **YeHoVaH** commands, Fill an omer of it to be kept for your generations; that they may see the bread that I have fed you in the wilderness, when I brought you forth from the land of Egypt. **33** And Moses said to Aaron, Take a pot, and put an omer full of manna in it, and lay it up before **YeHoVaH**, *to be kept for your generations*. *34* As **YeHoVaH** commanded Moses, so Aaron laid it up before the Testimony, to be kept. *35* And the children of Israel did eat manna *40 years*, until they came to a land inhabited; they did eat manna, until they came to the borders of the land of Canaan. *36* Now an omer is the tenth part of an ephah (about 5 pints).

Chapter 17

The people complain again about no water so YeHoVaH tells Moses to strike a rock to provide water. Moses doesn't follow the instructions exactly and YeHoVaH takes note. Amalek attacks but as Moses held up his arms, Joshua's army prevailed.

1 And all the congregation of the children of Israel journeyed from the wilderness of Sin, after their journeys, according to the commandment of *YeHoVaH*, and pitched in Rephidim: and there was no water for the people to drink. *2* Wherefore the people did protested to Moses, and said, Give us water that we may drink. And Moses said to them, Why protest you with me? why do you tempt **YeHoVaH**? *3* And the people were thirsty for water; and the people murmured against Moses, and said, What is this that you have brought us up out of Egypt, to kill us and our children and our cattle with thirst? *4* And Moses cried to **YeHoVaH**, saying, What shall I do to this people? they are almost ready to stone me. *5* And **YeHoVaH** said to Moses, Go on before the people, and take with you of the elders of Israel; and your rod, where you struck the river, take in your hand, and go. *6* Behold, I will stand before you there upon the rock in Horeb; and you shall strike the rock, and there shall come water out of it that the people may drink. And Moses did so in the sight of the elders of Israel. *7* And he called the name of the place Massah, and Meribah, because of the rebuke of the children of Israel, and because they tempted, saying, Is **YeHoVaH** among us, or not? *8* Then came Amalek, and fought with Israel in Rephidim. *9* And Moses said to Joshua, Choose us out men, and go out, fight with Amalek: tomorrow I will stand on the top of the hill with the rod of **Elohim** in my hand. *10* So Joshua did as Moses had said to him, and fought with Amalek: and Moses, Aaron, and Hur went up to the top of the hill.

11 And it came to pass, when Moses held up his hand, that Israel prevailed: and when he let down his hand, Amalek prevailed. *12* But Moses hands were heavy; and they took a stone, and put it under him, and he sat there; and Aaron and Hur held up his hands, the one on one side, and the other on the other side; and his hands were steady until the sun went down. *13* And Joshua embarrassed Amalek and his people with the edge of the sword. *14* And **YeHoVaH** said to Moses, Write this for a memorial in a book, and rehearse it in the ears of Joshua: for I will utterly put out the remembrance of Amalek from under heaven. *15* And Moses built an altar, and called the name of it Jehovahnissi: *16* For he said, Because **YeHoVaH** has sworn that He will fight against Amalek from generation to generation.
  Reading 16 ends

Chapter 18

Moses' father-in-law, Jethro comes and offers sacrifices to YeHoVaH. He tells Moses to appoint leaders to help him judge the needs of the people.
  Reading 17 begins
1 When Jethro, the priest of Midian, Moses' father-in-law, heard of all that **Elohim** had done for Moses, and for Israel his people, and that **YeHoVaH** had brought Israel out of Egypt; *2* Then Jethro, took Zipporah, Moses' wife, after he had sent her back, *3* And her two sons; of which the name of the one was Gershom; for he said, I have been an alien in a strange land: *4* And

the name of the other was Eliezer; for the **Elohim** of my father, said he, was my help, and delivered me from the sword of Pharaoh: **5** And Jethro, came with his sons and his wife to Moses into the wilderness, where he camped at the mount of **Elohim**: **6** And he said to Moses, I your father-in-law Jethro come to you, and your wife, and her two sons with her. **7** And Moses went out to meet his father-in-law, and did bow, and kissed him; and they asked each other of their welfare; and they came into the tent. **8** And Moses told his father-in-law all that **YeHoVaH** had done to Pharaoh and to the Egyptians for Israel's sake, and all the difficulty that had come upon them along the way, and how **YeHoVaH** delivered them. **9** And Jethro rejoiced for all the goodness that **YeHoVaH** had done to Israel, whom he had delivered out of the hand of the Egyptians. **10** And Jethro said, Blessed be **YeHoVaH**, who has delivered you out of the hand of the Egyptians, and out of the hand of Pharaoh, who has delivered the people from under the hand of the Egyptians.

11 Now I know that **YeHoVaH** is greater than all gods: for in the thing wherein they dealt proudly he was above them. **12** And Jethro, took a burnt offering and sacrifices for **Elohim**: and Aaron came, and all the elders of Israel, to eat bread with Jethro before **Elohim**. **13** And it came to pass on the next day, that Moses sat to judge the people: and the people stood by Moses from the morning to the evening. **14** And when Jethro saw all that he did to the people, he said, What is this thing that you do to the people? why do you sit alone, and all the people stand by you from morning to even? **15** And Moses said to Jethro, Because the people come to me to enquire of **YeHoVaH**; **16** When they have a matter, they come to me; and I judge between one and another, and I do make them know the statutes of **Elohim**, and His instructions. **17** And Jethro said to him, The thing that you do is not good. **18** You will surely wear away, both you, and this people that are with you: for this thing is too heavy for you; you are not able to perform it yourself alone. **19** Give ear now to my suggestion, and may **Elohim** be with you: you are to be the people's representative before **Elohim**, taking their causes to him: **20** And you shall teach them ordinances and instructions, and shall show them the way that they must walk, and the work that they must do.

21 Moreover you shall provide out of all the people able men, such as fear **Elohim**, men of truth, hating covetousness; and place such over them, to be rulers of thousands, and rulers of hundreds, rulers of fifties, and rulers of tens: **22** And let them judge the people at all seasons: and it shall be, that every great matter they shall bring to you, but every small matter they shall judge: so shall it be easier for yourself, and they shall bear the burden with you. **23** If you shall do this thing, and **Elohim** command you so, then you shall be able to endure, and this entire people shall also go to their place in peace. **24** So Moses listened to the voice of Jethro, and did all that he had said. **25** And Moses chose able men out of all Israel, and made them heads over the people, rulers of thousands, rulers of hundreds, rulers of fifties, and rulers of tens. **26** And they judged the people at all seasons: the hard causes they brought to Moses, but every small matter they judged themselves. **27** And Moses let his father-in-law depart; and he went his way into his own land.

Chapter 19

The Israelites camp near Mount Sinai and YeHoVaH speaks to Moses on the mountain and makes His covenant with Israel.

1 In the third month, when the children of Israel had gone forth out of the land of Egypt, the same day they came into the wilderness of Sinai. **2** For they were departed from Rephidim, and had come to the desert of Sinai, and had pitched in the wilderness; and there Israel camped before the mount. *3* And Moses went up to **Elohim. YeHoVaH** called to him out of the mountain, saying, Thus shall you say to the house of Jacob, and tell the children of Israel; *4* You have seen what I did to the Egyptians, and how I bore you on eagles' wings, and brought you to myself. *5* Now therefore, if you will obey my voice indeed, and keep my covenant, then you shall be an unusual treasure to me above all people: for all the earth is mine: *6* And you shall be to me a kingdom of priests, and a holy nation. These are the words that you shall speak to the children of Israel. *7* And Moses came and called for the elders of the people, and laid before their faces all these words that **YeHoVaH** commanded him. *8* And all the people answered together, and said, All that **YeHoVaH** has spoken we will do. And Moses returned the words of the people to **YeHoVaH**. *9* And **YeHoVaH** said to Moses, see, I come to you in a thick cloud, that the people may hear when I speak with you, and believe you forever. And Moses told the words of the people to **YeHoVaH**. *10* And **YeHoVaH** said to Moses, Go to the people, and sanctify them today and tomorrow, and let them wash their clothes,

11 And be ready on the third day: for the third day **YeHoVaH** *will come down in the sight of all the people upon Mount Sinai.* *12* And you shall set bounds to the people all around, saying, Take heed to yourselves, that you go not up into the mount, or touch the border of it: whosoever touches the mount shall be surely put to death: *13* There shall not a hand touch it, but he shall surely be stoned, or shot through; whether it be beast or man, it shall not live: when the trumpet sounds long, they shall come up to the mount. *14* And Moses went down from the mount to the people, and sanctified the people; and they washed their clothes. *15* And he said to the people, Be ready by the third day: do not come near a woman. *16* And it came to pass on the third day in the morning, that there were thunder and lighting, and a thick cloud upon the mount, and the voice of the trumpet exceeding loud; so that all the people that were in the camp trembled. *17* And *Moses brought forth the people out of the camp to meet with* **Elohim**; and they stood at the rear part of the mount. *18* And mount Sinai was altogether in smoke, because **YeHoVaH** descended upon it in fire: and the smoke there ascended like the smoke of a furnace, and the whole mount quaked greatly. *19* And when the voice of the trumpet sounded long, and continued louder and louder, Moses spoke, and **Elohim** answered him by a voice. *20* And **YeHoVaH** came down upon mount Sinai, on the top of the mount: and **YeHoVaH** called Moses up to the top of the mount; and Moses went up.

21 And **YeHoVaH** said to Moses, Go down, charge the people, in case they break through to Me to gaze, and many of them perish. *22* And let the priests also, which come near to Me, sanctify themselves, or else I break forth upon them. *23* And Moses said to **YeHoVaH**, The people cannot come up to mount Sinai: for you charged us, saying, Set bounds about the mount, and sanctify it. *24* And **YeHoVaH** said to him, Away, get you down, and you shall come up, you, and Aaron with you: but let not the priests and the people break through to come up to Me, or else I break forth upon them. *25* So Moses went down to the people, and spoke to them.

Chapter 20

YeHoVaH gives Moses the Ten Commandments.

1 And **YeHoVaH** spoke all these words, saying, *2* I am **YeHoVaH** your **Elohim**, which has brought you out of the land of Egypt, out of the house of bondage. *3* You shall have no other gods before me. *4* You shall not make before you any graven image (statues or idols), or any likeness of *anything that is in heaven above,* or that is in the earth beneath, or that is in the water under the earth. *5* You shall *not bow down to them, nor serve them*: for I **YeHoVaH** your **Elohim** am a jealous **Elohim**, visiting the iniquity of the fathers upon the children to the third and fourth generation of them that hate me; *6* And showing mercy to thousands of them that love me, and keep my commandments. *7* You shall not take the name of **YeHoVaH** your **Elohim** in vain (falsely); for **YeHoVaH** will not hold him guiltless that takes My name in vain. *8* Remember the **Sabbath** day, to keep it holy. *9* Six days shall you labor, and do all your work: *10* But the **seventh** day is the Sabbath of **YeHoVaH** your **Elohim**: in it you shall not do any work, you, nor your son, nor your daughter, your manservant, nor your maidservant, nor your cattle, nor your stranger that is within your gates:

11 For in six days **YeHoVaH** made heaven and earth, the sea, and all that in them is, and *rested* the **seventh** day: that is why **YeHoVaH** blessed the Sabbath day, and consecrated it. *12* Honor your father and your mother: that your days may be long upon the land which **YeHoVaH** your **Elohim** gives you. *13* You shall not murder. *14* You shall not commit adultery. *15* You shall not steal. *16* You shall not bear false witness against your neighbor. *17* You shall not covet your neighbor's house; you shall not covet your neighbor's wife, nor his manservant, nor his maidservant, nor his ox, nor his donkey, nor any thing that is your neighbor's. *18* And all the people heard the thunder, and saw the lightning, and the noise of the trumpet, and the mountain smoking: and when the people saw it, they backed away, and stood far off. *19* And they said to Moses, You speak with us, and we will hear: but let not **YeHoVaH** speak with us, or else we will die. *20* And Moses said to the people, Fear not: for **YeHoVaH** has come to test your character, and that his fear may be before your faces, that you do not sin.

21 And the people stood far off, and Moses drew near to the thick darkness where **Elohim** was. *22* And **YeHoVaH** said to Moses, Thus you shall say to the children of Israel, You have seen that I have talked with you from heaven. *23* You shall not make other gods of silver, neither shall you make to you gods of gold. *24* An altar of earth you shall make to me, and shall sacrifice there your burnt offerings, and your peace offerings, your sheep, and your oxen: in *all places where I record my name* I will come to you, and I will bless you. *25* And if you will make me an altar of stone, you shall not build it of hewn stone: for if you lift up your tool upon it, you have polluted it. *26* Neither shall you go up by steps to my altar, that your nakedness not be seen.
Reading 17 ends

CHAPTERS 21- 30

Chapter 21

A Hebrew slave shall be set free in the seventh year. Whoever kills shall be put to death and whoever injures shall compensate for that injury.
    Reading 18 begins
1 Now these are the judgments that you shall set before them. *2* If you buy a Hebrew servant, six years he shall serve: and in the seventh he shall go out free for nothing. *3* If he came in by himself, he shall go out by himself: if he were married, then his wife shall go out with him. *4* If his master has given him a wife, and she have born him sons or daughters; the wife and her children shall be her master's, and he shall go out by himself. *5* And if the servant shall plainly say, I love my master, my wife, and my children; I will not go out free: *6* Then his master shall

bring him to the judges; he shall also bring him to the door, or to the door post; and his master shall bore his ear through with a sharp-pointed instrument (aul); and he shall serve him forever. *7* And if a man sells his daughter to be a maidservant, she shall not go out as the menservants do. *8* If she please not her master, who has betrothed her to himself, then shall he let her be redeemed: to sell her to a strange nation he shall have no power, seeing he has dealt deceitfully with her. *9* And if he has betrothed her to his son, he shall deal with her after the manner of daughters. *10* If he takes another wife; her food, her needs, and her duty of marriage, shall he not diminish.

11 And if he does not these three to her, then shall she go out free without money. *12* He that kills a man, so that he dies, shall be surely put to death. *13* But if he had no evil purpose against him, and **Elohim** gave him into his hand, I will give you a place to which he may go in flight. *14* But if a man makes an attack on his neighbor intentionally, to put him to death by deceit, you are to take him from my altar and put him to death. *15* And he that kills his father, or his mother, shall be surely put to death. *16* And he that steals (kidnaps) a man, and sells him, or if he be found in his hand, he shall surely be put to death. *17* And he that curses his father, or his mother, shall surely be put to death. *18* And if men struggle together, and one kills another with a stone, or with his fist, and he does not die, but keeps his bed: *19* If he rise again, and walk around upon his staff, then shall he that harmed him be quit: only he shall pay for the loss of his time, and shall cause him to be thoroughly healed. *20* And if a man kills his servant, or his maid, with a rod, and he die under his hand; he shall be surely punished.

21 But, at the same time, if the servant goes on living for a day or two, the master is not to get punishment, for the servant is his property. *22* If men strive, and hurt a woman with child, so that her child is born early, and yet no injury follows: he shall be surely punished, according as the woman's husband will lay upon him; and he shall pay as the judges determine. *23* And if any injury follows, then you shall give life for life, *24* Eye for eye, tooth for tooth, hand for hand, foot for foot, *25* Burning for burning, wound for wound, stripe for stripe. *26* And if a man injures the eye of his servant, or the eye of his maid, that it perish; he shall let him go free for his eye's sake. *27* And if he knocks out his manservant's tooth, or his maidservant's tooth; he shall let him go free for his tooth's sake. *28* If an ox gores a man or a woman that they die: then the ox shall be surely stoned, and his flesh shall not be eaten; but the owner of the ox shall not be judged responsible. *29* But if the ox were known to push with his horn in times past, and it has been testified to his owner, and he has not kept him in, but that he has killed a man or a woman; the ox shall be stoned, and his owner also shall be put to death. *30* If a price is put on his life, let him make payment of whatever price is fixed.

31 Whether he has gored a son, or has gored a daughter, according to this judgment shall it be done to him. *32* If the ox shall push a manservant or a maidservant; he shall give to their master thirty shekels of silver, and the ox shall be stoned. *33* And if a man shall open a pit, or if a man shall dig a pit, and not cover it, and an ox or a donkey fall in it; *34* The owner of the pit shall make it good, and give money to the owner of them; and the dead beast shall be his. *35* And if one man's ox does damage to another man's ox, causing its death, then the living ox is to be exchanged for money, and division made of the price of it, and of the price of the dead one. *36* Or if it be known that the ox has used to push in times past, and his owner has not kept him in; he shall surely pay ox for ox; and the dead shall be his own.

Chapter 22

If a man steals he shall make restitution. If a man sleeps with a virgin he shall marry her. You are not to oppress strangers or the poor.

1 If a man shall steal an ox, or a sheep, and kill it, or sell it; he shall restore five oxen for the ox, and four sheep for a sheep. **2** If a thief be found breaking in, and be injured that he die, there shall be no blood shed for him. **3** But if it is after dawn, he will be responsible for he should make full restitution; if he has nothing, then he shall be sold for his theft. **4** If the theft is certainly found in his hand alive, whether it be ox, or donkey, or sheep; he shall restore double. **5** If a man shall cause a field or vineyard to be eaten, and shall put in his animals, and shall feed in another man's field; of the best of his own field, and of the best of his own vineyard, shall he make restitution. **6** If fire breaks out, and catch in thorns, so that the stacks of corn, or the standing corn, or the field, be consumed therein; he that kindled the fire shall surely make restitution. **7** If a man shall deliver to his neighbor money or items to keep, and it be stolen out of the man's house; if the thief be found, let him pay double. **8** If the thief be not found, then the master of the house shall be brought to the judges, to see whether he has put his hand to his neighbor's goods. **9** For all manner of trespass, whether it be for ox, for donkey, for sheep, for supplies, or for any manner of lost thing which another challenges to be his, the cause of both parties shall come before the judges; and whom the judges shall condemn, he shall pay double to his neighbor. **10** If a man deliver to his neighbor a donkey, or an ox, or a sheep, or any animal, to keep; and it dies, or be hurt, or driven away, no man seeing it:

11 Then shall an oath of **YeHoVaH** be between them both, that he has not put his hand to his neighbor's goods; and the owner of it shall accept thereof, and he shall not make it good. **12** And if it be stolen from him, he shall make restitution to the owner thereof. **13** If it be torn in pieces, then let him bring it for witness, and he shall not make good that which was torn. **14** If a man gets from his neighbor the use of one of his beasts, and it is damaged or put to death when the owner is not with it, he will certainly have to make payment for the loss. **15** If the owner is with it, he will not have to make payment: if he gave money for the use of it, the loss is covered by the payment. **16** And if a man entices a maid that is not betrothed, and lie with her, he shall surely endow her to be his wife. **17** If her father utterly refuses to give her to him, he shall pay money according to the dowry of virgins. **18** Any woman using unnatural powers (witch) or secret arts is to be put to death. **19** Whoever lies with an animal shall surely be put to death. **20** He that sacrifices to any god, except to **YeHoVaH** only, he shall be utterly destroyed.

21 You shall neither anger a stranger, nor oppress him: for you were strangers in the land of Egypt. **22** You shall not bother any widow, or fatherless child. **23** If you bother them in any way, and they cry at all to me, I will surely hear their cry; **24** And my wrath shall be hot, and I will kill you with the sword; and your wives shall be widows, and your children fatherless. **25** *If you lend money to any of my people that is poor by you, you shall not be to him as a lender, neither shall you lay upon him interest.* **26** If you at all take your neighbor's clothing to pledge collateral, you shall deliver it to him before the sun goes down: **27** For that is his covering only, it is his clothing for his skin: wherein shall he sleep? and it shall come to pass, when he cries to me, that I will hear; for I am gracious. **28** You shall not revile the gods, nor curse the ruler of your people. **29** *You shall not delay to offer the first of your ripe fruits, and of your liquors: the firstborn of your sons shall you give to me.* **30** Likewise shall you do with your oxen, and with your sheep: seven days it shall be with his mother; on the eighth day you shall give it me.

31 And you shall be holy men to me: neither shall you eat any flesh that is torn of beasts in the field; you shall cast it to the dogs.

Chapter 23

And YeHoVaH said, 'You shall not distort justice. Each year you shall hold feasts. My angel (messenger) will lead you and I will be an enemy to your enemies.

1 You shall not raise a false report: put not your hand with the wicked to be an unrighteous witness. *2* You shall not follow a multitude to do evil; neither shall you speak in a cause to decline after many to extort judgment: *3* Neither shall you tolerate a poor man in his cause. *4* If you meet your enemy's ox or his donkey going astray, you shall surely bring it back to him again. *5* If you see the donkey of one who has no love for you bent down to the earth under the weight that is put on it, you are to come to its help, *even against your desire.* *6* *Let no wrong decisions be given in the poor man's cause.* *7* Keep yourselves far from any false business; never let the upright or him who has done no wrong be put to death: for I will make the evildoer responsible for his sin. *8* And you shall take no gift: for the gift blinds the wise, and perverts the words of the righteous. *9* Also you shall not oppress a stranger: for you know the heart of a stranger, seeing you were strangers in the land of Egypt. *10* And six years you shall sow your land, and shall gather in the fruits thereof:

11 But the seventh year you shall let it rest and lie still; that the poor of your people may eat: and what they leave the beasts of the field shall eat. In like manner you shall deal with your vineyard, and with your olive yard. *12* Six days you shall do your work, and on the **seventh** day you shall rest: that your ox and your donkey may rest, and the son of your handmaid, and the stranger, may be refreshed. *13* And in all things that I have said to you be protected: and make no mention of the name of **other** gods, neither let it be heard out of your mouth. *14* **Three** times you shall keep a feast to me in the year. *15* You shall keep the (1) **Feast of Unleavened Bread**: (Starting the first day after Passover) you shall eat unleavened bread seven days, as I commanded you, in the time appointed of the month Abib; for in it you came out from Egypt: and none shall appear before me empty: *16* And the feast of harvest, *Also known as "Shavuot,"* the (2) **Feast of Weeks** *Exod. 34:22; Deut. 16:9-11* and the (3) **Feast of Harvest,** *the first-fruits of your labors, which you have sown in the field: and the feast of ingathering (also known as* **Sukkot"** *or* **Feast of Booths***, which is in the end of the year, when you have gathered in your labors out of the field. *17* Three items in the year all your males shall appear before **YeHoVaH**. *18* You shall not offer the blood of my sacrifice with leavened bread; neither shall the fat of my sacrifice remain until the morning. *19* The first of the first-fruits of your land you shall bring into the house of **YeHoVaH** your **Elohim**. *You shall not cook a young goat in his mother's milk.* (This has nothing to do with eating meat and milk/cheese together) *20* Behold, *I send a Messenger (Angel) before you*, to keep you in the way, and to bring you into the place that I have prepared.

21 Beware of him (Angel), and obey his voice, provoke him not; for he will not pardon your transgressions: for my name is in him. *22* But if you shall indeed obey his voice, and do all that I speak; then I will be an enemy to your enemies, and an adversary to your adversaries. *23* For my Messenger shall go before you, and bring you in to the Amorites, and the Hittites, and the Perizzites, and the Canaanites, the Hivites, and the Jebusites: and I will cut them off. *24* You shall not bow down to their gods, nor serve them, nor do after their works: but you shall utterly overthrow them, and quite break down their images. *25* And you shall serve **YeHoVaH** your **Elohim**, and He shall bless your bread, and your water; and I will take sickness away from the midst of you. *26* All your animals will give birth without loss, not one will be without young in all your land; I will give you a full measure of life. *27* I will send my fear before you, and will destroy all the people to whom you shall come, and I will make all your enemies turn their backs to you. *28* And I will send hornets before you, which shall drive out the Hivite, the Canaanite, and the Hittite, from before you. *29* I will not drive them out from before you in one year; to keep the land from becoming desolate, and the beast of the field multiply against you. *30* By little and little I will drive them out from before you, until you be increased, and inherit the land.

31 And I will set your bounds from the Red sea even to the sea of the Philistines, and from the desert to the river: for I will deliver the inhabitants of the land into your hand; and you shall drive them out before you. *32* You shall make no covenant with them, nor with their gods. *33* They shall not dwell in your land, for they will make you sin against me: for if you serve their gods, it will surely be it will certainly be a cause of sin to you.

Chapter 24

All the people agreed, "All that YeHoVaH has spoken we will do", and they offered sacrifices. YeHoVaH continues to talk to Moses on the mountain.

1 And he said to Moses, Come up to **YeHoVaH**, you, and Aaron, Nadab, and Abihu, and seventy of the elders of Israel; and worship you far off. *2* And Moses alone shall come near **YeHoVaH**: but they shall not come near; neither shall the people go up with him. *3* And Moses came and told the people all the words of **YeHoVaH**, and all the judgments: and all the people answered with one voice, and said, All the words which **YeHoVaH** has said will we do. *4* And Moses wrote all the words of **YeHoVaH**, and rose up early in the morning, and built an altar under the hill, and twelve pillars, according to the twelve tribes of Israel. *5* And he sent young men of the children of Israel, which offered burnt offerings, and sacrificed peace offerings of oxen to **YeHoVaH**. *6* And Moses took half of the blood, and put it in basins; and half of the blood he sprinkled on the altar. *7* And he took the book of the covenant, and read in the audience of the people: and they said, All that **YeHoVaH** has said will we do, and be obedient. *8* And Moses took the blood, and sprinkled it on the people, and said, Behold the blood of the covenant, which **YeHoVaH** has made with you concerning all these words. *9* Then Moses went up, and Aaron, Nadab, and Abihu, and seventy of the elders of Israel: *10* And they saw the **Elohim** of Israel; and under his feet there was, as it seemed, a jeweled floor, clear as the heavens.

11 And he put not his hand on the chiefs of the children of Israel: they saw **Elohim**, and took food and drink. *12* And **YeHoVaH** said to Moses, Come up to me into the mount, and be there: and I will give you tables of stone, and instructions, and commandments which I have written; that you may teach them. *13* And Moses rose up, and his minister *Joshua: and Moses went up* into the mount of **Elohim**. *14* And he said to the elders, Wait you here for us, until we come again to you: and, behold, Aaron and Hur are with you: if any man have any matters to do, let him come to them. *15* And Moses went up into the mount, and a cloud covered the mount. *16* And the glory of **YeHoVaH** dwelled upon Mount Sinai, and the cloud covered it six days: and the seventh day he called to Moses out of the midst of the cloud. *17* And the sight of the glory of **YeHoVaH** was like devouring fire on the top of the mount in the eyes of the children of Israel. *18* And Moses went into the midst of the cloud, and went up into the mountain: and Moses was there forty days and forty nights.
    Reading 18 ends

Chapter 25

YeHoVaH tells the Israelites to build a sanctuary for Him and to make an ark with a mercy seat, two winged guardians (cherubim), and a lamp stand.

Reading 19 begins

1 And **YeHoVaH** spoke to Moses, saying, **2** Speak to the children of Israel, that they bring me an offering: of every man that gives it willingly with his heart you shall take my offering. **3** And this is the offering which you shall take of them; gold, and silver, and brass, **4** And blue, and purple, and scarlet, and fine linen, and goats' hair, **5** And rams' skins dyed red, and badgers' skins, and acacia wood, **6** Oil for the light, spices for anointing oil, and for sweet incense, **7** Onyx stones, and stones to be set in the ephod, and in the breastplate. **8** And let them make me a sanctuary; that I may dwell among them. **9** According to all that I show you, after the pattern of the tabernacle, and the pattern of all the instruments thereof, even so shall you make it. **10** And they shall make an ark of acacia wood: two cubits and a half shall be the length, and a cubit (approximately 18-20 inches) and a half the breadth, and a cubit and a half the height.

11 And you shall overlay it with pure gold, within and without shall you overlay it, and shall make upon it a crown of gold all around. **12** And you shall cast four rings of gold for it, and put them in the four corners; and two rings shall be in the one side of it, and two rings in the other side of it. **13** And you shall make poles of acacia wood, and overlay them with gold. **14** And you shall put the poles into the rings by the sides of the ark that the ark may be carried with them. **15** The poles shall be in the rings of the ark: they shall not be taken from it. **16** And you shall put into the ark the testimony (tablets of commandments) that I shall give you. **17** And you shall make a mercy seat of pure gold: two cubits and a half shall be the length, and a cubit and a half the breadth. **18** And you shall make two winged guardians (cherubim) of gold; of beaten work shall you make them, in the two ends of the mercy seat. **19** And make one cherub on the one end, and the other cherub on the other end: even of the mercy seat shall you make the guardians on the two ends. **20** And the guardians shall stretch forth their wings on high, covering the mercy seat with their wings, and their faces shall look one to another; toward the mercy seat shall the faces of the angels be.

21 And you shall put the mercy seat above upon the ark; and in the ark you shall put the testimony that I shall give you. **22** And there I will meet with you, and I will commune with you from above the mercy seat, from between the two winged guardians that are upon the ark of the testimony, of all things that I will give you in commandment to the children of Israel. **23** You shall also make a table of acacia wood: two cubits shall be the length, and a cubit the breadth, and a cubit and a half for the height. **24** And you shall overlay it with pure gold, and make there a crown of gold all around. **25** And you shall make to it a border of a hand width around it, and you shall make a golden crown to the border all around. **26** And you shall make for it four rings of gold, and put the rings in the four corners that are on the four feet. **27** Over against the border shall the rings be for places of the poles to bear the table. **28** And you shall make the poles of acacia wood, and overlay them with gold, that the table may be carried with them. **29** And you shall make the dishes, and spoons, and covers, and bowls, to cover all: of pure gold shall you make them. **30** And you shall set upon the table showbread (Challah bread) before me always.

31 And you are to make a support for lights, of the best gold; its base and its pillar are to be of hammered gold; its cups, its buds, and its flowers are to be made of the same metal. **32** And six branches shall come out of the sides of it; three branches of the candlestick out of the one side, and three branches of the candlestick out of the other side (menorah): *33* Three bowls made like to almonds, with a bud and a flower in one branch; and three bowls made like almonds in the other branch, with a bud and a flower: so in the six branches that come out of the candlestick. *34* And in the candlesticks shall be four bowls made like almonds, with their buds and their flowers. *35* And there shall be a bud under two branches of the same, and a bud under two branches of the same, and a bud under two branches of the same, according to the six branches that proceed out of the candlestick. *36* Their buds and their branches shall be the same: all it shall be one beaten work of pure gold. *37* And you shall make the seven lamps thereof (menorah): and they shall light the lamps that they may give light over against it. *38* And the instruments and trays shall be of pure gold. *39* Of a talent (about *73* pounds) of pure gold shall he make it, with all these vessels. *40* And look that you make them after their pattern, which was shown you in the mount.

Chapter 26

YeHoVaH instructs Moses to make a tabernacle of fine linen, curtains of goat's hair to cover the tabernacle, boards of acacia wood and a linen veil.

1 Moreover you shall make the tabernacle with ten curtains of fine twined linen, and blue, and purple, and scarlet: with angels of delicate work shall you make them. *2* The length of one curtain shall be *28* cubits, and the width of one curtain four cubits: and every one of the curtains shall have one measure. *3* The five curtains shall be coupled together one to another; and other five curtains shall be coupled one to another. *4* And you are to put twists of blue cord on the edge of the outside curtain of the first group of five, and on the edge of the outside curtain of the second group of five; *5* 50 loops shall you make in the one curtain, and fifty loops shall you make in the edge of the curtain that is in the coupling of the second; that the loops may take hold one of another. *6* And you shall make fifty hooks of gold, and couple the curtains together with the hooks: and it shall be one tabernacle. *7* And you shall make curtains of goats' hair to be a covering upon the tabernacle: *11* curtains shall you make. *8* The length of one curtain shall be thirty cubits, and the width of one curtain four cubits: and the *11* curtains shall be all of one measure. *9* And you shall couple five curtains by themselves, and six curtains by themselves, and shall double the sixth curtain in the front of the tabernacle. *10* And you shall make 50 loops on the edge of the one curtain that is furthest out in the coupling, and fifty loops in the edge of the curtain that connects the second.

11 And you shall make 50 hooks of brass, and put the hooks into the loops, and couple the tent together, that it may be one. *12* And the remnant that remains of the curtains of the tent, the half curtain that remains, shall hang over the backside of the tabernacle. *13* And a cubit on the one side, and a cubit on the other side of that which remains in the length of the curtains of the tent, it shall hang over the sides of the tabernacle on this side and on that side, to cover it. *14* And you shall make a covering for the tent of rams' skins dyed red, and a covering above of badgers' skins. *15* And you shall make boards for the tabernacle of acacia wood standing up. *16* Ten cubits shall be the length of a board, and a cubit and a half shall be the breadth of one board. *17* Two tenons *(A projection on the end of a piece of wood shaped for insertion into a mortise (hole) to make a joint)* shall there be in one board, set in order one against another: thus shall you make for all the boards of the tabernacle. *18* And you shall make the boards for the tabernacle, twenty boards on the south side southward. *19* And you shall make 40 sockets of silver under the 20 boards; two sockets under one board for his two tenons, and two sockets under another board for his two tenons. *20* And for the second side of the tabernacle on the north side there shall be **20** boards:

21 And their 40 sockets of silver; two sockets under one board, and two sockets under another board. *22* And for the sides of the tabernacle westward you shall make six boards. *23* And two boards shall you make for the corners of the tabernacle in the two sides. *24* And they shall be coupled together beneath, and they shall be coupled together above the head of it to one ring: thus shall it be for them both; they shall be for the two corners. *25* And they shall be eight boards, and their sockets of silver, 16 sockets; two sockets under one board, and two sockets under another board. *26* And you shall make bars of acacia wood; five for the boards of the one side of the tabernacle, *27* And five bars for the boards of the other side of the tabernacle, and five bars for the boards of the side of the tabernacle, for the two sides westward. *28* And the middle bar in the midst of the boards shall reach from end to end. *29* And you shall overlay the boards with gold, and make their rings of gold for places for the bars: and you shall overlay the bars with gold. *30* And you shall rear up the tabernacle according to the fashion that was shown you in the mount.

31 And you shall make a veil of blue, and purple, and scarlet, and fine twined linen of cunning (fine crafted) work: with angels shall it be made: *32* And you shall hang it upon four pillars of acacia wood overlaid with gold: their hooks shall be of gold, upon the four sockets of silver. *33* And you are to put up the veil under the hooks, and put inside it the ark of the law (instruction): the veil is to be a division between the holy place and the most holy. *34* And you shall put the mercy seat upon the ark of the testimony in the most holy place. *35* And you shall set the table without the veil, and the candlestick over against the table on the side of the tabernacle toward the south: and you shall put the table on the north side. *36* And you shall make a hanging for the door of the tent, of blue, and purple, and scarlet, and fine twined linen, created with needlework. *37* And you shall make for the hanging five pillars of acacia wood, and overlay them with gold, and their hooks shall be of gold: and you shall cast five sockets of brass for them.

Chapter 27

YeHoVaH tells Moses to make an altar of acacia wood with bronze utensils, and a court for the tabernacle of fine linen hangings and bronze pillars.

1 And you shall make an altar of acacia wood, five cubits long, and five cubits broad; the altar shall be foursquare (4 equal sides): and the height shall be three cubits. *2* And you shall make the horns of it upon the four corners: the horns shall be of the same: and you shall overlay it with brass. *3* And you shall make its pans to receive its ashes, and its shovels, and its basins, and its flesh hooks, and its fire pans: all the vessels you shall make of brass. *4* And you shall make for it a grate of network of brass; and upon the net shall you make four brazen (brass) rings in the four corners thereof. *5* And you shall put it under the compass of the altar beneath that the net may be even to the midst of the altar. *6* And you shall make poles for the altar, poles of acacia wood, and overlay them with brass. *7* And the poles shall be put into the rings, and the poles shall be upon the two sides of the altar, to bear it. *8* Hollow with boards shall you make it: as it was shown you in the mount, so shall they make it. *9* And you shall make the court of the tabernacle: for the south side southward there shall be hangings for the court of fine twined linen of an hundred cubits long for one side: *10* And the 20 pillars and their 20 sockets shall be of brass; the hooks of the pillars and their bands shall be of silver.

11 And likewise for the north side in length there shall be hangings of 100 cubits long, and his 20 pillars and their 20 sockets of brass; the hooks of the pillars and their bands of silver. *12* And for the width of the court on the west side shall be hangings of 50 cubits: their pillars ten, and their sockets ten. *13* And the breadth of the court on the east side eastward shall be 50 cubits. *14* The hangings of one side of the gate shall be *15* cubits: their pillars three, and their sockets three. *15* And on the other side shall be hangings *15* cubits: their pillars three, and their sockets three. *16* And for the gate of the court shall be a hanging of 20 cubits, of blue, and purple, and scarlet, and fine twined linen, fashioned with needlework: and their pillars shall be four, and their sockets four. *17* All the pillars round about the court shall be banded with silver; their hooks shall be of silver, and their sockets of brass. *18* The length of the court shall be 100 cubits, and the breadth 50 everywhere, and the height five cubits of fine twined linen, and their sockets of brass. *19* All the vessels of the tabernacle in all the service, and all the pins, and all the pins of the court, shall be of brass.
Reading 19 ends

Reading 20 begins
20 And you shall command the children of Israel that they bring you pure olive oil beaten for the light, to cause the lamp to burn *always*. *21* In the tabernacle of the congregation without the veil, which is before the testimony, Aaron and his sons shall order it from evening to morning before **YeHoVaH**: it shall be a statute (instruction) *forever* to their generations on the behalf of the children of Israel.

Chapter 28

YeHoVaH sets Aaron and his sons apart to minister as priests. He designs a breastplate, an ephod, a robe, a tunic, a turban and a sash for them.

1 And take you to Aaron your brother, and his sons with him, from among the children of Israel, that he may minister to me in the priest's office, even Aaron, Nadab and Abihu, Eleazar and Ithamar, Aaron's sons. *2* And you shall make holy garments for Aaron your brother for glory and for beauty. *3* And you shall speak to all that are wise hearted, whom I have filled with the spirit of wisdom, that they may make Aaron's garments to consecrate him, that he may minister to me in the priest's office. *4* And these are the garments which they shall make; a breastplate, and an ephod (vest-like garment), and a robe, and a broidered coat, a headdress, and a girdle: and they shall make holy garments for Aaron your brother, and his sons, that he may minister to me in the priest's office. *5* And they shall take gold, and blue, and purple, and scarlet, and fine linen. *6* And they shall make the ephod of gold, of blue, and of purple, of scarlet, and fine twined linen, with cunning work. *7* It shall have the two shoulder pieces joined at the two edges; and so it shall be joined together. *8* And the beautifully worked band, which goes on it, is to be of the same work and the same material, of gold and blue and purple and red and twisted linen-work. *9* And you shall take two onyx stones, and engrave on them the names of the children of Israel: *10* Six of their names on one stone, and the other six names of the rest on the other stone, according to their birth.

11 With the work of an engraver in stone, like the engravings of a signet, shall you engrave the two stones with the names of the children of Israel: you shall make them to be set in settings of gold. *12* And you shall put the two stones upon the shoulders of the ephod for stones of memorial to the children of Israel: and Aaron shall bear their names before **YeHoVaH** upon his two shoulders for a memorial. *13* And you shall make settings of gold; *14* And two chains of pure gold at the ends; of wreathen (twisted like cords) work shall you make them, and fasten the wreathen chains to the pouches. *15* And you shall make the breastplate of judgment with crafted work; after the work of the ephod you shall make it; of gold, of blue, and of purple, and of scarlet, and of fine twined linen, shall you make it. *16* Foursquare it shall be being doubled; a span shall be the length, and a span shall be the width. *17* And you shall set in it settings of stones, four rows of stones: the first row shall be a sardius, a topaz, and a carbuncle: this shall be the first row. *18* And the second row shall be an emerald, a sapphire, and a diamond. *19* And the third row a ligure, an agate, and an amethyst. *20* And the fourth row a beryl, and an onyx, and a jasper: they shall be set in gold in their inclosing.

21 And the stones shall be with the names of the children of Israel, twelve, according to their names, like the engravings of a signet (stamp); every one with his name shall they be according to the twelve tribes. *22* And you are to make two chains of gold, twisted like cords, to be fixed to the priest's bag. *23* And you shall make upon the breastplate two rings of gold, and shall put the two rings on the two ends of the breastplate. *24* And you shall put the two twisted chains of gold in the two rings that are on the ends of the breastplate. *25* And the other two ends of the two twisted chains you shall fasten in the two settings, and put them on the shoulder pieces of the ephod before it. *26* And you shall make two rings of gold, and you shall put them upon the two ends of the breastplate in the border, which is in the side of the ephod inward. *27* And two other rings of gold you shall make, and shall put them on the two sides of the ephod underneath, toward the front, over against the other coupling, above the decorated band of the ephod. *28* And they shall bind the breastplate by the rings to the rings of the ephod with a lace of blue, that it may be above the decorated band of the ephod, and that the breastplate be not loosed from the ephod. *29* And Aaron shall bear the names of the children of Israel in the breastplate of judgment upon his heart, when he goes in to the holy place, for a memorial before **YeHoVaH** continually. *30* And you shall put in the breastplate of judgment the Urim and the Thummim (stones that would light by **YeHoVaH's command**); and they shall be upon Aaron's heart, when he goes in before **YeHoVaH**: and Aaron shall bear the judgment of the children of Israel upon his heart before **YeHoVaH** continually.

31 And you shall make the robe of the ephod all of blue. *32* And there shall be a hole in the top of it, in the midst thereof: it shall have a binding of woven work around the hole, as it were the hole of a habergeon (jacket-like), that it be not torn. *33* And beneath upon the hem of it you shall make pomegranates of blue, and of purple, and of scarlet, round about the hem thereof; and bells of gold between them all around: *34* A golden bell and a pomegranate, a golden bell and a pomegranate, upon the hem of the robe all around. *35* And it shall be upon Aaron to minister: and his sound shall be heard when he goes in to the holy place before **YeHoVaH**, and when he comes out, that he does not die. *36* And you shall make a plate of pure gold, and engrave upon it, like the engravings of a signet, **YeHoVaH Is Set Apart**. *37* And you shall put it on a blue lace that it may be upon the headdress; upon the front of the headdress it shall be. *38* And it shall be upon Aaron's forehead, that Aaron may bear the iniquity of the holy things, which the children of Israel shall bless in all their holy gifts; and it shall be always upon his forehead, that they may be accepted before **YeHoVaH**. *39* And you shall embroider the coat of fine linen, and you shall make the headdress of fine linen, and you shall make the girdle of needlework. *40* And for Aaron's sons you shall make coats, and you shall make for them girdles, and bonnets shall you make for them, for glory and for beauty.

41 And you shall put them upon Aaron your brother, and his sons with him; and shall anoint them, and consecrate them, and sanctify them that they may minister to me in the priest's office. **42** And you shall make them linen breeches (underclothes) to cover their nakedness; from the loins even to the thighs they shall reach: **43** And they shall be upon Aaron, and upon his sons, when they come in to the tabernacle of the congregation, or when they come near to the altar to minister in the holy place; that they bear not iniquity, and die: it shall be a statute (instruction) forever to him and his offspring after him.

Chapter 29

A young bull and two rams are sacrificed to consecrate Aaron and his sons and if they make daily sacrifices on the altar YeHoVaH will dwell with Israel.

1 And this is what you shall do to them to set them apart, to minister to me in the priest's office: Take one young bullock, and two rams without blemish, **2** and unleavened bread, and cakes unleavened tempered with oil, and wafers unleavened anointed with oil: of wheat flour shall you make them. **3** And you shall put them into one basket, and bring them in the basket, with the bullock and the two rams. **4** And Aaron and his sons you shall bring to the door of the tabernacle of the congregation, and shall wash them with water. **5** And you shall take the garments, and put upon Aaron the coat, and the robe of the ephod, and the ephod, and the breastplate, and gird him with the decorated girdle of the ephod **6** And you shall put the headdress upon his head, and put the holy crown upon the headdress. **7** Then shall you *take the anointing oil, and pour it upon his head*, and anoint him. **8** And you shall bring his sons, and put coats upon them. **9** And you shall gird them with girdles, Aaron and his sons, and put the bonnets on them: and the priest's office shall be theirs for a perpetual (everlasting) statute: and you shall consecrate Aaron and his sons. **10** And you shall cause a bullock to be brought before the tabernacle of the congregation: and Aaron and his sons shall put their hands upon the head of the bullock.

11 And you shall kill the bullock before **YeHoVaH**, by the door of the tabernacle of the congregation. **12** And you shall take of the blood of the bullock, and put it upon the horns of the altar with your finger, and pour all the blood beside the bottom of the altar. **13** And you shall take all the fat that covers the innards, and the appendage that is above the liver, and the two kidneys, and the fat that is upon them, and burn them upon the altar. **14** But the flesh of the bullock, and his skin, and his dung (feces), shall you burn with fire outside the camp: it is a sin offering. **15** You shall also take one ram; and Aaron and his sons shall put their hands upon the head of the ram. **16** And you shall slay the ram, and you shall take his blood, and sprinkle it upon the altar. **17** And you shall cut the ram in pieces, and wash the innards of him, and his legs, and put them to his pieces, and to his head. **18** And you shall burn the whole ram upon the altar: it is a burnt offering to **YeHoVaH**: it is a sweet savor, an offering made by fire to **YeHoVaH**. **19** And you shall take the other ram; and Aaron and his sons shall put their hands upon the head of the ram. **20** Then shall you kill the ram, and take of his blood, and put it upon the tip of the right ear of Aaron, and upon the tip of the right ear of his sons, and upon the thumb of their right hand, and upon the big toe of their right foot, and sprinkle the blood upon the altar round about.

21 And you shall take of the blood that is upon the altar, and of the anointing oil, and sprinkle it upon Aaron, and upon his garments, and upon his sons, and upon the garments of his sons with him: and he shall be blessed, and his garments, and his sons, and his sons' garments with him. *22* Also you shall take of the ram the fat and the rump, and the fat that covers the innards, and the appendage above the liver, and the two kidneys, and the fat that is upon them, and the right shoulder; for it is a ram of consecration: *23* And one loaf of bread, and one cake of oiled bread, and one wafer out of the basket of the unleavened bread that is before **YeHoVaH**: *24* And you shall put all in the hands of Aaron, and in the hands of his sons; and shall wave them for a *wave offering* before **YeHoVaH**. *25* And you shall receive them of their hands, and burn them upon the altar for a *burnt offering*, for a sweet savor before **YeHoVaH**: it is an offering made by fire to **YeHoVaH**. *26* And you shall take the breast of the ram of Aaron's consecration, and wave it for a *wave offering* before **YeHoVaH**: and it shall be your part. *27* And you shall sanctify the breast of the wave offering, and the shoulder of the heave offering, which is waved, and which is heaved up, of the ram of the consecration, even of that which is for Aaron, and of that which is for his sons *28* And it shall be Aaron's and his sons' by a statute forever from the children of Israel: for it is a *heave offering*: and it shall be a heave offering from the children of Israel of the sacrifice of their peace offerings, even their heave offering to **YeHoVaH**. *29* And the holy garments of Aaron shall be his sons' after him, to be anointed therein, and to be consecrated in them. *30* And that son that is priest in his stead shall put them on seven days, when he comes into the tabernacle of the congregation to minister in the holy place.

31 And you shall take the ram of the consecration, and see his flesh in the holy place. *32* And Aaron and his sons shall eat the flesh of the ram, and the bread that is in the basket by the door of the tabernacle of the congregation. *33* And they shall eat those things that the atonement was made, to consecrate and to sanctify them: but a stranger shall not eat thereof, because they are holy. *34* And if any of the flesh of the consecrations, or of the bread, remain to the morning, then you shall burn the remainder with fire: it shall not be eaten, because it is holy. *35* And thus shall you do to Aaron, and to his sons, according to all things that I have commanded you: seven days shall you consecrate them. *36* And you shall offer *every day* a bullock for a sin offering for atonement: and you shall cleanse the altar, when you have made atonement for it, and you shall anoint it, to sanctify it. *37* Seven days you shall make atonement for the altar, and sanctify it; and it shall be an altar most holy: whatsoever touches the altar shall be holy. *38* Now this is that which you shall offer upon the altar; two lambs of the first year day by day *continually*. *39* The one lamb you shall offer in the morning; and the other lamb you shall offer at evening *40* And with the one lamb a tenth ephah (a bushel) of flour mingled with the fourth part of a hin (1-1/2 gallon) of beaten oil; and the fourth part of an hin of wine for a drink offering.

41 And the other lamb you shall offer at twilight; and you shall offer with it the grain offering and the drink offering, as in the morning, for a sweet aroma, an offering made by fire to **YeHoVaH**. *42* This shall be a continual burnt offering throughout your generations at the door of the tabernacle of the congregation before **YeHoVaH**: where I will meet you, to speak there to you. *43* And there I will meet with the children of Israel, and the tabernacle shall be sanctified by My glory. *44* And I will sanctify the tabernacle of the congregation, and the altar: I will sanctify also both Aaron and his sons, to minister to Me in the priest's office. *45* And I will dwell among the children of Israel, and will be their **Elohim**. *46* And they shall know that I am **YeHoVaH** their **Elohim**, that brought them forth out of the land of Egypt, that I may dwell among them: I am **YeHoVaH** their **Elohim**.

EXODUS

Chapter 30

They make an altar for burning incense. The Israelites shall each give half a shekel to the sanctuary. They will make a bronze laver with anointing oil and incense.

1 And you shall make an altar to burn incense upon: of acacia wood shall you make it. *2* A cubit shall be the length, and a cubit the width; it shall be square: and two cubits shall be the height: the horns shall be of the same. *3* And you shall overlay it with pure gold, the top, and the sides all around, and the horns; and you shall make to it a crown of gold all around. *4* And two golden rings shall you make under the crown of it, by the two corners, upon the two sides of it; and they shall be for places for the poles to carry it. *5* And you shall make the poles of acacia wood, and overlay them with gold. *6* And you shall put it before the veil that is by the ark of the testimony (commandments), before the mercy seat that is over the testimony, where I will meet with you. *7* And Aaron shall burn sweet incense there every morning: when he dresses (trims the wicks) the lamps, he shall burn incense upon it. *8* And when Aaron lights the lamps at evening, he shall burn incense upon it, a perpetual incense before **YeHoVaH** throughout your generations. *9* You shall offer no *strange* incense thereon, nor burnt sacrifice, nor meal offering; neither shall you pour drink offering there. *10* And Aaron shall make atonement upon the horns of it once in a year with the blood of the sin offering of atonements: once in the year shall he make atonement upon it throughout your generations: it is most set apart to **YeHoVaH**.
  Reading 20 ends

  Reading 21 begins
11 And **YeHoVaH** spoke to Moses, saying, *12* When you take the sum of the children of Israel after their number, then shall they give every man a ransom (tithe) for his soul to **YeHoVaH**, when you number them; that there be no plague among them, when you number them. *13* This they shall give, every one that passes among them that are numbered, half a shekel after the shekel of the sanctuary: (a shekel is twenty gerahs:) a half shekel shall be the offering of **YeHoVaH**. *14* Every one that passes among them that are numbered, from **20** years old and above, shall give an offering to **YeHoVaH**. *15* The rich shall not give more, and the poor shall not give less than half a shekel, when they give an offering to **YeHoVaH**, to make an atonement for your souls. *16* And you shall take the atonement money of the children of Israel, and shall appoint it for the service of the tabernacle of the congregation; that it may be a memorial to the children of Israel before **YeHoVaH**, to make an *atonement* for your souls. *17* And **YeHoVaH** spoke to Moses, saying, *18* You shall also make a laver (basin or bowl) of brass, and its foot also of brass, to wash withal: and you shall put it between the tabernacle of the congregation and the altar, and you shall put water in it. *19* For Aaron and his sons shall wash their hands and their feet there: *20* When they go into the tabernacle of the congregation, they shall wash with water, that they do not die; or when they come near to the altar to minister, to burn offering made by fire to **YeHoVaH**:

21 So they shall wash their hands and their feet, that they do not die: and it shall be a statute forever to them, even to him and to his offspring throughout their generations. *22* Moreover **YeHoVaH** spoke to Moses, saying, *23* Take you also to you principal spices, of pure myrrh 500 shekels, and of sweet cinnamon half as much, 250 shekels, and of sweet calamus 250 shekels, *24* And of cassia 500 shekels, after the shekel of the sanctuary, and of oil olive a hin: *25* And you shall make it an oil of holy ointment, an ointment compound after the art of the apothecary (like a pharmacist) : it shall be a holy anointing oil. *26* And you shall anoint the tabernacle of the congregation there, and the ark of the testimony, *27* And the table and all its vessels, and the candlestick and its vessels, and the altar of incense, *28* And the altar of burnt offering with all its vessels, and the laver and its foot. *29* And you shall sanctify them, that they may be most holy: whatsoever touches them shall be holy. *30* And you shall anoint Aaron and his sons, and consecrate them, that they may minister to Me in the priest's office.

31 And you shall speak to the children of Israel, saying, This shall be a holy anointing oil to me throughout your generations. *32* Upon man's flesh shall it not be poured, *neither shall you make any other like it*, after the composition of it: it is set apart, and it shall be holy to you. *33* Whoever compounds any like it, or whosoever putts any of it upon a stranger, shall even be cut off from his people. *34* And **YeHoVaH** said to Moses, Take to you sweet spices, stacte, and onycha, and galbanum; these sweet spices with pure frankincense: of each shall there be a equal weight: *35* And you shall make it a perfume, a confection after the art of the apothecary, tempered together, pure and holy: *36* And you shall beat some of it very small, and put of it before the testimony in the tabernacle of the congregation, where I will meet with you: it shall be to you most holy. *37* And as for the perfume that you shall make, you *shall not* make to yourselves according to the composition thereof: it shall be to you holy for **YeHoVaH**. *38* Whosoever shall make like to that, to smell thereto, shall even be cut off from his people.

CHAPTERS 31- 40

Chapter 31

YeHoVaH spoke and said, 'I have filled Bezalel with my Spirit, with skill to make everything I have commanded. YeHoVaH commands the 'seventh' day is a Sabbath of rest.

1 And **YeHoVaH** spoke to Moses, saying, *2* See, I have called by name Bezaleel the son of Uri, the son of Hur, of the tribe of Judah: *3* And I have filled him with the spirit of **Elohim**, in wisdom, and in understanding, and in knowledge, and in all manner of workmanship, *4* To devise cunning works, to work in gold, and in silver, and in brass, *5* And in cutting of stones, to set them, and in carving of timber, to work in all manner of workmanship. *6* And I, behold, I have given with him Aholiab, the son of Ahisamach, of the tribe of Dan: and in the hearts of all that are wise hearted I have put wisdom, that they may make all that I have commanded you; *7* The tabernacle of the congregation, and the ark of the testimony, and the mercy seat that is there, and all the furniture of the tabernacle, *8* And the table and its furniture, and the pure candlestick with all its furniture, and the altar of incense, *9* And the altar of burnt offering with all its furniture, and the laver and its foot, *10* And the cloths of service, and the holy garments for Aaron the priest, and the garments of his sons, to minister in the priest's office,

11 And the anointing oil, and sweet incense for the holy place: according to all that I have commanded you shall they do. *12* And **YeHoVaH** spoke to Moses, saying, *13* Speak you also to the children of Israel, saying, truly my Sabbaths you shall keep (guard): for it is a sign between me and you throughout your generations; that you may know that I am **YeHoVaH** that does sanctify you. *14* You shall keep the Sabbath therefore; for it is holy to you: *every one that defiles it shall surely be put to death*: for whoever does any work therein, that soul shall be cut off from among his people. *15* Six days may work be done; but in the **seventh is the Sabbath** of rest, holy to **YeHoVaH**: whosoever does any work in the Sabbath day, he shall surely be put to death. *16* Wherefore the children of Israel shall keep the Sabbath, to observe the Sabbath *throughout their generations*, for a **perpetual** covenant. *17* It is a sign between me and the children of Israel forever: for in six days **YeHoVaH** made heaven and earth, and on the *seventh* day he rested, and was refreshed. *18* And he gave to Moses, when he had made an end of communing with him upon Mount Sinai, two tables of testimony, tables of stone, written with the finger of **YeHoVaH**.

Chapter 32

When Moses was on the mountain the people worshipped a golden calf. Moses pleaded with YeHoVaH for them. The Levites killed 3,000 people that day by YeHoVaH's command.

1 And when the people saw that Moses delayed to come down out of the mount, the people gathered themselves together to Aaron, and said to him, Up, make us gods, which shall go before us; for as for this Moses, the man that brought us up out of the land of Egypt, we know not what is become of him. *2* And Aaron said to them, Break off the golden earrings, which are in the ears of your wives, of your sons, and of your daughters, and bring them to me. *3* And all the people broke off the golden earrings that were in their ears, and brought them to Aaron. *4* And he received them at their hand, and fashioned it with a graving tool, after he had made it a molten calf: and they said, These be your gods, O Israel, which brought you up out of the land of Egypt. *5* And when Aaron saw it, he built an altar before it; and Aaron made proclamation, and said, tomorrow is a feast to **YeHoVaH**. *6* And they rose up early on the morning, and offered burnt offerings, and brought peace offerings; and the people sat down to eat and to drink, and rose up to play. *7* And **YeHoVaH** said to Moses, Go, get you down; for your people, which you brought out of the land of Egypt, have corrupted themselves: *8* They have turned aside quickly out of the way which I commanded them: they have made them a molten calf, and have worshipped it, and have sacrificed to it, and said, These be your gods, O Israel, which have brought you up out of the land of Egypt. *9* And **YeHoVaH** said to Moses, I have seen this people, and, behold, it is a stiff-necked (stubborn) people: *10* Now therefore let me alone, that my wrath may wax (grow) hot against them, and that I may consume them: and I will make of you a great nation.

11 And Moses begged **YeHoVaH** his **Elohim**, and said, my **Elohim**, why does your wrath stay hot against your people, which you have brought forth out of the land of Egypt with great power, and with a mighty hand? *12* Why should the Egyptians speak, and say, For mischief did he bring them out, to slay them in the mountains, and to consume them from the face of the earth? Turn from your fierce wrath, and repent of this evil against your people. *13* Remember Abraham, Isaac, and Jacob (Israel), your servants, to whom you swore by your own self, and said to them, I will multiply your seed as the stars of heaven, and all this land that I have spoken of will I give to your offspring, and they shall inherit it forever. *14* And **YeHoVaH** turned from the evil that he thought to do to his people. *15* And Moses turned, and went down from the mount, and the two tablets of the testimony were in his hand: the tablets were written on both their sides; on the one side and on the other they were written. *16* And the tables were the work of **Elohim**, and the writing was the writing of **YeHoVaH**, engraved upon the tablets. *17* And when *Joshua heard* the noise of the people as they shouted, he said to Moses, There is a noise of war in the camp.   *18* And he said, It is not the voice of them that shout for mastery, neither is it the voice of them that cry for being overcome: but the noise of them that sing do I hear. *19* And it came to pass, as soon as he came near to the camp, that he saw the calf, and the dancing: and Moses' anger grew hot, and he cast the tablets out of his hands, and broke them beneath the mount. *20* And he took the calf which they had made, and burnt it in the fire, and ground it to powder, and spread it upon the water, and made the children of Israel drink of it.

21 And Moses said to Aaron, What did this people do to you, that you have brought so great a sin upon them? *22* And Aaron said, Let not the anger of my lord grow hot: you know the people, that they are set on mischief. *23* For they said to me, Make us gods, which shall go before us: for as for this Moses, the man that brought us up out of the land of Egypt, we know not what is become of him. *24* And I said to them, Whoever has any gold, let them break it off. So they gave it me: then I cast it into the fire, and there came out this calf. *25* And Moses saw that the people were out of control, for Aaron had let them loose to their shame before their enemies: *26* Then Moses took his place at the way into the tents, and said, Whoever is on the side of **YeHoVaH**, let him come to me. And all the sons of Levi came together to him. *27* And he said to them, Thus says **YeHoVaH Elohim** of Israel, Put every man his sword by his side, and go in and out from gate to gate throughout the camp, and slay every man his brother, and every man his companion, and every man his neighbor. *28* And the children of Levi did according to the word of Moses: and there fell of the people that day about 3,000 men. *29* For Moses had said, Consecrate yourselves today to **YeHoVaH**, even every man upon his son, and upon his brother; that he may bestow upon you a blessing this day. *30* And it came to pass on the next day, that Moses said to the people, You have sinned a great sin: and now I will go up to **YeHoVaH**; to make an atonement for your sin.

31 And Moses returned to **YeHoVaH**, and said, Oh, this people have sinned a great sin, and have made them gods of gold. *32* Yet now, if you will forgive their sin--; and if not, blot me, I pray you, out of your book which you have written. *33* And **YeHoVaH** said to Moses, Whosoever has sinned against me, him will I blot out of my book. *34* Therefore now go, lead the people to the place of which I have spoken to you: behold, my Angel shall go before you: nevertheless in the day when I visit I will visit their sin upon them. *35* And **YeHoVaH** plagued the people, because they made the calf, which Aaron formed.

Chapter 33
Moses sets up a tent of meeting. He asks YeHoVaH not to send them out without His presence. YeHoVaH passes before Moses.

1 And **YeHoVaH** said to Moses, Depart, and go up therefore, you and the people which you have brought up out of the land of Egypt, to the land which I swore to Abraham, to Isaac, and to Jacob, saying, To your seed will I give it: *2* And I will send an angel before you; and I will drive out the Canaanite, the Amorite, and the Hittite, and the Perizzite, the Hivite, and the Jebusite: *3* To a land flowing with milk and honey: for I will not go up in the midst of you; for you are a stiff-necked (stubborn) people: for fear that I consume you in the way. *4* And when the people heard these evil tidings, they mourned: and no man put on him his ornaments. *5* For **YeHoVaH** had said to Moses, Say to the children of Israel, You are a stiff-necked people: I will come up into the midst of you in a moment, and consume you: therefore now put off your ornaments from you, that I may know what to do to you. *6* And the children of Israel stripped themselves of their ornaments (jewels, gold, and any flashy thing) by mount Horeb. *7* And Moses took the tabernacle, and pitched it without the camp, afar off from the camp, and called it the *Tabernacle of the congregation (Tent of Meeting).* And it came to pass, that every one that sought **YeHoVaH** went out to the tabernacle of the congregation, which was outside the camp. *8* And it came to pass, when Moses went out to the tabernacle that all the people rose up, and stood every man at his tent door, and looked after Moses, until he had gone into the tabernacle. *9* And it came to pass, as Moses entered into the tabernacle, the cloudy pillar descended, and stood at the door of the tabernacle, and **YeHoVaH** talked with Moses. *10* And all the people saw the cloudy pillar stand at the tabernacle door: and all the people rose up and worshipped, every man in his tent door.

11 And **YeHoVaH** spoke to Moses **face to face**, as a man speaks to his friend. And he turned again into the camp: but his servant Joshua, the son of Nun, a young man, departed not out of the tabernacle. *12* And Moses said to **YeHoVaH**, See, you say to me, Bring up this people: and you have not let me know whom you will send with me. Yet you have said, I know you by name, and you have also found grace in my sight. *13* Now therefore, I pray you, if I have found grace in your sight, show me now your way, that I may know you, that I may find grace in your sight: and consider that this nation is your people. *14* And he said, My presence shall go with you, and I will give you rest. *15* And he said to him, If your presence go not with me, carry us not up further. *16* For wherein shall it be known here that I and your people have found grace in your sight? is it not in that you go with us? so shall we be separated, I and your people, from all the people that are upon the face of the earth. *17* And **YeHoVaH** said to Moses, I will do this thing also that you have spoken: for you have found grace in my sight, and I know you by name. *18* And he said, I beseech you, show me your glory. *19* And he said, I will make all my goodness pass before you, and I will proclaim the name of **YeHoVaH** before you; and will be gracious to whom I will be gracious, and will show mercy on whom I will show mercy. *20* And he said, You cannot see my face: for there shall no man see me, and live.

21 And **YeHoVaH** said, Behold, there is a place by me, and you shall stand upon a rock: *22* And it shall come to pass, while my glory passes by, that I will put you in a cleft of the rock, and will cover you with my hand while I pass by: *23* And I will take away my hand, and you shall see my back: but my face shall not be seen.

Chapter 34

YeHoVaH tells Moses to make new tablets for the Torah (instruction). YeHoVaH makes a covenant with Israel.

1 And **YeHoVaH** said to Moses, Hew you two tablets of stone like the first: and I will write upon these tablets the words that were in the first tablets, which you broke. *2* And be ready in the morning, and come up in the morning to mount Sinai, and present yourself there to me in the top of the mount. *3* And no man shall come up with you, neither let any man be seen throughout the entire mount; neither let the flocks nor herds feed before that mount. *4* And he hewed two tablets of stone like the first; and Moses rose up early in the morning, and went up to mount Sinai, as **YeHoVaH** had commanded him, and took in his hand the two tablets of stone. *5* And **YeHoVaH** descended in the cloud, and stood with him there, and proclaimed the name of **YeHoVaH**. *6* And **YeHoVaH** passed by before him, and proclaimed, **YeHoVaH**, **Adonai Elohim**, merciful and gracious, longsuffering, and abundant in goodness and truth, *7* Keeping mercy for thousands, forgiving iniquity and transgression and sin, and that will by no means clear the guilty; visiting the iniquity of the fathers upon the children, and upon the children's children, to the third and to the fourth generation. *8* And Moses made haste, and bowed his head toward the earth, and worshipped. *9* And he said, If now I have found grace in your sight, O **YeHoVaH**, let my **Elohim**, I pray you, go among us; for it is a stiff-necked people; and pardon our iniquity and our sin, and take us for your inheritance. *10* And he said, Behold, I make a

EXODUS

covenant: before all your people I will do marvels, such as have not been done in all the earth, nor in any nation: and all the people among which you are shall see the work of **YeHoVaH**: for it is a terrible thing that I will do with you.

11 Observe you that which I command you this day: behold, I drive out before you the Amorite, and the Canaanite, and the Hittite, and the Perizzite, and the Hivite, and the Jebusite. **12** Take heed to yourself, or else you make a covenant with the inhabitants of the land or wherever you go, for fear that it be for a snare in the midst of you: **13** But you shall destroy their altars, break their images, and cut down their groves: **14** For you shall worship no other god: for **YeHoVaH**, whose name is Jealous, is a jealous god: **15** For fear that you make a covenant with the inhabitants of the land, and they go continually after their gods, and sacrifice to their gods, and one call you, and you eat of his sacrifice; **16** And you take of their daughters to your sons, and their daughters go continually after their gods, and make your sons go continuing after their gods. **17** You shall make you no molten (melted metal) gods. **18** The feast of unleavened bread shall you keep. Seven days you shall eat unleavened bread, as I commanded you, in the time of the month Abib: for in the month Abib you came out from Egypt. **19** Every first male child is mine; the first male birth of your cattle, the first male of every ox and sheep. **20** But the firstling of a donkey you shall redeem with a lamb: and if you redeem him not, then shall you break his neck. All the firstborn of your sons you shall redeem. And none shall appear before me empty.

21 Six days you shall work, but on the **seventh** day you shall rest: in plowing time and in harvest you shall rest. **22** And you shall observe the *feast of weeks*, of the *first-fruits* (offering) of *wheat harvest*, and the *feast of ingathering* at the year's end. **23** Three times in the year shall all your male children appear before **YeHoVaH**, the **Elohim** of Israel. **24** For I will cast out the nations before you, and enlarge your borders: neither shall any man desire your land, when you shall go up to appear before **YeHoVaH** your **Elohim** three times in the year. **25** You shall not offer the blood of my sacrifice with leaven; neither shall the sacrifice of the feast of the *Passover* be left to the morning. **26** The first of the first-fruits (offering) of your land you shall bring to the house of **YeHoVaH** your **Elohim**. You shall not cook a goat in its mother's milk. (This has nothing to do in any way, shape or form, with eating meat and cheese/milk together) **27** And **YeHoVaH** said to Moses, Write you these words: for after the tone of these words *I have made a covenant with you and with Israel.* **28** And he was there with **YeHoVaH** forty days and forty nights; he did neither eat bread, nor drink water. And he wrote upon the tablets the words of the covenant, the Ten Commandments. **29** And it came to pass, when Moses came down from mount Sinai with the two tables of testimony in Moses' hand, when he came down from the mount, that Moses knew not that the skin of his face shined white he talked with him. **30** And when Aaron and all the children of Israel saw Moses, behold, the skin of his face was shining; and they were afraid to come near him.

31 And Moses called to them; and Aaron and all the rulers of the congregation returned to him: and Moses talked with them. **32** And afterward all the children of Israel came near: and he gave them in commandment all that **YeHoVaH** had spoken with him in mount Sinai. **33** And until Moses was done speaking with them, he put a veil on his face. **34** But when Moses went in before **YeHoVaH** to speak with him, he took the veil off, until he came out. And he came out, and spoke to the children of Israel that which he was commanded. **35** And the children of Israel saw the face of Moses that the skin of Moses' face was shining: and Moses put the veil upon his face again, until he went in to speak with **YeHoVaH**.
Week 21 reading begins

Chapter 35

Moses tells the people to keep the Sabbath. He assembles craftsmen to make the tabernacle. The people donate gold and material for the work that needs done.
   Week 22 reading begins

1 And Moses gathered all the congregation of the children of Israel together, and said to them, These are the words which **YeHoVaH** has commanded, that you should do them. *2* Six days shall work be done, but on the **seventh** day there shall be to you a **holy day**, a **Sabbath of rest** to **YeHoVaH**: whosoever does work shall be put to death. *3* You shall kindle no fire throughout your dwellings upon the Sabbath day. *4* And Moses spoke to all the congregation of the children of Israel, saying, This is the thing which **YeHoVaH** commanded, saying, *5* Take from among you an offering to **YeHoVaH**: whosoever is of a willing heart, let him bring it, an offering of **YeHoVaH**; gold, and silver, and brass, *6* And blue, and purple, and scarlet, and fine linen, and goats' hair, *7* And rams' skins dyed red, and badgers' skins, and acacia wood, *8* And oil for the light, and spices for anointing oil, and for the sweet incense, *9* And onyx stones, and stones to be set for the ephod, and for the breastplate. *10* And every wise hearted among you shall come, and make all that **YeHoVaH** has commanded;

11 The tabernacle, his tent, and his covering, his hooks, and his boards, his bars, his pillars, and his sockets, *12* The ark, and the poles, with the mercy seat, and the veil of the covering, *13* The table, and its poles, and all his vessels, and the showbread, *14* The candlestick also for the light, and his furniture, and its lamps, with the oil for the light, *15* And the incense altar, and its poles, and the anointing oil, and the sweet incense, and the hanging for the door at the entering in of the tabernacle, *16* The altar of burnt offering, with his brass grate, its poles, and all its vessels, the laver and its foot, *17* The hangings of the court, its pillars, and their sockets, and the hanging for the door of the court, *18* The pins of the tabernacle, and the pins of the court, and their cords, *19* The cloths of service, to do service in the holy place, the holy garments for Aaron the priest, and the garments of his sons, to minister in the priest's office. *20* And all the congregation of the children of Israel departed from the presence of Moses.

21 And they came, every one whose heart was stirred, and every one whom his spirit made willing, and they brought **YeHoVaH**'s offering to the work of the tabernacle of the congregation, and for all his service, and for the holy garments. *22* And they came, both men and women, as many as were willing hearted, and brought bracelets, and earrings, and rings, and tablets, all jewels of gold: and every man that offered an offering of gold to **YeHoVaH**. *23* And every man, with whom was found blue, and purple, and scarlet, and fine linen, and goats' hair, and red skins of rams, and badgers' skins, brought them. *24* Every one that did offer an offering of silver and brass brought **YeHoVaH**'s offering: and every man, with whom was found acacia wood for any work of the service, brought it. *25* And all the women that were wise hearted did spin with their hands, and brought that which they had spun, both of blue, and of purple, and of scarlet, and of fine linen. *26* And all the women whose heart stirred them up in wisdom spun goats' hair. *27* And the rulers brought onyx stones, and stones to be set, for the ephod, and for the breastplate; *28* And spice, and oil for the light, and for the anointing oil, and for the sweet incense. *29* The children of Israel brought a willing offering to **YeHoVaH**, every man and woman, whose heart made them willing to bring for all manner of work, which **YeHoVaH** had commanded to be made by the hand of Moses. *30* And Moses said to the children of Israel, See, **YeHoVaH** has called by name Bezaleel the son of Uri, the son of Hur, of the tribe of Judah;

31 And he has filled him with the spirit of **YeHoVaH**, in wisdom, in understanding, and in knowledge, and in all manner of workmanship; *32* And to devise skilled works, to work in gold, and in silver, and in brass, *33* And in the cutting of stones, to set them, and in carving of wood, to make any manner of special work. *34* And he has put in his heart that he may teach, both he, and Aholiab, the son of Ahisamach, of the tribe of Dan. *35* They has he filled with wisdom of heart, to work all manner of work, of the engraver, and of the skilled workman, and of the embroiderer, in blue, and in purple, in scarlet, and in fine linen, and of the weaver, even of them that do any work, and of those that devise skilled work.

Chapter 36

The people give more than is needed. The curtains, the boards, the veil and the pillars are all constructed.

1 Then created Bezaleel and Aholiab, and every wise hearted man, in whom **YeHoVaH** put wisdom and understanding to know how to work all manner of work for the service of the sanctuary, according to all that **YeHoVaH** had commanded. *2* And Moses called Bezaleel and Aholiab, and every wise hearted man, in whose heart **YeHoVaH** had put wisdom, even every one whose heart stirred him up to come to the work to do it: *3* And they received of Moses all the offering, which the children of Israel had brought for the work of the service of the sanctuary, to make it all. And they brought yet to him free offerings every morning. *4* And all the wise men, that formed all the work of the sanctuary, came every man from his work which they made; *5* And they spoke to Moses, saying, The people bring much more than enough for the service of the work, which **YeHoVaH** commanded to make. *6* And Moses gave instructions, and they caused it to be proclaimed throughout the camp, saying, Let neither man nor woman make any more work for the offering of the sanctuary. So the people were restrained from bringing. *7* For the amount they had was sufficient for all the work to make it, and more. *8* And every wise hearted man among them that created the work of the tabernacle made ten curtains of fine twined linen, and blue, and purple, and scarlet: with winged guardians (cherubims) of cunning work made he them. *9* The length of one curtain was **28** cubits, and the breadth of one curtain four cubits: the curtains were all of one size. *10* And he coupled the five curtains one to another: and the other five curtains he coupled one to another.

11 And he made loops of blue on the edge of one curtain from the selvedge in the coupling: likewise he made in the uttermost side of another curtain, in the coupling of the second. *12* 50 loops he made in one curtain, and **50** loops made he in the edge of the curtain that was in the coupling of the second: the loops held one curtain to another. *13* And he made fifty hooks of gold, and coupled the curtains one to another with the hooks: so it became one tabernacle. *14* And he made curtains of goats' hair for the tent over the tabernacle: 11 curtains he made. *15* The length of one curtain was 30 cubits, and four cubits was the breadth of one curtain: the 11 curtains were of one size. *16* And he coupled five curtains by themselves, and six curtains by themselves. *17* And he made **50** loops upon the uttermost edge of the curtain in the coupling, and **50** loops made he upon the edge of the curtain that coupled the second. *18* And he made **50** hooks of brass to couple the tent together, that it might be one. *19* And he made a covering for the tent of rams' skins dyed red, and a covering of badgers' skins above that. *20* And he made boards for the tabernacle of acacia wood, standing up.

21 The length of a board was ten cubits, and the breadth of a board one cubit and a half. *22* One board had two tenons (*wooden pegs*), equally distant one from another: thus did he make for all the boards of the tabernacle. *23* And he made boards for the tabernacle; 20 boards for the south side southward: *24* And 40 sockets of silver he made under the 20 boards; two sockets under one board for his two tenons, and two sockets under another board for his two tenons. *25* And for the other side of the tabernacle, which is toward the north corner, he made 20 boards, *26* And their 40 sockets of silver; two sockets under one board, and two sockets under another board. *27* And for the sides of the tabernacle westward he made six boards. *28* And two boards made he for the corners of the tabernacle in the two sides. *29* And they were coupled beneath, and coupled together at the head thereof, to one ring: thus he did to both of them in both the corners. *30* And there were eight boards; and their sockets were 16 sockets of silver, under every board two sockets.

31 And he made bars of acacia wood; five for the boards of the one side of the tabernacle, *32* And five bars for the boards of the other side of the tabernacle, and five bars for the boards of the tabernacle for the sides westward. *33* And he made the middle bar to shoot through the boards from the one end to the other. *34* And he overlaid the boards with gold, and made their rings of gold to be places for the bars, and overlaid the bars with gold. *35* And he made a veil of blue, and purple, and scarlet, and fine twined linen: with winged guardians (cherubims) he made of crafted work. *36* And he made four pillars of acacia wood, and overlaid them with gold: their hooks were of gold; and he cast for them four sockets of silver. *37* And he made a hanging for the tabernacle door of blue, and purple, and scarlet, and fine twined linen, of needlework; *38* and five pillars for the curtain, with their hooks; the heads of the pillars were of gold and they were circled with bands of gold; and their five bases were of brass.

Chapter 37

Bezalel makes the ark with its cherubim, the table, the lamp stand and the incense altar. He made the anointing oil and the incense.

1 And Bezalel made the ark of acacia wood: two cubits and a half was the length of it, and a cubit and a half the breadth of it, and a cubit and a half the height of it: *2* And he overlaid it with pure gold within and without, and made a crown of gold to it all around. *3* And he cast for it four rings of gold, to be set by the four corners of it; two rings upon the one side of it, and two rings upon the other side of it. *4* And he made poles of acacia wood, and overlaid them with gold. *5* And he put the poles into the rings by the sides of the ark, to bear the ark. *6* And he made the mercy seat of pure gold: two cubits and a half was the length thereof, and one cubit and a half the breadth thereof. *7* And he made two winged guardians (cherubims) of gold, beaten out of one piece, on the two ends of the mercy seat; *8* One cherub on the end on this side, and another cherub on the other end on that side: out of the mercy seat made he the winged guardians on the two ends thereof. *9* And their wings were stretched out over the cover; the faces of the winged ones were opposite one another and facing the cover. *10* And he made the table of acacia wood: two cubits was the length thereof, and a cubit the breadth thereof, and a cubit and a half the height:

11 And he overlaid it with pure gold, and made there a crown of gold all around. *12* Also he made there a border of a handbreadth all around; and made a crown of gold for the border all around. *13* And he cast for it four rings of gold, and put the rings upon the four corners that were in the four feet. *14* Over against the border were the rings, the places for the poles to bear the table. *15* And he made the poles of acacia wood, and overlaid them with gold, to bear the table. *16* And he made the vessels that were upon the table, his dishes, and his spoons, and his bowls, and his covers to cover all, of pure gold. *17* And he made the candlestick of pure gold: of beaten work he made the candlestick; its shaft, and its branch, its bowls, its buds, and its flowers, were of the same: *18* And six branches going out of the sides thereof; three branches of the candlestick out of the one side thereof, and three branches of the candlestick out of the other side thereof: *19* Three bowls made after the fashion of almonds in one branch, a bud and a flower; and three bowls made like almonds in another branch, a bud and a flower: so throughout the six branches going out of the candlestick. *20* And in the candlestick were four bowls made like almonds, its buds, and its flowers:

21 And a bud under each set of two branches of the same, according to the six branches going out of it. *22* Their buds and their branches were of the same: all of it was one beaten work of pure gold. *23* And he made his seven lamps, and its snuffers, and its snuff dishes, of pure gold. *24* Of a talent (73 pounds) of pure gold made he it, and all the vessels. *25* And he made the incense altar of acacia wood: the length of it was a cubit, and the width of it a cubit; it was square; and two cubits was the height of it; the horns thereof were of the same. *26* And he overlaid it with pure gold, both the top of it, and the sides all around, and the horns of it: also he made to it a crown of gold all around. *27* And he made two rings of gold for it under the crown thereof, by the two corners of it, upon the two sides thereof, to be places for the poles to bear it all. *28* And he made the poles of acacia wood, and overlaid them with gold. *29* And he made the holy anointing oil, and the pure incense of sweet spices, according to the work of the apothecary (similar to a pharmacist).

Chapter 38

Bezalel makes the altar of burnt offering, the laver and the court. Ithamar keeps an inventory of the gold, silver and bronze used.

1 And he made the altar of burnt offering of acacia wood: five cubits was the length thereof, and five cubits the breadth thereof; it was square; and three cubits the height. *2* And he made the horns on the four corners of it; the horns were of the same: and he overlaid it with brass. *3* And he made all the vessels of the altar, the pots, and the shovels, and the basins, and the flesh hooks, and the fire pans: all the vessels were made of brass. *4* And he made a network of brass for the altar, under the frame round it, stretching halfway up; *5* And he cast four rings for the four ends of the grate of brass, to be places for the poles. *6* And he made the polls of acacia wood, and overlaid them with brass. *7* And he put the poles into the rings on the sides of the altar, to bear it all; he made the altar hollow with boards. *8* And he made the laver of brass, and the foot of it of brass, of the mirrors of the women assembling, which assembled at the door of the tabernacle of the congregation. *9* And he made the court: on the south side southward the hangings of the court were of fine twined linen, an hundred cubits: *10* Their pillars were 20, and their brass sockets 20; the hooks of the pillars and their fillets were of silver.

11 And for the north side the hangings were 100 cubits, their pillars were 20 and their sockets of brass 20; the hooks of the pillars and their binding rods of silver. *12* And for the west side were hangings of 50 cubits, their pillars ten, and their sockets ten; the hooks of the pillars and their binding rods of silver. *13* And for the east side eastward 50 cubits. *14* The hangings of the one side of the gate were 15 cubits; their pillars three, and their sockets three. *15* And for the other side of the court gate, on this hand and that hand, were hangings of 15 cubits; their pillars three, and their sockets three. *16* All the hangings of the court all around were of fine twined linen. *17* And the sockets for the pillars were of brass; the hooks of the pillars and their binding rods of silver; and the overlaying of their caps of silver; and all the pillars of the court were binding rods of silver. *18* And the hanging for the gate of the court was needlework, of blue, and purple, and scarlet, and fine twined linen: and 20 cubits was the length, and the height in the width was five cubits, answerable to the hangings of the court. *19* And their pillars were four, and their sockets of brass four; their hooks of silver, and the overlaying of their cap and their binding rods of silver. *20* And all the pins of the tabernacle, and of the court all around, were of brass.

21 This is the sum of the tabernacle, the tabernacle of testimony, as it was counted, according to the commandment of Moses, for the service of the Levites, by the hand of Ithamar, son to Aaron the priest. *22* And Bezalel the son Uri, the son of Hur, of the tribe of Judah, made all that **YeHoVaH** commanded Moses. *23* And with him was Aholiab, son of Ahisamach, of the tribe of Dan, an engraver, and a crafted workman, and an embroiderer in blue, and in purple, and in scarlet, and fine linen. *24* All the gold that was occupied for the work in all the work of the holy place, even the gold of the offering, was 29 talents (73 pounds each), and 730 shekels, after the shekel of the sanctuary. *25* And the silver of them that were numbered of the congregation was 100 talents (73 pounds each), and 1775 shekels, after the shekel of the sanctuary: *26* A bekah for every man, that is, half a shekel, after the shekel of the sanctuary, for every one that went to be numbered, from 20 years old and upward, for 603,550 men. *27* And of the 100 talents of silver were cast the sockets of the sanctuary, and the sockets of the veil; 100 sockets of the 100 talents (73 pounds each), a talent for a socket. *28* And of the 1775 shekels he made hooks for the pillars, and overlaid their caps, and filleted them. *29* And the brass of the offering was 70 talents (73 pounds each), and 2,400 shekels. *30* And therewith he made the sockets to the door of the tabernacle of the congregation, and the brass altar, and the brass grate for it, and all the vessels of the altar,

31 And the sockets of the court all around, and the sockets of the court gate, and all the pins of the tabernacle, and all the pins of the court round about.

Chapter 39

They made the ephod, breastplate, tunics, turban and sash for Aaron. Moses saw that it had all been made as YeHoVaH had commanded.

1 And of the blue, and purple, and scarlet, they made cloths of service, to do service in the holy place, and made the holy garments for Aaron; as **YeHoVaH** commanded Moses. *2* And he made the ephod of gold, blue, and purple, and scarlet, and fine twined linen. *3* And they did beat the gold into thin plates, and cut it into wires, to work it in the blue, and in the purple, and in the scarlet, and in the fine linen, with cunning work. *4* They made shoulder pieces for it, to couple it together: by the two edges was it coupled together. *5* And the crafted girdle of his ephod that was upon it was of the same, according to the work thereof; of gold, blue, and purple, and scarlet, and fine twined linen; as **YeHoVaH** commanded Moses. *6* Then they made the beryl stones, fixed in twisted frames of gold and cut like the cutting of a stamp, with the names of the children of Israel. *7* And he put them on the shoulders of the ephod, that they should be stones for a memorial to the children of Israel; as **YeHoVaH** commanded Moses. *8* And he made the breastplate of special crafted work, like the work of the ephod; of gold, blue, and purple, and scarlet, and fine twined linen. *9* It was square; they made the breastplate double: a span was the length, and a span the width, being doubled. *10* And they set in it four rows of stones: the first row was a sardius, a topaz, and a carbuncle: this was the first row of stones.

11 And the second row, an emerald, a sapphire, and a diamond. **12** And the third row, a ligure, an agate, and an amethyst. **13** And the fourth row, a beryl, an onyx, and a jasper stone: they were enclosed in twisted strands of gold in their inclosing. **14** And the stones were according to the names of the children of Israel, twelve, according to their names, like the engravings of a signet, everyone with his name, according to the **12** tribes. **15** And they made upon the breastplate chains at the ends, of twisted work of pure gold. **16** And they made two strands of gold, and two gold rings; and put the two rings in the two ends of the breastplate. **17** And they put the two strand chains of gold in the two rings on the ends of the breastplate. **18** And the other two ends of the chains were joined to the two frames and fixed to the front of the ephod over the armholes. **19** And they made two rings of gold, and put them on the two ends of the breastplate, upon the border of it, which was on the side of the ephod inward. **20** And they made two other golden rings, and put them on the two sides of the ephod underneath, toward the front part of it, over against the other coupling, above the crafted girdle of the ephod.

21 And they did bind the breastplate by his rings to the rings of the ephod with a lace of blue, that it might be above the crafted girdle of the ephod, and that the breastplate might not be loosened from the ephod; as **YeHoVaH** commanded Moses. **22** And he made the robe of the ephod of woven work, all of blue. **23** And there was a hole in the midst of the robe, as the hole of an habergeon (sleeveless coat), with a band around the hole, that it should not tear. **24** And they made upon the hems of the robe pomegranates of blue, and purple, and scarlet, and twined linen. **25** And they made bells of pure gold, and put the bells between the pomegranates upon the hem of the robe, all around between the pomegranates; **26** A bell and a pomegranate, a bell and a pomegranate, all around the hem of the robe to minister in; **YeHoVaH** commanded Moses. **27** And they made coats of fine linen of woven work for Aaron, and for his sons, **28** And a headdress of fine linen, and goodly bonnets of fine linen, and linen under garments of fine twined linen, **29** And a girdle of fine twined linen, and blue, and purple, and scarlet, of needlework; as **YeHoVaH** commanded Moses. **30** And they made the plate of the holy crown of pure gold, and wrote upon it a writing, like the engravings of a signet, "Holiness to **YeHoVaH**".

31 And they tied to it a lace of blue, to fasten it on high upon the headdress; as **YeHoVaH** commanded Moses. **32** Thus was all the work of the tabernacle of the tent of the congregation finished: and the children of Israel did according to all that **YeHoVaH** commanded Moses, so they did. **33** And they brought the tabernacle to Moses, the tent, and all his furniture, his hooks, his boards, his bars, and his pillars, and his sockets, **34** And the covering of rams' skins dyed red, and the covering of badgers' skins, and the veil of the covering, **35** The ark of the testimony, and the poles thereof, and the mercy seat, **36** The table, and all the vessels thereof, and the showbread, **37** The pure candlestick, with the lamps, even with the lamps to be set in order, and all the vessels, and the oil for light, **38** And the golden altar, and the anointing oil, and the sweet incense, and the hanging for the tabernacle door, **39** The brass altar, and its grate of brass, its poles, and all its vessels, the laver and his foot, **40** The hangings of the court, its pillars, and its sockets, and the hanging for the court gate, its cords, and its pins, and all the vessels of the service of the tabernacle, for the tent of the congregation, **41** The cloths of service to do service in the holy place, and the holy garments for Aaron the priest, and his sons' garments, to minister in the priest's office. **42** According to all that **YeHoVaH** commanded Moses, so the children of Israel made all the work. **43** And Moses looked upon all the work, and, behold, they had done it as **YeHoVaH** had commanded: and Moses blessed them.

Chapter 40

Moses set up the tabernacle and brought the ark into it, as YeHoVaH had commanded. Then the glory of YeHoVaH filled the tabernacle.

1 And **YeHoVaH** spoke to Moses, saying, *2* On the first day of the first month shall you set up the tabernacle of the tent of the congregation. *3* And you shall put in the ark of the testimony, and cover the ark with the veil. *4* And you shall bring in the table, and set in order the things that are to be set in order upon it; and you shall bring in the candlestick, and light the lamps there. *5* And you shall set the altar of gold for the incense before the ark of the testimony, and put the hanging of the door to the tabernacle. *6* And you shall set the altar of the burnt offering before the door of the tabernacle of the tent of the congregation. *7* And you shall set the laver (washing-vessel) between the tent of the congregation and the altar, and shall put water in it. *8* And you shall set up the court all around, and hang up the hanging at the court gate. *9* And you shall take the anointing oil, and anoint the tabernacle, and all that is therein, and shall consecrate it, and all the vessels there: and it shall be holy. *10* And you shall anoint the altar of the burnt offering, and all his vessels, and sanctify the altar: and it shall be an altar most holy.

11 And you shall anoint the laver and its foot, and sanctify it. *12* And you shall bring Aaron and his sons to the door of the tabernacle of the congregation, and wash them with water. *13* And you shall put upon Aaron the holy garments, and anoint him, and sanctify him; that he may minister to me in the priest's office. *14* And you shall bring his sons, and clothe them with coats: *15* And you shall anoint them, as you did anoint their father, that they may minister to me in the priest's office: for their anointing shall surely be an everlasting priesthood throughout their generations. *16* Thus did Moses: according to all that **YeHoVaH** commanded him to do. *17* And it came to pass in the first month in the second year, on the first day of the month that the tabernacle was set up. *18* And Moses set up the tabernacle, and fastened its sockets, and set up the boards, and put in the bars there, and set up its pillars. *19* And he spread across the tent over the tabernacle, and put the covering of the tent above upon it; as **YeHoVaH** commanded Moses. *20* And he took and put the testimony into the ark, and set the poles on the ark, and put the mercy seat above upon the ark:

21 And he brought the ark into the tabernacle, and set up the veil of the covering, and covered the ark of the testimony; as **YeHoVaH** commanded Moses. *22* And he put the table in the tent of the congregation, upon the side of the tabernacle northward, without the veil. *23* And he set the showbread (Challah bread) in order upon it before **YeHoVaH**; as **YeHoVaH** had commanded Moses. *24* And he put the candlestick in the tent of the congregation, over against the table, on the side of the tabernacle southward. *25* And he lit the lamps before **YeHoVaH**; as **YeHoVaH** commanded Moses. *26* And he put the golden altar in the tent of the congregation before the veil: *27* and he burnt sweet incense thereon; as **YeHoVaH** commanded Moses. *28* And he set up the hanging at the door of the tabernacle. *29* And he put the altar of burnt offering by the door of the tabernacle of the tent of the congregation, and offered upon it the burnt offering and the meal offering; as **YeHoVaH** commanded Moses. *30* And he set the laver between the tent of the congregation and the altar, and put water there, to wash.

31 And Moses and Aaron and his sons washed their hands and their feet there: *32* When they went into the tent of the congregation, and when they came near to the altar, they washed; as **YeHoVaH** commanded Moses. *33* And he set up the court all around the tabernacle and the altar, and set up the hanging of the court gate. So Moses finished the work. *34* Then a cloud covered the tent of the congregation, and the glory of **YeHoVaH** filled the tabernacle. *35* And Moses was not able to enter into the tent of the congregation, because the cloud stayed there, and the glory of **YeHoVaH** filled the tabernacle. *36* And when the cloud was taken up from over the tabernacle, the children of Israel went onward in all their journeys: *37* But if the cloud were not taken up, then they journeyed not till the day that it was taken up. *38* For the cloud of **YeHoVaH** was upon the tabernacle by day, and fire was on it by night, in the sight of all the house of Israel, throughout all their journeys.

Reading 22 ends

Thus Ends the Book Of Exodus   Praise **YeHoVaH**

True Name Torah Version

~LEVITICUS~

Genesis, Exodus, Leviticus, Numbers, Deuteronomy

The 3rd Book of Moses

Leviticus (Vayikra) meaning, 'And He called', gives YeHoVaH's laws concerning sacrifices, ceremonial laws regarding the priesthood, ceremonial laws concerning purification, laws regarding the sacred feasts and festivals, tithes, offerings, sabbatical and jubilee years, and vows.

READINGS FOR LEVITICUS

The name in (parentheses) is the Hebrew name for that week. For example: Week 24 'He Called' in Hebrew is 'Vayikra'

Reading 24 " He Called" (Vayikra) Leviticus **1:1 - 5:26**
YeHoVaH describes the laws (instructions) of animal sacrifice. *YeHoVaH* explains the different sacrifices that atone for guilt or sins, and distinguishes between sins committed inadvertently and sins committed on purpose.

Reading 25 *"Passover"* (Tzav) Leviticus **6:1 - 8:36**
YeHoVaH continues to describe the different laws (instruction) of sacrifices. A distinction is made between sin offerings, burnt offerings, and homage offerings, with each following its own process. *YeHoVaH* then commands the priests to make another offering that ordains themselves in their positions.

Reading 26 "Eighth" (Shmini) Leviticus **9:1 - 11:47**
YeHoVaH commands Aaron and his sons to make the burnt and sin offerings at the Tabernacle. When *YeHoVaH* accepts the offerings, the people shout with joy. *YeHoVaH* describes to Moses the laws (instruction) of kashrut.

Reading 27 "She Bears Seed" (Tazria) Leviticus **12:1 - 13:59**
YeHoVaH instructs Moses about the purification rituals for mothers following childbirth. *YeHoVaH* then describes to Moses and Aaron the procedures for identifying and responding to those infected with leprosy.

Reading 28 "Infected One" (Metzora) Leviticus **14:1 - 15:33**
YeHoVaH describes the purification ritual for people and homes afflicted with skin diseases. *Elohim* also instructs Moses and Aaron regarding the laws (instructions) of the emission of bodily fluids.

Reading 29 "After Death" (Achrei Mot)   Leviticus **16:1 - 18:30**
YeHoVaH speaks to Moses after the death of Aaron's two sons, who were killed for coming too close to the presence of *YeHoVaH*. *YeHoVaH* instructs Moses and Aaron on the procedures surrounding Yom Kippur, the Day of Atonement. *YeHoVaH* describes all the laws (instructions) surrounding sexual prohibitions. *ND*

Reading 30 "Holy One" (Kedoshim) Leviticus **19:1 - 20:27**
YeHoVaH describes to Moses many ethical and ritual laws (instructions) aimed at helping people live lives of holiness. The laws (instructions) described include some of those recorded in the Ten Commandments, such as respecting one's parents, keeping the Sabbath and not stealing. *YeHoVaH* also introduces laws (instructions) s about farming and about belief in supernatural beings.

Reading 31"Say" (Emor) Leviticus **21:1 - 24:23**
YeHoVaH describes the restrictions related to priests' sexuality and marriage. *YeHoVaH* then describes a variety of holidays, including Passover, Shabbat, Yom Kippur, and Sukkot. *YeHoVaH* outlines the omer period, asking the Israelites to bring food offerings to the priests for seven weeks.

Reading 32 "On The Mountain" (Behar) Leviticus **25:1 - 26:2**
YeHoVaH describes the laws (instructions) surrounding resting the land and crops every seven years, as well as the Jubilee year every **50** years. *YeHoVaH* permits the use of slaves but provides stipulations including the obligation to eventually free your slaves.

Reading 33 "**In My laws**" (instructions) (Bechukotai)   Leviticus **26:3 - 27:34**
YeHoVaH tells the people of Israel that if they follow *YeHoVaH*'s commandments, they will be provided with rain to feed their crops. *YeHoVaH* then describes the long list of punishments that will be inflicted on the Israelites if they do not follow *YeHoVaH*'s laws (instructions).

-End Torah Readings for Leviticus-

CHAPTERS 1- 10

Chapter 1

Whenever a burnt offering is brought they shall slaughter a bull, a sheep, a goat or a bird. The priest shall burn it on the altar to YeHoVaH.

Reading 24 begins

1 And **YeHoVaH** called to Moses, and spoke to him out of the tabernacle of the congregation, saying, **2** Speak to the children of Israel, and say to them, If any man of you bring an offering to **YeHoVaH**, you shall bring your offering of the cattle of the herd, and of the flock. **3** If his offering be a burnt sacrifice of the herd, let him offer a male without blemish: he shall offer it of his own voluntary will at the door of the tabernacle of the congregation before **YeHoVaH**. **4** And he shall put his hand upon the head of the burnt offering; and it shall be accepted for him to make atonement for him. **5** And he shall kill the steer before **YeHoVaH**: and the priests, Aaron's sons, shall bring the blood, and sprinkle the blood all around the altar that is by the door of the tabernacle of the congregation. **6** And the burned offering is to be skinned and cut up into its parts. **7** And the sons of Aaron the priest shall put fire upon the altar, and lay the wood in order upon the fire: **8** And the priests, Aaron's sons, shall lay the parts, the head, and the fat, in order upon the wood that is on the fire which is upon the altar: **9** But his innards and his legs shall he wash in water: and the priest shall burn all on the altar, to be a burnt sacrifice, an offering made by fire, of a sweet savor to **YeHoVaH**. **10** And if his offering were of the flocks, namely, of the sheep, or of the goats, for a burnt sacrifice; he shall bring it a male without blemish.

11 And he shall kill it on the side of the altar northward before **YeHoVaH**: and the priests, Aaron's sons, shall sprinkle his blood round about upon the altar. **12** And he shall cut it into pieces, with the head and the fat: and the priest shall lay them in order on the wood that is on the fire which is upon the altar: **13** But he shall wash the innards and the legs with water: and the priest shall bring it all, and burn it upon the altar: it is a burnt offering, an offering made by fire, of a sweet savor to **YeHoVaH**. **14** And if the burnt sacrifice for his offering to **YeHoVaH** be of birds, then he shall bring his offering of turtledoves, or of young pigeons. **15** And the priest shall bring it to the altar, and wring off his head, and burn it on the altar; and the blood shall be wrung out at the side of the altar: **16** And he shall pluck away his crop with his feathers, and cast it beside the altar on the east part, by the place of the ashes: **17** And he shall cleave it with the wings, but shall not divide it asunder: and the priest shall burn it upon the altar, upon the wood that is upon the fire: it is a burnt sacrifice, an offering made by fire, of a sweet savor to **YeHoVaH**.

Chapter 2

A grain offering consists of fine flour, oil and incense. After the priest burns a portion, the rest belongs to Aaron and his sons.

1 And when any will offer a meal offering to **YeHoVaH**, his offering shall be of fine flour; and he shall pour oil upon it, and put frankincense on it: **2** And let him take it to Aaron's sons, the priests; and having taken in his hand some of the meal and of the oil, with all the perfume, let him give it to the priest to be burned on the altar, as a sign, an offering made by fire, for a sweet smell to t **YeHoVaH**. **3** And the rest of the meal offering will be for Aaron and his sons; it is most holy among **YeHoVaH** 's fire offerings **4** And if you bring a sacrifice offering of meal baked in the oven, it shall be unleavened cakes of fine flour mingled with oil, or unleavened wafers anointed with oil. *5* And if your sacrifice be a meal offering baked in a pan, it shall be of fine flour unleavened, mingled with oil. *6* You shall part it in pieces, and pour oil on it: it is a meal offering. *7* And if your sacrifice be a meal offering baked in the frying pan, it shall be made of fine flour with oil. *8* And you shall bring the meal offering that is made of these things to **YeHoVaH**: and when it is presented to the priest, he shall bring it to the altar. *9* And the priest shall take from the meal offering a memorial, and shall burn it upon the altar: it is an offering made by fire, of a sweet savor to **YeHoVaH**. *10* And that which is left of the meal offering shall be Aaron's and his sons': it is a thing most holy of the offerings of **YeHoVaH** made by fire.

11 No meal offering, which you shall bring to **YeHoVaH**, shall be made with leaven: for you shall burn no leaven, or any honey, in any offering of **YeHoVaH** made by fire. *12* As for the offering of the first fruits, you shall offer them to **YeHoVaH**: but they shall not be burnt on the altar for a sweet savor. *13* And every offering of your meal offering shall you season with salt; neither shall you suffer the salt of the covenant of your **Elohim** to be lacking from your meal offering: with all your offerings you shall offer salt. *14* And if you offer a meal offering of your first fruits to **YeHoVaH**, you shall offer for the meal offering of your first fruits green ears of corn dried by the fire, even corn beaten out of full ears. *15* And you shall put oil upon it, and lay frankincense on it: it is a meal offering. *16* And the priest shall burn the memorial of it, part of the beaten corn, and part of the oil, with all the frankincense: it is an offering made by fire to **YeHoVaH**.

Chapter 3
Peace offerings are to be from the herd or the flock. It will be slaughtered at the tabernacle and the priest shall burn it on the altar as food.

1 And if his oblation be a sacrifice of peace offering, if he offers it of the herd; whether it be a male or female, he shall offer it without blemish before **YeHoVaH**. *2* And he shall lay his hand upon the head of his offering, and kill it at the door of the tabernacle of the congregation: and Aaron's sons the priests shall sprinkle the blood upon the altar all around. *3* And he shall offer of the sacrifice of the peace offering an offering made by fire to **YeHoVaH**; the fat that covers the innards, and all the fat that is upon the innards, *4* And the two kidneys, and the fat that is on them, which is by the flanks, and the tendon above the liver, with the kidneys, shall he take away. *5* And Aaron's sons shall burn it on the altar upon the burnt sacrifice, which is upon the wood that is on the fire: it is an offering made by fire, of a sweet savor to **YeHoVaH**. *6* And if his offering for a sacrifice of peace offering to **YeHoVaH** be of the flock; male or female, he shall offer it without blemish. *7* If he offers a lamb for his offering, then shall he offer it before **YeHoVaH**. *8* And he shall lay his hand upon the head of his offering, and kill it before the tabernacle of the congregation: and Aaron's sons shall sprinkle the blood all around the altar. *9* And he shall offer of the sacrifice of the peace offering an offering made by fire to **YeHoVaH**; the fat, and the whole rump, it shall he take off close to the backbone; and the fat that covers the innards, and all the fat that is upon the innards, *10* And the two kidneys, and the fat that is upon them, which is by the flanks, and the tendon above the liver, with the kidneys, shall he take away.

11 And the priest shall burn it upon the altar: it is the food of the offering made by fire to **YeHoVaH**. *12* And if his offering be a goat, then he shall offer it before **YeHoVaH**. *13* And he shall lay his hand upon the head of it, and kill it before the tabernacle of the congregation: and the sons of Aaron shall sprinkle the blood upon the altar all around. *14* And he shall offer his offering, even an offering made by fire to **YeHoVaH**; the fat that covers the innards, and all the fat that is upon the innards, *15* And the two kidneys, and the fat that is upon them, which is by the flanks, and the tendon above the liver, with the kidneys, it shall he take away. *16* And the priest shall burn them upon the altar: it is the food of the offering made by fire for a sweet savor: all the fat is **YeHoVaH**. *17* It shall be a perpetual statute for your generations throughout all your dwellings, that you eat neither fat nor blood.

Chapter 4
For any unintentional sin they shall slaughter a bull, a goat or a lamb. The priest shall burn it to YeHoVaH to make atonement.

1 And **YeHoVaH** spoke to Moses, saying, *2* Speak to the children of Israel, saying, If a soul shall sin through ignorance against any of the commandments of **YeHoVaH** concerning things which ought not to be done, and shall do against any of them: *3* If the priest that is anointed do sin according to the sin of the people; then let him bring for his sin, which he has sinned, a young steer without blemish to **YeHoVaH** for a sin offering. *4* And he shall bring the steer to the door of the tabernacle of the congregation before **YeHoVaH**; and shall lay his hand upon the steer's head, and kill the steer before **YeHoVaH**. *5* And the priest that is anointed shall take of the steer's blood, and bring it to the tabernacle of the congregation: *6* And the priest shall dip his finger in the blood, and sprinkle of the blood seven times before **YeHoVaH**, before the curtain of the sanctuary. *7* And the priest shall put some of the blood upon the horns of the altar of sweet incense before **YeHoVaH**, which is in the tabernacle of the congregation; and shall pour all the blood of the steer at the bottom of the altar of the burnt offering, which is at the door of the tabernacle of the congregation. *8* And he shall take off from it all the fat of the steer for the sin offering; the fat that covers the innards, and all the fat that is upon the innards, *9* And the two kidneys, and the fat that is upon them, which is by the flanks, and the tendon above the liver, with the kidneys, it shall he take away, *10* As it was taken off from the steer of the sacrifice of peace offerings: and the priest shall burn them upon the altar of the burnt offering.

11 And the skin of the steer, and all his flesh, with his head, and with his legs, and his innards, and his dung, *12* Even the whole steer shall he carry forth outside the camp to a clean place, where the ashes are poured out, and burn it on the wood with fire: where the ashes are poured out shall he be burnt. *13* And if the whole congregation of Israel sin through ignorance, and the thing be hid from the eyes of the assembly, and they have done anything against any of the commandments of **YeHoVaH** concerning things which should not be done, and are guilty; *14* When the sin, which they have sinned against it, is known, then the congregation shall offer a young steer for the sin, and bring him before the tabernacle of the congregation. *15* And the elders of the congregation shall lay their hands upon the head of the steer before **YeHoVaH**: and the steer shall be killed before **YeHoVaH**. *16* And the priest that is anointed shall bring of the steer's blood to the tabernacle of the congregation: *17* And the priest shall dip his finger in some of the blood, and sprinkle it seven times before **YeHoVaH**, even before the curtain. *18* And he shall put some of the blood upon the horns of the altar that is before **YeHoVaH**, that is in the tabernacle of the congregation, and shall pour out all the blood at the bottom of the altar of the burnt offering, which is at the door of the tabernacle of the congregation. *19* And he shall take all his fat from him, and burn it upon the altar. *20* And he shall do with the steer as he did with the steer for a sin offering, so shall he do with this: and the priest shall make atonement for them, and it shall be forgiven them.

21 And he shall carry forth the steer outside the camp, and burn him as he burned the first steer: it is a sin offering for the congregation. *22* When a ruler has sinned, and done somewhat through ignorance against any of the commandments of **YeHoVaH** his **Elohim** concerning things which should not be done, and is guilty; *23* Or if his sin, wherein he has sinned, come to his knowledge; he shall bring his offering, a kid of the goats, a male without blemish: *24* And he shall lay his hand upon the head of the goat, and kill it in the place where they kill the burnt offering before **YeHoVaH**: it is a sin offering. *25* And the priest shall take of the blood of the sin offering with his finger, and put it upon the horns of the altar of burnt offering, and shall pour out his blood at the bottom of the altar of burnt offering. *26* And he shall burn all his fat upon the altar, as the fat of the sacrifice of peace offerings: and the priest shall make atonement for him concerning his sin, and it shall be forgiven him. *27* And if any one of the common people sin through ignorance, while he does somewhat against any of the commandments of **YeHoVaH** concerning things which ought not to be done, and be guilty; *28* Or if his sin, which he has sinned, come to his knowledge: then he shall bring his offering, a kid of the goats, a female without blemish, for his sin which he has sinned. *29* And he shall lay his hand upon the head of the sin offering, and slay the sin offering in the place of the burnt offering. *30* And the priest shall take of the blood with his finger, and put it upon the horns of the altar of burnt offering, and shall pour out all the blood at the bottom of the altar.

31 And he shall take away all the fat, as the fat is taken away from off the sacrifice of peace offerings; and the priest shall burn it upon the altar for a sweet savor to **YeHoVaH**; and the priest shall make atonement for him, and it shall be forgiven him. *32* And if he brings a lamb for a sin offering, he shall bring a female without blemish. *33* And he shall lay his hand upon the head of the sin offering, and slay it for a sin offering in the place where they kill the burnt offering. *34* And the priest shall take of the blood of the sin offering with his finger, and put it upon the horns of the altar of burnt offering, and shall pour out all the blood at the bottom of the altar: *35* And he shall take away all the fat, as the fat of the lamb is taken away from the sacrifice of the peace offerings; and the priest shall burn them upon the altar, according to the offerings made by fire to **YeHoVaH**: and the priest shall make an atonement for his sin that he has committed, and it shall be forgiven him.

Chapter 5
If anyone sins by an oath or becomes unclean they should confess it and bring a sin offering. A guilt offering should be a ram.

1 And if a person sin, and hear the voice of swearing, and is a witness, whether he has seen or known of it; if he does not utter it, then he shall bear his iniquity. *2* Or if a soul touch any unclean thing, whether it be a carcass of an unclean animal, or a carcass of unclean cattle, or the carcass of unclean creeping things, and if it be hidden from him; he also shall be unclean, and guilty. *3* Or if he touch the uncleanness of man, whatsoever uncleanness it be that a man shall be defiled, and it be hid from him; when he knows of it, then he shall be guilty. *4* Or if a soul swear, pronouncing with his lips to do evil, or to do good, whatsoever it be that a man shall pronounce with an oath, and it be hid from him; when he knows of it, then he shall be guilty in one of these. *5* And it shall be, when he shall be guilty in one of these things, that he shall confess that he has sinned in that thing: *6* And he shall bring his trespass offering to **YeHoVaH** for his sin which he has sinned, a female from the flock, a lamb or a kid of the goats, for a sin offering; and the priest shall make atonement for him concerning his sin. *7* And if he be not able to bring a lamb, then he shall bring for his trespass, which he has committed, two turtledoves, or two young pigeons, to **YeHoVaH**; one for a sin offering, and the other for a burnt offering. *8* And he shall bring them to the priest, who shall offer that which is for the sin offering first, and wring off his head from his neck, but shall not divide it into pieces: *9* And he shall sprinkle of the blood of the sin offering upon the side of the altar; and the rest of the blood shall be wrung out at the bottom of the altar: it is a sin offering. *10* And he shall offer the second for a burnt offering, according to the manner: and the priest shall make atonement for him for his sin that he has sinned, and it shall be forgiven him.

11 But if he be not able to bring two turtledoves, or two young pigeons, then he that sinned shall bring for his offering the tenth part of an ephah (bushel) of fine flour for a sin offering; he shall put no oil upon it, neither shall he put any frankincense on it: for it is a sin offering. *12* Then shall he bring it to the priest, and the priest shall take his handful of it, as a memorial, and burn it on the altar, according to the offerings made by fire to **YeHoVaH**: it is a sin offering. *13* And the priest shall make atonement for him as touching his sin that he has sinned in one of these, and it shall be forgiven him: and the remnant shall be the priest's, as a meal offering. *14* And **YeHoVaH** spoke to Moses, saying, *15* If a person commit a trespass, and sin through ignorance, in the sacred things of **YeHoVaH**; then he shall bring for his trespass to **YeHoVaH** a ram without blemish out of the flocks, with your estimation by shekels of silver, after the shekel of the sanctuary, for a trespass offering. *16* And he shall make amends for the harm that he has done in the holy thing, and shall add the fifth part to it, and give it to the priest: and the priest shall make an atonement for him with the ram of the trespass offering, and it shall be forgiven him. *17* And if a soul sin, and commit any of these things that are forbidden to be done by the commandments of **YeHoVaH**; yet he knew it not, yet is he guilty, and shall bear his iniquity. *18* And he shall bring a ram without blemish out of the flock, with your estimation, for a trespass offering, to the priest: and the priest shall make an atonement for him concerning his ignorance wherein he erred and knew it not, and it shall be forgiven him. *19* It is a trespass offering: he has certainly trespassed against **YeHoVaH**. *20* And **YeHoVaH** spoke to Moses, saying,

21 If anyone does wrong, and is untrue to **YeHoVaH**, acting falsely to his neighbor in connection with something put in his care, or something given for a debt, or has taken away anything by force, or has been cruel to his neighbor, *22* Or have found that which was lost, and lies concerning it, and swears falsely; in any of all these that a man does, sinning: *23* Then it shall be, because he has sinned, and is guilty, that he shall restore that which he took violently away, or the thing which he has deceitfully gotten, or that which was delivered him to keep, or the lost thing which he found, *24* Or all that about which he has sworn falsely; he shall even restore it in the principal, and shall add the fifth part more to it, and give it to him to whom it belongs, in the day of his trespass offering. *25* And he shall bring his trespass offering to **YeHoVaH**, a ram without blemish out of the flock, with your estimation, for a trespass offering, to the priest: *26* And the priest shall make an atonement for him before **YeHoVaH**: and it shall be forgiven him for anything of all that he has done in trespassing.
  Reading 24 ends

Chapter 6
Any time someone cheats a neighbor they should make reimbursement and bring a guilt offering. The fire on the altar is never to go out.
  Reading 25 begins
1 And **YeHoVaH** spoke to Moses, saying, *2* Command Aaron and his sons, saying, This is the law (instruction) of the burnt offering: It is the burnt offering, because of the burning upon the

altar all night to the morning, and the fire of the altar shall be burning in it. *3* And the priest shall put on his linen garment, and his linen underclothes shall he put upon his flesh, and take up the ashes which the fire has consumed with the burnt offering on the altar, and he shall put them beside the altar. *4* And he shall put off his garments, and put on other garments, and carry forth the ashes outside the camp to a clean place. *5* And the fire upon the altar shall be burning; it shall not be put out: and the priest shall burn wood on it every morning, and lay the burnt offering in order upon it; and he shall burn on it the fat of the peace offerings. *6* The fire shall ever be burning upon the altar; it shall never go out. *7* And this is the law (instruction) of the meal offering: the sons of Aaron shall offer it before **YeHoVaH**, before the altar. *8* And he shall take of it his handful, of the flour of the meal offering, and of the oil, and all the frankincense that is upon the meal offering, and shall burn it upon the altar for a sweet savor, even the memorial of it, to **YeHoVaH**. *9* And the remainder shall Aaron and his sons eat: with unleavened bread shall it be eaten in the holy place; in the court of the tabernacle of the congregation they shall eat it. *10* It shall not be baked with leaven. I have given it to them for their portion of my offerings made by fire; it is most holy, as is the sin offering, and as the trespass offering.

11 All the males among the children of Aaron shall eat of it. It shall be a statute *forever* in your generations concerning the offerings of **YeHoVaH** made by fire: every one that touches them shall be holy. *12* And **YeHoVaH** spoke to Moses, saying, *13* This is the offering of Aaron and of his sons, which they shall offer to **YeHoVaH** in the day when he is anointed; the tenth part of an ephah (bushel) of fine flour for a meal offering perpetual, half of it in the morning, and half at night. *14* In a pan it shall be made with oil; and when it is baked, you shall bring it in: and the baked pieces of the meal offering shall you offer for a sweet savor to **YeHoVaH**. *15* And the priest of his sons that is anointed in his stead shall offer it: it is a statute forever to **YeHoVaH**; it shall be entirely burnt. *16* For every meal offering for the priest shall be entirely burnt: it shall not be eaten. *17* And **YeHoVaH** spoke to Moses, saying, *18* Speak to Aaron and to his sons, saying, This is the law (instruction) of the sin offering: In the place where the burnt offering is killed shall the sin offering be killed before **YeHoVaH**: it is most holy. *19* The priest that offers it for sin shall eat it: in the holy place shall it be eaten, in the court of the tabernacle of the congregation. *20* Whatsoever shall touch the flesh shall be holy: and when there is sprinkled of the blood upon any garment, you shall wash that where it was sprinkled in the holy place.

21 But the earthen vessel wherein it is wet through shall be broken: and if it be wet through in a brass pot, it shall be both scoured, and rinsed in water. *22* All the males among the priests shall eat: it is most holy. *23* And no sin offering, any of the blood is brought into the tabernacle of the congregation to reconcile withal in the holy place, shall be eaten: it shall be burnt in the fire.

Chapter 7
All the meal of a peace offering shall be eaten within two days. Do not eat the fat or the blood of an animal. For a wave offering it belongs to Aaron and his sons.

1 Likewise this is the law (instruction) of the trespass offering: it is most holy. *2* In the place where they kill the burnt offering shall they kill the trespass offering: and the blood shall he sprinkled all around upon the altar. *3* And he shall offer of it all the fat; the rump, and the fat that covers the innards, *4* And the two kidneys, and the fat that is on them, which is by the flanks, and the tendon that is above the liver, with the kidneys, it shall he take away: *5* And the priest shall burn them upon the altar for an offering made by fire to **YeHoVaH**: it is a trespass offering. *6* Every male among the priests shall eat: it shall be eaten in the holy place: it is most holy. *7* As the sin offering is, so is the trespass offering: there is one law (instruction) for them: the priest that makes atonement shall have it. *8* And the priest that offers any man's burnt offering, even the priest shall have to himself the skin of the burnt offering that he has offered. *9* And all the meal offering that is baked in the oven, and all that is dressed in the frying pan, and in the pan, shall be the priest's that offers it. *10* And every meal offering, mingled with oil, and dries, shall all the sons of Aaron have, one as much as another.

11 And this is the law (instruction) of the sacrifice of peace offerings, which he shall offer to *YeHoVaH*. *12* If he offers it for a thanksgiving, then he shall offer with the sacrifice of thanksgiving unleavened cakes mingled with oil, and unleavened wafers anointed with oil, and cakes mingled with oil, of fine flour, fried. *13* Besides the cakes, he shall offer for his offering leavened bread with the sacrifice of thanksgiving of his peace offerings. *14* And of it he shall offer one out of the whole sacrifice for a heave offering to *YeHoVaH*, and it shall be the priest's that sprinkles the blood of the peace offerings. *15* And the flesh of the sacrifice of his peace offerings for thanksgiving shall be eaten the same day that it is offered; he shall not leave any of it until the morning. *16* But if the sacrifice of his offering be a vow, or a voluntary offering, it shall be eaten the same day that he offers his sacrifice: and on the next day also the remainder of it shall be eaten: *17* But the remainder of the flesh of the sacrifice on the third day shall be burnt with fire. *18* And if any of the flesh of the sacrifice of his peace offerings be eaten at all on the third day, it shall not be accepted; neither shall it be imputed to him that offers it: it shall be a disgrace, and the soul that eats of it shall bear his iniquity. *19* And the flesh that touches any unclean thing shall not be eaten; it shall be burnt with fire: and as for the flesh, all that be clean shall eat. *20* But the soul that eats of the flesh of the sacrifice of peace offerings, that pertain to *YeHoVaH*, having his uncleanness upon him, even that soul shall be cut off from his people.

21 Moreover the soul that shall touch any unclean thing, as the uncleanness of man, or any unclean animal, or any disgraceful unclean thing, and eat of the flesh of the sacrifice of peace offerings, which pertain to *YeHoVaH*, even that soul shall be cut off from his people. *22* And *YeHoVaH* spoke to Moses, saying, *23* Speak to the children of Israel, saying, You shall eat no manner of fat, of ox, or of sheep, or of goat. *24* And the fat of the animal that dies of itself, and the fat of that which is torn with animals, may be used in any other use: but you shall not eat of it. *25* For whosoever eats the fat of the animal, of which men offer an offering made by fire to *YeHoVaH*, even the soul that eats it shall be cut off from his people. *26* Moreover you shall eat no manner of blood, whether it is of fowl or of animal, in any of your dwellings. *27* Whatsoever soul that eats any manner of blood, even that soul shall be cut off from his people. *28* And *YeHoVaH* spoke to Moses, saying, *29* Speak to the children of Israel, saying, He that offers the sacrifice of his peace offerings to *YeHoVaH* shall bring his offering to *YeHoVaH* of the sacrifice of his peace offerings. *30* His own hands shall bring the offerings of *YeHoVaH* made by fire, the fat with the breast, shall he bring, that the breast may be waved for a wave offering before *YeHoVaH*.

31 And the priest shall burn the fat upon the altar: but the breast shall be Aaron's and his sons'. *32* And the right shoulder shall you give to the priest for a heave offering of the sacrifices of your peace offerings. *33* He among the sons of Aaron, that offers the blood of the peace offerings, and the fat, shall have the right shoulder for his part. *34* For the wave breast and the heave shoulder have I taken of the children of Israel from off the sacrifices of their peace offerings, and have given them to Aaron the priest and to his sons by a statute forever from among the children of Israel. *35* This is the portion of the anointing of Aaron, and of the anointing of his sons, out of the offerings of *YeHoVaH* made by fire, in the day when he presented them to minister to **YeHoVaH** in the priest's office; *36* Which **YeHoVaH** commanded to be given them of the children of Israel, in the day that he anointed them, by a statute forever throughout their generations. *37* This is the law (instruction) of the burnt offering, of the meal offering, and of the sin offering, and of the trespass offering, and of the consecrations, and of the sacrifice of the peace offerings; *38* Which **YeHoVaH** commanded Moses in mount Sinai, in the day that he commanded the children of Israel to offer their oblations to **YeHoVaH**, in the wilderness of Sinai.

Chapter 8

Moses brought the people together at the tabernacle. He makes offerings on the altar and consecrates Aaron and his sons with oil and blood.

1 And **YeHoVaH** spoke to Moses, saying, *2* Take Aaron and his sons with him, and the garments, and the anointing oil, and a steer for the sin offering, and two rams, and a basket of unleavened bread; *3* And gather you all the congregation together to the door of the tabernacle of the congregation. *4* And Moses did as **YeHoVaH** commanded him; and the assembly was gathered together to the door of the tabernacle of the congregation. *5* And Moses said to the congregation, This is the thing which **YeHoVaH** commanded to be done. *6* And Moses brought Aaron and his sons, and washed them with water. *7* He put the coat on him, making it tight with its band, and then the robe, and over it the ephod, with its band of needlework to keep it in place. *8* And he put the breastplate upon him: also he put in the breastplate the *Urim and the Thummim* (jeweled lights). *9* And he put the *mitre* (official headdress) upon his head; also upon the mitre, upon his forefront, did he put the golden plate, the holy crown; as **YeHoVaH** commanded Moses. *10* And Moses took the anointing oil, and anointed the tabernacle and all that was therein, and sanctified them.

11 And he sprinkled upon the altar seven times, and anointed the altar and all his vessels, both the laver and his foot, to sanctify them. *12* And he poured of the anointing oil upon Aaron's head, and anointed him, to sanctify him. *13* And Moses brought Aaron's sons, and put coats upon them, and girded them with girdles, and put bonnets upon them; as **YeHoVaH** commanded Moses. *14* And he brought the steer for the sin offering: and Aaron and his sons laid their hands upon the head of the steer for the sin offering. *15* And he slew it; and Moses took the blood, and put it upon the horns of the altar all around with his finger, and purified the altar, and poured the blood at the bottom of the altar, and sanctified it, to make reconciliation upon it. *16* And he took all the fat that was upon the innards, and the tendon above the liver, and the two kidneys, and their fat, and Moses burned it upon the altar. *17* But the steer, and his hide, his flesh, and his dung, he burnt with fire outside the camp; as **YeHoVaH** commanded Moses. *18* And he brought the ram for the burnt offering: and Aaron and his sons laid their hands upon the head of the ram. *19* And he killed it; and Moses sprinkled the blood upon the altar round about. *20* And he cut the ram into pieces; and Moses burnt the head, and the pieces, and the fat.

21 And he washed the innards and the legs in water; and Moses burnt the whole ram upon the altar: it was a burnt sacrifice for a sweet savor, and an offering made by fire to **YeHoVaH**; as **YeHoVaH** commanded Moses. *22* And he brought the other ram, the ram of consecration: and Aaron and his sons laid their hands upon the head of the ram. *23* And he slew it; and Moses took of the blood of it, and put it upon the tip of Aaron's right ear, and upon the thumb of his right hand, and upon the great toe of his right foot. *24* And he brought Aaron's sons, and Moses put of the blood upon the tip of their right ear, and upon the thumbs of their right hands, and upon the great toes of their right feet: and Moses sprinkled the blood upon the altar round about. *25* And he took the fat, and the rump, and all the fat that was upon the innards, and the tendon above the liver, and the two kidneys, and their fat, and the right shoulder: *26* And out of the basket of unleavened bread, that was before **YeHoVaH**, he took one unleavened cake, and a cake of oiled bread, and one wafer, and put them on the fat, and upon the right shoulder: *27* And he put all upon Aaron's hands, and upon his sons' hands, and waved them for a wave offering before **YeHoVaH**. *28* And Moses took them from off their hands, and burnt them on the altar upon the burnt offering: they were consecrations for a sweet savor: it is an offering made by fire to **YeHoVaH**. *29* And Moses took the breast, and waved it for a wave offering before **YeHoVaH**: for of the ram of consecration it was Moses' part; as **YeHoVaH** commanded Moses. *30* And Moses took of the anointing oil, and of the blood which was upon the altar, and sprinkled it upon Aaron, and upon his garments, and upon his sons, and upon his sons' garments with him; and sanctified Aaron, and his garments, and his sons, and his sons' garments with him.

31 And Moses said to Aaron and to his sons, Boil the flesh at the door of the tabernacle of the congregation: and there eat it with the bread that is in the basket of consecrations, as I commanded, saying, Aaron and his sons shall eat it. *32* And that which remains of the flesh and of the bread shall you burn with fire. *33* And you shall not go out of the door of the tabernacle of the congregation in seven days, until the days of your consecration be at an end: for seven days shall he consecrate you. *34* As he has done this day, so **YeHoVaH** has commanded to do, to make atonement for you. *35* Therefore shall you abide at the door of the tabernacle of the congregation day and night seven days, and keep the charge of **YeHoVaH**, that you die not: for so I am commanded. *36* So Aaron and his sons did all things that **YeHoVaH** commanded by the hand of Moses.
   Reading 25 ends

Chapter 9
Aaron brings a sin offering and a burnt offering to make atonement. The glory of YeHoVaH appears and the offerings are consumed by fire.
   Reading 26 begins
1 And it came to pass on the eighth day, that Moses called Aaron and his sons, and the elders of Israel; *2* And he said to Aaron, Take thee a young calf for a sin offering, and a ram for a burnt offering, without blemish, and offer them before **YeHoVaH**. *3* And to the children of Israel you shall speak, saying, Take you a kid of the goats for a sin offering; and a calf and a lamb, both of the first year, without blemish, for a burnt offering; *4* Also a steer and a ram for peace offerings, to sacrifice before **YeHoVaH**; and a meal offering mingled with oil: for today **YeHoVaH** will *appear* to you. *5* And they brought that which Moses commanded before the tabernacle of the congregation: and the entire congregation drew near and stood before **YeHoVaH**. *6* And Moses said, This is the thing which **YeHoVaH** commanded that you should do: and the glory of **YeHoVaH** shall *appear* to you. *7* And Moses said to Aaron, Go to the altar, and offer your sin offering, and your burnt offering, and make atonement for yourself, and for the people: and offer the offering of the people, and make atonement for them; as **YeHoVaH** commanded. *8* Aaron went to the altar, and slew the calf of the sin offering, which was for him. *9* And the sons of Aaron brought the blood to him: and he dipped his finger in the blood, and put it upon the horns of the altar, and poured out the blood at the bottom of the altar: *10* But the fat, and the kidneys,

and the tendon above the liver of the sin offering, he burnt upon the altar; as **YeHoVaH** commanded Moses.

11 And the flesh and the hide he burnt with fire outside the camp. *12* And he slew the burnt offering; and Aaron's sons presented to him the blood, which he sprinkled round about upon the altar. *13* And they presented the burnt offering to him, with the pieces, and the head: and he burnt them upon the altar. *14* And he did wash the innards and the legs, and burnt them upon the burnt offering on the altar. *15* And he brought the people's offering, and took the goat, which was the sin offering for the people, and slew it, and offered it for sin, as the first. *16* And he brought the burnt offering, and offered it according to the manner. *17* And he brought the meal offering, and took a handful, and burnt it upon the altar, beside the burnt sacrifice of the morning. *18* He slew also the steer and the ram for a sacrifice of peace offerings, which was for the people: and Aaron's sons presented to him the blood, which he sprinkled upon the altar all around, *19* And the fat of the steer and of the ram, the rump, and that which covers the innards, and the kidneys, and the tendon above the liver: *20* And they put the fat upon the breasts, and he burnt the fat upon the altar:

21 And the breasts and the right shoulder Aaron waved for a wave offering before **YeHoVaH**, as Moses commanded. *22* And Aaron lifted up his hand toward the people, and blessed them, and came down from offering of the sin offering, and the burnt offering, and peace offerings. *23* And Moses and Aaron went into the tabernacle of the congregation, and came out, and blessed the people: and the glory of **YeHoVaH** appeared to all the people. *24* And there came a fire out from before **YeHoVaH**, and consumed upon the altar the burnt offering and the fat: which when all the people saw, they shouted, and fell on their faces.

Chapter 10

Nadab and Abihu, the sons of Aaron offer strange fire, so YeHoVaH consumes them in fire. Aaron and his other sons are instructed not to mourn their deaths and stayed at the tabernacle.

1 And Nadab and Abihu, the sons of Aaron, took both of them his censer, and put fire in them, and put incense on it, and offered *strange* fire before **YeHoVaH**, which he commanded them not. *2* And there went out fire from **YeHoVaH**, and devoured them, and they died before **YeHoVaH**. *3* Then Moses said to Aaron, This is it that **YeHoVaH** spoke, saying, I will be sanctified in them that come near me, and before all the people I will be glorified. And Aaron held his peace. *4* And Moses called Mishael and Elzaphan, the sons of Uzziel the uncle of Aaron, and said to them, Come near, carry your brethren from before the sanctuary out of the camp. *5* So they went near, and carried them in their coats out of the camp; as Moses had said. *6* And Moses said to Aaron, and to Eleazar and to Ithamar, his sons, Uncover not your heads, neither tear your clothes; for fear that you die, and for fear that wrath come upon all the people: but let your brethren, the whole house of Israel, grieve the burning which **YeHoVaH** has kindled. *7* And you shall not go out from the door of the tabernacle of the congregation, for fear that you die: for the anointing oil of **YeHoVaH** is upon you. And they did according to the word of Moses. *8* And **YeHoVaH** spoke to Aaron, saying, *9* Do not drink wine nor strong drink, you, nor your sons with thee, when you go into the tabernacle of the congregation, for fear that you die: it shall be a statute forever throughout your generations: *10* And that you may put difference between holy and unholy, and between unclean and clean;

11 And that you may teach the children of Israel all the statutes that **YeHoVaH** has spoken to them by the hand of Moses. *12* And Moses spoke to Aaron, and to Eleazar and to Ithamar, his sons that were left, Take the meal offering that remains of the offerings of **YeHoVaH** made by fire, and eat it without leaven beside the altar: for it is most holy: *13* And you shall eat it in the holy place, because it is your due, and your sons' due, of the sacrifices of **YeHoVaH** made by fire: for so I am commanded. *14* And the wave breast and heave shoulder shall you eat in a clean place; you, and your sons, and your daughters with thee: for they be your due, and your sons' due, which are given out of the sacrifices of peace offerings of the children of Israel. *15* The heave shoulder and the wave breast shall they bring with the offerings made by fire of the fat, to wave it for a wave offering before **YeHoVaH**; and it shall be yours, and your sons' with you, by a statute forever; as **YeHoVaH** has commanded. *16* And Moses diligently sought the goat of the sin offering, and, behold, it was burnt: and he was angry with Eleazar and Ithamar, the sons of Aaron which were left alive, saying, *17* Why have you not eaten the sin offering in the holy place, seeing it is most holy, and **Elohim** has given it you to bear the iniquity of the congregation, to make atonement for them before **YeHoVaH**? *18* Behold, the blood of it was not brought in within the holy place: you should indeed have eaten it in the holy place, as I commanded. *19* And Aaron said to Moses, Behold, this day have they offered their sin offering and their burnt offering before **YeHoVaH**; and such things have happened to me: and if I had eaten the sin offering today, should it have been accepted in the sight of **YeHoVaH**? *20* And when Moses heard that, he was content.

CHAPTERS 11- 20

Chapter 11
YeHoVaH defines clean and unclean animals. Animals with cloven hooves that chew the cud, and fish with scales and fins may be eaten. Anything that touches a carcass becomes unclean.

1 And **YeHoVaH** spoke to Moses and to Aaron, saying to them, *2* Speak to the children of Israel, saying, These are the animals which you shall eat among all the animals that are on the earth. *3* Whatever parts the hoof, and is *cloven footed* (having split hoofs), and *chews the cud* (cud is a portion of food that returns from an animal with four compartment stomachs to the mouth to be chewed for the second time like a cow), among the animals, that you shall eat. *4* Nevertheless these shall you not eat of them that chew the cud, or of them that divide the hoof: as the camel, because he chews the cud, but divides not the hoof; he is unclean to you. *5* And the coney (rabbit), because he chews the cud, but divides not the hoof; he is unclean to you. *6* And the hare, because he chews the cud, but divides not the hoof; he is unclean to you. *7* And the swine, although he divides the hoof, and is cloven footed (split hoof), he does not chew the cud; he is unclean to you. *8* Of their flesh shall you not eat, and their carcass shall you not touch; they are unclean to you. *9* These shall you eat of all that are in the waters: whatever has fins and scales in the waters, in the seas, and in the rivers, those shall you eat. *10* And all that have no fins and scales in the seas, and in the rivers, of all that move in the waters, and of any living thing which is in the waters, they shall be forbidden to you: *11* They shall be even an abomination (disgrace) to you; you shall not eat of their flesh, but you shall have their carcasses in abomination. *12* Whatsoever has neither fins nor scales in the waters that shall be an abomination to you. *13* And these are they which you shall have in abomination among the fowls; they shall not be eaten, they are an abomination: the eagle, and the ossifrage (bearded vulture), and the ospray (large hawk), **14** And the vulture, and the kite after its kind; **15** Every raven after its kind; **16** And the owl, and the night hawk, and the cuckow (grayish bird, cuckoo), and the hawk after its kind, **17** And the little owl, and the cormorant, and the great owl, **18** And the swan, and the pelican, and the gier eagle (Egyptian vulture), **19** And the stork, the heron after its kind, and the lapwing (small dark green bird), and the bat. **20** All fowls that creep, going upon all four, shall be an abomination to you.

21 Yet these may you eat of every flying creeping thing that goes upon all four, which have legs above their feet, to leap upon the earth; **22** Even these of them you may eat; the locust after its kind, and the bald locust after its kind, and the beetle after its kind, and the grasshopper after its kind. **23** But all other flying creeping things, which have four feet, shall be an abomination to you. **24** And for these you shall be unclean: whosoever touches the carcass of them shall be unclean until the even. **25** Whoever takes away the dead body of one of them is to have his clothing washed, and will be unclean till evening. **26** The carcasses of every animal that divides the hoof, and is not cloven footed, nor chews the cud, are unclean to you: every one that touches them shall be unclean. **27** And whatsoever goes upon his paws, among all manner of animals that go on all four, those are unclean to you: whoever touches their carcass shall be unclean until the evening. **28** And he that touches the carcass of them shall wash his clothes, and be unclean until the evening: they are unclean to you. **29** These also shall be unclean to you among the creeping things that creep upon the earth; the weasel, and the mouse, and the tortoise after his kind, **30** And the ferret, and the chameleon, and the lizard, and the snail, and the mole.

31 These are unclean to you among all that creep: whosoever does touch them, when they be dead, shall be unclean until the evening. **32** And upon whatever any of them, when they are dead, does fall, it shall be unclean; whether it be any vessel of wood, or cloth, or skin, or sack, whatever vessel it be, where any work is done, it must be put into water, and it shall be unclean until the evening; so it shall be cleansed. **33** And every earthen vessel, that any of them falls, whatever is in it shall be unclean; and you shall break it. **34** Of all food, which may be eaten, that on which such water comes shall be unclean: and all drink that may be drunk in every such vessel shall be unclean. **35** And everything upon any part of their carcass falls shall be unclean; whether it be oven, or ranges for pots, they shall be broken down: for they are unclean and shall be unclean to you. **36** Nevertheless a fountain or pit, where there is plenty of water, shall be clean: but that which touches their carcass shall be unclean. **37** And if any part of their carcass falls upon any sowing seed that is to be sown, it shall be clean. **38** But if any water be put upon the seed, and any part of their carcass fall on it, it shall be unclean to you. **39** And if any animal, of which you may eat, die; he that touches the carcass shall be unclean until the evening. **40** And he that eats of the carcass shall wash his clothes, and be unclean until the evening: he also that bears the carcass shall wash his clothes, and be unclean until the evening.

41 And every creeping thing that creeps upon the earth shall be an abomination; it shall not be eaten. **42** Whatsoever goes upon the belly, and whatsoever goes upon all four, or whatsoever has more feet among all creeping things that creep upon the earth, you shall not eat; for they are an abomination. **43** You shall not make yourselves abominable with any creeping thing that creeps; neither shall you make yourselves unclean with them, that you should be defiled by them. **44** For I am **YeHoVaH** your **Elohim**: you shall therefore sanctify yourselves, and you shall be holy; for I am holy: neither shall you defile yourselves with any manner of creeping thing that creeps upon the earth. *45* For I am **YeHoVaH** that brings you up out of the land of Egypt, to be your **Elohim**: you shall therefore be holy, for I am holy. *46* This is the law (instruction) of the animals, and of the fowl, and of every living creature that moves in the waters, and of every creature that creeps upon the earth: *47* To make a difference between the unclean and the clean, and between the animal that may be eaten and the animal that may not be eaten.

Reading 26 ends

Chapter 12

Every male child is to be circumcised on the eighth day. Women who give birth shall bring offerings after her days (33) of purification.

Reading 27 begins

1 And **YeHoVaH** spoke to Moses, saying, *2* Speak to the children of Israel, saying, If a woman has conceived seed, and born a man child: then she shall be unclean seven days; according to the days of the separation for her medical condition shall she be unclean. *3* And in the eighth day the flesh of his foreskin shall be circumcised. *4* And she shall then continue in the blood of her purifying *33* days; she shall touch no hallowed thing, nor come into the sanctuary, until the days of her purifying be fulfilled. *5* But if she bear a woman child, then she shall be unclean two weeks, as in her separation: and she shall continue in the blood of her purifying 66 days. *6* And when the days of her purifying are fulfilled, for a son, or for a daughter, she shall bring a lamb of the first year for a burnt offering, and a young pigeon, or a turtledove, for a sin offering, to the door of the tabernacle of the congregation, to the priest: *7* Who shall offer it before **YeHoVaH**, and make atonement for her; and she shall be cleansed from the issue of her blood. This is the law (instruction) for her that has born a male or a female. *8* And if she be not able to bring a lamb, then she shall bring two turtles, or two young pigeons; the one for the burnt offering, and the other for a sin offering: and the priest shall make atonement for her, and she shall be clean.

Chapter 13

Anyone who has leprosy: the priest shall declare him or her unclean and they shall live outside the camp. Any leprous garment shall be burned.

1 And **YeHoVaH** spoke to Moses and Aaron, saying, *2* When a man shall have in the skin of his flesh a rising, a scab, or bright spot, and it be in the skin of his flesh like the plague of leprosy; then he shall be brought to Aaron the priest, or to one of his sons the priests: *3* And the priest shall look on the plague in the skin of the flesh: and when the hair in the plague is turned white, and the plague in sight be deeper than the skin of his flesh, it is a plague of leprosy: and the priest shall look on him, and pronounce him unclean. *4* If the bright spot be white in the skin of his flesh, and in sight be not deeper than the skin, and the hair be not turned white; then the priest shall quarantine him that has the plague seven days: *5* And the priest shall look on him the seventh day: and, behold, if the plague in his sight be at a stay, and the plague spread not in the skin; then the priest shall quarantine seven days more: *6* And the priest shall look on him again the seventh day: and, behold, if the plague be somewhat dark, and the plague spread not in the skin, the priest shall pronounce him clean: it is but a scab: and he shall wash his clothes, and be clean. *7* But if the scab spread much abroad in the skin, after that he has been seen of the priest for his cleansing, he shall be seen of the priest again. *8* And if the priest sees that, behold, the scab spreads in the skin, then the priest shall pronounce him unclean: it is a leprosy. *9* When the plague of leprosy is in a man, then he shall be brought to the priest; *10* And the priest shall see him: and, behold, if the rising be white in the skin, and it have turned the hair white, and there be quick raw flesh in the rising;

11 It is an old leprosy in the skin of his flesh, and the priest shall pronounce him unclean, and shall not quarantine him: for he is unclean. *12* And if a leprosy break out abroad in the skin, and the leprosy cover all the skin of him that has the plague from his head even to his foot, wherever the priest looks; *13* Then the priest shall consider: and, behold, if the leprosy have covered all his flesh, he shall pronounce him clean that has the plague: it is all turned white: he is clean. *14* But when raw flesh appears in him, he shall be unclean. *15* And the priest shall see the raw flesh, and pronounce him to be unclean: for the raw flesh is unclean: it is a leprosy. *16* Or if the raw flesh turn again, and be changed to white, he shall come to the priest; *17* And the priest shall see him: and, behold, if the plague be turned into white; then the priest shall pronounce him clean that has the plague: he is clean. *18* The flesh also, in which, even in the skin, was a boil, and is healed, *19* And in the place of the boil there be a white rising, or a bright spot, white, and somewhat reddish, and it be showed to the priest; *20* And if, when the priest sees it, behold, it be in sight lower than the skin, and the hair be turned white; the priest shall pronounce him unclean: it is a plague of leprosy broken out of the boil.

21 But if the priest look on it, and, behold, there be no white hairs therein, and if it be not lower than the skin, but be somewhat dark; then the priest shall quarantine him seven days: *22* And if it spread much abroad in the skin, then the priest shall pronounce him unclean: it is a plague. *23* But if the bright spot stay in his place, and spread not, it is a burning boil; and the priest shall pronounce him clean. *24* Or if there be any flesh, in the skin whereof there is a hot burning, and the quick flesh that burns have a white bright spot, somewhat reddish, or white; *25* Then the priest shall look upon it: and, behold, if the hair in the bright spot has turned white, and it is in sight deeper than the skin; it is a leprosy broken out of the burning: wherefore the priest shall pronounce him unclean: it is the plague of leprosy. *26* But if the priest look on it, and, behold, there be no white hair in the bright spot, and it be no lower than the other skin, but be somewhat dark; then the priest shall quarantine him seven days: *27* And the priest shall look upon him the seventh day: and if it be spread much abroad in the skin, then the priest shall pronounce him unclean: it is the plague of leprosy. *28* And if the bright spot stay in his place, and spread not in the skin, but it be somewhat dark; it is a rising of the burning, and the priest shall pronounce him clean: for it is an inflammation of the burning. *29* If a man or woman have a plague upon the head or the beard; *30* Then the priest shall see the plague: and, behold, if it be in sight deeper than the skin; and there be in it a yellow thin hair; then the priest shall pronounce him unclean: it is a dry *scab*, even a leprosy upon the head or beard.

31 And if the priest look on the plague of the scab, and, behold, it be not in sight deeper than the skin, and that there is no black hair in it; then the priest shall shut up him that has the plague of the scab seven days: *32* And in the seventh day the priest shall look on the plague: and, behold, if the scab spread not, and there be in it no yellow hair, and the scab be not in sight deeper than the skin; *33* He shall be shaven, but the scab shall he not shave; and the priest shall quarantine him that has the scab seven days more: *34* And in the seventh day the priest shall look on the scab: and, behold, if the scab be not spread in the skin, nor be in sight deeper than the skin; then the priest shall pronounce him clean: and he shall wash his clothes, and be clean. *35* But if the scab spread much in the skin after his cleansing; *36* Then the priest shall look on him: and, behold, if the scab be spread in the skin, the priest shall not seek for yellow hair; he is unclean. *37* But if the scab be in his sight at a stay, and that there is black hair grown up therein; the scab is healed, he is clean: and the priest shall pronounce him clean.

38 If a man also or a woman have in the skin of their flesh bright spots, even white bright spots; *39* Then the priest shall look: and, behold, if the bright spots in the skin of their flesh be darkish white; it is a freckled spot that grows in the skin; he is clean. *40* And the man whose hair is fallen off his head, he is bald; yet is he clean.

41 And he that has his hair fallen off from the part of his head toward his face, he is forehead bald: yet is he clean. *42* And if there be in the bald head, or bald forehead, a white reddish sore; it is a leprosy sprung up in his bald head, or his bald forehead. *43* Then the priest shall look upon it: and, behold, if the rising of the sore be white reddish in his bald head, or in his bald forehead, as the leprosy appears in the skin of the flesh; *44* He is a leprous man, he is unclean: the priest shall pronounce him utterly unclean; his plague is in his head. *45* And the leper in whom the plague is, his clothes shall be rent, and his head bare, and he shall put a covering upon his upper lip, and shall cry, Unclean, unclean. *46* All the days wherein the plague shall be in him he shall be defiled; he is unclean: he shall dwell alone; without the camp shall his habitation be. *47* The garment also that the plague of leprosy is in, whether it be a woolen garment, or a linen garment; *48* Whether it be in the warp, or woof; of linen, or of wool; whether in a skin, or in anything made of skin; *49* And if the plague be greenish or reddish in the garment, or in the skin, either in the warp, or in the woof, or in anything of skin; it is a plague of leprosy, and shall be shown to the priest: *50* And the priest shall look upon the plague, and quarantine he that has the plague seven days:

51 And he shall look on the plague on the seventh day: if the plague be spread in the garment, either in the warp, or in the woof, or in a skin, or in any work that is made of skin; the plague is a fretting leprosy; it is unclean. *52* He shall therefore burn that garment, whether warp or woof, in woolen or in linen, or anything of skin, wherein the plague is: for it is a fretting leprosy; it shall be burnt in the fire. *53* And if the priest shall look, and, behold, the plague be not spread in the garment, either in the warp, or in the woof, or in anything of skin; *54* Then the priest shall command that they wash the thing wherein the plague is, and he shall shut it up seven days more: *55* And the priest shall look on the plague, after that it is washed: and, behold, if the plague have not changed his color, and the plague be not spread; it is unclean; you shall burn it in the fire; it is fret inward, whether it be bare within or without. *56* And if the priest look, and, behold, the plague be somewhat dark after the washing of it; then he shall rend it out of the garment, or out of the skin, or out of the warp, or out of the woof: *57* And if it appear still in the garment, either in the warp, or in the woof, or in anything of skin; it is a spreading plague: you shall burn that wherein the plague is with fire. *58* And the garment, either warp, or woof, or whatsoever thing of skin it be, which you shall wash, if the plague be departed from them, then it shall be washed the second time, and shall be clean. *59* This is the law (instruction) of the plague of leprosy in a garment of woolen or linen, either in the warp, or woof, or anything of skins, to pronounce it clean, or to pronounce it unclean.

Reading 27 ends

Chapter 14
Anyone who is healed of leprosy shall shave their hair and bring offerings. If a house has leprosy the priest shall inspect it.

Reading 28 begins

1 And **YeHoVaH** spoke to Moses, saying, *2* This shall be the law (instruction) of the leper in the day of his cleansing: He shall be brought to the priest: *3* And the priest shall go forth out of the camp; and the priest shall look, and, behold, if the plague of leprosy be healed in the leper;

4 Then shall the priest command to take for him that is to be cleansed two birds alive and clean, and cedar wood, and scarlet, and hyssop: *5* And the priest shall command that one of the birds be killed in an earthen vessel over running water: *6* As for the living bird, he shall take it, and the cedar wood, and the scarlet, and the hyssop, and shall dip them and the living bird in the blood of the bird that was killed over the running water: *7* And he shall sprinkle upon him that is to be cleansed from the leprosy seven times, and shall pronounce him clean, and shall let the living bird loose into the open field. *8* And he who is to be made clean will have his clothing washed and his hair cut and have a bath, and he will be clean. And after that he will come back to the tent-circle; but he is to keep outside his tent for seven days. *9* But it shall be on the seventh day, that he shall shave all his hair off his head and his beard and his eyebrows, even all his hair he shall shave off: and he shall wash his clothes, also he shall wash his flesh in water, and he shall be clean. *10* And on the eighth day he shall take two he lambs without blemish, and one ewe lamb of the first year without blemish, and three tenth deals of fine flour for a meal offering, mingled with oil, and one log of oil.

11 And the priest that makes him clean shall present the man that is to be made clean, and those things, before **YeHoVaH**, at the door of the tabernacle of the congregation: *12* And the priest shall take one male lamb, and offer him for a trespass offering, and the log of oil, and wave them for a wave offering before **YeHoVaH**: *13* And he shall slay the lamb in the place where he shall kill the sin offering and the burnt offering, in the holy place: for as the sin offering is the priest's, so is the trespass offering: it is most holy: *14* And the priest shall take some of the blood of the trespass offering, and the priest shall put it upon the tip of the right ear of him that is to be cleansed, and upon the thumb of his right hand, and upon the great toe of his right foot: *15* And the priest shall take some of the log of oil, and pour it into the palm of his own left hand: *16* And the priest shall dip his right finger in the oil that is in his left hand, and shall sprinkle of the oil with his finger seven times before **YeHoVaH**: *17* And of the rest of the oil that is in his hand shall the priest put upon the tip of the right ear of him that is to be cleansed, and upon the thumb of his right hand, and upon the great toe of his right foot, upon the blood of the trespass offering: *18* And the remnant of the oil that is in the priest's hand he shall pour upon the head of him that is to be cleansed: and the priest shall make an atonement for him before **YeHoVaH**. *19* And the priest shall offer the sin offering, and make atonement for him that is to be cleansed from his uncleanness; and afterward he shall kill the burnt offering: *20* And the priest shall offer the burnt offering and the meal offering upon the altar: and the priest shall make an atonement for him, and he shall be clean.

21 And if he be poor, and cannot get so much; then he shall take one lamb for a trespass offering to be waved, to make an atonement for him, and one tenth deal of fine flour mingled with oil for a meal offering, and a log of oil; *22* And two turtledoves, or two young pigeons, such as he is able to get; and the one shall be a sin offering, and the other a burnt offering. *23* And he shall bring them on the eighth day for his cleansing to the priest, to the door of the tabernacle of the congregation, before **YeHoVaH**. *24* And the priest shall take the lamb of the trespass offering, and the log of oil, and the priest shall wave them for a wave offering before **YeHoVaH**: *25* And he shall kill the lamb of the trespass offering, and the priest shall take some of the blood of the trespass offering, and put it upon the tip of the right ear of him that is to be cleansed, and upon the thumb of his right hand, and upon the great toe of his right foot: *26* And the priest shall pour of the oil into the palm of his own left hand: *27* And the priest shall sprinkle with his right finger some of the oil that is in his left hand seven times before **YeHoVaH**: *28* And the priest shall put of the oil that is in his hand upon the tip of the right ear of him that is to be cleansed, and upon the thumb of his right hand, and upon the great toe of his right foot, upon the place of the blood of the trespass offering: **29** And the rest of the oil that is in the priest's hand he shall put upon the head of him that is to be cleansed, to make an atonement for him before *YeHoVaH*. **30** And he shall offer the one of the turtledoves, or of the young pigeons, such as he can get;

31 Even such as he is able to get, the one for a sin offering, and the other for a burnt offering, with the meal offering: and the priest shall make an atonement for him that is to be cleansed before *YeHoVaH* **32** This is the law (instruction) of him in whom is the plague of leprosy, whose hand is not able to get that which pertains to his cleansing. **33** And *YeHoVaH* spoke to Moses and to Aaron, saying, **34** When you come into the land of Canaan, which I give to you for a possession, and I put the plague of leprosy in a house of the land of your possession; *YeHoVaH* And he that owns the house shall come and tell the priest, saying, It seems to me there is a plague in the house: **36** Then the priest shall command that they empty the house, before the priest go into it to see the plague, that all that is in the house be not made unclean: and afterward the priest shall go in to see the house: **37** And he shall look on the plague, and, behold, if the plague be in the walls of the house with hollow strakes, greenish or reddish, which in sight are lower than the wall; **38** Then the priest shall go out of the house to the door of the house, and shut up the house seven days: **39** And the priest shall come again the seventh day, and shall look: and, behold, if the plague be spread in the walls of the house; **40** Then the priest shall command that they take away the stones in which the plague is, and they shall cast them into an unclean place outside the city:

41 And he shall cause the house to be scraped within all around, and they shall pour out the dust that they scrape off without the city into an unclean place: **42** And they shall take other stones, and put them in the place of those stones; and he shall take other mortar, and shall plaster the house. **43** And if the plague come again, and break out in the house, after that he has taken away the stones, and after he has scraped the house, and after it is plastered; **44** Then the priest shall come and look, and, behold, if the plague be spread in the house, it is a fretting leprosy in the house; it is unclean. **45** And he shall break down the house, the stones of it, and the timber, and all the mortar of the house; and he shall carry them forth out of the city into an unclean place. **46** Moreover he that goes into the house all the while that it is shut up shall be unclean until the evening. **47** And he that lies in the house shall wash his clothes; and he that eats in the house shall wash his clothes. **48** And if the priest shall come in, and look upon it, and, behold, the plague has not spread in the house, after the house was plastered: then the priest shall pronounce the house clean, because the plague is healed. **49** And he shall take to cleanse the house two birds, and cedar wood, and scarlet, and hyssop: **50** And he shall kill the one of the birds in an earthen vessel over running water:

51 And he shall take the cedar wood, and the hyssop, and the scarlet, and the living bird, and dip them in the blood of the slain bird, and in the running water, and sprinkle the house seven times: **52** And he shall cleanse the house with the blood of the bird, and with the running water, and with the living bird, and with the cedar wood, and with the hyssop, and with the scarlet: **53** But he shall let go the living bird out of the city into the open fields, and make an atonement for the house: and it shall be clean. **54** This is the law (instruction) for all manner of plague of leprosy, and scab, **55** And for the leprosy of a garment, and of a house, **56** And for a rising, and for a scab, and for a bright spot: **57** To teach when it is unclean, and when it is clean: this is the law (instruction) of leprosy.

LEVITICUS

Chapter 15
YeHoVaH defines when a man or women is clean or unclean.

1 And **YeHoVaH** spoke to Moses and to Aaron, saying, *2* Say to the children of Israel: If a man has an unclean flow from his flesh, it will make him unclean. *3* If the flow goes on or if the part is stopped up, to keep back the flow, he is still unclean. *4* Every bed on which he has been resting will be unclean, and everything on which he has been seated will be unclean. *5* And anyone touching his bed is to have his clothing washed and his body bathed in water and is unclean till evening. *6* And he who has been seated on anything on which the unclean man has been seated is to have his clothing washed and his body bathed in water and be unclean till evening. *7* And anyone touching the flesh of the unclean man is to have his clothing washed and his body bathed in water and will be unclean till evening. *8* And if liquid from the mouth of the unclean man comes on to him who is clean, then he is to have his clothing washed and his body bathed in water and be unclean till evening. *9* Any saddle that the person with the discharge rides on will be unclean. *10* Whoever touches anything that was under him will be unclean until evening; he who carries those things is to wash his clothes and bathe himself in water; he will be unclean until evening.

11 And whomever he touches that has the issue, and has not rinsed his hands in water, he shall wash his clothes, and bathe himself in water, and be unclean until the evening. *12* And the vessel of earth, that he touches which has the issue, shall be broken: and every vessel of wood shall be rinsed in water. *13* And when he that has an issue is cleansed of his issue; then he shall number to himself seven days for his cleansing, and wash his clothes, and bathe his flesh in running water, and shall be clean. *14* And on the eighth day he shall take to him two turtledoves, or two young pigeons, and come before **YeHoVaH** to the door of the tabernacle of the congregation, and give them to the priest: *15* And the priest shall offer them, the one for a sin offering, and the other for a burnt offering; and the priest shall make an atonement for him before **YeHoVaH** for his issue. *16* And if any man's seed of copulation go out from him, then he shall wash all his flesh in water, and be unclean until the evening. *17* And every garment, and every skin, whereon is the seed of copulation, shall be washed with water, and be unclean until the evening. *18* The woman also with whom the man shall lie with seed of copulation, they shall both bathe themselves in water, and be unclean until the evening. *19* And if a woman has a flow of blood from her body (monthly period), she will have to be kept separate for seven days, and anyone touching her will be unclean till evening. *20* And everything that she lies upon in her separation shall be unclean: everything also that she sits upon shall be unclean.

21 And whoever touches her bed shall wash his clothes, and bathe himself in water, and be unclean until the evening. *22* And whoever touches anything that she sat upon shall wash his clothes, and bathe himself in water, and be unclean until the evening. *23* And if it is on her bed, or on anything where she sits, when he touches it, he shall be unclean until the evening. *24* And if any man has relations with her so that her blood comes on him, he will be unclean for seven days and every bed on which he has been resting will be unclean. *25* And if a woman has an issue of her blood many days out of the time of her separation (monthly period), or if it run beyond the time of her separation; all the days of the issue of her uncleanness shall be as the days of her separation: she shall be unclean. *26* Every bed where she lies all the days of her issue shall be to her as the bed of her separation: and whatsoever she sits upon shall be unclean, as the uncleanness of her separation. *27* And whosoever touches those things shall be unclean, and shall wash his clothes, and bathe himself in water, and be unclean until the evening. *28* But if she be cleansed of her issue, then she shall number to herself seven days, and after that she shall be clean. *29* And on the eighth day she shall take to her two turtles, or two young pigeons, and bring them to the priest, to the door of the tabernacle of the congregation. *30* And the priest shall offer the one for a sin offering, and the other for a burnt offering; and the priest shall make atonement for her before **YeHoVaH** for the issue of her uncleanness.

31 Thus shall you separate the children of Israel from their uncleanness; that they die not in their uncleanness, when they defile my tabernacle that is among them. *32* This is the law (instruction) of him that has an issue, and of him whose seed goes from him, and is defiled therewith; *33* And for her who has a flow of blood, and for any man or woman who has an unclean flow, and for him who has sex relations with a woman when she is unclean.
   Reading 28 ends

Chapter 16

Once a year Aaron shall make atonement for the people. He shall bring one goat as a sin offering and release another as a scapegoat.
   Reading 29 begins

1 And **YeHoVaH** spoke to Moses after the death of the two sons of Aaron, when they offered strange incense before **YeHoVaH**, and died; *2* And **YeHoVaH** said to Moses, Speak to Aaron your brother, that he come not at all times into the holy place within the curtain before the mercy seat, which is upon the ark; that he die not: for I will appear in the cloud upon the mercy seat. *3* Thus shall Aaron come into the holy place: with a young steer for a sin offering, and a ram for a burnt offering. *4* He shall put on the holy linen coat, and he shall have the linen underclothes upon his flesh, and shall be girded with a linen girdle, and with the linen mitre (headdress) shall he be attired: these are holy garments; therefore shall he wash his flesh in water, and so put them on. *5* And he shall take of the congregation of the children of Israel two kids of the goats for a sin offering, and one ram for a burnt offering. *6* And Aaron shall offer his steer of the sin offering, which is for himself, and make an atonement for himself, and for his house. *7* And he shall take the two goats, and present them before **YeHoVaH** at the door of the tabernacle of the congregation. *8* And Aaron shall cast lots upon the two goats; one lot for **YeHoVaH**, and the other lot for the *scapegoat*. *9* And Aaron shall bring the goat upon which **YeHoVaH** lot fell, and offer him for a sin offering. *10* But the goat, on which the lot fell to be the scapegoat, shall be presented alive before **YeHoVaH**, to make atonement with him, and to let him go for a *scapegoat* into the wilderness.

11 And Aaron shall bring the steer of the sin offering, which is for himself, and shall make an atonement for himself, and for his house, and shall kill the steer of the sin offering: *12* And he shall take a censer full of burning coals of fire from off the altar before **YeHoVaH**, and his hands full of sweet incense beaten small, and bring it within the curtain: *13* And he shall put the incense upon the fire before **YeHoVaH**, that the cloud of the incense may cover the mercy seat that is upon the testimony, that he die not: *14* And he shall take of the blood of the steer, and sprinkle it with his finger upon the mercy seat eastward; and before the mercy seat shall he sprinkle of the blood with his finger seven times. *15* Then shall he kill the goat of the sin offering, that is for the people, and bring his blood within the curtain, and do with that blood as he did with the blood of the steer, and sprinkle it upon the mercy seat, and before the mercy seat: *16* And he shall make an atonement for the holy place, because of the uncleanness of the children of Israel, and because of their transgressions in all their sins: and so shall he do for the tabernacle of the congregation, that remains among them in the midst of their uncleanness. *17* And there shall be no man in the tabernacle of the congregation when he goes in to make an atonement in the holy place, until he come out, and have made atonement for himself, and for his household, and for all the congregation of Israel. *18* And he shall go out to the altar that is before **YeHoVaH**, and make an atonement for it; and shall take of the blood of the steer, and of the blood of the goat, and put it upon the horns of the altar all around. *19* And he shall sprinkle of the blood upon it with his finger seven times, and cleanse it, and consecrate it from the uncleanness of the children of Israel. *20* And when he has made an end of reconciling the holy place, and the tabernacle of the congregation, and the altar, he shall bring the live goat:

21 And Aaron shall lay both his hands upon the head of the live goat, and confess over him all the iniquities of the children of Israel, and all their transgressions in all their sins, putting them upon the head of the goat, and shall send him away by the hand of a fit man into the wilderness: *22* And the goat shall bear upon him all their iniquities to a land not inhabited: and he shall let go the goat in the wilderness. *23* And Aaron shall come into the tabernacle of the congregation, and shall put off the linen garments, which he put on when he went into the holy place, and shall leave them there: *24* And he shall wash his flesh with water in the holy place, and put on his garments, and come forth, and offer his burnt offering, and the burnt offering of the people, and make an atonement for himself, and for the people. *25* And the fat of the sin offering shall he burn upon the altar. *26* And he that let go the goat for the scapegoat shall wash his clothes, and bathe his flesh in water, and afterward come into the camp. *27* And the steer for the sin offering, and the goat for the sin offering, whose blood was brought in to make atonement in the holy place, shall one carry forth without the camp; and they shall burn in the fire their skins, and their flesh, and their dung. *28* And he that burns them shall wash his clothes, and bathe his flesh in water, and afterward he shall come into the camp. *29* And this shall be a statute for ever to you: that in the seventh month, on the tenth day of the month, you shall afflict your souls, and do no work at all, whether it be one of your own country, or a stranger that sojourned among you: *30* For on that day shall the priest make an atonement for you, to cleanse you, that you may be clean from all your sins before **YeHoVaH**.

31 It shall be a Sabbath of rest to you, and you shall afflict your souls, by a statute forever. *32* And the priest, whom he shall anoint, and whom he shall consecrate to minister in the priest's office in his father's stead, shall make the atonement, and shall put on the linen clothes, even the holy garments: *33* And he shall make an atonement for the holy sanctuary, and he shall make an atonement for the tabernacle of the congregation, and for the altar, and he shall make an atonement for the priests, and for all the people of the congregation. *34* And this shall be an everlasting statute to you, to make atonement for the children of Israel for all their sins once a year. And he did as **YeHoVaH** commanded Moses.

Chapter 17
Anyone who kills an animal and does not bring an offering is guilty. The life is in the blood said YeHoVaH and I have given it to make atonement.

1 And **YeHoVaH** spoke to Moses, saying, *2* Speak to Aaron, and to his sons, and to all the children of Israel, and say to them; This is the thing which **YeHoVaH** has commanded, saying, *3* What man so ever there be of the house of Israel, that kills an ox, or lamb, or goat, in the camp, or that kills it out of the camp, *4* And brings it not to the door of the tabernacle of the congregation, to offer an offering to **YeHoVaH** before the tabernacle of **YeHoVaH**; blood shall be imputed to that man; he has shed blood; and that man shall be cut off from among his people: **5** To the end that the children of Israel may bring their sacrifices, which they offer in the open field, even that they may bring them to **YeHoVaH**, to the door of the tabernacle of the congregation, to the priest, and offer them for peace offerings to **YeHoVaH**. **6** And the priest shall sprinkle the blood upon the altar of **YeHoVaH** at the door of the tabernacle of the congregation, and burn the fat for a sweet savor to **YeHoVaH**. **7** And they shall no more offer their sacrifices to devils, after which they have worshiped. This shall be a statute forever to them throughout their generations. **8** And you shall say to them, Whatsoever man there be of the house of Israel, or of the strangers which sojourn among you, that offers a burnt offering or sacrifice, **9** And brings it not to the door of the tabernacle of the congregation, to offer it to **YeHoVaH**; even that man shall be cut off from among his people. **10** And whatever man there be of the house of Israel, or of the strangers that sojourn (temporarily lives) among you, that eats any manner of blood; I will even set my face against that soul that eats blood, and will cut him off from among his people.

11 For the life of the flesh is in the blood: and I have given it to you upon the altar to make an atonement for your souls: for it is the blood that makes an atonement for the soul. **12** Therefore I said to the children of Israel, No soul of you shall eat blood, neither shall any stranger that sojourned among you eat blood. **13** And whatever man there be of the children of Israel, or of the strangers that sojourn among you, which hunts and catches any animal or fowl that may be eaten; he shall even pour out the blood, and cover it with dust. **14** For it is the life of all flesh; the blood of it is for the life: therefore I said to the children of Israel, You shall eat the blood of no manner of flesh: for the life of all flesh is the blood: whosoever eats it shall be cut off. **15** And every soul that eats that which died of itself, or that which was torn with animals, whether it be one of your own country, or a stranger, he shall both wash his clothes, and bathe himself in water, and be unclean until the evening: then shall he be clean. **16** But if he wash them not, nor bathe his flesh; then he shall bear his iniquity.

Chapter 18
Don't have sex with a relative, a woman on her period, your neighbor's wife, another man or an animal. These things are an abomination.

1 And **YeHoVaH** spoke to Moses, saying, **2** Speak to the children of Israel, and say to them, I am **YeHoVaH** your **Elohim**. **3** After the doings of the land of Egypt, wherein you dwelt, shall you not do: and after the doings of the land of Canaan, where I brought you, shall you not do: neither shall you walk in their ordinances. **4** You shall do my judgments, and keep my ordinances, to walk therein: I **YeHoVaH** am your **Elohim**. **5** You shall therefore keep my statutes, and my judgments: which if a man do, he shall live in them: I am **YeHoVaH**. **6** None of you shall approach to any that is near of kin to him, to uncover their nakedness: I am **YeHoVaH**. **7** The nakedness of your father, or the nakedness of your mother, shall you not uncover: she is your mother; you shall not uncover her nakedness. **8** The nakedness of your father's wife shall you not uncover: it is your father's nakedness. **9** The nakedness of your sister, the daughter of your father, or daughter of your mother, whether she be born at home, or born abroad, even their nakedness you shall not uncover. **10** You may not have sex relations with your son's daughter or your daughter's daughter, for they are part of yourself;

11 The nakedness of your father's wife's daughter, begotten of your father, she is your sister, you shall not uncover her nakedness. **12** You shall not uncover the nakedness of your father's sister: she is your father's near kinswoman. *13* You shall not uncover the nakedness of your mother's sister: for she is your mother's near kinswoman. *14* You shall not uncover the nakedness of your father's brother, you shall not approach to his wife: she is your aunt. *15* You shall not uncover the nakedness of your daughter-in-law: she is your son's wife; you shall not uncover her nakedness. *16* You shall not uncover the nakedness of your brother's wife: it is your brother's nakedness.*17* You shall not uncover the nakedness of a woman and her daughter, neither shall you take her son's daughter, or her daughter's daughter, to uncover her nakedness; for they are her near kinswomen: it is wickedness. *18* Neither shall you take a wife to her sister, to vex her, to uncover her nakedness, beside the other in her lifetime. *19* Also you shall not approach to a woman to uncover her nakedness, as long as she is put apart for her uncleanness. *20* Moreover you shall not lie carnally with your neighbor's wife, to defile yourself with her.

21 And you shall not let any of your seed pass through the fire to Molech, neither shall you profane the name of your *Elohim*: I am *YeHoVaH*. *22 You shall not lie with a man, as with a woman: it is an abomination*. *23* Neither shall you lie with any animal to defile yourself therewith: neither shall any woman stand before an animal to lie down there: it is confusion. *24* Defile not you yourselves in any of these things: for in all these the nations are defiled which I cast out before you: *25* And the land is defiled: therefore I do visit the iniquity upon it, and the land itself vomits out her inhabitants. *26* You shall therefore keep my statutes and my judgments, and shall not commit any of these abominations; neither any of your own nation, nor any stranger that traveled among you: *27* (For all these abominations have the men of the land done, which were before you, and the land is defiled;) *28* That the land spew not you out also, when you defile it, as it spewed out the nations that were before you. *29* For whosoever shall commit any of these abominations, even the souls that commit them shall be cut off from among their people. *30* Therefore shall you keep my ordinance, that you commit not any one of these abominable customs, which were committed before you, and that you defile not yourselves therein: I *YeHoVaH* am your *Elohim*.

Reading 29 ends

Chapter 19

YeHoVaH commands to keep His Sabbaths. Don't turn to idols. Love your neighbor as yourself. Don't mix livestock. Do no injustice.

Reading 30 begins

1 And *YeHoVaH* spoke to Moses, saying, *2* Speak to all the congregation of the children of Israel, and say to them, You shall be holy: for I *YeHoVaH* your *Elohim* am holy. *3* You shall fear every man his mother, and his father, and keep my Sabbaths: I am *YeHoVaH* your *Elohim*. *4* Turn you not to idols, nor make to yourselves molten gods: I am *YeHoVaH* your *Elohim*. *5* And if you offer a sacrifice of peace offerings to *YeHoVaH*, you shall offer it at your own will. *6* It shall be eaten the same day you offer it, and on the next day: and if any remain until the third day, it shall be burnt in the fire. *7* And if it be eaten at all on the third day, it is abominable; it shall not be accepted. *8* Therefore every one that eats it shall bear his iniquity, because he has profaned the hallowed thing of *YeHoVaH*: and that soul shall be cut off from among his people. *9* And when you reap the harvest of your land, you shall not wholly reap the corners of your field, neither shall you gather the gleanings of your harvest. *10* And you shall not glean your vineyard, neither shall you gather every grape of your vineyard; you shall leave them for the poor and stranger: I am *YeHoVaH* your *Elohim*.

11 You shall not steal, neither deal falsely, neither lie one to another. **12** And you shall not swear by my name falsely, neither shall you profane the name of your *Elohim*: I am *YeHoVaH*. **13** You shall not defraud your neighbor, neither rob him: the wages of him that is hired shall not abide with thee all night until the morning. **14** You shall not curse the deaf, nor put a stumbling block before the blind, but shall fear your *Elohim*: I am *YeHoVaH*. **15** You shall do no unrighteousness in judgment: you shall not respect the person of the poor, nor honor the person of the mighty: but in righteousness shall you judge your neighbor. **16** You shall not go up and down as a talebearer among your people: neither shall you stand against the blood of your neighbor; I am *YeHoVaH*. **17** Let there be no hate in your heart for your brother; but you may make a protest to your neighbor, so that he may be stopped from doing evil. **18** You shall not avenge, nor bear any grudge against the children of your people, but you shall *love your neighbor as yourself*: I am *YeHoVaH*. **19** " 'Keep my decrees. " 'Do not mate different kinds of animals. " 'Do not plant your field with two kinds of seed. " 'Do not wear clothing woven of two kinds of material. **20** And whosoever lies carnally with a woman, that is a bondmaid, betrothed to a husband, and not at all redeemed, nor freedom given her; she shall be a curse; they shall not be put to death, because she was not free.

21 And he shall bring his trespass offering to *YeHoVaH*, to the door of the tabernacle of the congregation, even a ram for a trespass offering. **22** And the priest shall make an atonement for him with the ram of the trespass offering before *YeHoVaH* for his sin which he has done: and the sin which he has done shall be forgiven him. **23** And when you shall come into the land, and shall have planted all manner of trees for food, then you shall count the fruit as uncircumcised: three years shall it be as uncircumcised to you: it shall not be eaten of. **24** But in the fourth year all the fruit shall be holy to praise *YeHoVaH*. **25** And in the fifth year shall you eat of the fruit, that it may yield to you the increase: I am *YeHoVaH* your *Elohim*. **26** You shall not eat anything with the blood: neither shall you use enchantment, nor observe times. **27** You shall not round the corners of your head; neither shall you mar the corners of your beard. **28** You shall not make any cuttings in your flesh for the dead, nor print any marks upon you: I am *YeHoVaH*. **29** Do not prostitute your daughter, to cause her to be a whore; lest the land fall to whoredom, and the land become full of wickedness. **30** You shall keep my Sabbaths, and reverence my sanctuary: I am *YeHoVaH*.

31 Regard not them that have familiar spirits, neither seek after wizards, to be defiled by them: I am *YeHoVaH* your *Elohim*. **32** 'Stand up in the presence of the aged, show respect for the elderly and revere your *Elohim*. I am *YeHoVaH*. **33** And if a stranger sojourn with thee in your land, you shall not vex him. **34** But the stranger that dwells with you shall be to you as one born among you, and you shall love him as yourself; for you were strangers in the land of Egypt: I am *YeHoVaH* your *Elohim*. **35** You shall do no unrighteousness in judgment, in *meteyard* (a yard, staff, or rod used as a measuring device), in weight, or in measure. **36** Just balances, just weights, a just ephah (bushel), and a just *hin* (ancient Hebrew unit of liquid measure equal to about **1.5** U.S. gallons), shall you have: I am *YeHoVaH* your *Elohim*, which brought you out of the land of Egypt. **37** Therefore shall you observe all my statutes, and all my judgments, and do them: I am *YeHoVaH*.

Chapter 20
Any man, who worships Molech, curses their parents, commits adultery or has sex with another man or animal shall be put to death.

1 And **YeHoVaH** spoke to Moses, saying, *2* Again, you shall say to the children of Israel, Whoever of the children of Israel, or of the strangers that sojourn in Israel, that gives any of his seed to Molech; he shall surely be put to death: the people of the land shall stone him with stones. *3* And I will set my face against that man, and will cut him off from among his people; because he has given of his seed to Molech, to defile my sanctuary, and to profane my holy name. *4* But if the common people choose to look the other way when someone gives their children to Molech and do not execute such a person,   *5* I will set my own face against such a person and their extended family, cutting off from their people - both the guilty party and anyone with them who faithlessly followed Molech. *6* I will also oppose anyone who resorts to dead spirits or spirits of divination and faithlessly follows those things. I will cut such an individual off from their people. *7* Sanctify yourselves therefore, and be you holy: for I am **YeHoVaH** your **Elohim**. *8* And you shall keep my statutes, and do them: I am **YeHoVaH** that sanctify you. *9* For every one that curses his father or his mother shall be surely put to death: he has cursed his father or his mother; his blood shall be upon him. *10* And the man that commits adultery with another man's wife, even he that commits adultery with his neighbor's wife, the adulterer and the adulteress shall surely be put to death.

11 And the man that lies with his father's wife has uncovered his father's nakedness: both of them shall surely be put to death; their blood shall be upon them. *12* And if a man lie with his daughter-in-law, both of them shall surely be put to death: they have created confusion; their blood shall be upon them. *13 If a man also lie with man, as he lies with a woman, both of them have committed an abomination: they shall surely be put to death; their blood shall be upon them*. *14* And if a man take a wife and her mother, it is wickedness: they shall be burnt with fire, both he and they; that there be no wickedness among you. *15* And if a man lies with an animal, he shall surely be put to death: and you shall slay the animal. *16* And if a woman approach to any animal, and lie down with, you shall kill the woman, and the animal: they shall surely be put to death; their blood shall be upon them. *17* And if a man shall take his sister, his father's daughter, or his mother's daughter, and see her nakedness, and she see his nakedness; it is a wicked thing; and they shall be cut off in the sight of their people: he has uncovered his sister's nakedness; he shall bear his iniquity. *18* If a man sleeps with a woman during her menstrual period and has sexual contact with her, he has exposed the source of her blood flow and she has uncovered the same. Both of them will be cut off from their people. *19* And you shall not uncover the nakedness of your mother's sister, nor of your father's sister: for he uncovers his near kin: they shall bear their iniquity. *20* And if a man shall lie with his uncle's wife, he has uncovered his uncle's nakedness: they shall bear their sin; they shall die childless.

21 And if a man shall take his brother's wife, it is an unclean thing: he has uncovered his brother's nakedness; they shall be childless. *22* You must keep all my rules and all my regulations, and do them so that the land I am bringing you to, where you will live, won't vomit you out. *23* And you shall not walk in the manners of the nation, which I cast out before you: for they committed all these things, and therefore I detest them. *24* But I have said to you, You shall inherit their land, and I will give it to you to possess it, a land that flows with milk and honey: I am **YeHoVaH** your **Elohim**, which have separated you from other people. *25* You shall therefore put difference between clean animals and unclean, and between unclean fowls and clean: and you shall not make your souls detestable by animal, or by fowl, or by any manner of living thing that creeps on the ground, which I have separated from you as unclean. *26* And you shall be holy to me: for I **YeHoVaH** am holy, and have severed you from other people, that you should be mine. **27** If someone, whether male or female, is an intermediate with the dead or a psychic, they must be executed. They will be stoned; their blood is on their own head.

Reading 30 ends

CHAPTERS 21-27

Chapter 21

A priest must not make himself unclean and must only marry a virgin. No descendant of Aaron with a defect may offer the offerings.

Reading 31 begins

1 *YeHoVaH* said to Moses, Say to the priests, Aaron's sons: None of you are allowed to make yourselves unclean by any dead person among your community **2** except for your closest relatives: for your mother, father, son, daughter, brother; **3** also for your unmarried sister, who is close to you because she isn't married - you may be polluted for her sake. **4** But he shall not defile himself, being a chief man among his people, to profane himself. **5** They shall not make baldness upon their head, neither shall they shave off the corner of their beard, nor make any cuttings in their flesh. **6** They shall be holy to their *Elohim*, and not profane the name of their *Elohim*: for the offerings of *YeHoVaH* made by fire, and the bread of their *Elohim*, they do offer: therefore they shall be holy. **7** Priests must not marry a woman who is immoral and defiled, nor can they marry a woman divorced from her husband, because priests must be holy to their *Elohim*. **8** You shall sanctify him therefore; for he offers the bread of your *Elohim*: he shall be holy to thee: for I *YeHoVaH*, which sanctify you, am holy. **9** If the daughter of a priest defiles herself by being immoral, she defiles her father. She must be burned with fire.. **10** And he that is the high priest among his brethren, upon whose head the anointing oil was poured, and that is consecrated to put on the garments, shall not uncover his head, nor tear his clothes;

11 Neither shall he go in to any dead body, nor defile himself for his father, or for his mother; **12** Neither shall he go out of the sanctuary, nor profane the sanctuary of his *Elohim*; for the crown of the anointing oil of his *Elohim* is upon him: I am *YeHoVaH*. **13** And he shall take a wife in her virginity. **14** A widow, or a divorced woman, or profane, or a harlot, these shall he *not* take: but he shall take a virgin of his own people to wife. **15** Neither shall he profane his seed among his people: for I *YeHoVaH* do sanctify him. **16** And *YeHoVaH* spoke to Moses, saying, **17** Speak to Aaron, saying, Whoever he be of your seed in their generations that has any blemish, let him not approach to offer the bread of his *Elohim*. **18** For whatever man he be that has a blemish, he shall not approach: a blind man, or a lame, or he that has a flat nose, or anything in excess, **19** Or a man that is has a broken foot, or broken hand, **20** anyone who is a hunchback or too small; anyone who has an eye disease, a rash, scabs, or a crushed testicle.

21 No man that has a blemish of the seed of Aaron the priest shall come near to offer the offerings of *YeHoVaH* made by fire: he that has a blemish; he shall not come near to offer the bread of his *Elohim*. **22** He shall eat the bread of his *Elohim*, both of the most holy, and of the holy. **23** Only he shall not go in to the curtain, nor come near to the altar, because he has a blemish; that he profane not my sanctuaries: for I *YeHoVaH* do sanctify them. **24** And Moses told it to Aaron, and to his sons, and to all the children of Israel.

Chapter 22
A priest shall not eat the offerings if he is unclean. No outsider shall eat the offerings. Offerings must be animals without defect.

1 And **YeHoVaH** spoke to Moses, saying, *2* Speak to Aaron and to his sons, that they separate themselves from the holy things of the children of Israel, and that they profane not my holy name in those things which they consecrate to me: I am **YeHoVaH**. *3* Say to them, Whoever he be of all your seed among your generations, that goes to the holy things, which the children of Israel consecrate to **YeHoVaH**, having his uncleanness upon him, that soul shall be cut off from my presence: I am **YeHoVaH**. *4* What man of the seed of Aaron is a leper, or has a running issue; he shall not eat of the holy things, until he be clean. And whoever touches anything that is unclean by the dead, or a man whose seed goes from him; *5* Or whosoever touches any creeping thing, whereby he may be made unclean, or a man of whom he may take uncleanness, whatever uncleanness he has; *6* The soul which has touched any such shall be unclean until evening, and shall not eat of the holy things, unless he wash his flesh with water. *7* And when the sun is down, he shall be clean, and shall afterward eat of the holy things, because it is his food. *8* That which dies of itself, or is torn with animals, he shall not eat to defile himself; I am **YeHoVaH**. *9* They shall therefore keep my ordinance, or else they bear sin for it, and die, if they profane it: I **YeHoVaH** do sanctify them. *10* There shall no stranger eat of the holy thing: a sojourner of the priest, or a hired servant, shall not eat of the holy thing.

11 But if a priest purchases a servant, that person can eat it, and servants born into the priest's household can also eat his food. *12* If the priest's daughter also were married to a stranger, she may not eat of an offering of the holy things. *13* But if the priest's daughter be a widow, or divorced, and have no child, and is returned to her father's house, as in her youth, she shall eat of her father's food: but there shall be no stranger eat of it. *14* And if a man eats of the holy thing unwittingly, then he shall add a fifth part to it, and shall give it to the priest with the holy thing. *15* And they shall not profane the holy things of the children of Israel, which they offer to **YeHoVaH**; *16* Or suffer them to bear the iniquity of trespass, when they eat their holy things: for I **YeHoVaH** do sanctify them. *17* And **YeHoVaH** spoke to Moses, saying, *18* Speak to Aaron, and to his sons, and to all the children of Israel, and say to them, Whatever he be of the house of Israel, or of the strangers in Israel, that will offer his gift for all his vows, and for all his freewill offerings, which they will offer to **YeHoVaH** for a burnt offering; *19* You shall offer at your own will a male without blemish, of the cattle, of the sheep, or of the goats. *20* But whatever has a blemish shall you not offer: for it shall not be acceptable for you.

21 And whoever offers a sacrifice of peace offerings to **YeHoVaH** to accomplish his vow, or a freewill offering in cattle or sheep, it shall be perfect to be accepted; there shall be no blemish therein. *22* Blind, or broken, or maimed, or having a *wen (a sore)*, or scurvy, or scabbed, you shall not offer these to **YeHoVaH**, nor make an offering by fire of them upon the altar to **YeHoVaH**. *23* An ox or a lamb which has more or less than its natural parts, may be given as a free offering; but it will not be taken in payment of an oath. *24* An animal which has its reproductive parts damaged or crushed or broken or cut, may not be offered to **YeHoVaH**; such a thing may not be done anywhere in your land. *25* And from one who is not an Israelite you may not take any of these for an offering to **YeHoVaH**; for they are unclean, there is a mark on them, and **YeHoVaH** will not be pleased with them. *26* And **YeHoVaH** spoke to Moses, saying, *27* When a steer, or a sheep, or a goat, is brought forth, then it shall be seven days under the dam; and from the eighth day forward it shall be accepted for an offering made by fire to

YeHoVaH. *28* And whether it is cow, or ewe, you shall not kill it and her young both in one day. *29* And when you will offer a sacrifice of thanksgiving to *YeHoVaH*, offer it at your own will. *30* On the same day it shall be eaten up; you shall leave none of it until tomorrow: I am *YeHoVaH*.

31 Therefore shall you keep my commandments, and do them: I am *YeHoVaH*. *32* Neither shall you profane my holy name; but I will be blessed among the children of Israel: I am *YeHoVaH* which consecrate you, *33* That brought you out of the land of Egypt, to be your *Elohim*: I am *YeHoVaH*.

Chapter 23
YeHoVaH proclaims feast days: Passover, Unleavened Bread, First Fruits, Fifty Days Later, the Day of Trumpets, the Day of Atonement and Booths.

1 And *YeHoVaH* spoke to Moses, saying, *2* Speak to the children of Israel, and say to them, Concerning the feasts of *YeHoVaH*, which you shall proclaim to be holy gatherings, even these are my feasts. *3* Six days shall work be done: but the *seventh* day is the Sabbath of rest, a holy gathering; you shall do no work therein: it is the Sabbath of *YeHoVaH* in all your dwellings. *4* These are the feasts of *YeHoVaH*, even holy gatherings, which you shall proclaim in their seasons. *5* In the **14**th day of the first month at evening is *YeHoVaH's* Passover. *6* And on the 15th day of the same month is the feast of unleavened bread to *YeHoVaH*: seven days you must eat unleavened bread. *7* In the first day you shall have a holy gathering: you shall do no servile work. *8* But you shall offer an offering made by fire to *YeHoVaH* seven days: in the seventh day is a holy gathering: you shall do no servile (slave like) work therein. *9* And *YeHoVaH* spoke to Moses, saying, *10* Speak to the children of Israel, and say to them, When you come into the land which I give to you, and shall reap the harvest, then you shall bring a sheaf of the *first fruits* (the earliest fruit of the season) of your harvest to the priest:

11 And he shall wave the sheaf before *YeHoVaH*, to be accepted for you: on the day after the Sabbath the priest shall wave it. *12* And you shall offer that day when you wave the sheaf a male lamb without blemish of the first year for a burnt offering to *YeHoVaH*. *13* And the meal offering shall be two tenth deals of fine flour mingled with oil, an offering made by fire to *YeHoVaH* for a sweet savor: and the drink offering shall be of wine, the fourth part of an hin (1.5 gallons). *14* And you shall eat neither bread, nor parched corn, nor green ears, until the same day that you have brought an offering to your *Elohim*: it shall be a statute *forever* throughout your generations in all your dwellings. *15* And you shall count to you from the day after the Sabbath, from the day that you brought the sheaf of the wave offering; seven Sabbaths shall be complete: *16* Even to the day after the seventh Sabbath shall you number 50 days; and you shall offer a new meal offering to *YeHoVaH*. *17* You shall bring out of your habitations two wave loaves of two tenth deals; they shall be of fine flour; they shall be baked with leaven; they are the first fruits to *YeHoVaH*. *18* And you shall offer with the bread seven lambs without blemish of the first year, and one young steer, and two rams: they shall be for a burnt offering to *YeHoVaH*, with their meal offering, and their drink offerings, even an offering made by fire, of sweet savor to *YeHoVaH*. *19* Then you shall sacrifice one kid of the goats for a sin offering, and two lambs of the first year for a sacrifice of peace offerings. *20* And the priest shall wave them with the bread of the first fruits for a *wave offering* before *YeHoVaH*, with the two lambs: they shall be holy to *YeHoVaH* for the priest.

21 And you shall proclaim on the same day, that it may be a holy gathering to you: you shall do no servile work: it shall be a statute forever in all your dwellings throughout your generations. *22* And when you reap the harvest of your land, you shall not completely clean the corners of your field when you reap, neither shall you gather any gleaning (small pieces) of your harvest: you shall leave them to the poor, and to the stranger: I am **YeHoVaH** your **Elohim**. *23* And **YeHoVaH** spoke to Moses, saying, *24* Speak to the children of Israel, saying, In the seventh month, in the first day of the month, shall you have a Sabbath, a memorial of blowing of trumpets, a holy gathering. *25* You shall do no servile work: but you shall offer an offering made by fire to **YeHoVaH**. *26* And **YeHoVaH** spoke to Moses, saying, *27* Also on the tenth day of this seventh month there shall be a day of atonement: it shall be a holy gathering to you; and you shall make miserable your souls, and offer an offering made by fire to **YeHoVaH**. *28* And you shall do no work in that day: for it is a day of atonement, to make atonement for you before **YeHoVaH** your **Elohim**. *29* For whatever soul it is that shall not be afflicted in that same day, he shall be cut off from among his people. *30* And whatever soul it is that does any work in that same day, the same soul will I destroy from among his people.

31 You shall do no manner of work: it shall be a statute *forever* throughout your generations in all your dwellings. *32* It shall be to you a Sabbath of rest, and you shall afflict your souls: in the ninth day of the month at evening, from **evening to evening**, shall you **celebrate your Sabbath**. *(Note: This is why the biblical day begins at sundown and ends at sundown the next day. So the Sabbath begins at sundown on Friday and ends at sundown on Saturday)* *33* And **YeHoVaH** spoke to Moses, saying, *34* Speak to the children of Israel, saying, The **15**th day of this seventh month shall be the feast of tabernacles for seven days to **YeHoVaH**. *35* On the first day shall be a holy gathering: you shall do no servile work. *36* Seven days you shall offer an offering made by fire to **YeHoVaH**: on the eighth day shall be a holy gathering to you; and you shall offer an offering made by fire to **YeHoVaH**: it is a solemn assembly; and you shall do no servile work. *37* These are the feasts of **YeHoVaH**, which you shall proclaim to be holy gatherings, to offer an offering made by fire to **YeHoVaH**, a burnt offering, and a meal offering, a sacrifice, and drink offerings, everything upon his day: *38* Beside the Sabbaths of **YeHoVaH**, and beside your gifts, and beside all your vows, and beside all your freewill offerings, which you give to **YeHoVaH**. *39* Also in the **15**th day of the seventh month, when you have gathered in the fruit of the land, you shall keep a feast to **YeHoVaH** seven days: on the first day shall be a Sabbath, and on the eighth day shall be a Sabbath. *40* And you shall take you on the first day the boughs (larger branch of a tree) of goodly trees, branches of palm trees, and the boughs of thick trees, and willows of the brook; and you shall rejoice before **YeHoVaH** your **Elohim** seven days.

41 And you shall keep it a feast to **YeHoVaH** seven days in the year. It shall be a statute *forever* in your generations: you shall celebrate it in the seventh month. *42* You shall dwell in booths seven days; all that are Israelites born shall dwell in booths: *43* That your generations may know that I made the children of Israel to dwell in booths, when I brought them out of the land of Egypt: I am **YeHoVaH** your **Elohim**. *44* And Moses declared to the children of Israel the feasts of **YeHoVaH**.

Chapter 24
Aaron the priest is to tend the lamps (menorah) and set out the bread before YeHoVaH. An Israelite blasphemed so they took him outside and stoned him.

LEVITICUS

1 And **YeHoVaH** spoke to Moses, saying, *2* Command the children of Israel that they bring to thee pure oil olive beaten for the light, to cause the lamps to burn continually. *3* Without the veil of the testimony, in the tabernacle of the congregation, shall Aaron order it from the evening to the morning before **YeHoVaH** continually: it shall be a statute forever in your generations. *4* He shall order the lamps upon the pure candlestick before **YeHoVaH** continually. *5* And you shall take fine flour, and bake twelve cakes: two tenth deals shall be in one cake. *6* And you shall set them in two rows, six on a row, upon the pure table before **YeHoVaH**. *7* And you shall put pure frankincense upon each row that it may be on the bread for a memorial, even an offering made by fire to **YeHoVaH**. *8* Every Sabbath he shall set it in order before **YeHoVaH** continually, being taken from the children of Israel by an everlasting covenant. *9* And it shall be Aaron's and his sons'; and they shall eat it in the holy place: for it is most holy to him of the offerings of **YeHoVaH** made by fire by a perpetual statute. *10* And the son of an Israelite woman, whose father was an Egyptian, went out among the children of Israel: and this son of the Israelite woman and a man of Israel strove together in the camp;

11 And the Israelite woman's son blasphemed the name of **YeHoVaH**, and cursed. And they brought him to Moses: (and his mother's name was Shelomith, the daughter of Dibri, of the tribe of Dan:) *12* And they put him in ward, that the mind of **YeHoVaH** might be shown them. *13* And **YeHoVaH** spoke to Moses, saying, *14* Bring forth him that has cursed outside the camp; and let all that heard him lay their hands upon his head, and let all the congregation stone him. *15* And you shall speak to the children of Israel, saying, Whoever curses his **Elohim** shall bear his sin. *16* And he that blasphemed the name of **YeHoVaH**, he shall surely be put to death, and all the congregation shall certainly stone him: as well the stranger, as he that is born in the land, when he blasphemed the name of **YeHoVaH**, shall be put to death. *17* And he that kills any man shall surely be put to death. *18* And he that kills an animal shall make it good; animal for animal. *19* And if a man cause a blemish in his neighbor; as he has done, so shall it be done to him; *20* Breach for breach, eye for eye, tooth for tooth: as he has caused a blemish in a man, so shall it be done to him again.

21 And he that kills an animal, he shall restore it: and he that kills a man, he shall be put to death. *22* You shall have *one manner of* law (instruction), as well for the stranger, as for one of your own country: for I am **YeHoVaH** your **Elohim**. *23* And Moses spoke to the children of Israel that they should bring forth him that had cursed outside the camp, and stone him with stones. And the children of Israel did as **YeHoVaH** commanded Moses.
Reading 31 ends

Chapter 25
The land shall rest every seventh year. Every 50th year there shall be a jubilee, when property shall be restored to their owners and slaves released from bondage.
Reading 32 begins
1 And **YeHoVaH** spoke to Moses in mount Sinai, saying, *2* Speak to the children of Israel, and say to them, When you come into the land which I give you, then shall the land keep a Sabbath to **YeHoVaH**. *3* Six years you shall sow your field, and six years you shall prune your vineyard, and gather in the fruit; *4* But in the seventh year shall be a Sabbath of rest to the land, a Sabbath for **YeHoVaH**: you shall neither sow your field, nor prune your vineyard. *5* That which grows of its own accord of your harvest you shall not reap, neither gather the grapes of your vine undressed: for it is a year of rest to the land. *6* And the Sabbath of the land shall be food for you; for thee, and for your servant, and for your maid, and for your hired servant, and for

your stranger that sojourned with thee. *7* And for your cattle, and for the animal that are in your land, shall all the increase be food. *8* And you shall number seven Sabbaths of years to thee, seven times seven years; and the space of the seven Sabbaths of years shall be to thee 49 years. *9* Then shall you cause the trumpet of the jubilee to sound on the tenth day of the seventh month, in the Day of Atonement shall you make the trumpet sound throughout all your land. *10* And you shall consecrate the 50th year, and proclaim liberty throughout all the land to all the inhabitants: it shall be a jubilee to you; and you shall return every man to his possession, and you shall return every man to his family.

11 Let this 50th year be the Jubilee: no seed may be planted, and that which comes to growth of itself may not be cut, and the grapes may not be taken from the uncared-for vines. *12* For it is the jubilee; it shall be holy to you: you shall eat the increase out of the field. *13* In the year of this jubilee you shall return every man to his possession. *14* And in the business of trading goods for money, do no wrong to one another. *15* Let your exchange of goods with your neighbors have relation to the number of years after the year of Jubilee, and the number of times the earth has given her produce. *16* If the number of years is great, the price will be increased, and if the number of years is small, the price will be less, for it is the produce of a certain number of years which the man is giving you. *17* And do no wrong, one to another, but let the fear of **YeHoVaH** be before you; for I am **YeHoVaH** your **Elohim**. *18* So keep my rules and my decisions and do them, and you will be safe in your land. *19* And the land will give her fruit, and you will have food in full measure and be safe in the land. *20* And if you shall say, What shall we eat the seventh year? Behold, we shall not sow, nor gather in our increase:

21 Then I will command my blessing upon you in the sixth year, and it shall bring forth fruit for three years. *22* And you shall sow the eighth year, and eat yet of old fruit until the ninth year; until her fruits come in you shall eat of the old store. *23* The land shall not be sold forever: for the land is mine, for you are strangers and sojourners with me. *24* And in all the land of your possession you shall grant redemption for the land. *25* If your brother becomes poor, and has to give up some of his land for money, his nearest relation may come and get back that which his brother has given up. *26* And if the man have none to redeem it, and himself be able to redeem it; *27* Then let him count the years of the sale, and restore the overage to the man to whom he sold it; that he may return to his possession. *28* But if he be not able to restore it to him, then that which is sold shall remain in the hand of him that has bought it until the year of jubilee: and in the jubilee it shall go out, and he shall return to his possession. *29* And if a man sells a dwelling house in a walled city, then he may redeem it within a whole year after it is sold; within a full year may he redeem it. *30* And if he does not get it back by the end of the year, then the house in the town will become the property of him who gave the money for it, and of his children forever; it will not go from him in the year of Jubilee.

31 But the houses of the villages that have no wall round about them shall be counted as the fields of the country: they may be redeemed, and they shall go out in the jubilee. *32* Notwithstanding the cities of the Levites, and the houses of the cities of their possession, may the Levites redeem at any time. *33* And if a man purchase of the Levites, then the house that was sold, and the city of his possession, shall go out in the year of jubilee: for the houses of the cities of the Levites are their possession among the children of Israel. *34* But the field of the suburbs of their cities may not be sold; for it is their perpetual possession. *35* And if your brother becomes poor and is not able to make a living, then you are to keep him with you, helping him as you would a man from another country who is living among you. *36* Take no

LEVITICUS

interest from him, in money or in goods, but have the fear of your **Elohim** before you, and let your brother make a living among you. **37** Do not take interest on the money that you let him have or on the food that you give him. **38** I am **YeHoVaH** your **Elohim**, which brought you forth out of the land of Egypt, to give you the land of Canaan, and to be your **Elohim**. **39** And if your brother that dwells by thee be continuously poor, and be sold to thee; you shall not compel him to serve as a bondservant: **40** But as a hired servant, and as a sojourner, he shall be with thee, and shall serve thee to the year of jubilee.

41 And then shall he depart from thee, both he and his children with him, and shall return to his own family, and to the possession of his fathers shall he return. **42** For they are my servants, which I brought forth out of the land of Egypt: they shall not be sold as bondmen. **43** You shall not rule over him with rigor; but shall fear **YeHoVaH** your **Elohim**. **44** Both your bondmen, and your bondmaids, which you shall have, shall be of the heathen (does not believe in god) that are all around you; of them shall you buy bondmen and bondmaids. **45** Moreover of the children of the strangers that do sojourn among you, of them shall you buy, and of their families that are with you, which they begat in your land: and they shall be your possession. **46** And you shall take them as an inheritance for your children after you, to inherit them for a possession; they shall be your bondmen forever: but over your brethren the children of Israel, you shall not rule one over another with rigor. **47** If an immigrant or foreign guest prospers financially among you, but your fellow Israelite faces financial difficulty and so sells themselves to the immigrant or foreign guest, or to a descendant of a foreigner, **48** After that he is sold he may be redeemed again; one of his brethren may redeem him: **49** Either his uncle, or his uncle's son, may redeem him, or any that is next of kin to him of his family may redeem him; or if he be able, he may redeem himself. **50** And he shall reckon with him that bought him from the year that he was sold to him to the year of jubilee: and the price of his sale shall be according to the number of years, according to the time of an hired servant shall it be with him.

51 If there be yet many years behind, according to them he shall give again the price of his redemption out of the money that he was bought for. **52** And if there remain but few years to the year of jubilee, then he shall count with him, and according to his years shall he give him again the price of his redemption. **53** And as a yearly hired servant shall he be with him: and the other shall not rule with rigor over him in your sight. **54** And if he be not redeemed in these years, then he shall go out in the year of jubilee, both he, and his children with him. **55** For to me the children of Israel are servants; they are my servants whom I brought forth out of the land of Egypt: I am **YeHoVaH** your **Elohim**.

Chapter 26
YeHoVaH says to keep His law (instructions) and He will give peace in the land and make you fruitful. If not He will scatter you, but He will not break His covenant.

1 You shall not make idols nor graven images, neither rear you up a standing image, neither shall you set up any image of stone in your land, to bow down to it: for I am **YeHoVaH** your **Elohim**. **2** You shall keep my Sabbaths, and reverence my sanctuary: Mine, **YeHoVaH**.
   Reading 32 ends

   Reading 33 begins
3 If you walk in my statutes, and keep my commandments, and do them; **4** Then I will give you rain in due season, and the land shall yield her increase, and the trees of the field shall yield

their fruit. **5** And your threshing shall reach to the vintage, and the vintage shall reach to the sowing time: and you shall eat your bread to the full, and dwell in your land safely. **6** And I will give peace in the land, and you shall lie down, and none shall make you afraid: and I will rid evil animals out of the land, neither shall the sword go through your land. **7** And you shall chase your enemies, and they shall fall before you by the sword. **8** And five of you shall chase 100, and 100 of you shall put 10,000 to flight: and your enemies shall fall before you by the sword. **9** For I will have respect to you, and make you fruitful, and multiply you, and establish my covenant with you. **10** And you shall eat old store, and bring forth the old because of the new.

11 And I set my tabernacle among you: and my soul shall not detest you. **12** And I will walk among you, and will be your **Elohim**, and you shall be my people. **13** I am **YeHoVaH** your **Elohim**, which brought you forth out of the land of Egypt, that you should not be their bondmen; and I have broken the bands of your yoke, and made you go upright. **14** But if you will not listen to me, and will not do all these commandments; **15** And if you shall despise my statutes, or if your soul detest my judgments, so that you will not do all my commandments, but that you break my covenant: **16** I also will do this to you; I will even appoint over you terror, consumption, and the burning fever, that shall consume the eyes, and cause sorrow of heart: and you shall sow your seed in vain, for your enemies shall eat it. **17** And I will set my face against you, and you shall be slain before your enemies: they that hate you shall reign over you; and you shall flee when none pursues you. **18** And if you will not yet listen to me, then I will punish you seven times more for your sins. **19** And I will break the pride of your power; and I will make your heaven as iron, and your earth as brass: **20** And your strength shall be spent in vain: for your land shall not yield her increase, neither shall the trees of the land yield their fruits.

21 And if you walk contrary to me, and will not listen to me; I will bring seven times more plagues upon you according to your sins. **22** I will also send wild animals among you, which shall rob you of your children, and destroy your cattle, and make you few in number; and your roads shall be desolate. **23** And if you will not be reformed by me by these things, but will walk contrary to me; **24** Then will I also walk contrary to you, and will punish you yet seven times for your sins. **25** And I will bring a sword upon you, that shall avenge the quarrel of my covenant: and when you are gathered together within your cities, I will send the pestilence among you; and you shall be delivered into the hand of the enemy. **26** And when I have broken the staff of your bread, ten women shall bake your bread in one oven, and they shall deliver you your bread again by weight: and you shall eat, and not be satisfied. **27** And if you will not for all this listen to me, but walk contrary to me; **28** Then I will walk contrary to you also in fury; and I, even I, will chastise you seven times for your sins. **29** And you shall eat the flesh of your sons, and the flesh of your daughters shall you eat. **30** And I will destroy your high places, and cut down your images, and cast your carcass upon the carcass of your idols, and my soul shall detest you.

31 And I will make your cities waste, and bring your sanctuaries to misery, and I will not smell the savor of your sweet odors. **32** And I will bring the land into misery: and your enemies that dwell there shall be astonished at it. **33** And I will scatter you among the heathens (godless), and will draw out a sword after you: and your land shall be desolate, and your cities waste. **34** Then shall the land enjoy her Sabbaths, as long as it lies desolate, and you are in your enemies' land; even then shall the land rest, and enjoy her Sabbaths. **35** As long as it lies desolate it shall rest; because it did not rest in your Sabbaths, when you dwelt upon it. **36** And upon them that are left alive of you I will send faintness into their hearts in the lands of their enemies; and the sound of a shaken leaf shall chase them; and they shall flee, as fleeing from a sword; and they shall fall when none pursues. **37** And they shall fall one upon another, as it were before a sword, when none pursues: and you shall have no power to stand before your enemies. **38** And you shall perish among the heathens, and the land of your enemies shall eat you up. **39** And they that are left of you shall pine away in their iniquity in your enemies' lands; and also in the iniquities of their fathers shall they pine away with them. **40** If they shall confess their iniquity, and the iniquity of their fathers, with their trespass which they trespassed against me, and that also they have walked contrary to me;

41 And that I also have walked contrary to them, and have brought them into the land of their enemies; if then their uncircumcised hearts be humbled, and they then accept of the punishment of their iniquity: **42** Then will I remember my covenant with Jacob, and also my covenant with Isaac, and also my covenant with Abraham will I remember; and I will remember the land. **43** The land also shall be left of them, and shall enjoy her Sabbaths, while she lies desolate with them: and they shall accept of the punishment of their iniquity: because, even because they despised my judgments, and because their soul detested my statutes. **44** And yet for all that, when they be in the land of their enemies, I will not cast them away, neither will I abhor them, to destroy them utterly, and to break my covenant with them: for I am **YeHoVaH** their **Elohim**. **45** But I will for their sakes remember the covenant of their ancestors, whom I brought forth out of the land of Egypt in the sight of the heathen, that I might be their **Elohim**: I am **YeHoVaH**. **46** These are the statutes and judgments and laws (instructions), which **YeHoVaH** made between him and the children of Israel in Mount Sinai by the hand of Moses.

Chapter 27

Anyone who dedicates a person or land to YeHoVaH shall make a valuation. A tithe of everything from the land belongs to YeHoVaH.

1 And **YeHoVaH** spoke to Moses, saying, **2** Speak to the Israelites and say to them: When a person makes a solemn promise to **YeHoVaH** involving the value of a person. **3** And your estimation shall be of the male from 20 years old to 60 years old; your estimation shall be 50 shekels of silver, after the shekel of the sanctuary. **4** And if it is a female, then your estimation shall be 30 shekels. **5** And if it is from 5 years to 20 years old, then your estimation shall be of the male 20 shekels, and for the female 10 shekels. **6** And if it is from a month old to five years old, then your estimation shall be of the male **5** shekels of silver, and for the female your estimation shall be **3** shekels of silver. **7** And if it be from 60 years old and above; if it be a male, then your estimation shall be 15 shekels, and for the female 10 shekels. **8** But if he is poorer than your estimation, then he shall present himself before the priest, and the priest shall value him; according to his ability that vowed shall the priest value him. **9** And if it is an animal, whereof men bring an offering to **YeHoVaH**, all that any man gives of such to **YeHoVaH** shall be holy. **10** He shall not alter it, nor change it, a good for a bad, or a bad for a good: and if he shall at all change animal for animal, then it and the exchange shall be holy.

11 And if it be any unclean animal, of which they do not offer a sacrifice to **YeHoVaH**, then he shall present the animal before the priest: **12** And the priest shall value it, whether it be good or bad: as you value it, who is the priest, so shall it be. **13** But if he will at all redeem it, then he shall add a fifth part to your estimation. **14** And when a man shall sanctify his house to be holy to **YeHoVaH**, then the priest shall estimate it, whether it be good or bad: as the priest shall estimate it, so shall it stand. **15** And if he that sanctified it will redeem his house, then he shall add the fifth part of the money of your estimation to it, and it shall be his. *16* And if a man shall sanctify to *YeHoVaH* some part of a field of his possession, then your estimation shall be according to the seed: an homer of barley seed shall be valued at 50 shekels of silver. *17* If he sanctifies his field from the year of jubilee, according to your estimation it shall stand. *18* But if he sanctifies his field after the jubilee, then the priest shall reckon to him the money according to the years that remain, even to the year of the jubilee, and it shall be abated from your estimation. *19* And if he that sanctified the field will in any wise redeem it, then he shall add the fifth part of the money of your estimation to it, and it shall be assured to him. *20* And if he will not redeem the field, or if he has sold the field to another man, it shall not be redeemed any more.

21 But the field, when it goes out in the jubilee, shall be holy to *YeHoVaH*, as a field devoted; the possession shall be the priest's. *22* And if a man sanctify to *YeHoVaH* a field which he has bought, which is not of the fields of his possession; *23* Then the priest shall reckon to him the worth of your estimation, even to the year of the jubilee: and he shall give your estimation in that day, as a holy thing to *YeHoVaH*. *24* In the year of the jubilee the field shall return to him of whom it was bought, even to him to whom the possession of the land did belong. *25* And all your estimations shall be according to the shekel of the sanctuary: 20 gerahs shall be the shekel. *26* Only the firstling of the animals, which should be *YeHoVaH's* firstling, no man shall sanctify it; whether it be ox, or sheep: it is *YeHoVaH's*. And if it be of an unclean animal, then he shall redeem it according to your estimation, and shall add a fifth part of it thereto: or if it be not redeemed, then it shall be sold according to your estimation. *28* Notwithstanding no devoted thing, that a man shall devote to *YeHoVaH* of all that he has, both of man and animal, and of the field of his possession, shall be sold or redeemed: every devoted thing is most holy to *YeHoVaH*. *29* None devoted, which shall be devoted of men, shall be redeemed; but shall surely be put to death. *30* And all the tithe of the land, whether of the seed of the land, or of the fruit of the tree, is *YeHoVaH's*: it is holy to *YeHoVaH*.

31 If someone wants to redeem any of his tenth, he must add to it one-fifth. *32* And concerning the tithe of the herd, or of the flock, even of whatever passes under the rod, the tenth shall be holy to *YeHoVaH*. *33* He shall not search whether it be good or bad, neither shall he change it: and if he change it at all, then both it and the change shall be holy; it shall not be redeemed. *34* These are the commandments, which *YeHoVaH* commanded Moses for the children of Israel in Mount Sinai.
   Reading 33 ends

Thus Ends the Book of Leviticus   Praise *YeHoVaH*

True Name Torah Version

~NUMBERS~

Genesis, Exodus, Leviticus, Numbers, Deuteronomy

The 4th Book of Moses

Numbers in Hebrew is Bamidbar (ba-midBAR) which means "In the desert," details the travels, battles and struggles of the Jews during their 50-year sojourn in the desert after the Exodus. It records a census of the tribes, the positioning of each tribe when they camped and traveled Korach's rebellion, and the events surrounding sending the spies to Israel. Numbers ends with the capture of the East Bank of the Jordan River and the subsequent settlement there of the tribes of Reuben and Gad.

READINGS FOR NUMBERS

The name in (parentheses) is the Hebrew name for that week. For example: Week 34 'In the desert' in Hebrew is 'Bamidbar'.

Reading 34 "In the Desert" (Bamidbar) Numbers **1:1 - 4:20**
YeHoVaH tells Moses to conduct a census of all the Israelite men over the age of 20. Moses takes up a second census to count all of the Levite men. *YeHoVaH* gives specific instructions to the Levites about their roles in the Tent of Meeting.

Reading 35 "Elevate" (Nasso) Numbers **4:21 - 7:89**
YeHoVaH describes the service of the Gershon family of Levites. The laws relating to the suspected adulteress and the nazirite are given. *YeHoVaH* tells Moses and Aaron the priestly blessing. The heads of tribes bring gifts to the Tabernacle.

Reading 36 "When You Raise (the Lamps)" (Beha'alotcha) Numbers **8:1 - 12:16**
The Israelites receive instructions regarding Passover. They journey forth from Sinai and complain to *YeHoVaH* on several occasions, provoking *Elohim*'s anger. Miriam and Aaron speak against Moses.

Reading 37 "Send" (Sh'lach) Numbers **13:1 - 15:51**
Moses sends **12** spies to explore the Land of Israel. Ten of them convince the people that it will be too difficult to conquer the land. *YeHoVaH* responds to their lack of confidence by punishing them with 50 years of wandering in the wilderness. *YeHoVaH* commands the Israelites to put fringes on the ends of their clothing.

Reading 38 "Korach" (Korach) Numbers **16:1 - 18:32**
Korach and his followers accuse Moses and Aaron of taking power and prestige for themselves at the expense of the community. Moses defends himself against the rebels by saying that *YeHoVaH* will make His presence known by how He kills these rebels. Then *YeHoVaH* opens the ground and swallows Korach and his followers.

Reading 39 "Law Of" (Chukat) Numbers **19:1 - 22:1**
YeHoVaH instructs Moses and Aaron regarding the red heifer. Miriam, who is the sister of Moses and Aaron, dies. Moses hits a rock to bring forth water rather than speaking to it. At the end of the portion, Aaron dies.

Reading 40 "Balak" (Balak) Numbers **22:2 - 25:9**
Balak, the king of Moab, asks Balaam to curse the Israelites after he sees them defeat various nations in battle. Balaam's donkey sees an angel of *YeHoVaH* and refuses to move any further. Balaam hits the donkey. *YeHoVaH* speaks through the mouth of the donkey to tell him not to curse the Israelites. Instead of cursing the Israelites, Balaam blesses them.

Reading 41 "Pinchas" (Pinchas) Numbers **25:10 - 30:1**
YeHoVaH gives Phinehas a covenant of peace. *YeHoVaH* explains the apportionment of the Land of Israel. The daughters of Zelophehad petition to inherit their father's portion. Moses appoints Joshua as his successor.

Reading 42 "Tribes" (Matot)   Numbers **30:2 - 32:52**
Moses describes the laws of oaths. The Israelites battle the Midianites. The tribes of Reuben and Gad request to dwell outside of the Land of Israel.

Reading 43 "Journeys Of" (Masei) Numbers **33:1 - 36:13**
The year is 2488 and the 40 years in the desert are drawing to a close. Miriam and Aaron have passed on, and Joshua has been appointed as the successor. In these last two portions of Numbers, (Mattoth – Massey), YeHoVaH begins to wrap things up.

-End Torah Readings for Numbers-

CHAPTERS 1- 10

Chapter 1

YeHoVaH tells Moses to count the Israelite armies. The number of men over 20 years old was 603,550. The Levites were not included in the count.

Reading 34 begins

1 And **YeHoVaH** spoke to Moses in the wilderness of Sinai, in the tabernacle of the congregation, on the first day of the second month, in the second year after they came out of the land of Egypt, saying, 2 Take you the sum (census) of all the congregation of the children of Israel, after their families, by the house of their fathers, with the number of names, every male head by head; 3 From 20 years old and upward, all that are able to go forth to war in Israel: you and Aaron shall number them by their armies. 4 And with you there shall be a man of every tribe; every one head of the house of his fathers. 5 And these are the names of the men that shall stand with you: of the tribe of Reuben; Elizur the son of Shedeur. 6 Of Simeon; Shelumiel the son of Zurishaddai. 7 Of Judah; Nahshon the son of Amminadab. 8 Of Issachar; Nethaneel the son of Zuar. 9 Of Zebulun; Eliab the son of Helon. 10 Of the children of Joseph: of Ephraim; Elishama the son of Ammihud: of Manasseh; Gamaliel the son of Pedahzur.

11 Of Benjamin; Abidan the son of Gideoni. 12 Of Dan; Ahiezer the son of Ammishaddai. 13 Of Asher; Pagiel the son of Ocran. 14 Of Gad; Eliasaph the son of Deuel. 15 Of Naphtali; Ahira the son of Enan. 16 These were the renowned of the congregation, princes of the tribes of their fathers, heads of thousands in Israel. 17 And Moses and Aaron took these men which are expressed by their names: 18 And they assembled all the congregation together on the first day of the second month, and they declared their ancestry after their families, by the house of their fathers, according to the number of the names, from 20 years old and upward, head by head. 19 As **YeHoVaH** commanded Moses, so he numbered them in the wilderness of Sinai. 20 And the children of Reuben, Israel's eldest son, by their generations, after their families, by the house of their fathers, according to the number of the names, every male from 20 years old and upward, all that were able to go forth to war;

21 Those that were numbered, of the tribe of Reuben, were 56,500. 22 Of the children of Simeon, by their generations, after their families, by the house of their fathers, those that were numbered, according to the number of the names, every male from 20 years old and upward, all that were able to go forth to war; 23 Those that were numbered of the tribe of Simeon, were 59,300. 24 Of the children of Gad, by their generations, after their families, by the house of their fathers, according to the number of the names, from 20 years old and upward, all that were able to go forth to war; 25 Those that were numbered of the tribe of Gad, were 55,650. 26 Of the children of Judah, by their generations, after their families, by the house of their fathers, according to the number of the names, from 20 years old and upward, all that were able to go forth to war; 27 Those that were numbered of the tribe of Judah, were 75,600 28 Of the children of Issachar, by their generations, after their families, by the house of their fathers, according to the number of the names, from 20 years old and upward, all that were able to go forth to war; 29 Those that were numbered of the tribe of Issachar, were 55,500. 30 Of the children of Zebulun, by their generations, after their families, by the house of their fathers, according to the number of the names, from 20 years old and upward, all that were able to go forth to war;

31 Those that were numbered of the tribe of Zebulun, were 57,500. *32* Of the children of Joseph, namely, of the children of Ephraim, by their generations, after their families, by the house of their fathers, according to the number of the names, from 20 years old and upward, all that were able to go forth to war; *33* Those that were numbered of the tribe of Ephraim, were 50,500. *34* Of the children of Manasseh, by their generations, after their families, by the house of their fathers, according to the number of the names, from 20 years old and upward, all that were able to go forth to war; *35* Those that were numbered of the tribe of Manasseh, were 32,200. *36* Of the children of Benjamin, by their generations, after their families, by the house of their fathers, according to the number of the names, from 20 years old and upward, all that were able to go forth to war; *37* Those that were numbered of the tribe of Benjamin, were 35,500. *38* Of the children of Dan, by their generations, after their families, by the house of their fathers, according to the number of the names, from 20 years old and upward, all that were able to go forth to war; *39* Those that were numbered of the tribe of Dan, were 62,700. *40* Of the children of Asher, by their generations, after their families, by the house of their fathers, according to the number of the names, from 20 years old and upward, all that were able to go forth to war;

41 Those that were numbered of the tribe of Asher, were 51,500. *42* Of the children of Naphtali, throughout their generations, after their families, by the house of their fathers, according to the number of the names, from 20 years old and upward, all that were able to go forth to war; *43* Those that were numbered of the tribe of Naphtali, were 53,500. *44* These are those that were numbered, which Moses and Aaron numbered, and the princes of Israel, being *12* men: each one was for the house of his fathers. *45* So were all those that were numbered of the children of Israel, by the house of their fathers, from 20 years old and upward, all that were able to go forth to war in Israel; *46* Even all they that were numbered were 603,550. *47* But the Levites after the tribe of their fathers were *not numbered* among them. *48* For **YeHoVaH** had spoken to Moses, saying, *49* Only you shall *not* number the tribe of Levi, neither take the sum of them among the children of Israel: *50* But you shall appoint the Levites over the tabernacle of testimony, and over all the vessels thereof, and over all things that belong to it: they shall bear the tabernacle, and all the vessels thereof; and they shall minister to it, and shall encamp round about the tabernacle.

51 And when the tabernacle goes forward, the Levites shall take it down: and when the tabernacle is to be pitched, the Levites shall set it up: and the stranger (non-Levite) that comes near shall be put to death. *52* And the children of Israel shall pitch their tents, every man by his own camp, and every man by his own banner (tribe), throughout their divisions. *53* But the Levites shall pitch round about the tabernacle of testimony, so there be no wrath upon the congregation of the children of Israel: and the Levites shall keep the charge of the tabernacle of testimony. *54* And the children of Israel did according to all that **YeHoVaH** commanded Moses, so did they.

Chapter 2
The Israelites were to camp around the tabernacle: Judah to the east, Reuben to the south, Ephraim to the west and Dan to the north.

1 And **YeHoVaH** spoke to Moses and Aaron, saying, *2* The children of Israel are to put up their tents in the order of their families, by the flags of their fathers' houses, facing the Tent of meeting on every side. **3** And on the east side toward the rising of the sun shall they of the camp of Judah pitch throughout their armies: and Nahshon the son of Amminadab shall be captain of the children of Judah. **4** And his army, and those numbered were 75,600. **5** And those that do pitch next to him shall be the tribe of Issachar: and Nethaneel the son of Zuar shall be captain of the children of Issachar. **6** And his army, and those numbered there, were 55,500. **7** Then the tribe of Zebulun: and Eliab the son of Helon shall be captain of the children of Zebulun. **8** And his army, and those that were numbered there, were 57,500. **9** All that were numbered in the camp of Judah were 186,500, throughout their armies. These shall first set forth. **10** On the south side shall be the standard of the camp of Reuben according to their army: and the captain of the children of Reuben shall be Elizur the son of Shedeur.

11 And his host, and those that were numbered there, were 56,500. **12** And those which pitch by him shall be the tribe of Simeon: and the captain of the children of Simeon shall be Shelumiel the son of Zurishaddai. **13** And his army, and those that were numbered were 59,300. **14** Then the tribe of Gad: and the captain of the sons of Gad shall be Eliasaph the son of Reuel. **15** And his army, and those that were numbered were 55,650. **16** All that were numbered in the camp of Reuben were 151,550, throughout their army. And they shall set forth in the second rank. **17** Then the tabernacle of the congregation shall set forward with the camp of the Levites in the midst of the camp: as they encamp, so shall they set forward, every man in his place by their banners. **18** On the west side shall be the banner of the camp of Ephraim according to their army: and the captain of the sons of Ephraim shall be Elishama the son of Ammihud. **19** And his army, and those that were numbered were 50,500. **20** And by him shall be the tribe of Manasseh: and the captain of the children of Manasseh shall be Gamaliel the son of Pedahzur.

21 And his host, and those that were numbered were 32,200. **22** Then the tribe of Benjamin: and the captain of the sons of Benjamin shall be Abidan the son of Gideoni. **23** And his army, and those that were numbered were 35,500. **24** All that were numbered of the camp of Ephraim were 108,100, throughout their armies. And they shall go forward in the third rank. **25** The banner of the camp of Dan shall be on the north side by their armies: and the captain of the children of Dan shall be Ahiezer the son of Ammishaddai. **26** And his army, and those that were numbered were 62,700. **27** And those that encamp by him shall be the tribe of Asher: and the captain of the children of Asher shall be Pagiel the son of Ocran. **28** And his army, and those that were numbered were 51,500. **29** Then the tribe of Naphtali: and the captain of the children of Naphtali shall be Ahira the son of Enan. **30** And his host, and those that were numbered were 53,500.

31 All they that were numbered in the camp of Dan were 157,600. They shall go last with their banners. **32** These are those that were numbered of the children of Israel by the house of their fathers: all those that were numbered throughout their army were 603,550. **33** But the Levites were **not** numbered among the children of Israel; as **YeHoVaH** commanded Moses. **34** And the children of Israel did according to all that **YeHoVaH** commanded Moses: so they pitched by their banners, and so they set forward, every one after their families, according to the house of their fathers.

Chapter 3
The Levites are to assist Aaron. "I have taken them in place of every firstborn". The number of Levites over one month old was 22,000. YeHoVaH outlines their duties.

1 These also are the generations of Aaron and Moses in the day that **YeHoVaH** spoke with Moses in Mount Sinai. **2** And these are the names of the sons of Aaron; Nadab the firstborn, and Abihu, Eleazar, and Ithamar. **3** These are the names of the sons of Aaron, the priests that were anointed, whom he consecrated to minister in the priest's office. **4** And Nadab and Abihu died before **YeHoVaH**, when they offered strange fire before **YeHoVaH**, in the wilderness of Sinai, and they had no children: and Eleazar and Ithamar ministered in the priest's office in the sight of Aaron their father. **5** And **YeHoVaH** spoke to Moses, saying, **6** Bring the tribe of Levi near, and present them before Aaron the priest, that they may minister to him. **7** And they shall keep his charge, and the charge of the whole congregation before the tabernacle of the congregation, to do the service of the tabernacle. **8** And they shall keep all the instruments of the tabernacle of the congregation, and the charge of the children of Israel, to do the service of the tabernacle. **9** And you shall give the Levites to Aaron and to his sons: they are completely given to him out of the children of Israel. **10** And you shall appoint Aaron and his sons, and they shall wait on their priest's office: and the stranger (non-Levite) that comes near shall be put to death.

11 And **YeHoVaH** spoke to Moses, saying, **12** "I have taken the Levites from among the Israelites in place of the first male offspring of every Israelite woman. The Levites are mine, **13** For all the first sons are mine; on the day when I put to death all the first sons in the land of Egypt, I took for myself every first male birth of man and beast. They are mine; I am **YeHoVaH**. **14**And **YeHoVaH** spoke to Moses in the wilderness of Sinai, saying, **15** Number the children of Levi after the house of their fathers, by their families: every male from a month old and upward shall you number them. **16** And Moses numbered them according to the word of **YeHoVaH**, as he was commanded. **17** And these were the sons of Levi by their names; Gershon, and Kohath, and Merari. **18** And these are the names of the sons of Gershon by their families; Libni, and Shimei. **19** And the sons of Kohath by their families; Amram, and Izehar, Hebron, and Uzziel. **20** And the sons of Merari by their families; Mahli, and Mushi. These are the families of the Levites according to the house of their fathers.

21 Of Gershon was the family of the Libnites, and the family of the Shimites: these are the families of the Gershonites. **22** Those that were numbered of them, according to the number of all the males, from a month old and upward, even those that were numbered of them were 7,500. **23** The families of the Gershonites shall pitch their tents behind the tabernacle westward. **24** And the chief of the house of the father of the Gershonites shall be Eliasaph the son of Lael. **25** And the charge of the sons of Gershon in the tabernacle of the congregation shall be the tabernacle, and the tent, the covering thereof, and the hanging for the door of the tabernacle of the congregation, **26** And the hangings of the court, and the curtain for the door of the court, which is by the tabernacle, and by the altar around it, and the cords of it for all the service thereof. **27** And of Kohath was the family of the Amramites, and the family of the Izeharites, and the family of the Hebronites, and the family of the Uzzielites: these are the families of the Kohathites. **28** In the number of all the males, from a month old and upward, were 8,600, keeping the charge of the sanctuary. **29** The families of the sons of Kohath shall pitch their tents on the side of the tabernacle southward. *30* And the chief of the house of the father of the families of the Kohathites shall be Elizaphan the son of Uzziel.

31 And their charge shall be the ark, and the table, and the candlestick, and the altars, and the vessels of the sanctuary wherewith they minister, and the hanging, and all the service thereof. *32* And Eleazar the son of Aaron the priest shall be chief over the chief of the Levites, and have the oversight of them that keep the care of the sanctuary. *33* Of Merari was the family of the Mahlites, and the family of the Mushites: these are the families of Merari. *34* And those that were numbered of them, according to the number of all the males, from a month old and upward, were 6,200. *35* And the chief of the house of the father of the families of Merari was Zuriel the son of Abihail: these shall pitch their tents on the side of the tabernacle northward. *36* And under the custody and charge of the sons of Merari shall be the boards of the tabernacle, and the bars thereof, and the pillars thereof, and the sockets thereof, and all the vessels thereof, and all that serves there, *37* And the pillars of the court all around, and their sockets, and their pins, and their cords. *38* But those that camp before the tabernacle toward the east, even before the tabernacle of the congregation eastward, shall be Moses, and Aaron and his sons, keeping the care of the sanctuary for the care of the children of Israel; and the stranger that comes near shall be put to death. *39* All that were numbered of the Levites, which Moses and Aaron numbered at the commandment of *YeHoVaH*, throughout their families, all the males from a month old and upward, were 22,000. *40* And *YeHoVaH* said to Moses, Number all the firstborn of the males of the children of Israel from a month old and upward, and take the number of their names.

41 And you shall take the Levites for me for I am *YeHoVaH,* instead of all the firstborn among the children of Israel; and the cattle of the Levites instead of all the firstlings among the cattle of the children of Israel. *42* And Moses numbered, as *YeHoVaH* commanded him, all the firstborn among the children of Israel. *43* And all the firstborn males by the number of names, from a month old and upward, of those that were numbered of them, were 22,273. *44* And *YeHoVaH* spoke to Moses, saying, *45* Take the Levites instead of all the firstborn among the children of Israel, and the cattle of the Levites instead of their cattle; and the Levites shall be mine: I am *YeHoVaH*. *46* And for those that are to be redeemed of the 273 of the firstborn of the children of Israel, which are more than the Levites; *47* You shall even take *five shekels* apiece by the head, after the shekel of the sanctuary shall you take them: (the shekel is 20 gerahs:) *48* Give the money for the redemption of the additional Israelites to Aaron and his sons. *49* And Moses took the redemption money of those that were over and above them that were redeemed by the Levites: *50* From the firstborn of the Israelites he collected silver weighing 1,365 shekels, according to the sanctuary shekel.

51 And Moses gave the money of those that were redeemed to Aaron and to his sons, according to the word of *YeHoVaH*, as *YeHoVaH* commanded Moses.

Chapter 4
The Kohathites are to carry the most holy things. The Gershonites are to carry the coverings. The Merarites are to carry the frame.

1 And *YeHoVaH* spoke to Moses and to Aaron, saying, *2* Take the sum of the sons of Kohath from among the sons of Levi, after their families, by the house of their fathers, *3* From 30 years old and upward to 50 years old, all that enter into the host, to do the work in the tabernacle of the congregation. *4* This shall be the service of the sons of Kohath in the tabernacle of the congregation, about the most holy things: *5* And when the camp moves forward, Aaron shall come, and his sons, and they shall take down the covering veil, and cover the ark of testimony with it: *6* And shall put on the covering of badgers' skins, and shall spread over it a cloth completely of blue, and shall put in the poles. *7* And upon the table of show-bread they shall spread a cloth of blue, and put thereon the dishes, and the spoons, and the bowls, and covers to cover withal: and the continual bread shall be there: *8* And they shall spread upon them a cloth of scarlet, and cover the same with a covering of badgers' skins, and shall put in the poles there. *9* And they shall take a cloth of blue, and cover the candlestick of the light, and his lamps, and his tongs, and his snuff-dishes, and all the oil vessels thereof, wherewith they minister to it: *10* And they shall put it and all the vessels within a covering of badgers' skins, and shall put it upon a bar.

11 And upon the golden altar they shall spread a cloth of blue, and cover it with a covering of badgers' skins, and shall put to the poles thereof: *12* And they shall take all the instruments of ministry, which they minister in the sanctuary, and put them in a cloth of blue, and cover them with a covering of badgers' skins, and shall put them on a bar: *13* And they shall take away the ashes from the altar, and spread a purple cloth there: *14* And they shall put upon it all the vessels, that they minister about it, even the censers, the flesh-hooks, and the shovels, and the basins, all the vessels of the altar; and they shall spread upon it a covering of badgers' skins, and put to the poles. *15* And when Aaron and his sons have made an end of covering the sanctuary, and all the vessels of the sanctuary, as the camp is to set to move forward; after that, the sons of Kohath shall come to bear it: but they shall not touch any holy thing, or they will die. These things are the burden of the sons of Kohath in the tabernacle of the congregation. *16* And to the office of Eleazar the son of Aaron the priest pertains the oil for the light, and the sweet incense, and the daily meal offering, and the anointing oil, and the oversight of all the tabernacle, and of all that is within, in the sanctuary, and in the vessels there. *17* And **YeHoVaH** spoke to Moses and to Aaron saying, *18* Cut not off the tribe of the families of the Kohathites from among the Levites: *19* But do to them, that they may live, and not die, when they approach the most holy things: Aaron and his sons shall go in, and appoint them every one to his service and to his burden: *20* But they shall not go in to see when the holy things are covered, or they will die.
Reading 34 ends

Reading 35 begins
21 And **YeHoVaH** spoke to Moses, saying, *22* Take also all the sons of Gershon, throughout the houses of their fathers, by their families; *23* From 30 years old and upward until 50 years old shall you number them; all that enter in to perform the service, to do the work in the tabernacle of the congregation. *24* This is the service of the families of the Gershonites, to serve, and for labors: *25* And they shall bear the curtains of the tabernacle, and the tabernacle of the congregation, his covering, and the covering of the badgers' skins that is above it, and the hanging for the door of the tabernacle of the congregation, *26* And the hangings of the court, and the hanging for the door of the gate of the court, which is by the tabernacle and by the altar all around, and their cords, and all the instruments of their service, and all that is made for them: so shall they serve. *27* At the appointment of Aaron and his sons shall be all the service of the sons of the Gershonites, in all their work, and in all their service: and you shall appoint to them in charge all their labors. *28* This is the service of the families of the sons of Gershon in

the tabernacle of the congregation: and their charge shall be under the hand of Ithamar the son of Aaron the priest. *29* As for the sons of Merari, you shall number them after their families, by the house of their fathers; *30* From 30 years old and upward to 50 years old shall you number them, every one that enters into the service, to do the work of the tabernacle of the congregation.

31 And this is the charge of their labor, according to all their service in the tabernacle of the congregation; the boards of the tabernacle, and the bars, and the pillars, and sockets, *32* And the pillars of the court all around, and their sockets, and their pins, and their cords, with all their instruments, and with all their service: and by name you shall reckon the instruments of the charge of their labor. *33* This is the service of the families of the sons of Merari, according to all their service, in the tabernacle of the congregation, under the hand of Ithamar the son of Aaron the priest. *34* And Moses and Aaron and the chief of the congregation numbered the sons of the Kohathites after their families, and after the house of their fathers, *35* From 30 years old and upward to 50 years old, every one that enters into the service, for the work in the tabernacle of the congregation: *36* And those that were numbered by their families were 2,750. *37* These were they that were numbered of the families of the Kohathites, all that might do service in the tabernacle of the congregation, which Moses and Aaron did number according to the commandment of *YeHoVaH* by the hand of Moses. *38* And those that were numbered of the sons of Gershon, throughout their families, and by the house of their fathers, *39* From 30 years old and upward to 50 years old, every one that enters into the service, for the work in the tabernacle of the congregation, *40* Even those that were numbered, throughout their families, by the house of their fathers, were 2,630.

41 These are the numbered of the families of the sons of Gershon, of all that might do service in the tabernacle of the congregation, whom Moses and Aaron did number according to the commandment of *YeHoVaH*. *42* And those that were numbered of the families of the sons of Merari, throughout their families, by the house of their fathers, *43* From 30 years old and upward to 50 years old, every one that enters into the service, for the work in the tabernacle of the congregation, *44* Even those that were numbered of them after their families, were 3,200. *45* These are those that were numbered of the families of the sons of Merari, whom Moses and Aaron numbered according to the word of *YeHoVaH* by the hand of Moses. *46* All those that were numbered of the Levites, whom Moses and Aaron and the chief of Israel numbered, after their families, and after the house of their fathers, *47* From 30 years old and upward to 50 years old, every one that came to do the service of the ministry, and the service of the burden in the tabernacle of the congregation. *48* Even those that were numbered of them, were 8,580, *49* According to the commandment of *YeHoVaH* they were numbered by the hand of Moses, every one according to his service, and according to his burden: thus were they numbered of him, as *YeHoVaH* commanded Moses.

Chapter 5
Anyone who sins shall make restitution and add a fifth to it. If a man suspects his wife of unfaithfulness he shall take her to the priest.

1 And *YeHoVaH* spoke to Moses, saying, *2* Command the children of Israel, that they put out of the camp every leper, and every one that has a health issue, and whosoever is defiled by the dead: *3* Both male and female shall you put out, outside the camp shall you put them; that they defile not their camps, in the midst where I dwell. *5* And the children of Israel did so, and put them out of the camp: as **YeHoVaH** spoke to Moses, so did the children of Israel. *5* And **YeHoVaH** spoke to Moses, saying, *6* Speak to the children of Israel, When a man or woman shall commit any sin that men commit, to do a trespass against **YeHoVaH**, and that person be guilty; *7* Then they shall confess their sin which they have done: and he shall compensate his trespass with the principal party, and add to it one-fifth part, and give it to him against whom he has trespassed. *8* But if the man has no kinsman to compensate the trespass to, let the trespass be compensated to **YeHoVaH**, even to the priest; beside the ram of the atonement, whereby atonement shall be made for him. *9* And every offering of all the holy things of the children of Israel, which they bring to the priest, shall be his. *10* And every man's hallowed things shall be his: whatever any man gives the priest, it shall be his.

11 And **YeHoVaH** spoke to Moses, saying, *12* Speak to the children of Israel, and say to them, If any man's wife go aside, and sin against him, *13* And a man lie with her physically, and it be hid from the eyes of her husband, and be kept close, and she be defiled, and there be no witness against her, neither she be taken with the manner; *15* And the spirit of jealousy come upon him, and he be jealous of his wife, and she be defiled: or if the spirit of jealousy come upon him, and he be jealous of his wife, and she be not defiled: *15* Then shall the man bring his wife to the priest, and he shall bring her offering for her, the tenth part of an ephah of barley meal; he shall pour no oil upon it, nor put frankincense thereon; for it is an *offering of jealousy*, an offering of memorial, bringing iniquity to remembrance. *16* And the priest shall bring her near, and set her before **YeHoVaH**: *17* And the priest shall take holy water in an earthen vessel; and of the dust that is in the floor of the tabernacle the priest shall take, and put it into the water: *18* And the priest shall set the woman before **YeHoVaH**, and uncover the woman's head, and put the offering of memorial in her hands, which is the jealousy offering: and the priest shall have in his hand the bitter water that causes the curse: *19* And the priest shall charge her by an oath, and say to the woman, If no man have lain with you, and if you have not gone aside to uncleanness with another instead of thy husband, be you free from this bitter water that causes the curse: *20* But if you have gone aside to another instead of thy husband, and if you be defiled, and some man have laid with you besides your husband:

21 Then the priest shall charge the woman with an oath of cursing, and the priest shall say to the woman, **YeHoVaH** make you a curse and an oath among thy people, when **YeHoVaH** does make your thigh to rot, and thy belly to swell; *22* And this water that causes the curse shall go into thy bowels, to make thy belly to swell, and your thigh to rot: And the woman shall say, Amen, amen. *23* And the priest shall write these curses in a book, and he shall blot them out with the bitter water: *25* And he shall cause the woman to drink the bitter water that causes the curse: and the water that causes the curse shall enter into her, and become bitter. *25* Then the priest shall take the jealousy offering out of the woman's hand, and shall wave the offering before **YeHoVaH**, and offer it upon the altar: *26* And the priest shall take a handful of the offering, even the memorial, and burn it upon the altar, and afterward shall cause the woman to drink the water. *27* And when he has made her to drink the water, then it shall come to pass, that, if she be defiled, and have done sin against her husband, that the water that causes the curse shall enter into her, and become bitter, and her belly shall swell, and her thigh shall rot: and the woman shall be a curse among her people. *28* And if the woman be not defiled, but be clean; then she shall be free, and shall conceive child. *29* *This is the law of jealousies*, when a wife goes aside to another instead of her husband, and is defiled; *30* Or when the spirit of jealousy comes upon him, and he be jealous over his wife, and shall set the woman before **YeHoVaH**, and the priest shall execute upon her all this law (instruction).

31 Then shall the man be guiltless from iniquity, and this woman shall bear her iniquity.

Chapter 6
Anyone who makes a Nazirite vow shall not drink wine or cut their hair. Aaron's blessing shall be: "YeHoVaH bless you and keep you . . ."

1 And **YeHoVaH** spoke to Moses, saying, **2** Speak to the children of Israel, and say to them, When either man or woman shall separate themselves to vow a vow of a Nazarite (denotes generally one who is separated from others and consecrated to **Elohim**), to separate themselves to **YeHoVaH**   **3** He shall separate himself from wine and strong drink, and shall drink no vinegar of wine, or vinegar of strong drink, neither shall he drink any liquor of grapes, nor eat moist grapes, or dried. **5** All the days of his separation shall he eat nothing that is made of the vine tree, from the kernels even to the husk. **5** All the days of the vow of his separation there shall no razor come upon his head: until the days be fulfilled, in which he separates himself to **YeHoVaH**, he shall be holy, and shall let the locks of the hair of his head grow. **6** All the days that he separates himself to **YeHoVaH** he shall come at no dead body. **7** He shall not make himself unclean for his father, or for his mother, for his brother, or for his sister, when they die: because the consecration of his **Elohim** is upon his head. **8** All the days of his separation he is holy to **YeHoVaH**. **9** And if any man die very suddenly by him, and he has defiled the head of his consecration; then he shall shave his head in the day of his cleansing, on the seventh day shall he shave it. **10** And on the eighth day he shall bring two turtles, or two young pigeons, to the priest, to the door of the tabernacle of the congregation:

11 And the priest shall offer the one for a sin offering, and the other for a burnt offering, and make atonement for him, for that he sinned by the dead, and shall hallow his head that same day. **12** And he shall consecrate to **YeHoVaH** the days of his separation, and shall bring a lamb of the first year for a trespass offering: but the days that were before shall be lost, because his separation was defiled. **13** And this is the law of the Nazarite, when the days of his separation are fulfilled: he shall be brought to the door of the tabernacle of the congregation: **15** And he shall offer his offering to **YeHoVaH**, one male lamb of the first year without blemish for a burnt offering, and one ewe lamb of the first year without blemish for a sin offering, and one ram without blemish for peace offerings, **15** And a basket of unleavened bread, cakes of fine flour mingled with oil, and wafers of unleavened bread anointed with oil, and their meal offering, and their drink offerings. **16** And the priest shall bring them before **YeHoVaH**, and shall offer his sin offering, and his burnt offering: **17** And he shall offer the ram for a sacrifice of peace offerings to **YeHoVaH**, with the basket of unleavened bread: the priest shall offer also his meal offering, and his drink offering. **18** And the Nazarite shall shave the head of his separation at the door of the tabernacle of the congregation, and shall take the hair of the head of his separation, and put it in the fire that is under the sacrifice of the peace offerings. **19** And the priest shall take the sodden shoulder of the ram, and one unleavened cake out of the basket, and one unleavened wafer, and shall put them upon the hands of the Nazarite, after the hair of his separation is shaven: **20** And the priest shall wave them for a wave offering before **YeHoVaH**: this is holy for the priest, with the wave breast and heave shoulder: and after that the Nazarite may drink wine.

21 "This is the law of the Nazirite who vows offerings to **YeHoVaH** in accordance with their dedication, in addition to whatever else they can afford. They must fulfill the vows they have made, according to the law of the Nazirite." *22* And **YeHoVaH** spoke to Moses, saying, *23* Speak to Aaron and to his sons, saying, This is how you shall bless the children of Israel, saying to them, (The Priestly Blessing) *24* **YeHoVaH** bless you, and keep you: *25* **YeHoVaH** make his face shine upon you, and be gracious to you: *26* **YeHoVaH** lift up his countenance upon you, and give you peace. *27* And they shall put my name upon the children of Israel, and I will bless them.

Chapter 7
The leader of each tribe brought a grain offering, a burnt offering, a sin offering and peace offering. Moses spoke with YeHoVaH.

1 And it came to pass on the day that Moses had fully set up the tabernacle, and had anointed it, and sanctified it, and all the instruments there, both the altar and all the vessels there, and had anointed them, and sanctified them; *2* That the princes of Israel, heads of the house of their fathers, who were the princes of the tribes, and were over them that were numbered, offered: *3* And they brought their offering before **YeHoVaH**, six covered wagons, and twelve oxen; a wagon for two of the princes, and for each one an ox: and they brought them before the tabernacle. *4* And **YeHoVaH** spoke to Moses, saying, *5* Take it of them, that they may be to do the service of the tabernacle of the congregation; and you shall give them to the Levites, to every man according to his service. *6* And Moses took the wagons and the oxen, and gave them to the Levites. *7* Two wagons and four oxen he gave to the sons of Gershon, according to their service: *8* And four wagons and eight oxen he gave to the sons of Merari, according to their service, under the hand of Ithamar the son of Aaron the priest. *9* But to the sons of Kohath he gave none: because the service of the sanctuary belonging to them was that they should bear upon their shoulders. *10* And the princes offered for dedicating of the altar in the day that it was anointed, even the princes offered their offering before the altar.

11 And **YeHoVaH** said to Moses, They shall offer their offering, each prince on his day, for the dedicating of the altar. *12* And he that offered his offering the first day was Nahshon the son of Amminadab, of the tribe of Judah: *13* And his offering was one silver charger, the weight of was 130 shekels, one silver bowl of 70 shekels, after the shekel of the sanctuary; both of them were full of fine flour mingled with oil for a meal offering: *14* One spoon of ten shekels of gold, full of incense: *15* One young bullock, one ram, one lamb of the first year, for a burnt offering: *16* One kid of the goats for a sin offering: *17* And for a sacrifice of peace offerings, two oxen, five rams, five he goats, five lambs of the first year: this was the offering of Nahshon the son of Amminadab. *18* On the second day Nethaneel the son of Zuar, prince of Issachar, did offer: *19* He offered for his offering one silver charger, the weight of was *130* shekels, one silver bowl of 70 shekels, after the shekel of the sanctuary; both of them full of fine flour mingled with oil for a meal offering: *20* One spoon of gold of ten shekels, full of incense:

21 One young bullock, one ram, one lamb of the first year, for a burnt offering: *22* One kid of the goats for a sin offering: *23* And for a sacrifice of peace offerings, two oxen, five rams, five male goats, five lambs of the first year: this was the offering of Nethaneel the son of Zuar. *24* On the third day Eliab the son of Helon, prince of the children of Zebulun, did offer: *25* His offering was one silver charger, the weight was 130 shekels, one silver bowl of 70 shekels, after the shekel of the sanctuary; both of them full of fine flour mingled with oil for a meal offering: *26* One golden spoon of ten shekels, full of incense: *27* One young bullock, one ram, one lamb of the first year, for a burnt offering: *28* One kid of the goats for a sin offering: *29* And for a sacrifice of peace offerings, two oxen, five rams, five male goats, five lambs of the first year: this was the offering of Eliab the son of Helon. *30* On the fourth day Elizur the son of Shedeur, prince of the children of Reuben, did offer:

31 His offering was one silver charger of the weight of 130 shekels, one silver bowl of 70 shekels, after the shekel of the sanctuary; both of them full of fine flour mingled with oil for a meal offering: *32* One golden spoon of ten shekels, full of incense: *33* One young bullock, one ram, one lamb of the first year, for a burnt offering: *34* One kid of the goats for a sin offering: *35* And for a sacrifice of peace offerings, two oxen, five rams, five male goats, five lambs of the first year: this was the offering of Elizur the son of Shedeur. *36* On the fifth day Shelumiel the son of Zurishaddai, prince of the children of Simeon, did offer: *37* His offering was one silver charger, the weight was 130 shekels, one silver bowl of seventy shekels, after the shekel of the sanctuary; both of them full of fine flour mingled with oil for a meal offering: *38* One golden spoon of ten shekels, full of incense: *39* One young bullock, one ram, one lamb of the first year, for a burnt offering: *40* One kid of the goats for a sin offering:

41 And for a sacrifice of peace offerings, two oxen, five rams, five male goats, five lambs of the first year: this was the offering of Shelumiel the son of Zurishaddai. *42* On the sixth day Eliasaph the son of Deuel, prince of the children of Gad, offered: *43* His offering was one silver charger of the weight of 130 shekels, a silver bowl of 70 shekels, after the shekel of the sanctuary; both of them full of fine flour mingled with oil for a meal offering: *44* One golden spoon of ten shekels, full of incense: *45* One young bullock, one ram, one lamb of the first year, for a burnt offering: *46* One kid of the goats for a sin offering: *47* And for a sacrifice of peace offerings, two oxen, five rams, five male goats, five lambs of the first year: this was the offering of Eliasaph the son of Deuel. *48* On the seventh day Elishama the son of Ammihud, prince of the children of Ephraim, offered: *49* His offering was one silver charger, the weight of was 130 shekels, one silver bowl of 70 shekels, after the shekel of the sanctuary; both of them full of fine flour mingled with oil for a meal offering: *50* One golden spoon of ten shekels, full of incense:

51 One young bullock, one ram, one lamb of the first year, for a burnt offering: *52* One kid of the goats for a sin offering: *53* And for a sacrifice of peace offerings, two oxen, five rams, five male goats, five lambs of the first year: this was the offering of Elishama the son of Ammihud. *54* On the eighth day offered Gamaliel the son of Pedahzur, prince of the children of Manasseh: *55* His offering was one silver charger of the weight of **130** shekels, one silver bowl of **70** shekels, after the shekel of the sanctuary; both of them full of fine flour mingled with oil for a meal offering: *56* One golden spoon of ten shekels, full of incense: *57* One young bullock, one ram, one lamb of the first year, for a burnt offering: *58* One kid of the goats for a sin offering: *59* And for a sacrifice of peace offerings, two oxen, five rams, five male goats, five lambs of the first year: this was the offering of Gamaliel the son of Pedahzur. *60* On the ninth day Abidan the son of Gideoni, prince of the children of Benjamin, offered:

61 His offering was one silver charger, the weight was a 130 shekels, one silver bowl of 70 shekels, after the shekel of the sanctuary; both of them full of fine flour mingled with oil for a meal offering: *62* One golden spoon of ten shekels, full of incense: *63* One young bullock, one ram, one lamb of the first year, for a burnt offering: *64* One kid of the goats for a sin offering:

65 And for a sacrifice of peace offerings, two oxen, five rams, five male goats, five lambs of the first year: this was the offering of Abidan the son of Gideoni. **66** On the tenth day Ahiezer the son of Ammishaddai, prince of the children of Dan, offered: **67** His offering was one silver charger, the weight was 130 shekels, one silver bowl of 70 shekels, after the shekel of the sanctuary; both of them full of fine flour mingled with oil for a meal offering: **68** One golden spoon of ten shekels, full of incense: **69** One young bullock, one ram, one lamb of the first year, for a burnt offering: **70** One kid of the goats for a sin offering:

71 And for a sacrifice of peace offerings, two oxen, five rams, five male goats, five lambs of the first year: this was the offering of Ahiezer the son of Ammishaddai. **72** On the eleventh day Pagiel the son of Ocran, prince of the children of Asher, offered: **73** His offering was one silver charger, the weight was 130 shekels, one silver bowl of 70 shekels, after the shekel of the sanctuary; both of them full of fine flour mingled with oil for a meal offering: **74** One golden spoon of ten shekels, full of incense: **75** One young bullock, one ram, one lamb of the first year, for a burnt offering: **76** One kid of the goats for a sin offering: **77** And for a sacrifice of peace offerings, two oxen, five rams, five male goats, five lambs of the first year: this was the offering of Pagiel the son of Ocran. **78** On the twelfth day Ahira the son of Enan, prince of the children of Naphtali, offered: **79** His offering was one silver charger, the weight was **130** shekels, one silver bowl of **70** shekels, after the shekel of the sanctuary; both of them full of fine flour mingled with oil for a meal offering: **80** One golden spoon of ten shekels, full of incense:

81 One young bullock, one ram, one lamb of the first year, for a burnt offering: **82** One kid of the goats for a sin offering: **83** And for a sacrifice of peace offerings, two oxen, five rams, five male goats, five lambs of the first year: this was the offering of Ahira the son of Enan. **84** This *was* the dedication offering for the altar from the leaders of Israel when it was anointed: twelve silver dishes, twelve silver bowls, twelve gold pans, **85** each silver dish weighing one hundred and thirty shekels and each bowl seventy; all the silver of the utensils *was* 2,400 shekels, according to the shekel of the sanctuary; **86** the twelve gold pans, full of incense, weighing ten shekels apiece, according to the shekel of the sanctuary, all the gold of the pans 120 shekels; **87** all the oxen for the burnt offering twelve bulls, all the rams twelve, the male lambs one year old with their grain offering twelve, and the male goats for a sin offering twelve; **88** and all the oxen for the sacrifice of peace offerings 24 bulls, all the rams 60, the male goats 60, the male lambs one year old 60. This *was* the dedication offering for the altar after it was anointed. **89** Now when Moses went into the tent of meeting to speak with Him, he heard the voice speaking to him from above the mercy seat that was on the ark of the testimony, from between the two cherubim, so He spoke to him.
Reading 35 ends

Chapter 8
The Levites are presented as a wave offering to YeHoVaH and make atonement for them. YeHoVaH sets them apart to serve at the tent of meeting.
Reading 36 begins
1 And **YeHoVaH** spoke to Moses, saying, **2** Speak to Aaron and say to him, When you light the lamps, the seven lamps shall give light over against the candle stand. **3** And Aaron did so; he lit the lamps there against the candle stand, as **YeHoVaH** commanded Moses. **4** And this work of the candle stand was of beaten gold, to the shaft, to the flowers, were beaten work: according to the pattern that **YeHoVaH** had shown Moses, so he made the candle stand. **5** And **YeHoVaH**

spoke to Moses, saying, *6* Take the Levites from among the children of Israel, and cleanse them. *7* And thus shall you do to them, to cleanse them: Sprinkle water of purifying upon them, and let them shave all their flesh, and let them wash their clothes, and so make themselves clean. *8* Then let them take a young bullock with his meal offering, even fine flour mingled with oil, and another young bullock shall you take for a sin offering. *9* And you shall bring the Levites before the tabernacle of the congregation: and you shall gather the whole assembly of the children of Israel together: *10* And you shall bring the Levites before **YeHoVaH**: and the children of Israel shall put their hands upon the Levites:

11 And Aaron shall offer the Levites before **YeHoVaH** for an offering of the children of Israel, that they may execute the service of **YeHoVaH**. *12* And the Levites shall lay their hands upon the heads of the bullocks: and you shall offer the one for a sin offering, and the other for a burnt offering, to **YeHoVaH**, to make an atonement for the Levites. *13* And you shall set the Levites before Aaron, and before his sons, and offer them for an offering to **YeHoVaH**. *14* *Thus shall you separate the Levites from among the children of Israel: and the Levites shall be mine.* *15* And after that shall the Levites go in to do the service of the tabernacle of the congregation: and you shall cleanse them, and offer them for an offering. *16* For they are wholly given to me from among the children of Israel; instead of every womb, even firstborn of all the children of Israel, have I taken them to me. *17* For all the firstborn of the children of Israel are mine, both man and beast: on the day that I destroyed every firstborn in the land of Egypt I sanctified them for myself. *18* And I have taken the Levites for all the firstborn of the children of Israel. *19* And I have given the Levites as a gift to Aaron and to his sons from among the children of Israel, to do the service of the children of Israel in the tabernacle of the congregation, and to make atonement for the children of Israel: that there be no plague among the children of Israel, when the children of Israel come near to the sanctuary. *20* And Moses, and Aaron, and all the congregation of the children of Israel, did to the Levites according to all that **YeHoVaH** commanded Moses concerning the Levites, so did the children of Israel.

21 And the Levites were purified, and they washed their clothes; and Aaron offered them as an offering before **YeHoVaH**; and Aaron made atonement for them to cleanse them. *22* And after that went the Levites in to do their service in the tabernacle of the congregation before Aaron, and before his sons: as **YeHoVaH** had commanded Moses concerning the Levites, so did they to them. *23* And **YeHoVaH** spoke to Moses, saying, *24* This is it that belongs to the Levites: from 25 years old and upward they shall go in to wait upon the service of the tabernacle of the congregation: *25* And from the age of 50 years they shall cease waiting upon the service thereof, and shall serve no more: *26* But shall minister with their brethren in the tabernacle of the congregation, to keep the charge, and shall do no service. Thus shall you do to the Levites touching their work.

Chapter 9
In the first month of the second year the Israelites are told to keep the Passover. When the cloud lifted from the tabernacle they would journey on but when it remained, they remained according to YeHoVaH's command.

1 And **YeHoVaH** spoke to Moses in the wilderness of Sinai, in the first month of the second year after they came out of the land of Egypt, saying, *2* Let the children of Israel keep the Passover at his appointed season. *3* In the fourteenth day of this month, at evening (sunset), you shall keep it in his appointed season: according to all the rites of it, and according to all the ceremonies thereof, shall you keep it. *4* And Moses spoke to the children of Israel, that they should keep the Passover. *5* And they kept the Passover on the fourteenth day of the *first* month at evening in the wilderness of Sinai: according to all that **YeHoVaH** commanded Moses, so did the children of Israel. *6* And there were certain men, who were defiled by a dead body of a man, that they could not keep the Passover on that day: and they came before Moses and before Aaron on that day: *7* And those men said to him, We are defiled by the dead body of a man: why are we kept back, that we may not offer an offering of **YeHoVaH** in his appointed season among the children of Israel? *8* And Moses said to them, Stand still, and I will hear what **YeHoVaH** will command concerning you. *9* And **YeHoVaH** spoke to Moses, saying, *10* "Tell the Israelites: 'When any of you or your descendants are unclean because of a dead body or are away on a journey, they are still to celebrate the **YeHoVaH**'s Passover.

11 The fourteenth day of the *second* month at evening they shall keep it, and eat it with unleavened bread and bitter herbs. *12* They shall leave none of it to the morning, nor break any bone of it: according to all the ordinances of the Passover they shall keep it. *13* But if anyone who is ceremonially clean and not on a journey fails to celebrate the Passover, they must be cut off from their people for not presenting **YeHoVaH**'s offering at the appointed time. They will bear the consequences of their sin. *14* And if a stranger shall sojourn among you, and will keep the Passover to **YeHoVaH**; according to the ordinance of the Passover, and according to the manner thereof, so shall he do: you *shall have one ordinance, both for the stranger, and for him that was born in the land.* *15* And on the day that the tabernacle was reared up the cloud covered the tabernacle, namely, the tent of the testimony: and at evening there was upon the tabernacle as it were the appearance of fire, until the morning. *16* So it was always: the cloud covered it by day, and the appearance of fire by night. *17* And when the cloud was taken up from the tabernacle, then after that the children of Israel journeyed: and in the place where the cloud stayed, there the children of Israel pitched their tents. *18* At the commandment of **YeHoVaH** the children of Israel journeyed, and at the commandment of **YeHoVaH** they pitched their tents: as long as the cloud stayed upon the tabernacle they rested in their tents. *19* And when the cloud remained long upon the tabernacle many days, then the children of Israel kept the charge of **YeHoVaH**, and journeyed not. *20* And so it was, when the cloud was a few days upon the tabernacle; according to the commandment of **YeHoVaH** they stayed in their tents, and according to the commandment of **YeHoVaH** they journeyed.

21 And so it was, when the cloud abode from evening to the morning, and that the cloud was taken up in the morning, then they journeyed: whether it was by day or by night that the cloud was taken up, they journeyed. *22* Or whether it were two days, or a month, or a year, that the cloud remained upon the tabernacle, not moving, the children of Israel abode in their tents, and journeyed not: but when it was taken up, they journeyed. *23* At the commandment of **YeHoVaH** they rested in the tents, and at the commandment of **YeHoVaH** they journeyed: they kept the charge of **YeHoVaH**, at the commandment of **YeHoVaH** by the hand of Moses.

Chapter 10

YeHoVaH tells Moses to make two silver trumpets to direct the congregation when needed. In the second month the cloud lifted and they set out just as YeHoVaH commanded.

1 And **YeHoVaH** spoke to Moses, saying, *2* Make two trumpets of silver; of a whole piece shall you make them: that you may use them for the calling of the assembly, and for the journeying of the camps. *3* And when they shall blow with them, all the assembly shall assemble themselves to you at the door of the tabernacle of the congregation. *4*And if they blow just one trumpet, then the princes, who are heads of the thousands of Israel, shall gather themselves to you. *5* When you blow an alarm, then the camps that lie on the east parts shall go forward. *6* When you blow an alarm the second time, then the camps that lie on the south side shall take their journey: they shall blow an alarm for their journeys. *7* But when the congregation is to be gathered together, you shall blow, but you shall not sound an alarm. *8* And the sons of Aaron, the priests, shall blow with the trumpets; and they shall be to you for an ordinance forever throughout your generations. *9* And if you go to war in your land against the enemy that oppresses you, then you shall blow an alarm with the trumpets; and you shall be remembered before **YeHoVaH** your **Elohim**, and you shall be saved from your enemies. *10* Also in the day of your gladness, and in your solemn days, and in the beginnings of your months, you shall blow with the trumpets over your burnt offerings, and over the sacrifices of your peace offerings; that they may be to you for a memorial before your **Elohim**: I am **YeHoVaH** your **Elohim**.

11 And it came to pass on the twentieth day of the second month, in the second year, that the cloud was taken up from off the tabernacle of the testimony. *12* And the children of Israel took their journeys out of the wilderness of Sinai; and the cloud rested in the wilderness of Paran. *13* And they first took their journey according to the commandment of **YeHoVaH** by the hand of Moses. *14* In the first place went the standard of the camp of the children of Judah according to their armies: and over his host was Nahshon the son of Amminadab. *15* And over the tribe of the children of Issachar was Nethaneel the son of Zuar. *16* And over the tribe of the children of Zebulun was Eliab the son of Helon. *17* And the tabernacle was taken down; and the sons of Gershon and the sons of Merari set forward, bearing the tabernacle. *18* And the banner of the camp of Reuben set forward according to their armies: and over his group was Elizur the son of Shedeur. *19* And over the tribe of the children of Simeon was Shelumiel the son of Zurishaddai. *20* And over the group of the tribe of the children of Gad was Eliasaph the son of Deuel.

21 And the Kohathites set forward, bearing the sanctuary: and the other did set up the tabernacle where they came. *22* And the banner of the camp of the children of Ephraim set forward according to their armies: and over his group was Elishama the son of Ammihud. *23* And over the tribe of the children of Manasseh was Gamaliel the son of Pedahzur. *24* And over the tribe of the children of Benjamin was Abidan the son of Gideoni. *25* Finally, as the rear guard for all the units, the divisions of the camp of Dan set out under their banner. Ahiezer son of Ammishaddai was in command. *26* And over the tribe of the children of Asher was Pagiel the son of Ocran. *27* And over the tribe of the children of Naphtali was Ahira the son of Enan. *28* Thus were the journeys of the children of Israel according to their armies, when they set forward. *29* And Moses said to Hobab, the son of Raguel the Midianite, Moses' father-in-law, We are journeying to the place of which **YeHoVaH** said, I will give you it: come with us, and we will do you good: for **YeHoVaH** has spoken good concerning Israel. *30* And he said to him, I will not go; but I will depart to my own land, and to my kindred.

31 And he said, Leave us not, I pray you; forasmuch as you know how we are to camp in the wilderness, and you may be to us instead of eyes. *32* And it shall be, if you go with us, it shall be, that what goodness **YeHoVaH** shall do to us, the same will we do to you. *33* And they departed from the mount of **YeHoVaH** three days' journey: and the ark of the covenant of

YeHoVaH went before them in the three days' journey, to search out a resting place for them. *34* And the cloud of *YeHoVaH* was upon them by day, when they went out of the camp. *35* And it came to pass, when the ark set forward, that Moses said, Rise up, *YeHoVaH*, and let your enemies be scattered; and let them that hate you flee before you. *36* And when it rested, he said, Return, O *YeHoVaH*, to the many thousands of Israel.

CHAPTERS 11- 20

Chapter 11
When the people grumbled that they had no meat, YeHoVaH was angry but sent quails for them to eat. He put his Spirit on seventy elders to help Moses.

1 And when the people complained, it displeased *YeHoVaH*: and *YeHoVaH* heard it; and his anger was kindled; and the fire of *YeHoVaH* burnt among them, and *consumed* them that were in the outermost parts of the camp. *2* And the people cried to Moses; and when Moses prayed to *YeHoVaH*, the fire was quenched. *3* And he called the name of the place Taberah: because the fire of *YeHoVaH* burnt among them. *4* And the mixed multitude that was among them began to crave other food, and again the Israelites started wailing and said, "If only we had meat to eat! *5* We remember the fish, which we did eat in Egypt freely; the cucumbers, and the melons, and the leeks, and the onions, and the garlic: *6* But now our soul is dried away: there is nothing at all, beside this manna, before our eyes. *7* And the manna was as coriander seed, and the color thereof was pale yellow. *8* And the people went about, and gathered it, and ground it in mills, or beat it in a mortar, and baked it in pans, and made cakes of it: and the taste of it was as the taste of fresh oil. *9* And when the dew fell upon the camp in the night, the manna fell upon it. *10* Then Moses heard the people weep throughout their families, every man in the door of his tent: and the anger of *YeHoVaH* was kindled greatly; Moses also was displeased.

11 And Moses said to *YeHoVaH*, Why have you afflicted your servant? and why have I not found favor in your sight, that you lay the burden of all the people upon me? *12* Have I conceived this entire people? have I begotten them, that you should say to me, Carry them in thy bosom, as a nursing father bears the sucking child, to the land which you swore to their fathers? *13* When should I have meat to give to all these people? for they weep to me, saying, Give us meat, that we may eat. *14* I am not able to bear all these people alone, because it is too heavy for me. *15* And if you deal this way with me, kill me, I pray you, out of hand, if I have found favor in thy sight; and let me not see my misery. *16* And *YeHoVaH* said to Moses, Gather to me seventy men of the elders of Israel, whom you know to be the elders of the people, and officers over them; and bring them to the tabernacle of the congregation, that they may stand there with you. *17* And I will come down and talk with you there: and I will take of the spirit which is upon you, and will put it upon them; and they shall bear the burden of the people with you, that you bear it not thyself alone. *18* And say to the people, Sanctify yourselves against tomorrow, and you shall eat meat: for you have wept in the ears of *YeHoVaH*, saying, Who shall give us meat to eat? for it was well with us in Egypt: therefore *YeHoVaH* will give you meat, and you shall eat. *19* Ye shall not eat one day, nor two days, nor five days, neither ten days, nor 20 days; *20* But even a whole month, until it come out at your nostrils, and it be loathsome to you:

because you have despised **YeHoVaH** which is among you, and have wept before him, saying, Why did we come forth out of Egypt?

21 And Moses said, The people, among whom I am, are 600,000 footmen; and you have said, I will give them meat, that they may eat a whole month. *22* Shall the flocks and the herds be slain for them, to suffice them? or shall all the fish of the sea be gathered together for them, to suffice them? *23* And **YeHoVaH** said to Moses, Is **YeHoVaH**'s arm too short? you shall see now whether my word shall come to pass to you or not. *24* And Moses went out, and told the people the words of **YeHoVaH**, and gathered the seventy men of the elders of the people, and set them round about the tabernacle. *25* And **YeHoVaH** came down in a cloud, and spoke to him, and took of the spirit that was upon him, and gave it to the seventy elders: and it came to pass, that, when the spirit rested upon them, they prophesied, and did not cease. *26* But there remained two of the men in the camp, the name of the one was Eldad, and the name of the other Medad: and the spirit rested upon them; and they were of them that were written, but went not out to the tabernacle: and they prophesied in the camp. *27* And there ran a young man, and told Moses, and said, Eldad and Medad do prophesy in the camp. *28* And Joshua the son of Nun, the servant of Moses, one of his young men, answered and said, My lord Moses, forbid them. *29* But Moses replied, "Are you jealous for my sake? I wish that all of **YeHoVaH**'s people were prophets and that **YeHoVaH** would put his Spirit on them!" *30* Then Moses and the elders of Israel returned to the camp.

31 And there went forth a wind from **YeHoVaH**, and brought quails from the sea, and let them fall by the camp, as it were a day's journey on this side, and as it were a day's journey on the other side, round about the camp, and as it were two cubits high upon the face of the earth. *32* And the people stood up all that day, and all that night, and all the next day, and they gathered the quails: he that gathered least gathered ten homers (about 38 bushels): and they spread them all abroad for themselves all around the camp. *33* But while the meat was still between their teeth and before it could be consumed, the anger of **YeHoVaH** burned against the people, and he struck them with a severe plague. *34* And he called the name of that place Kibroth Hattaavah: because there they buried the people that lusted. *35* And the people journeyed from Kibroth Hattaavah to Hazeroth; and abode at Hazeroth.

Chapter 12
Miriam and Aaron speak against Moses and YeHoVaH is angry. He punishes Miriam with leprosy. Moses prayed and after seven days she returned.

1 And *Miriam and Aaron spoke against Moses* because he had married an Ethiopian woman. *2* And they said, Has **YeHoVaH** indeed spoken only by Moses? has he not spoken also by us? And **YeHoVaH** heard them. *3* (Now Moses was a very humble man, more humble than anyone else on the face of the earth.) *4* And **YeHoVaH** spoke suddenly to Moses, and to Aaron, and to Miriam, Come out you three to the tabernacle of the congregation. And the three came out. *5* And **YeHoVaH** came down in the pillar of the cloud, and stood in the door of the tabernacle, and called Aaron and Miriam: and they both came forth. *6* And he said, Hear now my words: If there be a prophet among you, I **YeHoVaH** will make myself known to him in a vision, and will speak to him in a dream. *7* My servant Moses is not so, who is faithful in all my house. *8* With him I speak face to face, clearly and not in riddles; he sees the form of **YeHoVaH**. Why then were you not afraid to speak against my servant Moses?" *9* And the anger of **YeHoVaH** was kindled against them; and he departed. *10* And the cloud departed from off the tabernacle; and, behold, Miriam became leprous, white as snow: and Aaron looked upon Miriam, and, behold, she was leprous.

11 And Aaron said to Moses, Alas, my lord, I beseech you, lay not the sin upon us, wherein we have done foolishly, and wherein we have sinned. *12* Let her not be as one dead, of whom the flesh is half consumed when he comes out of his mother's womb. *13* And Moses cried to **YeHoVaH**, saying, Heal her now, O my **Elohim**, I beseech you. *14* And **YeHoVaH** said to Moses, If her father had but spit in her face, should she not be ashamed seven days? let her be shut out from the camp seven days, and after that let her be received in again. *15* And Miriam was shut out from the camp seven days: and the people journeyed not till Miriam was brought in again. *16* And afterward the people removed from Hazeroth, and pitched in the wilderness of Paran.
Reading 36 ends

Chapter 13
Moses sends men to spy out the land of Canaan. Only Caleb and Joshua say, "Let us go up," but the others said that the inhabitants were too strong and scared the people.
Reading 37 begins

1 And **YeHoVaH** spoke to Moses, saying, *2* Send men, that they may search the land of Canaan, which I give to the children of Israel: of every tribe of their fathers shall you send a man, everyone a ruler among them. *3* And Moses by the commandment of **YeHoVaH** sent them from the wilderness of Paran: all those men were heads of the children of Israel. *4* And these were their names: of the tribe of Reuben, Shammua the son of Zaccur. *5* Of the tribe of Simeon, Shaphat the son of Hori. *6* Of the tribe of Judah, Caleb the son of Jephunneh. *7* Of the tribe of Issachar, Igal the son of Joseph. *8* Of the tribe of Ephraim, Oshea the son of Nun. *9* Of the tribe of Benjamin, Palti the son of Raphu. *10* Of the tribe of Zebulun, Gaddiel the son of Sodi.

11 Of the tribe of Joseph, namely, of the tribe of Manasseh, Gaddi the son of Susi. *12* Of the tribe of Dan, Ammiel the son of Gemalli. *13* Of the tribe of Asher, Sethur the son of Michael. *14* Of the tribe of Naphtali, Nahbi the son of Vophsi. *15* Of the tribe of Gad, Geuel the son of Machi. *16* These are the names of the men that Moses sent to spy out the land. And Moses gave to Hoshea, the son of Nun, the name of Joshua. *17* And Moses sent them to spy out the land of Canaan, and said to them, Go up this way southward, and go up into the mountain: *18* And see the land, what it is, and the people that dwell there, whether they be strong or weak, few or many; *19* And what the land is that they dwell in, whether it be good or bad; and what cities they dwell in, whether in tents, or in strong holds; *20* And what the land is, whether it be fat or lean, whether there be wood there, or not. And *be you of good courage*, and bring of the fruit of the land. Now the time was the time of the first ripe grapes.

21 So they went up, and searched the land from the wilderness of Zin to Rehob, as men come to Hamath. *22* And they ascended by the south, and came to Hebron; where Ahiman, Sheshai, and Talmai, the children of Anak, were. *23* And they came to the brook of Eshcol, and cut down from there a branch with one cluster of grapes, and they bore it between two polls; and they brought of the pomegranates, and of the figs. *24* The place was called the brook Eshcol, because of the cluster of grapes which the children of Israel cut down from there. *25* And they returned from searching of the land after forty days. **26** And they came to Moses, and to Aaron, and to all the congregation of the children of Israel, to the wilderness of Paran, to Kadesh; and brought back word to them, and to all the congregation, and showed them the fruit of the land. **27** And they told him, and said, We came to the land where you sent us, and surely it flows with milk and honey; and this is the fruit of it. **28** Nevertheless the people be strong that dwell in the land, and the cities are walled, and very great: and moreover we saw the children of Anak there. **29** The Amalekites dwell in the land of the south: and the Hittites, and the Jebusites, and the Amorites, dwell in the mountains: and the Canaanites dwell by the sea, and by the coast of Jordan. **30** And *Caleb* stilled the people before Moses, and said, Let us go up at once, and possess it; for we are well able to overcome it.

31 But the men that went up with him said, We be not able to go up against the people; for they are stronger than we. **32** And they brought up an evil report of the land which they had searched to the children of Israel, saying, The land, through which we have gone to search, is a land that eats up the inhabitants thereof; and all the people that we saw in it are men of a great stature. **33** We saw there the Nephilim (the descendants of Anak come from the Nephilim). We saw ourselves as grasshoppers, and that's how we appeared to them."

Chapter 14

The people grumbled so YeHoVaH said that they would spend forty years in the wilderness. Moses tells them they are not to go up now, but they ignored Moses and went up to the land and were defeated.

1 And the entire congregation lifted up their voice, and cried; and the people wept that night. **2** All the Israelites criticized Moses and Aaron. The entire community said to them, "If only we had died in the land of Egypt or if only we had died in this desert! **3** And why has **YeHoVaH** brought us to this land, to fall by the sword, that our wives and our children should be a prey? were it not better for us to return into Egypt? **4** And they said one to another, Let us make a captain, and let us return to Egypt. **5** Then Moses and Aaron fell on their faces before all the assembly of the congregation of the children of Israel. **6** And Joshua the son of Nun, and Caleb the son of Jephunneh, which were of them that searched the land, tore their clothes: **7** And they spoke to all the company of the children of Israel, saying, The land, which we passed through to search it, is an exceeding good land. **8** If **YeHoVaH** delight in us, then he will bring us into this land, and give us it; a land that flows with milk and honey. **9** Only don't rebel against **YeHoVaH** and don't be afraid of the people of the land. They are our prey. Their defense has deserted them, but **YeHoVaH** is with us. So don't be afraid of them."**10** But *all the congregation bade stone them with stones.* And the glory of **YeHoVaH** appeared in the tabernacle of the congregation before all the children of Israel.

11 And **YeHoVaH** said to Moses, How long will this people provoke me? and how long will it be before they believe me, for all the signs which I have showed among them? **12** I will destroy them with the pestilence, and disinherit them, and will make of you a greater nation and mightier than they. **13** And Moses said to **YeHoVaH**, Then the Egyptians shall hear it, (for you brought up this people in thy might from among them;) **14** And they will tell it to the inhabitants of this land: for they have heard that **YeHoVaH** is among this people, that **YeHoVaH** is seen face to face, and that His cloud stands over them, and that you go before them, by day time in a pillar of a cloud, and in a pillar of fire by night. **15** Now if you shall kill all this people as one man, then the nations which have heard the fame of you will speak, saying, *16* Because **YeHoVaH** was not able to bring this people into the land which he swore to them, therefore he has slain them in the wilderness. *17* And now, I beseech you, let the power of my **Elohim** be great, according as you have spoken, saying, *18* **YeHoVaH** is longsuffering, and of great mercy, forgiving iniquity and transgression, and by no means clearing the guilty, visiting the iniquity of the fathers upon the children to the third and fourth generation. *19* Pardon, I beseech you, the iniquity of this people according to the greatness of thy mercy, and as you have forgiven this people, from Egypt even until now. *20* And **YeHoVaH** said, I have pardoned according to your word:

21 But as I live and as the **YeHoVaH**'s glory fills the entire earth,. *22* Because all those men which have seen my glory, and my miracles, which I did in Egypt and in the wilderness, and have tempted me now these ten times, and have not hearkened to my voice; *23* Surely they shall not see the land which I swore to their fathers, neither shall any of them that provoked me see it: *24* But my servant Caleb, because he had a different spirit in him, and has been true to me with all his heart, him I will take into that land into which he went, and his seed will have it for their heritage. *25* Tomorrow turn you, and get you into the wilderness by the way of the Red sea. *26* And **YeHoVaH** spoke to Moses and to Aaron, saying, *27* How long shall I bear with this evil congregation, which murmur against me? I have heard the murmurings of the children of Israel, which they say against me. *28* Say to them, As truly as I live, says **YeHoVaH**, as you have spoken in my ears, so will I do to you: *29* Your carcasses shall fall in this wilderness; and all that were numbered of you, according to your whole number, from 20 years old and upward which have murmured against me. *30* Doubtless you shall not come into the land, concerning which I swore to make you dwell, except for Caleb the son of Jephunneh, and Joshua the son of Nun.

31 But your little ones, which you said should be a prey, they will I bring in, and they shall know the land that you have despised. *32* But as for you, your carcasses, they shall fall in this wilderness. *33* And your children shall wander in the wilderness forty years, and bear your whoredoms (faithless, unworthy, or idolatrous practices or pursuits), until your carcasses be wasted in the wilderness. *34* For forty years - 'one year for each of the forty days you explored the land' - you will suffer for your sins and know what it is like to have me against you'. *35* I **YeHoVaH** have said, I will surely do it to this entire evil congregation that are gathered together against me: in this wilderness they shall be consumed, and there they shall die. *36* And the men, which Moses sent to search the land, who returned, and made all the congregation to murmur against him, by bringing up a slander upon the land, *37* Even those men that did bring up the evil report upon the land, *died by the plague* before **YeHoVaH**. *38* But Joshua the son of Nun, and Caleb the son of Jephunneh, which were of the men that went to search the land, lived onl. *39* And Moses told these sayings to all the children of Israel: and the people mourned greatly. *40* And they rose up early in the morning, and got them up into the top of the mountain, saying, Lo, we be here, and will go up to the place which **YeHoVaH** has promised: for we have sinned.

41 And Moses said, Why now do you transgress the commandment of **YeHoVaH**? but it shall not prosper. *42* Do *not* go up, for **YeHoVaH** is *no longer* among you; that you be not destroyed before your enemies. *43* For the Amalekites and the Canaanites are there before you, and you shall fall by the sword: *because you turned away from* **YeHoVaH**, therefore **YeHoVaH** will **not** be with you. *44* But they assumed to go up to the hilltop *anyway*: nevertheless the ark of the covenant of **YeHoVaH**, and Moses, departed not out of the camp. *45* Then the Amalekites and the Canaanites who lived in that hill country came down and attacked them and beat them down all the way to Hormah.

Chapter 15
There is one law (instruction) for you and for strangers. Make an offering if you sin unintentionally. Anyone who sins defiantly shall be cut off.

1Now **YeHoVaH** spoke to Moses, saying, **2** "Speak to the sons of Israel and say to them, 'When you enter the land where you are to live, which I am giving you, **3** then make an offering by fire to **YeHoVaH**, a burnt offering or a sacrifice to fulfill a special vow, or as a freewill offering or in your appointed times, to make a soothing aroma to **YeHoVaH**, from the herd or from the flock. **4** The one who presents his offering shall present to **YeHoVaH** a grain offering of one-tenth *of an ephah* of fine flour mixed with one-fourth of a hin of oil, **5** and you shall prepare wine for the drink offering, one-fourth of a hin, with the burnt offering or for the sacrifice, for each lamb. **6** Or for a ram you shall prepare as a grain offering two-tenths *of an ephah* of fine flour mixed with one-third of a hin of oil; **7** and for the drink offering you shall offer one-third of a hin of wine as a soothing aroma to **YeHoVaH**. **8** When you prepare a bull as a burnt offering or a sacrifice, to fulfill a special vow, or for peace offerings to **YeHoVaH**, **9** then you shall offer with the bull a grain offering of three-tenths *of an ephah* of fine flour mixed with one-half a hin of oil; **10** and you shall offer as the drink offering one-half a hin of wine as an offering by fire, as a soothing aroma to **YeHoVaH**.

11 This is to be done for every young ox and for every male sheep or male lamb or young goat. **12** Whatever number you make ready, so you are to do for everyone. *13* All that are born of the country shall do these things after this manner, in offering an offering made by fire, of a sweet savor to **YeHoVaH**. *14* And if a stranger sojourn (travel) with you, or whoever be among you in your generations, and will offer an offering made by fire, of a sweet savor to **YeHoVaH**; as you do, so he shall do. **15** One ordinance shall be both for you of the congregation, and also for the stranger that travels with you, an ordinance forever in your generations: as you are, so shall the stranger be before **YeHoVaH**. **16** *One* **law** (instruction) ***and one manner shall be for you, and for the stranger that travels with you**. *17* And **YeHoVaH** spoke to Moses, saying, *18* Speak to the children of Israel, and say to them, When you come into the land where I bring you, *19* Then it shall be, that, when you eat of the bread of the land, you shall offer up a heave-offering to **YeHoVaH**. *20* You shall offer up a cake of the first of your dough for a heave-offering: as you do the heave-offering of the threshing floor, so shall you heave it.

21 Of the first of your dough you shall give to **YeHoVaH** a heave-offering in your generations. **22** And if you have erred, and not observed all these commandments, which **YeHoVaH** has spoken to Moses, *23* All the laws (instructions) which **YeHoVaH** has given you by the hand of Moses, from the day when **YeHoVaH** gave them, and ever after from generation to generation; **24** Then it shall be, if it should be committed by ignorance without the knowledge of the congregation, that all the congregation shall offer one young bullock for a burnt offering, for a sweet savor to **YeHoVaH**, with his meal offering, and his drink offering, according to the manner, and one kid of the goats for a sin-offering. *25* And the priest shall make an atonement for all the congregation of the children of Israel, and it shall be forgiven them; for it is ignorance: and they shall bring their offering, a sacrifice made by fire to **YeHoVaH**, and their sin-offering before **YeHoVaH**, for their ignorance: **26** And it shall be forgiven all the congregation of the children of Israel, and the stranger that travels among them; seeing all the people were in ignorance. **27** And if any soul sin through ignorance, then he shall bring a female goat of the first year for a sin-offering. **28** And the priest shall make atonement for the soul that sins ignorantly, when he sins by ignorance before **YeHoVaH**, to make atonement for him; and it shall be forgiven him. **29** *You shall have one law for him that sins through ignorance, both for him that is born among the children of Israel, and for the stranger that travels among them.* **30** " 'But anyone who sins defiantly, whether native-born or foreigner, blasphemes **YeHoVaH** and must be cut off from the people of Israel.

31 Because he has despised the word of **YeHoVaH**, and has broken his commandment, that soul shall utterly be cut off; his iniquity shall be upon him. **32** And while the children of Israel were in the wilderness, they found a man that gathered sticks upon the Sabbath day. **33** And they that found him gathering sticks brought him to Moses and Aaron, and to the entire congregation. **34** They placed him in custody, because it wasn't clear what should be done to him. **35** And **YeHoVaH** said to Moses, The man shall surely be put to death: all the congregation shall stone him with stones without the camp. **36** And all the congregation brought him outside the camp, and stoned him, and he died; as **YeHoVaH** commanded Moses. **37** And **YeHoVaH** spoke to Moses, saying, **38** Speak to the children of Israel, and bid them that they make them fringes in the borders of their garments throughout their generations, and that they put upon the fringe of the borders a strand of blue: **39** And it shall be to you for a fringe, that you may look upon it, and *remember all the commandments* of **YeHoVaH**, and do them; and that you seek not after your own heart and your own eyes, after which you use to go a whoring (to pursue a faithless, unworthy, or idolatrous desire): **40** That you may remember, and do all my commandments, and be holy to your **Elohim**.

41 I am **YeHoVaH** your **Elohim**, who brought you out of the land of Egypt, to be your **Elohim**: I am **YeHoVaH** your **Elohim**.
  Reading 37 ends

Chapter 16

Korah, Dathan and Abiram rise against Moses and Aaron. Moses says, "YeHoVaH will choose." YeHoVaH did choose and the ground swallowed up those with Korah. But the people still continued to complain and YeHoVaH again responds to their disobedience.
  Reading 38 begins
1 Now Korah, the son of Izhar, the son of Kohath, the son of Levi, and Dathan and Abiram, the sons of Eliab, and On, the son of Peleth, sons of Reuben, took men: **2** And they rose up before Moses, with others of the children of Israel, 250 princes of the assembly, famous in the congregation, men of renown: **3** And they gathered themselves together against Moses and against Aaron, and said to them, You take too much upon you, seeing all the congregation are holy, every one of them, and **YeHoVaH** is among them: why then do you lift up yourselves above the congregation of **YeHoVaH**? **4** And when Moses heard it, he fell upon his face: **5** And he spoke to Korah and to all his company, saying, tomorrow **YeHoVaH** will show who are his, and who is holy; and will cause him to come near to him: even him whom he has chosen will he cause to come near to him. **6** Take you censers, Korah, and all his company; **7** And put fire therein, and put incense in them before **YeHoVaH** tomorrow: and it shall be that the man whom **YeHoVaH** does choose, he shall be holy: you take too much upon you, you sons of Levi. **8** And

Moses said to Korah, Hear, I pray you, you sons of Levi: *9* Seems it is but a small thing to you, that the **Elohim** of Israel has separated you from the congregation of Israel, to bring you near to himself to do the service of the tabernacle of **YeHoVaH**, and to stand before the congregation to minister to them? *10* And he has brought you near to him, and all your brethren the sons of Levi with you: and seek you the priesthood also?

11 For which cause both you and all thy company are gathered together against **YeHoVaH**: and what is Aaron that you murmur against him? *12* And Moses sent to call Dathan and Abiram, the sons of Eliab: which said, We will not come up: *13* Is it a small thing that you have brought us up out of a land that flows with milk and honey, to kill us in the wilderness, except you make yourself altogether a prince over us? *14* Moreover you have not brought us into a land that flows with milk and honey, or given us inheritance of fields and vineyards: will you put out the eyes of these men? we will not come up. *15* And Moses was very angry, and said to **YeHoVaH**, Respect not you their offering: I have not taken one donkey from them, neither have I hurt one of them. *16* And Moses said to Korah, Be you and all your company before **YeHoVaH**, you, and they, and Aaron, tomorrow: *17* And take every man his censer, and put incense in them, and bring you before **YeHoVaH** every man his censer, 250 censers; you also, and Aaron, each of you his censer. *18* And they took every man his censer, and put fire in them, and laid incense thereon, and stood in the door of the tabernacle of the congregation with Moses and Aaron. *19* And Korah gathered the entire congregation against them to the door of the tabernacle of the congregation: and the glory of **YeHoVaH** appeared to the entire congregation. *20* And **YeHoVaH** spoke to Moses and to Aaron, saying,

21 *Separate* yourselves from among this congregation, that I may *consume* them in a moment. *22* And they fell upon their faces, and said, O **YeHoVaH**, the **Elohim** of the spirits of all flesh, shall one man sin, and will you be angry with all the congregation? *23* And **YeHoVaH** spoke to Moses, saying, *24* Speak to the congregation, saying, Get you away from about the tabernacle of Korah, Dathan, and Abiram. *25* And Moses rose up and went to Dathan and Abiram; and the elders of Israel followed him. *26* And he spoke to the congregation, saying, Depart, I pray you, from the tents of these wicked men, and touch nothing of theirs, or you will be consumed in all their sins. *27* So they got up from the tabernacle of Korah, Dathan, and Abiram, on every side: and Dathan and Abiram came out, and stood in the door of their tents, and their wives, and their sons, and their little children. *28* And Moses said, Hereby you shall know that **YeHoVaH** has sent me to do all these works; for *I have not done them of my own mind*. *29* If these men die the common death of all men, or if they be visited after the visitation of all men; then **YeHoVaH** has not sent me. *30* But if **YeHoVaH** make a new thing, and the earth open her mouth, and swallow them up, with all that belong to them, and they go down quick into the pit; then you shall understand that these men have provoked **YeHoVaH**.

31 And it came to pass, as he had ended speaking all these words, that the ground gave way that was under them: *32* And the earth opened her mouth, and swallowed them up, and their houses, and all the men that belonged to Korah, and all their goods. *33* They, and all that belonged to them, went down alive into the pit, and the earth closed upon them: and they perished from among the congregation. *34* And all Israel that were around them fled at the cry of them: for they said, Or the earth swallow us up also. *35* And there came out a fire from **YeHoVaH**, and consumed the 250 men that offered incense. *36* And **YeHoVaH** spoke to Moses, saying, *37* Speak to Eleazar the son of Aaron the priest, that he take up the censers out of the burning, and scatter you the fire about; for they are hallowed. *38* The censers of these sinners against their own souls, let them make them broad plates for a covering of the altar: for they offered them before **YeHoVaH**, therefore they are hallowed: and they shall be a sign to the children of Israel. *39* And Eleazar the priest took the brass censers, where they that were burnt had offered; and they were made broad plates for a covering of the altar: *40* To be a memorial to the children of Israel, that no stranger, which is not of the seed of Aaron, come near to offer incense before **YeHoVaH**; that he be not as Korah, and as his company: as **YeHoVaH** said to him by the hand of Moses.

41 But the next day all the congregation of the children of Israel murmured against Moses and against Aaron, saying, You have killed the people of **YeHoVaH**. *42* And it came to pass, when the congregation was gathered against Moses and against Aaron that they looked toward the tabernacle of the congregation: and, behold, the cloud covered it, and the glory of **YeHoVaH** appeared. *43* And Moses and Aaron came before the tabernacle of the congregation. *44* And **YeHoVaH** spoke to Moses, saying, *45* Get up from among this congregation, that I may consume them as in a moment. And they fell upon their faces. *46* And Moses said to Aaron, Take a censer, and put fire in from off the altar, and put on incense, and go quickly to the congregation, and make an atonement for them: for there is wrath gone out from **YeHoVaH**; the plague is begun. *47* And Aaron took as Moses commanded, and ran into the midst of the congregation; and, behold, the plague was begun among the people: and he put on incense, and made atonement for the people. *48* And he stood between the dead and the living; and the plague was stopped. *49* Now they that died in the plague were 15,700, beside them that died about the matter of Korah. *50* And Aaron returned to Moses to the door of the tabernacle of the congregation: and the plague was stopped.

Chapter 17
The people continue to complain 'again' and YeHoVaH tells Moses to bring a staff from each tribal leader to the Tent of Meeting to stop the grumbling. Aaron's staff was the only one that blossomed.

1 And **YeHoVaH** spoke to Moses, saying, *2* Speak to the children of Israel, and take of every one of them a rod according to the house of their fathers, of all their princes according to the house of their fathers 12 rods: write you every man's name upon his rod. *3* And you shall write Aaron's name upon the rod of Levi: for one rod shall be for the head of the house of their fathers. *4* And you shall lay them up in the tabernacle of the congregation before the testimony, where I will meet with you. *5* And it shall come to pass, that the man's rod, whom I shall choose, shall blossom: and I will make to cease from me the murmurings of the children of Israel, whereby they murmur against you. *6* And Moses spoke to the children of Israel, and every one of their princes gave him a rod, for each prince one, according to their fathers' houses, for a total of 12 rods: and the rod of Aaron was among their rods. *7* And Moses laid up the rods before **YeHoVaH** in the tabernacle of witness. *8* And it came to pass, that on the next morning Moses went into the tabernacle of witness; and, behold, the rod of Aaron for the house of Levi was budded, and brought forth buds, and bloomed blossoms, and yielded almonds. *9* And Moses brought out all the rods from before **YeHoVaH** to all the children of Israel: and they looked, and took every man his rod. *10* And **YeHoVaH** said to Moses, Bring Aaron's rod again before the testimony, to be kept for a token against the rebels; and you shall take away their murmurings from me, so that they do not die.

11 And Moses did so: as **YeHoVaH** commanded him. *12* And the children of Israel spoke to Moses, saying, Behold, we die, we perish, we all perish. *13* Whoever comes any way near to the tabernacle of **YeHoVaH** shall die: shall we be consumed with dying?

Chapter 18

YeHoVaH tells Aaron: "I have given you the Levites to work at the Tent of Meeting. Everything that is devoted to YeHoVaH is yours." He assigns the service of the tabernacle to Aaron and his sons and the Levites.

1 And **YeHoVaH** said to Aaron, You and your sons and your father's house with you shall bear the iniquity of the sanctuary: and you and thy sons with you shall bear the iniquity of your priesthood. *2* And thy brethren also of the tribe of Levi, the tribe of thy father, with you, that they may be joined to you, and minister to you: but you and thy sons with you shall minister before the tabernacle of witness. *3* And they shall keep thy charge, and the charge of the entire tabernacle: only they shall not come near the vessels of the sanctuary and the altar that neither they, nor you also, die. *4* And they shall be joined to you, and keep the charge of the tabernacle of the congregation, for all the service of the tabernacle: and a stranger shall not come near to you. *5* And you shall keep the charge of the sanctuary, and the charge of the altar: that there be no wrath any more upon the children of Israel. *6* And I, behold, I have taken your brethren the Levites from among the children of Israel: to you they are given as a gift for **YeHoVaH**, to do the service of the tabernacle of the congregation. *7* Therefore you and thy sons with you shall keep your priest's office for everything of the altar, and within the veil; and you shall serve: I have given your priest's office to you as a service of gift: and the stranger (non-Levite) that comes near shall be put to death. *8* And **YeHoVaH** spoke to Aaron, Behold, I also have given you the charge of my heave-offerings of all the hallowed things of the children of Israel; to you have I given them by reason of the anointing, and to thy sons, by an ordinance forever. *9* This shall be yours of the most holy things, reserved from the fire: every offering of theirs, every meal offering of theirs, and every sin offering of theirs, and every trespass offering of theirs which they shall render to me, shall be most holy for you and for thy sons. *10* In the most holy place shall you eat it; every male shall eat it: it shall be holy to you.

11 And this is yours; the heave-offering of their gift, with all the wave-offerings of the children of Israel: I have given them to you, and to thy sons and to thy daughters with you, by a statute forever: every one that is clean in thy house shall eat of it. *12* All the best of the oil, and all the best of the wine, and of the wheat, the first fruits of them which they shall offer to **YeHoVaH**, them have I given you. *13* And whatsoever is first ripe in the land, which they shall bring to **YeHoVaH**, shall be yours; every one that *is clean* in your house shall eat of it. *14* Everything devoted in Israel shall be yours. *15* The first offspring of every womb, both human and animal, that is offered to **YeHoVaH** is yours. But you must redeem every firstborn son and every firstborn male of unclean animals. *16* And those that are to be redeemed from a month old shall you redeem, according to your estimation, for the money of five shekels, after the shekel of the sanctuary, which is 20 gerahs (1 gerah is one-twentieth of a shekel). *17* But the first offspring of a cow, or the first offspring of a sheep, or the first offspring of a goat, you shall not redeem; they are holy: you shall sprinkle their blood upon the altar, and shall burn their fat for an offering made by fire, for a sweet savor to **YeHoVaH**. *18* And the flesh of them shall be yours, as the wave breast and as the right shoulder are yours. *19* All the heave-offerings of the holy things, which the children of Israel offer to **YeHoVaH**, have I given you, and thy sons and thy daughters with you, by a statute forever: it is a covenant of salt (a binding promise) forever before **YeHoVaH** to you and to your seed with you. *20* And **YeHoVaH** spoke to Aaron, *You shall have no inheritance in their land, and neither shall you have any part among them: I am your part and your inheritance among the children of Israel.*

21 And, behold, I have given the children of Levi all the tenth in Israel for an inheritance, for their service that they serve, even the service of the tabernacle of the congregation. *22* Neither must the children of Israel come near the tabernacle of the congregation, or else they bear sin, and die. *23* But the Levites shall do the service of the tabernacle of the congregation, and they shall bear their iniquity: it shall be a statute forever throughout your generations, that among the children of Israel they have no inheritance. *24* But the tithes of the children of Israel, which they offer as a heave-offering to **YeHoVaH**, I have given to the Levites to inherit: therefore I have said to them, Among the children of Israel they shall have no inheritance. *25* And **YeHoVaH** spoke to Moses, saying, *26* Thus speak to the Levites, and say to them, When you take of the children of Israel the tithes which I have given you from them for your inheritance, then you shall offer up a heave-offering of it for **YeHoVaH**, even a tenth part of the tithe. *27* And this, your heave-offering shall be reckoned to you, as though it were the corn of the threshing floor, and as the fullness of the winepress. *28* Thus you also shall offer a heave-offering to **YeHoVaH** of all your tithes, which you receive of the children of Israel; and you shall give thereof **YeHoVaH**'s heave-offering to Aaron the priest. *29* Out of all your gifts you shall offer every heave-offering of **YeHoVaH**, of all the best thereof, even the hallowed part thereof out of it. *30* Therefore you shall say to them, When you have heaved the best thereof from it, then it shall be counted to the Levites as the increase of the threshing floor, and as the increase of the winepress.

31 And you shall eat it in every place, you and your households: for it is your reward for your service in the tabernacle of the congregation. *32* And you shall bear no sin by reason of it, when you have heaved from it the best of it: neither shall you pollute the holy things of the children of Israel, or else you die.
Reading 38 ends

Chapter 19
YeHoVaH tells them to burn a heifer outside the camp for the water of cleansing. Anyone who is unclean and does not cleanse themselves shall be cut off.
Reading 39 begins
1 And **YeHoVaH** spoke to Moses and to Aaron, saying, *2* This is the ordinance of the law (instruction) which **YeHoVaH** has commanded, saying, Speak to the children of Israel, that they bring you a *red heifer* without spot, wherein is no blemish, and upon which never came a yoke: *3* And you shall give her to Eleazar the priest, that he may bring her forth outside the camp, and one shall slay her before his face: *4* And Eleazar the priest shall take of her blood with his finger, and sprinkle of her blood directly before the tabernacle of the congregation seven times: *5* And one shall burn the heifer in his sight; her skin, and her flesh, and her blood, with her dung, shall he burn: *6* And the priest shall take cedar wood, and hyssop, and scarlet, and cast it into the midst of the burning of the heifer. *7* Then the priest shall wash his clothes, and he shall bathe his flesh in water, and afterward he shall come into the camp, and the priest shall be unclean until the evening. *8* And he that burns her shall wash his clothes in water, and bathe his flesh in water, and shall be unclean until the evening. *9* And a man that is clean shall gather up the ashes of the heifer, and lay them up outside the camp in a clean place, and it shall be

kept for the congregation of the children of Israel for a water of separation: it is a purification for sin. *10* And he that gathers the ashes of the heifer shall wash his clothes, and be unclean until the evening: and it shall be to the children of Israel, and to the stranger that travels among them, for a statute forever.

11 He that touches the dead body of any man shall be unclean seven days. *12* He shall purify himself with it on the third day, and on the seventh day he shall be clean: but if he purify not himself the third day, then the seventh day he shall not be clean. *13* Whosoever touches the dead body of any man and purifies not himself, defiles the tabernacle of **YeHoVaH**; and that soul shall be cut off from Israel: because the water of separation was not sprinkled upon him, he shall be unclean; his uncleanness is yet upon him. *14* This is the law, when a man dies in a tent: all that come into the tent, and all that is in the tent, shall be unclean seven days. *15* And every open vessel, which has no covering bound upon it, is unclean. *16* And whosoever touches one that is slain with a sword in the open fields, or a dead body, or a bone of a man, or a grave, shall be unclean seven days. *17* And for an unclean person they shall take of the ashes of the burnt heifer of purification for sin, and running water shall be put thereto in a vessel: *18* And a clean person shall take hyssop, and dip it in the water, and sprinkle it upon the tent, and upon all the vessels, and upon the persons that were there, and upon him that touched a bone, or one slain, or one dead, or a grave: *19* And the clean person shall sprinkle upon the unclean on the third day, and on the seventh day: and on the seventh day he shall purify himself, and wash his clothes, and bathe himself in water, and shall be clean at evening. *20* But the man that shall be unclean, and shall not purify himself, that soul shall be cut off from among the congregation, because he has defiled the sanctuary of **YeHoVaH**: the water of separation has not been sprinkled upon him; he is unclean.

21 And it shall be a perpetual statute to them, that he that sprinkles the water of separation shall wash his clothes; and he that touches the water of separation shall be unclean until evening. *22* And whatsoever the unclean person touches shall be unclean; and the soul that touches it shall be unclean until evening.

Chapter 20
YeHoVaH tells Moses to speak to a rock to produce water but he struck the rock instead. Edom refused Israel passage. Miriam and Aaron both die.

1 Then came the children of Israel, even the whole congregation, into the desert of Zin in the first month: and the people abode in Kadesh; and Miriam died there, and was buried there. *2* And there was no water for the congregation: and they gathered themselves together against Moses and against Aaron. *3* And the people were angry with Moses and said, If only death had overtaken us when our brothers came to their death before **YeHoVaH**! *4* And why have you brought up the congregation of **YeHoVaH** into this wilderness, that we and our cattle should die here? *5* And why have you made us to come up out of Egypt, to bring us in to this evil place? it is no place of seed, or of figs, or of vines, or of pomegranates; neither is there any water to drink. *6* And Moses and Aaron went from the presence of the assembly to the door of the tabernacle of the congregation, and they fell upon their faces: and the glory of **YeHoVaH** appeared to them. *7* And **YeHoVaH** spoke to Moses, saying, *8* Take the rod, and gather you the assembly together, you, and Aaron thy brother, and '*speak you to the rock*' before their eyes; and it shall give forth its water, and you shall bring forth to them water out of the rock: so you shall give the congregation and their animals drink. **9** And Moses took the rod from before **YeHoVaH**, as he commanded him. **10** And Moses and Aaron gathered the congregation together before the rock, and he said to them, Hear now, you rebels; must we fetch you water out of this rock?

11 And Moses lifted up his hand, and '*with his rod*' he hit the rock twice: and the water came out abundantly, and the congregation drank, and their animals also. **12** And **YeHoVaH** spoke to Moses and Aaron, Because you *believed me not*, to sanctify me in the eyes of the children of Israel, therefore you *shall not* bring this congregation into the land which I have given them. **13** This is the water of Meribah; because the children of Israel strove with **YeHoVaH**, and he was sanctified in them. **14** And Moses sent messengers from Kadesh to the king of Edom, Thus says thy brother Israel, You know all the travail (difficult and hard work) that has befallen us: **15** How our fathers went down into Egypt, and we have dwelt in Egypt a long time; and the Egyptians provoked us, and our fathers: **16** And when we cried to **YeHoVaH**, he heard our voice, and sent an angel, and has brought us forth out of Egypt: and, behold, we are in Kadesh, a city in the uttermost of thy border: **17** Let us pass, I pray you, through thy country: we will not pass through the fields, or through the vineyards, neither will we drink of the water of the wells: we will go by the king's highway, we will not turn to the right hand nor to the left, until we have passed thy borders. **18** And Edom said to him, You shall not pass by me, or else I come out against you with the sword. **19** And the children of Israel said to him, We will go by the highway: and if I and my cattle drink of thy water, then I will pay for it: I will only, without doing anything else, go through on my feet. **20** And he said, You shall not go through. And Edom came out against him with many people, and with a strong hand.

21 Thus Edom refused to give Israel passage through his border: where Israel turned away from him. **22** And the children of Israel, even the whole congregation, journeyed from Kadesh, and came to mount Hor. **23** And **YeHoVaH** spoke to Moses and Aaron in mount Hor, by the coast of the land of Edom, saying, **24**Aaron shall be gathered to his people: for he shall not enter into the land which I have given to the children of Israel, '*because* you *rebelled*' against my word at the water of Meribah. **25** Take Aaron and Eleazar his son, and bring them up to mount Hor: **26** And strip Aaron of his garments, and put them upon Eleazar his son: and Aaron shall be gathered to his people, and shall die there. **27** And Moses did as **YeHoVaH** commanded: and they went up into mount Hor in the sight of the entire congregation. **28** And Moses stripped Aaron of his garments, and put them upon Eleazar his son; and Aaron died there in the top of the mount: and Moses and Eleazar came down from the mount. **29** And when the entire congregation saw that Aaron was dead, they mourned for Aaron **30** days, all the house of Israel.

CHAPTERS 21- 30

Chapter 21
The people continue to grumble so YeHoVaH sends snakes. Moses makes a bronze snake and whoever looked at it lived. Israel defeated the Amorites.

1 And when king Arad the Canaanite, which dwelt in the south, heard tell that Israel came by the way of the spies; then he fought against the Israelites, and took some of them prisoners. *2* And Israel vowed a vow to *YeHoVaH*, and said, If you will indeed deliver this people into my hand, then I will utterly destroy their cities. *3* And *YeHoVaH* listened to the voice of Israel, and delivered up the Canaanites; and they utterly destroyed them and their cities: and he called the name of the place Hormah. *4* And they journeyed from mount Hor by the way of the Red sea, to compass the land of Edom: and the soul of the people was much discouraged because of the way. *5* And the people spoke against *Elohim*, and against Moses, Why have you brought us up out of Egypt to die in the wilderness? for there is no bread, neither is there any water; and our soul hates this light bread. *6* And *YeHoVaH* sent fiery serpents among the people, and they bit the people; and many people of Israel died. *7* Therefore the people came to Moses, and said, We have sinned, for we have spoken against *YeHoVaH*, and against you; pray to *YeHoVaH*, that he take away the serpents from us. And Moses prayed for the people. *8* And *YeHoVaH* said to Moses, Make you a fiery serpent, and set it upon a pole: and it shall come to pass, that every one that is bitten, when he looks upon it, shall live. *9* And Moses made a serpent of brass, and put it upon a pole, and it came to pass, that if a serpent had bitten any man, when he beheld the serpent of brass, he lived. *10* And the children of Israel set forward, and pitched in Oboth.

11 And they journeyed from Oboth, and pitched at Ijeabarim, in the wilderness which is before Moab, toward the sun rising. *12* From there they removed, and pitched in the valley of Zared. *13* From there they removed, and pitched on the other side of Arnon, which is in the wilderness that comes out of the coasts of the Amorites: for Arnon is the border of Moab, between Moab and the Amorites. *14* Where it is said in the book of the wars (the book has been completely lost but it is generally thought to be a collection of victory songs or poems) of *YeHoVaH*, What he did in the Red sea, and in the brooks of Arnon, *15* And at the stream of the brooks that goes down to the dwelling of Ar, and lies upon the border of Moab. *16* And from there they went to Beer: that is the well where *YeHoVaH* spoke to Moses, Gather the people together, and I will give them water. *17* Then Israel sang this song, Spring up, O well; sing you to it: *18* The princes dug the well, the nobles of the people dug it, by the direction of the lawgiver, with their staves. And from the wilderness they went to Mattanah: *19* And from Mattanah to Nahaliel: and from Nahaliel to Bamoth: *20* And from Bamoth in the valley, that is in the country of Moab, to the top of Pisgah, which looks toward Jeshimon.

21 And the Israelites sent messengers to Sihon king of the Amorites, saying, *22* Let me pass through thy land: we will not turn into the fields, or into the vineyards; we will not drink of the waters of the well: but we will go along by the king's high way, until we are past thy borders. *23* And Sihon would not suffer the Israelites to pass through his border: but Sihon gathered all his people together, and went out against the Israelites into the wilderness: and he came to Jahaz, and fought against the Israelites. *24* And the Israelites destroyed him with the edge of the sword, and possessed his land from Arnon to Jabbok, even to the children of Ammon: for the border of the children of Ammon was strong. *25* And the Israelites took all these cities: and dwelt in all the cities of the Amorites, in Heshbon, and in all the villages thereof. *26* For Heshbon was the city of Sihon the king of the Amorites, who had fought against the former king of Moab, and taken all his land out of his hand, even to Arnon. *27* Where they that speak in proverbs say, Come into Heshbon, let the city of Sihon be built and prepared: *28* For there is a fire gone out of Heshbon, a flame from the city of Sihon: it has consumed Ar of Moab, and the lords of the high places of Arnon. *29* Woe to you, Moab! you are undone, O people of

Chemosh: he has given his sons that escaped, and his daughters, into captivity to Sihon king of the Amorites. *30* We have shot at them; Heshbon is perished even to Dibon, and we have laid them waste even to Nophah, which reaches to Medeba.

31 Thus the Israelites dwelt in the land of the Amorites. *32* And Moses sent to spy out Jaazer, and they took the villages there, and drove out the Amorites that were there. *33* And they turned and went up by the way of Bashan: and Og the king of Bashan went out against them, he, and all his people, to the battle at Edrei. *34* And **YeHoVaH** said to Moses, Fear him not: for I have delivered him into thy hand, and all his people, and his land; and you shall do to him as you did to Sihon king of the Amorites, which dwelt at Heshbon. *35* So they killed him, and his sons, and all his people, until there was none left alive: and they possessed his land.
   Reading 39 ends

Chapter 22
Balak sends for Balaam to curse the Israelites. Balaam's donkey warns him. The Angel of YeHoVaH says, "Go, but speak only what I tell you."
   Reading 40 begins
1 And the children of Israel set forward, and pitched in the plains of Moab on this side Jordan by Jericho. *2* And Balak the son of Zippor saw all that Israel had done to the Amorites. *3* And Moab was much afraid of the people, because they were many: and Moab was distressed because of the children of Israel. *4* And Moab said to the elders of Midian, Now shall this company lick up all that are round about us, as the ox licks up the grass of the field. And Balak the son of Zippor was king of the Moabites at that time. *5* He sent messengers to Balaam the son of Beor to Pethor, which is by the river of the land of the children of his people, to call him, saying, Behold, there is a people come out from Egypt: behold, they cover the face of the earth, and they abide over against me: *6* Come now, in answer to my prayer, and put a curse on this people, for they are greater than I: and then I may be strong enough to overcome them and send them out of the land: for it is clear that good comes to him who has your blessing, but he on whom you put your curse is cursed. *7* And the elders of Moab and the elders of Midian departed with the rewards of divination (knowledge of how a future event will happen) in their hand; and they came to Balaam, and spoke to him the words of Balak. *8* And he said to them, Lodge here this night, and I will bring you word again, as **YeHoVaH** shall speak to me: and the princes of Moab abode with Balaam. *9* And **Elohim** came to Balaam, and said, What men are these with you? *10* And Balaam said to **YeHoVaH**, Balak the son of Zippor, king of Moab, hath sent to me, saying,

11 Behold, there is a people come out of Egypt, which covers the face of the earth: come now, curse me them; perhaps I shall be able to overcome them, and drive them out. *12* And **YeHoVaH** said to Balaam, You shall not go with them; you shall not curse the people: for they are blessed. *13* And Balaam rose up in the morning, and said to the princes of Balak, Get you into your land: for **YeHoVaH** refuses to give me leave to go with you. *14*And the princes of Moab rose up, and they went to Balak, and said, Balaam refuses to come with us. *15* And Balak sent yet again princes, more, and more honorable than they. *16* And they came to Balaam, and said to him, Thus says Balak the son of Zippor, Let nothing, I pray you, hinder you from coming to me: *17* For I will promote you to very great honor, and I will do whatever you say to me: come therefore, I pray you, curse me this people. *18* And Balaam answered and said to the servants of Balak, If Balak would give me his house full of silver and gold, I cannot go beyond the word of **YeHoVaH** my **Elohim**, to do less or more. *19* Now therefore, I pray you, stay also here this night that I may know what **YeHoVaH** will say to me more. *20* And **YeHoVaH** came to Balaam at night, and said to him, If the men come to call you, rise up, and go with them; but yet the word which I shall say to you, that shall you do.

21 And Balaam rose up in the morning, and saddled his donkey, and went with the princes of Moab. *22* And **YeHoVaH**'s anger was kindled because he went: and the angel of **YeHoVaH** stood in the way for an adversary against him. Now he was riding upon his donkey, and his two servants were with him. *23* And the donkey saw the angel of **YeHoVaH** standing in the way, and his sword drawn in his hand: and the donkey turned aside out of the way, and went into the field: and Balaam struck the donkey, to turn her into the way. *24* But the angel of **YeHoVaH** stood in a path of the vineyards, a wall being on this side, and a wall on that side. *25* And when the donkey saw the angel of **YeHoVaH**, she thrust herself to the wall, and crushed Balaam's foot against the wall: and he struck her again. *26* And the angel of **YeHoVaH** went further, and stood in a narrow place, where there was no way to turn either to the right hand or to the left. *27* And when the donkey saw the angel of **YeHoVaH**, she fell down under Balaam: and Balaam's anger was kindled, and he struck the donkey with a staff. *28* And **YeHoVaH** opened the mouth of the donkey, and she said to Balaam, What have I done to you, that you have stuck me these three times? *29* And Balaam said to the donkey, because you have mocked me: I wish there were a sword in my hand, for now would I kill you. *30* And the donkey said to Balaam, Am not I your donkey, upon which you have ridden ever since I was yours to this day? was I ever not to do so to you? And he said, No.

31 Then **YeHoVaH** opened the eyes of Balaam, and he saw the angel of **YeHoVaH** standing in the way, and his sword drawn in his hand: and he bowed down his head, and fell flat on his face. *32* And the angel of **YeHoVaH** said to him, Where have you struck your donkey these three times? behold, I went out to withstand you, because your way is perverse before me: *33* And the donkey saw me, and turned from me these three times: unless she had turned from me, surely now also I had slain you, and saved her alive. *34* And Balaam said to the angel of **YeHoVaH**, I have sinned; for I knew not that you stood in the way against me: now therefore, if it displeases you, I will get back again. *35* And the angel of **YeHoVaH** said to Balaam, Go with the men: but only the word that I shall speak to you, that you shall speak. So Balaam went with the princes of Balak. *36* And when Balak heard that Balaam had come, he went out to meet him to a city of Moab, which is in the border of Arnon, which is in the utmost coast. *37* And Balak said to Balaam, Did I not earnestly send to you to call you? Why didn't you come to me? am I not able indeed to promote you to honor? *38* And Balaam said to Balak, Lo, I have come to you: have I now any power at all to say anything? the word that **YeHoVaH** puts in my mouth, that shall I speak. *39* And Balaam went with Balak, and they came to Kirjathhuzoth. *40* And Balak offered oxen and sheep, and sent to Balaam, and to the princes that were with him.

41 And it came to pass the next day, that Balak took Balaam, and brought him up into the high places of Baal, that he might see the utmost part of the people.

Chapter 23
*YeHoVaH gives Balaam a word: "How can I curse whom **Elohim** has not cursed?" Then at another place: "YeHoVaH their **Elohim** is with Israel."*

1 And Balaam said to Balak, Build here seven altars, and prepare here seven oxen and seven rams. *2* And Balak did as Balaam had spoken; and Balak and Balaam offered on every altar a bullock and a ram. *3* And Balaam said to Balak, Stand by thy burnt offering, and I will go: perhaps *YeHoVaH* will come to meet me: and whatever he shows me I will tell you. And he went to a high place. *4* And *YeHoVaH* met Balaam: and he said to him, I have prepared seven altars, and I have offered upon every altar a bullock and a ram. *5* And *YeHoVaH* put a word in Balaam's mouth, and said, Return to Balak, and thus you shall say. *6* And he returned to him, and while he stood by his burnt sacrifice, he, and all the princes of Moab. *7* And he took up his parable, and said, Balak the king of Moab has brought me from Aram, out of the mountains of the east, saying, Come, curse me Jacob, and come, defy Israel. *8* How shall I curse, whom *YeHoVaH* has not cursed? or how shall I defy, whom *YeHoVaH* has not defied? *9* For from the top of the rocks I see him, and from the hills I behold him: thus, the people shall dwell alone, and shall not be reckoned among the nations. *10* Who can count the dust of Jacob, and the number of the fourth part of Israel? Let me die the death of the righteous, and let my last end be like his!

11 And Balak said to Balaam, What have you done to me? I took you to curse my enemies, and, behold, you have blessed them altogether. *12* And he answered and said, Must I not take heed to speak that which *YeHoVaH* has put in my mouth? *13* And Balak said to him, Come, I pray you, with me to another place, from where you may see them: you shall see but the utmost part of them, and shall not see them all: and curse me them from there. *14*And he brought him into the field of Zophim, to the top of Pisgah, and built seven altars, and offered a bullock and a ram on every altar. *15* And he said to Balak, Stand here by thy burnt offering, while I meet *YeHoVaH* yonder. *16* And *YeHoVaH* met Balaam, and put a word in his mouth, and said, Go again to Balak, and say thus. *17* And when he came to him, behold, he stood by his burnt offering, and the princes of Moab with him. And Balak said to him, What has *YeHoVaH* spoken? *18* And he took up his parable, and said, Rise up, Balak, and hear; listen to me, you son of Zippor: *19* *YeHoVaH* is not a man, that he should lie; *neither the son of man, that he should repent*: has he said, and shall he not do it? or has he spoken, and shall he not make it good? *20* Behold, I have received commandment to bless: and he has blessed; and I cannot reverse it.

21 He has not beheld iniquity in Jacob, neither has he seen unreasonableness in Israel: *YeHoVaH* his *Elohim* is with him, and the shout of a king is among them. *22* *YeHoVaH* brought them out of Egypt; he has as it were the strength of a unicorn. *23* Surely there is no enchantment against Jacob, neither is there any foretelling against the children of Israel: according to this time it shall be said of Jacob and of Israel, What has *Elohim* wrought! *24* Behold, the people shall rise up as a great lion, and lift up himself as a young lion: he shall not lie down until he eat of the prey, and drink the blood of the slain. *25* And Balak said to Balaam, Neither curse them at all, nor bless them at all. *26* But Balaam answered and said to Balak, didn't I tell you, saying, All that *YeHoVaH* speaks, that I must do? *27* And Balak said to Balaam, Come, I pray you, I will bring you to another place; perhaps it will please *YeHoVaH* that you may curse them from there. *28* And Balak brought Balaam to the top of Peor that looks toward Jeshimon. *29* And Balaam said to Balak, Build here seven altars, and prepare here seven bullocks and seven rams. *30* And Balak did as Balaam had said, and offered a bullock and a ram on every altar.

Chapter 24

Balak was angry that Balaam did not curse Israel but blessed them three times. Balaam said, "Blessed is he that blesses you, and cursed is he that curses you.

1 Now when Balaam saw that it pleased **YeHoVaH** to bless Israel, he did not rely on his own understanding as at other times, but turned his face toward the wilderness. *2* And Balaam lifted up his eyes, and he saw Israel abiding in his tents according to their tribes; and the spirit of **YeHoVaH** came upon him. *3* and he spoke his message: "The prophecy of Balaam son of Beor, the prophecy of one whose eye sees clearly, *4* He has said, which heard the words of **YeHoVaH**, which saw the vision of the Almighty, falling into a trance, but having his eyes open: *5* How goodly are your tents, O Jacob, and your tabernacles, O Israel! *6* "Like valleys they spread out, like gardens beside a river, like aloes planted by **YeHoVaH**, like cedars beside the waters. *7* He shall pour the water out of his buckets, and his seed shall be in many waters, and his king shall be higher than Agag, and his kingdom shall be exalted. *8* **YeHoVaH** brought him forth out of Egypt; he has as it were the strength of a *unicorn*: he shall eat up the nations his enemies, and shall break their bones, and pierce them through with his arrows. *9* He couched, he lay down as a lion, and as a great lion: who shall stir him up? *Blessed is he that blesses you, and cursed is he that curses you. 10* And Balak's anger was kindled against Balaam, and he hit his hands together: and Balak said to Balaam, I called you to curse my enemies, and, behold, you have altogether blessed them these three times.

11 Therefore now flee you to thy place: I thought to promote you to great honor; but, **YeHoVaH** has kept you back from honor. *12* And Balaam said to Balak, Spoke I not also to thy messengers which you sent to me, saying, *13* If Balak would give me his house full of silver and gold, I cannot go beyond the commandment of **YeHoVaH**, to do either good or bad of mine own mind; but what **YeHoVaH** say, that will I speak? *14* And now, behold, I go to my people: come therefore, and I will tell you what this people shall do to thy people in the latter days. *15* And he took up his story, and said, Balaam the son of Beor has said, and the man whose eyes are open has said: *16* He has said, which heard the words of **YeHoVaH**, and knew the knowledge of the most High, which saw the vision of the Almighty, falling into a trance, but having his eyes open: *17* I shall see him, but not now: I shall behold him, but not near: there shall come a Star out of Jacob, and a Scepter shall rise out of Israel, and shall destroy the corners of Moab, and destroy all the children of Sheth. *18* And Edom shall be a possession, Seir also shall be a possession for his enemies; and Israel shall do valiantly. *19* Out of Jacob shall come he that shall have dominion, and shall destroy him that remains of the city. *20* And when he looked on Amalek, he took up his story, and said, Amalek was the first of the nations; but his latter end shall be that he perishes forever.

21 And he looked on the Kenites, and continued his story, and said, Strong is your dwelling place, and you put your nest in a rock. *22* Nevertheless the Kenite shall be wasted, until Asshur shall carry you away captive. *23* And he continued his story, and said, Alas, who shall live when **YeHoVaH** does this! *24* And ships shall come from the coast of Chittim, and shall afflict Asshur, and shall afflict Eber, and he also shall perish forever. *25* And Balaam rose up, and went and returned to his place: and Balak also went his way.

Chapter 25

The people are unfaithful with Moabite women and worship their gods. Phinehas kills one couple and YeHoVaH commends his zeal.

1 And Israel abode in Shittim, and the people began to commit prostitution with the daughters of Moab. *2* And they called the people to the sacrifices of their gods: and the people did eat, and bowed down to their gods. *3* And Israel joined himself to Baalpeor: and the anger of **YeHoVaH** was kindled against Israel. *4* And **YeHoVaH** said to Moses, Take all the heads of the people, and hang them up before **YeHoVaH** against the sun, that the fierce anger of **YeHoVaH** may be turned away from Israel. *5* And Moses said to the judges of Israel, Slay you every one his men that were joined to Baalpeor. *6* And, behold, one of the children of Israel came and brought to his brethren a Midianitish woman in the sight of Moses, and in the sight of all the congregation of the children of Israel, who were weeping before the door of the tabernacle of the congregation. *7* And when Phinehas, the son of Eleazar, the son of Aaron the priest, saw it, he rose up from among the congregation, and took a javelin in his hand; *8* And he went after the man of Israel into the tent, and thrust both of them through, the man of Israel, and the woman through her belly. So the plague was stayed from the children of Israel. *9* And those that died in the plague were 25,000.

Reading 40 ends

Reading 41 begins
10 And **YeHoVaH** speaks to Moses, saying, kill the Midianites.

11 Phinehas, the son of Eleazar, the son of Aaron the priest, has turned my wrath away from the children of Israel, while he was zealous for my sake among them, that I consumed not the children of Israel in my jealousy. *12* Why say, Behold, I give to him my covenant of peace: *13* And he shall have it, and his seed after him, even the covenant of an everlasting priesthood; because he was zealous for his **Elohim**, and made an atonement for the children of Israel. *14*Now the name of the Israelite that was slain, even that was slain with the Midianitish woman, was Zimri, the son of Salu, a prince of a chief house among the Simeonites. *15* And the name of the Midianitish woman that was slain was Cozbi, the daughter of Zur; he was head over a people, and of a chief house in Midian. *16* And **YeHoVaH** spoke to Moses, saying, *17* Anger the Midianites, and kill them: *18* For they are a danger to you with their false ways, causing sin to come on you in the question of Peor, and because of Cozbi, their sister, the daughter of the chief of Midian, who was put to death at the time of the disease which came on you because of Peor.

Chapter 26

YeHoVaH tells Moses and Eleazar to take a census. There were 601,730 fighting men and 23,000 Levites. Of the original families that fled Egypt, only Joshua and Caleb remained.

1 And it came to pass after the plague, that **YeHoVaH** spoke to Moses and to Eleazar the son of Aaron the priest, saying, *2* Take the sum of all the congregation of the children of Israel, from 20 years old and upward, throughout their fathers' house, all that are able to go to war in Israel. *3* And Moses and Eleazar the priest spoke with them in the plains of Moab by Jordan near Jericho, saying, *4* Take the sum of the people, from 20 years old and upward; as **YeHoVaH** commanded Moses and the children of Israel, which went forth out of the land of Egypt.

5 Reuben, the eldest son of Israel: the children of Reuben; Hanoch, of whom cometh the family of the Hanochites: of Pallu, the family of the Palluites: *6* Of Hezron, the family of the Hezronites: of Carmi, the family of the Carmites. *7* These are the families of the Reubenites: and they that were numbered of them were forty and three thousand and 750. *8* And the sons of Pallu; Eliab. *9* And the sons of Eliab; Nemuel, and Dathan, and Abiram. This is that Dathan and Abiram, which were famous in the congregation, who strove against Moses and against Aaron in the company of Korah, when they strove against *YeHoVaH*: *10* And the earth opened her mouth, and swallowed them up together with Korah, when that company died, at the same time the fire devoured 250 men: and they became a sign.

11 Nevertheless the children of Korah did not die. *12* The sons of Simeon after their families: of Nemuel, the family of the Nemuelites: of Jamin, the family of the Jaminites: of Jachin, the family of the Jachinites: *13* Of Zerah, the family of the Zarhites: of Shaul, the family of the Shaulites. *14* These are the families of the Simeonites, 22,220. *15* The children of Gad after their families: of Zephon, the family of the Zephonites: of Haggi, the family of the Haggites: of Shuni, the family of the Shunites: *16* Of Ozni, the family of the Oznites: of Eri, the family of the Erites: *17* Of Arod, the family of the Arodites: of Areli, the family of the Arelites. *18* These are the families of the children of Gad according to those that were numbered, 50,500. *19* The sons of Judah were Er and Onan: and Er and Onan died in the land of Canaan. *20* And the sons of Judah after their families were; of Shelah, the family of the Shelanites: of Pharez, the family of the Pharzites: of Zerah, the family of the Zarhites.

21 And the sons of Pharez were; of Hezron, the family of the Hezronites: of Hamul, the family of the Hamulites. *22* These are the families of Judah according to those that were numbered, 76,500. *23* Of the sons of Issachar after their families: of Tola, the family of the Tolaites: of Pua, the family of the Punites: *24* Of Jashub, the family of the Jashubites: of Shimron, the family of the Shimronites. *25* These are the families of Issachar according to those that were numbered, 65,300. *26* Of the sons of Zebulun after their families: of Sered, the family of the Sardites: of Elon, the family of the Elonites: of Jahleel, the family of the Jahleelites. *27* These are the families of the Zebulunites according to those that were numbered, 60,500. *28* The sons of Joseph after their families were Manasseh and Ephraim. *29* Of the sons of Manasseh: of Machir, the family of the Machirites: and Machir begat Gilead: of Gilead come the family of the Gileadites. *30* These are the sons of Gilead: of Jeezer, the family of the Jeezerites: of Helek, the family of the Helekites:

31 And of Asriel, the family of the Asrielites: and of Shechem, the family of the Shechemites: *32* And of Shemida, the family of the Shemidaites: and of Hepher, the family of the Hepherites. *33* And Zelophehad the son of Hepher had no sons, but daughters: and the names of the daughters of Zelophehad were Mahlah, and Noah, Hoglah, Milcah, and Tirzah. *34* These are the families of Manasseh, and those that were numbered, 52,700. *35* These are the sons of Ephraim after their families: of Shuthelah, the family of the Shuthalhites: of Becher, the family of the Bachrites: of Tahan, the family of the Tahanites. *36* And these are the sons of Shuthelah: of Eran, the family of the Eranites. *37* These are the families of the sons of Ephraim according to those that were numbered, 32,500. These are the sons of Joseph after their families. *38* The sons of Benjamin after their families: of Bela, the family of the Belaites: of Ashbel, the family of the Ashbelites: of Ahiram, the family of the Ahiramites: *39* Of Shupham, the family of the Shuphamites: of Hupham, the family of the Huphamites. *40* And the sons of Bela were Ard and Naaman: of Ard, the family of the Ardites: and of Naaman, the family of the Naamites.

41 These are the sons of Benjamin after their families: and they that were numbered were 55,600. *42* These are the sons of Dan after their families: of Shuham, the family of the Shuhamites. These are the families of Dan after their families. *43* All the families of the Shuhamites, according to those that were numbered of them, were 5,500. *44* Of the children of Asher after their families: of Jimna, the family of the Jimnites: of Jesui, the family of the Jesuites: of Beriah, the family of the Beriites. *45* Of the sons of Beriah: of Heber, the family of the Heberites: of Malchiel, the family of the Malchielites. *46* And the name of the daughter of Asher was Sarah. *47* These are the families of the sons of Asher according to those that were numbered; were 53,500. *48* Of the sons of Naphtali after their families: of Jahzeel, the family of the Jahzeelites: of Guni, the family of the Gunites: *49* Of Jezer, the family of the Jezerites: of Shillem, the family of the Shillemites. *50* These are the families of Naphtali according to their families: and they that were numbered were 55,500.

51 These were the numbered of the children of Israel, 601,730. *52* And **YeHoVaH** spoke to Moses, saying, *53* Unto these the land shall be divided for an inheritance according to the number of names. *54* To many you shall give the more inheritance, and to few you shall give the less inheritance: to every one shall his inheritance be given according to those that were numbered of him. *55* Nevertheless the land shall be divided by lot: according to the names of the tribes of their fathers they shall inherit. *56* According to the lot shall the possession thereof be divided between many and few. *57* And these are they that were numbered of the Levites after their families: of Gershon, the family of the Gershonites: of Kohath, the family of the Kohathites: of Merari, the family of the Merarites. *58* These are the families of the Levites: the family of the Libnites, the family of the Hebronites, the family of the Mahlites, the family of the Mushites, the family of the Korathites. And Kohath begat Amram. *59* And the name of Amram's wife was Jochebed, the daughter of Levi, whom her mother bare to Levi in Egypt: and she bare to Amram Aaron and Moses, and Miriam their sister. *60* And to Aaron was born Nadab, and Abihu, Eleazar, and Ithamar.

61 And Nadab and Abihu died, when they offered strange fire before **YeHoVaH**. *62* And those that were numbered were 23,000, all males from a month old and upward: for they were not numbered among the children of Israel, because there was no inheritance given them among the children of Israel. *63* These are they that were numbered by Moses and Eleazar the priest, who numbered the children of Israel in the plains of Moab by Jordan near Jericho. *64* But among these there was not a man of them whom Moses and Aaron the priest numbered, when they numbered the children of Israel in the wilderness of Sinai. *65* For **YeHoVaH** had said of them, They shall surely die in the wilderness. And there was not left a man of them, except Caleb the son of Jephunneh, and Joshua the son of Nun.

Chapter 27
The daughters of Zelophehad were given an inheritance. YeHoVaH tells Moses that he was to die. Moses commissions Joshua as the next leader.

1 Then came the daughters of Zelophehad, the son of Hepher, the son of Gilead, the son of Machir, the son of Manasseh, of the families of Manasseh the son of Joseph: and these are the names of his daughters; Mahlah, Noah, and Hoglah, and Milcah, and Tirzah. *2* And they stood before Moses, and before Eleazar the priest, and before the princes and all the congregation, by the door of the tabernacle of the congregation, saying, *3* Our father died in the wilderness, and he was not in the company of them that gathered themselves together against **YeHoVaH** in the company of Korah; but died in his own sin, and had no sons. **4** Why should the name of our father be done away from among his family, because he has no son? Give to us therefore a possession among the brethren of our father. **5** And Moses brought their cause before **YeHoVaH**. **6** And **YeHoVaH** spoke to Moses, saying, **7** The daughters of Zelophehad speak right: you shall surely give them a possession of an inheritance among their father's brethren; and you shall cause the inheritance of their father to pass to them. **8** And you shall speak to the children of Israel, saying, If a man die, and have no son, then you shall ensure his inheritance passes to his daughter(s). **9** If he has no daughter, give his inheritance to his brothers. **10** If he has no brothers, give his inheritance to his father's brothers (uncles).

11 And if his father have no brothers, then you shall give his inheritance to his kinsman (a male blood relative) that is next to him of his family, and he shall possess it: and it shall be to the children of Israel a statute (decree) of judgment, as **YeHoVaH** commanded Moses. **12** And **YeHoVaH** said to Moses, Get you up into this mount Abarim, and see the land that I have given to the children of Israel. **13** And when you have seen it, you also shall be gathered to thy people, as Aaron thy brother was gathered. **14** For you rebelled against my commandment in the desert (Numbers 20:7, 20:11) of Zin, in the fighting of the congregation, to sanctify me at the water before their eyes: that is the water of Meribah in Kadesh in the wilderness of Zin. **15** And Moses spoke to **YeHoVaH**, saying, **16** Let **YeHoVaH**, the **Elohim** of the spirits of all flesh, set a man over the congregation, **17** Which may go out before them, and which may go in before them, and which may lead them out, and which may bring them in; that the congregation of **YeHoVaH** be not as sheep which have no shepherd. **18** And **YeHoVaH** said to Moses, Take you *Joshua* the son of Nun, a man in whom is the spirit, and lay your hand upon him; **19** And set him before Eleazar the priest, and before all the congregation; and give him a charge in their sight. **20** And you shall put '*some*' of your honor upon him, that all the congregation of the children of Israel may be obedient.

21 And he shall stand before Eleazar the priest, who shall ask counsel for him after the judgment of Urim before **YeHoVaH**: at his word shall they go out, and at his word they shall come in, both he, and all the children of Israel with him, even all the congregation. **22** And Moses did as **YeHoVaH** commanded him: and he took Joshua, and set him before Eleazar the priest, and before the entire congregation: **23** And he laid his hands upon him, and gave him a charge, as **YeHoVaH** commanded by the hand of Moses.

Chapter 28
YeHoVaH commands the people to bring offerings each morning and evening, on the Sabbath and on the first of the month and to celebrate Passover and the Feast of Weeks (Shavuote or Pentecost) Shavuot occurs 50 days or seven weeks after Passover.

1 And **YeHoVaH** spoke to Moses, saying, **2** Command the children of Israel, and say to them, My offering, and my bread for my sacrifices made by fire, for a sweet savor to me, shall you observe to offer to me in their due season. **3** And you shall say to them, This is the offering made by fire which you shall offer to **YeHoVaH**; two lambs of the first year without blemish, for a continual burnt offering. **4** The one lamb shall you offer in the morning, and the other lamb shall you offer at evening; **5** And a tenth part of an ephah of flour for a meal offering, mingled with the fourth part of an hin of beaten oil. **6** It is a continual burnt offering, which was ordained in mount

Sinai for a sweet savor, a sacrifice made by fire to **YeHoVaH**. *7* And the drink offering shall be the fourth part of a hin for the one lamb: in the holy place shall you ensure the strong wine is poured to **YeHoVaH** for a drink offering. *8* And the other lamb shall you offer at evening: as the meal offering of the morning **YeHoVaH**, and as the drink offering, you shall offer it, a sacrifice made by fire, of a sweet savor to **YeHoVaH**. *9* And on the *Sabbath* day (day seven), two lambs of the first year without blemish, and two tenth deals of flour for a meal offering, mingled with oil, and the drink offering: *10* This is the burnt offering of every Sabbath, beside the continual burnt offering, and his drink offering.

11 And in the beginnings of your months you shall offer a burnt offering to **YeHoVaH**; two young bulls, and one ram, seven lambs of the first year without blemish; *12* And three tenth deals of flour for a meal offering, mingled with oil, for one bullock; and two tenth deals of flour for a meal offering, mingled with oil, for one ram; *13* And a tenth of an ephah of flour mingled with oil for a meal offering to one lamb; for a burnt offering of a sweet savor, a sacrifice made by fire to **YeHoVaH**. *14* And their drink offerings shall be half a hin of wine to a bullock, and the third part of a hin to a ram, and a fourth part of a hin to a lamb: this is the burnt offering of every month throughout the months of the year. *15* And one kid of the goats for a sin offering to **YeHoVaH** shall be offered, beside the continual burnt offering, and his drink offering. *16* And in the 15th day of the first month is the **Passover** of **YeHoVaH**. *17* And in the 15th day of this month is the feast: seven days shall unleavened bread be eaten. *18* In the first day shall be a holy assembly; you shall do no manner of servile (physical) work therein: *19* But you shall offer a sacrifice made by fire for a burnt offering to **YeHoVaH**; two young bullocks, and one ram, and seven lambs of the first year: they shall be to you without blemish: *20* And their meal offering shall be of flour mingled with oil: three tenth deals shall you offer for a bullock, and two tenth deals for a ram;

21 Two-tenths of an ephah shall you offer for every lamb, throughout the seven lambs: *22* And one goat for a sin offering, to make an atonement for you. *23* Ye shall offer these beside the burnt offering in the morning, which is for a continual burnt offering. *24* After this manner you shall offer daily, throughout the seven days, the meal of the sacrifice made by fire, of a sweet savor to **YeHoVaH**: it shall be offered beside the continual burnt offering, and his drink offering. *25* And on the seventh day you shall have a holy assembly; you shall do no physical work. *26* Also in the day of the first-fruits, when you bring a new meal offering to **YeHoVaH**, after your weeks (50) be out, you shall have a holy assembly; you shall do no physical work: *27* But you shall offer the burnt offering for a sweet savor to **YeHoVaH**; two young bullocks, one ram, seven lambs of the first year; *28* And their meal offering of flour mingled with oil, three tenth of an ephah to one bullock, two tenths to one ram, *29* Two tenths deal to one lamb, throughout the seven lambs; *30* And one kid of the goats, to make an atonement for you.

31 Ye shall offer them beside the continual burnt offering, and his meal offering, (they shall be to you without blemish) and their drink offerings.

Chapter 29

YeHoVaH commands: In the seventh month on the first day sound the trumpets (Rosh Hashanah); on the tenth day make atonement; on the fifteenth day celebrate for seven days.

1 And in the seventh month, on the first day of the month, you shall have a holy assembly; you shall do no physical work: it is a day of blowing the trumpets to you (Feast of Trumpets or Rosh Hashanah). *2* And you shall offer a burnt offering for a sweet savor to **YeHoVaH**; one young bullock, one ram, and seven lambs of the first year without blemish: *3* And their meal offering shall be of flour mingled with oil, three tenth of an ephah for a bullock, and two tenth of an ephah for a ram, *4* And one tenth of an ephah for one lamb, throughout the seven lambs: *5* And one kid of the goats for a sin offering, to make an atonement for you: *6* Beside the burnt offering of the month, and his meal offering, and the daily burnt offering, and his meal offering, and their drink offerings, according to their manner, for a sweet savor, a sacrifice made by fire to **YeHoVaH**. *7* And you shall have on the tenth day of this seventh month a holy assembly; and you shall search your souls: you shall not do any work: *8* But you shall offer a burnt offering to **YeHoVaH** for a sweet savor; one young bullock, one ram, and seven lambs of the first year; they shall be without blemish: *9* And their meal offering shall be of flour mingled with oil, three tenth of an ephah to a bullock, and two tenth of an ephah to one ram, *10* A two tenth of an ephah for one lamb, throughout the seven lambs:

11 One kid of the goats for a sin offering; beside the sin offering of atonement, and the continual burnt offering, and the meal offering of it, and their drink offerings. *12* And on the fifteenth day of the seventh month you shall have a holy assembly; you shall do no work, and you shall keep a feast to **YeHoVaH** seven days: *13* And you shall offer a burnt offering, a sacrifice made by fire, of a sweet savor to **YeHoVaH**; thirteen young bullocks, two rams, and 15 lambs of the first year; they shall be without blemish: *14* And their meal offering shall be of flour mingled with oil, three tenth of an ephah to every bullock of the 13 bullocks, two tenth of an ephah to each ram of the two rams, *15* And a two tenth of an ephah to each lamb of the 15 lambs: *16* And one kid of the goats for a sin offering; beside the continual burnt offering, his meal offering, and his drink offering. *17* And on the second day you shall offer 12 young bullocks, two rams, 15 lambs of the first year without spot: *18* And their meal offering and their drink offerings for the bullocks, for the rams, and for the lambs, shall be according to their number, after the manner: *19* And one kid of the goats for a sin offering; beside the continual burnt offering, and the meal offering thereof, and their drink offerings. *20* And on the third day 11 bullocks, two rams, 15 lambs of the first year without blemish.

21 And their meal offering and their drink offerings for the bullocks, for the rams, and for the lambs, shall be according to their number, after the manner: *22* And one goat for a sin offering; beside the continual burnt offering, and his meal offering, and his drink offering. *23* And on the fourth day ten bullocks, two rams, and 15 lambs of the first year without blemish: *24* Their meal offering and their drink offerings for the bullocks, for the rams, and for the lambs, shall be according to their number, after the manner: *25* And one kid of the goats for a sin offering; beside the continual burnt offering, his meal offering, and his drink offering. *26* And on the fifth day nine bullocks, two rams, and 15 lambs of the first year without spot: *27* And their meal offering and their drink offerings for the bullocks, for the rams, and for the lambs, shall be according to their number, after the manner: *28* And one goat for a sin offering; beside the continual burnt offering, and his meal offering, and his drink offering. *29* And on the sixth day eight bullocks, two rams, and 15 lambs of the first year without blemish: *30* And their meal offering and their drink offerings for the bullocks, for the rams, and for the lambs, shall be according to their number, after the manner:

31 And one goat for a sin offering; beside the continual burnt offering, his meal offering, and his drink offering. *32* And on the seventh day seven bullocks, two rams, and 15 lambs of the first year without blemish: *33* And their meal offering and their drink offerings for the bullocks, for the rams, and for the lambs, shall be according to their number, after the manner: *34* And one goat for a sin offering; beside the continual burnt offering, his meal offering, and his drink offering. *35* On the eighth day you shall have a solemn assembly: you shall do no servile work therein: *36* But you shall offer a burnt offering, a sacrifice made by fire, of a sweet savor to **YeHoVaH**: one bullock, one ram, seven lambs of the first year without blemish: *37* Their meal offering and their drink offerings for the bullock, for the ram, and for the lambs, shall be according to their number, after the manner: *38* And one goat for a sin offering; beside the continual burnt offering, and his meal offering, and his drink offering. *39* These things you shall do to **YeHoVaH** in your set feasts, beside your vows, and your freewill offerings, for your burnt offerings, and for your meal offerings, and for your drink offerings, and for your peace offerings. *40* And Moses told the children of Israel according to all that **YeHoVaH** commanded Moses.

Reading 41 ends

Chapter 30

When a man makes a vow he must not break his word. When a woman makes a vow it shall stand unless her father or husband forbids it.

Reading 42 begins

1 And Moses spoke to the heads of the tribes concerning the children of Israel, saying, This is what **YeHoVaH** has commanded. *2* If a man vows a vow to **YeHoVaH**, or swear an oath to bind his soul with a bond, he shall not break his word, he shall do according to all that proceeds out of his mouth. *3* If a woman also vow a vow to **YeHoVaH**, and bind herself by a bond, being in her father's house in her youth; *4* And her father hear her vow, and her bond that she has bound her soul, and her father shall hold his peace at her; then all her vows shall stand, and every bond that she has bound her soul shall stand. *5* But if her father disallow her in the day that he hears; not any of her vows, or of her bonds wherewith she has bound her soul, shall stand: and **YeHoVaH** shall forgive her, because her father disallowed her. *6* And if she had a husband, when she vowed, or uttered out of her lips, that she bound her soul; *7* And her husband heard it, and held his peace at her in the day that he heard it: then her vows shall stand, and her bonds that she bound her soul shall stand. *8* But if her husband disallowed her on the day that he heard it; then he shall make her vow which she vowed, and that which she uttered with her lips, that she bound her soul, of no effect: and **YeHoVaH** shall forgive her. *9* But every vow of a widow, and of her that is divorced, wherewith they have bound their souls, shall stand against her. *10* And if she vowed in her husband's house, or bound her soul by a bond with an oath;

11 And her husband heard it, and held his peace at her, and disallowed her not: then all her vows shall stand, and every bond that she bound her soul shall stand. *12* But if her husband has utterly made them void on the day he heard them; then whatever proceeded out of her lips concerning her vows, or concerning the bond of her soul, shall not stand: her husband has made them void; and **YeHoVaH** shall forgive her. *13* Every vow, and every binding oath to afflict the soul, her husband may establish it, or her husband may make it void. *14* But if her husband altogether hold his peace at her from day to day; then he establishes all her vows, or all her bonds, which are upon her: he confirms them, because he held his peace at her in the day that he heard them. *15* But if he in any way makes them void after that he has heard them; then he shall bear her iniquity. *16* These are the statutes (instructions), which **YeHoVaH** commanded Moses, between a man and his wife, between the father and his daughter, being yet in her youth in her father's house.

CHAPTERS 31- 36

Chapter 31
YeHoVaH tells Moses to take vengeance on the Midianites. The Israelites killed the men, burned their cities and divided the spoils.

1 And **YeHoVaH** spoke to Moses, saying, *2* Give the Midianites punishment for the wrong they did to the children of Israel: and after that you will go to rest with your people. *3* And Moses spoke to the people, saying, Arm some of yourselves to the war, and let them go against the Midianites, and avenge **YeHoVaH** of Midian. *4* Of every tribe a thousand, throughout all the tribes of Israel, shall you send to the war. *5* So there were delivered out of the thousands of Israel, a thousand of every tribe, twelve thousand armed for war. *6* And Moses sent them to the war, a thousand of every tribe, them and Phinehas the son of Eleazar the priest, to the war, with the holy instruments, and the trumpets to blow in his hand. *7* And they fought against the Midianites, as **YeHoVaH** commanded Moses; and they slew all the males. *8* And they slew the kings of Midian, beside the rest of them that were slain; namely, Evi, and Rekem, and Zur, and Hur, and Reba, five kings of Midian: Balaam also the son of Beor they slew with the sword. *9* And the children of Israel took all the women of Midian captives, and their little ones, and took the spoil of all their cattle, and all their flocks, and all their goods. *10* And they burnt all their cities where they dwelt, and all their castles, with fire.

11 And they took all the spoil, and all the prey, both of men and of animals. *12* And they brought the captives, and the prey, and the spoil, to Moses, and Eleazar the priest, and to the congregation of the children of Israel, to the camp at the plains of Moab, which are by Jordan near Jericho. *13* And Moses, and Eleazar the priest, and all the princes of the congregation, went forth to meet them outside the camp. *14* And Moses was angry with the officers of the host, with the captains over thousands, and captains over hundreds, which came from the battle. *15* And Moses said to them, Have you saved all the women alive? *16* Behold, these caused the children of Israel, through the counsel of Balaam, to commit trespass against **YeHoVaH** in the matter of Peor, and there was a plague among the congregation of **YeHoVaH**. *17* Now kill every male among the little ones, and kill every woman that has known man by lying with him. *18* But all the women children, that have not known a man by lying with him, keep alive for yourselves. *19* And do you abide outside the camp seven days: whosoever has killed any person, and whoever has touched any slain, purify both yourselves and your captives on the third day, and on the seventh day. *20* And purify all your clothing, and all that is made of skins, and all work of goats' hair, and all things made of wood.

21 And Eleazar the priest said to the men of war which went to the battle, This is the ordinance of the law which **YeHoVaH** commanded Moses; *22* Only the gold, and the silver, the brass, the iron, the tin, and the lead, *23* Everything that may abide the fire, you shall make it go through the fire, and it shall be clean: nevertheless it shall be purified with the water of separation: and all that abides not the fire you shall make go through the water. *24* And you shall wash your clothes on the seventh day, and you shall be clean, and afterward you shall come into the camp. *25* And *YeHoVaH* spoke to Moses, saying, *26* Take the sum of the prey that was taken, both of man and of beast, you, and Eleazar the priest, and the chief fathers of the congregation: *27* And divide the prey into two parts; between them that took the war upon them, who went out to battle, and between all the congregation: *28* And levy a tribute to *YeHoVaH* of the men of war which went out to battle: one soul of 500, both of the persons, and of the cattle, and of the donkeys, and of the sheep: *29* Take it of their half, and give it to Eleazar the priest, for a heave-offering of *YeHoVaH*. *30* And of the children of Israel's half, you shall take one portion of 50, of the persons, of the cattle, of the donkeys, and of the flocks, of all manner of animals, and give them to the Levites, which keep the charge of the tabernacle of *YeHoVaH*.

31 And Moses and Eleazar the priest did as *YeHoVaH* commanded Moses. *32* And the booty, being the rest of the prey which the men of war had caught, was 675,000 sheep, *33* 72,000 oxen, *34* And 61,000 donkeys, *35* And 32,000 persons in all, of women that had not known having relations with man by lying with him. *36* And the half, which was the portion of them that went out to war, was in number 337,500 sheep: *37* And *YeHoVaH's* tribute of the sheep was 675. *38* And the oxen were 6,030; of which *YeHoVaH's* tribute was 72. *39* And the donkeys were 30,500; of which *YeHoVaH's* tribute was 61. *40* And the persons were 16,000; of which *YeHoVaH's* tribute was 32 persons.

41 And Moses gave the tribute, which was *YeHoVaH's* heave-offering, to Eleazar the priest, as *YeHoVaH* commanded Moses. *42* And of the children of Israel's half, which Moses divided from the men that fought, *43* (Now the half that pertained to the congregation was 300,000 and 37,500 sheep, *44* And 36,000 cattle, *45* And 30,500 donkeys, *46* And 16,000 persons;) *47* Even of the children of Israel's half, Moses took one portion of 50, both of man and of animal, and gave them to the Levites, which kept the charge of the tabernacle of *YeHoVaH*; as YeHoVaH commanded Moses. *48* And the officers which were over thousands of the host, the captains of thousands, and captains of hundreds, came near to Moses: *49* And they said to Moses, Thy servants have taken the sum of the men of war which are under our charge, and there lacks not one man of us. *50* We have therefore brought a holy offering for *YeHoVaH*, what every man has gotten, of jewels of gold, chains, and bracelets, rings, earrings, and tablets, to make an atonement for our souls before *YeHoVaH*.

51 And Moses and Eleazar the priest took the gold items, even all shaped jewels. *52* And all the gold of the offering that they offered up to *YeHoVaH*, of the captains of thousands, and of the captains of hundreds, was 16,750 shekels. *53* (For the men of war had taken spoil, every man for himself.) *54* And Moses and Eleazar the priest took the gold of the captains of thousands and of hundreds, and brought it into the tabernacle of the congregation, for a memorial for the children of Israel before *YeHoVaH*.

Chapter 32
Reuben and Gad ask to settle in Gilead. Moses agreed if they helped to conquer the land, so Reuben, Gad and Manasseh built cities then helped subdue the land in battle.

1 Now the children of Reuben and the children of Gad had a very great multitude of cattle: and when they saw the land of Jazer, and the land of Gilead, that, behold, the place was a place for cattle; *2* The children of Gad and the children of Reuben came and spoke to Moses, and to Eleazar the priest, and to the princes of the congregation, saying, *3* Ataroth, and Dibon, and Jazer, and Nimrah, and Heshbon, and Elealeh, and Shebam, and Nebo, and Beon, *4* Even the country which *YeHoVaH* destroyed before the congregation of Israel, is a land for cattle, and your servants have cattle: *5* So they said, if we have found grace in thy sight, let this land be given to your servants for a possession, and bring us not over the Jordan. *6* And Moses said to the children of Gad and to the children of Reuben, Shall your brethren go to war, and shall you sit here? *7* And why discourage the heart of the children of Israel from going over into the land that *YeHoVaH* has given them? *8* Thus did your fathers, when I sent them from Kadeshbarnea to see the land. *9* For when they went up to the valley of Eshcol, and saw the land, they discouraged the heart of the children of Israel, that they should not go into the land which *YeHoVaH* had given them. *10* And *YeHoVaH*'s anger was kindled the same time, and he swore, saying,

11 Surely none of the men that came up out of Egypt, from 20 years old and upward, shall see the land which I swore to Abraham, to Isaac, and to Jacob; because they have not wholly followed me: *12* except Caleb the son of Jephunneh the Kenezite, and Joshua the son of Nun: for they have wholly followed *YeHoVaH*. *13* And *YeHoVaH*'s anger was kindled against the children of Israel, and he made them wander in the wilderness forty years, until all the generation, that had done evil in the sight of *YeHoVaH*, was consumed. *14* And, behold, you are risen up in your fathers' stead, an increase of sinful men, to augment yet the fierce anger of *YeHoVaH* toward Israel. *15* For if you turn away from after him, he will yet again leave him or her in the wilderness; and you shall destroy this entire people. *16* And they came near to him, and said, We will build sheepfolds here for our cattle, and cities for our little ones: *17* But we ourselves will go ready armed before the children of Israel, until we have brought them to their place: and our little ones shall dwell in the fenced cities because of the inhabitants of the land. *18* We will not return to our houses, until the children of Israel have inherited every man his inheritance. *19* For we will not inherit with them on yonder side Jordan, or forward; because our inheritance is fallen to us on this side Jordan eastward. *20* And Moses said to them, If you will do this thing, if you will go armed before *YeHoVaH* to war,

21 And will go all of you armed over Jordan before *YeHoVaH*, until he has driven out his enemies from before him, *22* And the land be subdued before *YeHoVaH*: then afterward you shall return, and be guiltless before *YeHoVaH*, and before Israel; and this land shall be your possession before *YeHoVaH*. *23* But if you will not do so, behold, you have sinned against *YeHoVaH*: and be sure your sin will find you out. *24* Build you cities for your little ones, and folds for your sheep; and do that which has come out of your mouth. *25* And the children of Gad and the children of Reuben spoke to Moses, saying, Thy servants will do as my lord commands. *26* Our little ones, our wives, our flocks, and all our cattle, shall be there in the cities of Gilead: *27* But thy servants will pass over, every man armed for war, before *YeHoVaH* to battle, as my lord says. *28* So concerning them Moses commanded Eleazar the priest, and Joshua the son of Nun, and the chief fathers of the tribes of the children of Israel: *29* And Moses said to them, If the children of Gad and the children of Reuben will pass with you over Jordan, every man armed to battle, before *YeHoVaH*, and the land shall be subdued before you; then you shall give them the land of Gilead for a possession: *30* But if they will not pass over with you armed, they shall have possessions among you in the land of Canaan.

31 And the children of Gad and the children of Reuben answered, saying, As **YeHoVaH** has said to your servants, so will we do. *32* We will pass over armed before **YeHoVaH** into the land of Canaan, that the possession of our inheritance on this side Jordan may be ours. *33* And Moses gave to them, even to the children of Gad, and to the children of Reuben, and to half the tribe of Manasseh the son of Joseph, the kingdom of Sihon king of the Amorites, and the kingdom of Og king of Bashan, the land, with the cities thereof in the coasts, even the cities of the country all around. *34* And the children of Gad built Dibon, and Ataroth, and Aroer, *35* And Atroth, Shophan, and Jaazer, and Jogbehah, *36* And Bethnimrah, and Bethharan, fenced cities: and folds for sheep. *37* And the children of Reuben built Heshbon, and Elealeh, and Kirjathaim, *38* And Nebo, and Baalmeon, (their names being changed,) and Shibmah: and gave other names to the cities that they built. *39* And the children of Machir the son of Manasseh went to Gilead, and took it, and dispossessed the Amorite that was in it. *40* And Moses gave Gilead to Machir the son of Manasseh; and he dwelt therein.

41 And Jair the son of Manasseh went and took the small towns thereof, and called them Havothjair. *42* And Nobah went and took Kenath, and the villages thereof, and called it Nobah, after his own name.
  Reading 42 ends

Chapter 33
The Israelites journeyed from Egypt. In the 40th year Aaron dies. Moses records their travels. They camp by the Jordan and YeHoVaH tells them to, "Take the land."
  Reading 43 begins

1 These are the journeys of the children of Israel, which went forth out of the land of Egypt with their armies under the hand of Moses and Aaron. *2* And **Moses wrote** their travels according to their journeys **by the commandment of YeHoVaH**: and these are their journeys according to their travels. *3* And they departed from Rameses in the first month, on the fifteenth day of the first month; on the morning after the Passover the children of Israel went out with a high hand in the sight of all the Egyptians. *4* For the Egyptians buried all their firstborn, which **YeHoVaH** had taken from among them: upon their gods also **YeHoVaH** executed judgments. *5* And the children of Israel removed from Rameses, and pitched in Succoth. *6* And they departed from Succoth, and pitched in Etham, which is in the edge of the wilderness. *7* And they moved from Etham, and turned again to Pihahiroth, which is before Baalzephon: and they pitched before Migdol. *8* And they departed from before Pihahiroth, and passed through the midst of the sea into the wilderness, and went three days' journey in the wilderness of Etham, and pitched in Marah. *9* And they moved from Marah, and came to Elim: and in Elim were *12* fountains of water, and 70 palm trees; and they pitched there. *10* And they moved from Elim, and camped by the Red sea.

11 And they moved from the Red sea, and camped in the wilderness of Sin. *12* And they took their journey out of the wilderness of Sin, and camped in Dophkah. *13* And they departed from Dophkah, and camped in Alush. *14* And they removed from Alush, and camped at Rephidim, where there was no water for the people to drink. *15* And they departed from Rephidim, and pitched in the wilderness of Sinai. *16* And they moved from the desert of Sinai, and pitched at Kibrothhattaavah. *17* And they departed from Kibrothhattaavah, and camped at Hazeroth. *18* And they departed from Hazeroth, and pitched in Rithmah. *19* And they departed from

Rithmah, and pitched at Rimmonparez. *20* And they departed from Rimmonparez, and pitched in Libnah.

21 And they moved from Libnah, and pitched at Rissah. *22* And they journeyed from Rissah, and pitched in Kehelathah. *23* And they went from Kehelathah, and pitched in mount Shapher. *24* And they moved from mount Shapher, and encamped in Haradah. *25* And they removed from Haradah, and pitched in Makheloth. *26* And they moved from Makheloth, and camped at Tahath. *27* And they departed from Tahath, and pitched at Tarah. *28* And they moved from Tarah, and pitched in Mithcah. *29* And they went from Mithcah, and pitched in Hashmonah. *30* And they departed from Hashmonah, and camped at Moseroth.

31 And they departed from Moseroth, and pitched in Benejaakan. *32* And they moved from Benejaakan, and camped at Horhagidgad. *34* And they moved from Jotbathah, and camped at Ebronah. *35* And they departed from Ebronah, and camped at Eziongaber. *36* And they moved from Eziongaber, and pitched in the wilderness of Zin, which is Kadesh. *37* And they moved from Kadesh, and pitched in mount Hor, in the edge of the land of Edom. *38* And **Aaron** the priest went up into mount Hor at the commandment of **YeHoVaH**, and **died** there, in the 40th year after the children of Israel were come out of the land of Egypt, in the first day of the fifth month. *39* And Aaron was **123** years old when he died in mount Hor. *40* And king Arad the Canaanite, which dwelt in the south in the land of Canaan, heard of the coming of the children of Israel.

41 And they departed from mount Hor, and pitched in Zalmonah. *42* And they departed from Zalmonah, and pitched in Punon. *43* And they departed from Punon, and pitched in Oboth. *44* And they departed from Oboth, and pitched in Ijeabarim, in the border of Moab. *45* And they departed from Iim, and pitched in Dibongad. *46* And they moved from Dibongad, and camped in Almondiblathaim. *47* And they moved from Almondiblathaim, and pitched in the mountains of Abarim, before Nebo. *48* And they departed from the mountains of Abarim, and pitched in the plains of Moab by Jordan near Jericho. *49* And they pitched by Jordan, from Bethjesimoth even to Abelshittim in the plains of Moab. *50* And **YeHoVaH** spoke to Moses in the plains of Moab by Jordan near Jericho, saying,

51 Speak to the children of Israel, and say to them, When you are passed over Jordan into the land of Canaan; *52* drive out all the inhabitants of the land before you. Destroy all their carved images and their cast idols, and demolish all their high places: *53* Take possession of the land and settle in it, for I have given you the land to possess. *54*And you shall divide the land by lot for an inheritance among your families: and to the more you shall give the more inheritance, and to the fewer you shall give the less inheritance: every man's inheritance shall be in the place where his lot falls; according to the tribes of your fathers you shall inherit. *55* But if you will not drive out the inhabitants of the land from before you; then it shall come to pass, that those which you let remain of them shall be needles in your eyes, and thorns in your sides, and shall aggravate you in the land wherein you dwell. *56* Moreover it shall come to pass, that I shall do to you, as I thought to do to them.

Chapter 34
YeHoVaH declares the borders in Canaan shall be Edom, the Great Sea, Mount Hor and the Jordan. Eleazar and Joshua shall divide the land among them.

1 And **YeHoVaH** spoke to Moses, saying, *2* Command the children of Israel, and say to them, When you come into the land of Canaan; (this is the land that shall fall to you for an inheritance, even the land of Canaan with the coasts included) *3* Then your south quarter shall be from the wilderness of Zin along by the coast of Edom, and your south border shall be the outmost coast of the salt sea eastward: *4* And your border shall turn from the south to the ascent of Akrabbim, and pass on to Zin: and the going forth there shall be from the south to Kadeshbarnea, and shall go on to Hazaraddar, and pass on to Azmon: *5* And the border shall fetch a compass from Azmon to the river of Egypt, and the boundaries of it shall be at the sea. *6* And as for the western border, you shall even have the great sea for a border: this shall be your west border. *7* And this shall be your north border: from the great sea you shall point out for you mount Hor: *8* From mount Hor you shall point out your border to the entrance of Hamath; and the goings forth of the border shall be to Zedad: *9* And the border shall go on to Ziphron, and the boundaries of it shall be at Hazarenan: this shall be your north border. *10* And you shall point out your east border from Hazarenan to Shepham:

11 And the coast shall go down from Shepham to Riblah, on the east side of Ain; and the border shall descend, and shall reach to the side of the sea of Chinnereth eastward: *12* And the border shall go down to Jordan, and the boundaries of it shall be at the salt sea: this shall be your land with the coasts there all around. *13* And Moses commanded the children of Israel, saying, This is the land which you shall inherit by lot, which **YeHoVaH** commanded to give to the nine tribes, and to the half tribe: *14* For the tribe of the children of Reuben according to the house of their fathers, and the tribe of the children of Gad according to the house of their fathers, have received their inheritance; and half the tribe of Manasseh have received their inheritance: *15* The two tribes and the half tribe have received their inheritance on this side Jordan near Jericho eastward, toward the sun rising. *16* And **YeHoVaH** spoke to Moses, saying, *17* These are the names of the men which shall divide the land to you: Eleazar the priest, and Joshua the son of Nun. *18* And you shall take one prince of every tribe, to divide the land by inheritance. *19* And the names of the men are these: Of the tribe of Judah, Caleb the son of Jephunneh. *20* And of the tribe of the children of Simeon, Shemuel the son of Ammihud.

21 Of the tribe of Benjamin, Elidad the son of Chislon. *22* And the prince of the tribe of the children of Dan, Bukki the son of Jogli. *23* The prince of the children of Joseph, for the tribe of the children of Manasseh, Hanniel the son of Ephod. *24* And the prince of the tribe of the children of Ephraim, Kemuel the son of Shiphtan. *25* And the prince of the tribe of the children of Zebulun, Elizaphan the son of Parnach. *26* And the prince of the tribe of the children of Issachar, Paltiel the son of Azzan. *27* And the prince of the tribe of the children of Asher, Ahihud the son of Shelomi. *28* And the prince of the tribe of the children of Naphtali, Pedahel the son of Ammihud. *29* These are the ones **YeHoVaH** commanded to divide the inheritance to the children of Israel in the land of Canaan.

Chapter 35
YeHoVaH declares: You shall give cities to the Levites. Appoint cites of refuge for anyone who has killed accidentally. A murderer shall be put to death.

1 And **YeHoVaH** spoke to Moses in the plains of Moab by Jordan near Jericho, saying, *2* Command the children of Israel, that they give to the Levites of the inheritance of their possession cities to dwell in; and you shall give also to the Levites suburbs for the cities round about them. *3* And the cities shall they have to dwell in; and the suburbs of them shall be for their cattle, and for their goods, and for all their livestock. *4* And the suburbs of the cities, which you shall give to the Levites, shall reach from the wall of the city and outward a thousand cubits (cubit = about 20 inches) round about. *5* And you shall measure from without the city on the east side two thousand cubits, and on the south side two thousand cubits, and on the west side two thousand cubits, and on the north side two thousand cubits; and the city shall be in the midst: this shall be to them the suburbs of the cities. *6* And among the cities which you shall give to the Levites there shall be six cities for refuge, which you shall appoint for the manslayer (one who kills another unintentionally), that he may flee there: and to them you shall add 52 cities. *7* So all the cities that you shall give to the Levites shall be 58 cities: these shall you give with their suburbs. *8* And the cities which you shall give shall be of the possession of the children of Israel: from them that have many you shall give many; but from them that have few you shall give few: every one shall give of his cities to the Levites according to his inheritance which he inherits. *9* And **YeHoVaH** spoke to Moses, saying, *10* Speak to the children of Israel, and say to them, When you come over to Jordan into the land of Canaan;

11 Then you shall appoint you cities to be cities of refuge for you; that the manslayer (one who kills another unintentionally) may flee there, which kills any person accidentally. *12* And they shall be to you cities for refuge from the avenger; that the manslayer die not, until he stand before the congregation in judgment. *13* And of these cities which you shall give six cities shall you have for refuge. *14* You shall give three cities on this side Jordan, and three cities shall you give in the land of Canaan, which shall be cities of refuge. *15* These six cities shall be a refuge, both for the children of Israel, and for the stranger, and for the sojourner among them: that every one that kills any person accidentally may flee thither. *16* And if he kills him with an instrument of iron, so that he die, he is a murderer: the murderer shall surely be put to death. *17* And if he kills him with throwing a stone, wherewith he may die, and he does die, he is a murderer: the *murderer shall surely be put to death*. *18* Or if he kills him with a hand weapon of wood, wherewith he may die, and he does die, he is a murderer: the murderer shall surely be put to death. *19* He whose right it is to give punishment for blood, may himself put to death the taker of life when he comes face to face with him. *20* But if he thrust him of hatred, or hurl at him by lying in wait, that he die;

21 Or in hate gave him blows with his hand, causing death; he who gave the death-blow is to be put to death; *he is a taker of life*: he whose right it is to give punishment for blood may put to death the murderer when he comes face to face with him. *22* But if a man has given a wound to another suddenly and not in hate (accidentally), or without design has sent something against him, *23* Or has given him a blow with a stone, without seeing him, so causing his death, though he had nothing against him and no desire to do him evil: *24* Then let the meeting of the people be judge between the man responsible for the death and him who has the right of punishment for blood, acting by these rules: *25* And let the people keep the man responsible for the death safe from the hands of him who has the right of punishment for blood, and send him back to his safe town where he had gone in flight: there let him be till the death of the high priest who was marked with the holy oil. *26* But if ever he goes outside the walls of the safe town where he had gone in flight, *27* And the giver of punishment, meeting him outside the walls of the town, puts him to death, he will not be responsible for his blood: *28* Because he should have remained in the city of his refuge until the death of the high priest: but after the death of the high priest the slayer shall return into the land of his possession. *29* So these things shall be for a statute of judgment to you throughout your generations in all your dwellings. *30* Whoever kills any person, the murderer shall be put to death by the mouth of witnesses: but one witness shall not testify against any person to cause him to die (must be two or more witnesses).

31 Moreover you shall take no satisfaction for the life of a murderer, which is guilty of death: but he shall be surely put to death. **32** And you shall take no satisfaction for him that fled to the city of his refuge, that he should come again to dwell in the land, until the death of the priest. **33** So you shall not pollute the land where you are: for blood it defiles the land: and the land cannot be cleansed of the blood that is shed therein, but by the blood of him that shed it. **34** Defile not therefore the land which you shall inhabit, wherein I dwell: for I **YeHoVaH** dwell among the children of Israel.

Chapter 36
The clan of Gilead asks about Zelophehad's daughters. Moses says, "Daughters who inherit land must marry within their own tribe."

1 And the chief fathers of the families of the children of Gilead, the son of Machir, the son of Manasseh, of the families of the sons of Joseph, came near, and spoke before Moses, and before the princes, the chief fathers of the children of Israel: **2** And they said, **YeHoVaH** commanded my lord to give the land for an inheritance by lot to the children of Israel: and my lord was commanded by **YeHoVaH** to give the inheritance of Zelophehad our brother to his daughters. **3** And if they be married to any of the sons of the *other tribes* of the children of Israel, then shall their inheritance be *taken* from the inheritance of our fathers, and shall be put to the inheritance of the tribe where they are received: so shall it be taken from the lot of our inheritance. **4** And when the jubilee of the children of Israel shall be, then shall their inheritance be put to the inheritance of the tribe where they are received: so shall their inheritance be taken away from the inheritance of the tribe of our fathers. **5** And Moses commanded the children of Israel according to the word of **YeHoVaH**, saying, The tribe of the sons of Joseph have said well. **6** This is the thing which **YeHoVaH** does command concerning the daughters of Zelophehad, saying, Let them marry to whom they think best; but only to the family of the tribe of their father shall they marry. **7** So shall not the inheritance of the children of Israel remove from tribe to tribe: for every one of the children of Israel shall keep himself to the inheritance of the tribe of his fathers. **8** And every daughter, that possesses an inheritance in any tribe of the children of Israel, shall be wife to one of the family of the tribe of her father, that the children of Israel may enjoy every man the inheritance of his fathers. **9** *Neither shall the inheritance remove from one tribe to another tribe*; but every one of the tribes of the children of Israel shall keep himself to his own inheritance. **10** Even as **YeHoVaH** commanded Moses, so did the daughters of Zelophehad:

11 For Mahlah, Tirzah, and Hoglah, and Milcah, and Noah, the daughters of Zelophehad, were married to their father's brothers' sons: **12** And they were married into the families of the sons of Manasseh the son of Joseph, and their inheritance remained in the tribe of the family of their father. **13** These are the commandments and the judgments, which **YeHoVaH** commanded by the hand of Moses to the children of Israel in the plains of Moab by Jordan near Jericho.
   Reading 43 ends

Thus Ends the Book of Numbers   Praise **YeHoVaH**

True Name Torah Version

DEUTERONOMY

~DEUTERONOMY~

Genesis, Exodus, Leviticus, Numbers, Deuteronomy

The 5th Book of Moses

The word "Deuteronomy" comes from the Greek word for "the second law (instruction)" or "the laws (instructions) copied or repeated." In the book of Deuteronomy Moses is writing a series of speeches to the people of Israel in the plains of Moab on the day before they entered the land of Canaan, the Promised Land. These messages are intended to speak to every member of the congregation of Israel, not just the religious. The purpose of Moses was to remind them of YeHoVaH's law (instruction), and everything that YeHoVaH did for them, and every promise YeHoVaH made to them. Moses explained to them that their new life in the land of Canaan would be blessed or cursed depending on their ability to walk after YeHoVaH and His laws (instructions). These words were spoken to them on the 11th month of the final year of Israel's wandering in the wilderness, the 40th year after they left Egypt.

READINGS FOR DEUTERONOMY

The name in (parentheses) is the Hebrew name for that week. For example: Week 44 'Words' in Hebrew is 'Devarim'.

Reading 44 *"Words"* (Devarim*)* Deuteronomy **1:1 - 3:22**
In this Torah portion, Moses recounts the Israelites' episodes from their 40 years in the wilderness. Moses encourages the Israelites in their upcoming conquest of the land of Canaan.

Reading 45 *"And I Pleaded"* (Vaetchanan*)* Deuteronomy **3:23 - 7:11**
In this Torah portion, Moses stresses to the Israelites the importance of keeping YeHoVaH's commandments when they enter the Land of Israel. Moses repeats the Ten Commandments and utters the Shema and Ve'ahavta prayers.

Reading 46 *"As a Result"* (Eikev*)* Deuteronomy **7:12 - 11:25**
In this Torah portion, Moses continues his speech to the Israelites. He tells them they will have to annihilate people who are not believers in YeHoVaH. Moses reminds them not to forget YeHoVaH's commandments even after they enter the land of Israel, and that they must continue to fear YeHoVaH's.

Reading 47 *"See"* (Re'eh*)* Deuteronomy **11:26 - 16:17**
In this Torah portion, Moses tells the Israelites that if they worship idols, they will be punished. Moses explains the laws (instructions) of kosher food, and he details the three pilgrimage festivals: Passover, Shavuot, and Sukkot.

Reading 48 *"Judges"* (Shoftim*)* Deuteronomy **16:18 - 21:9**
In this Torah portion, Moses reviews the justice system for the Israelites. Moses talks about the limits future kings should have on their possessions. Moses explains that the priests and Levites should not be paid and should survive on donations from the people. Finally, Moses explains the laws of warfare.

Reading 49 *"When You Go Out"* (Ki Teitzei*)* Deuteronomy **21:10 - 25:19**
In this Torah portion, Moses delivers specific rules about proper family relationships. He continues with laws (instructions) involving many aspects of daily living, justice, family responsibility, work and sexuality.

Reading 50 *"When You Enter In"* (Ki Tavo*)* Deuteronomy **26:1 - 29:8**
In this Torah portion, Moses instructs the Israelites regarding the first fruit offering. Moses then lists the blessings the people will enjoy if they keep the commandments, and the punishments they will suffer for disobeying them.

Reading 51 *"You Are Standing"* (Nitzavim*)* Deuteronomy **29:9 - 30:20**
In this Torah portion, Moses describes the Covenant between YeHoVaH and the Israelites, urging the Israelites to uphold the Covenant and honor the Torah so that they may be rewarded with life in the Land of Israel.

Reading 52 *"And He Went"* (Vayeilech*)* Deuteronomy **31:1 - 31:30**
In this Torah portion, Moses concludes his speech to the Israelites, blesses Joshua, and instructs the community to gather every seven years to read publicly from the Torah. YeHoVaH predicts the eventual straying of the Israelite

Reading 53 *"Listen"* (Ha'Azinu) Deuteronomy **32:1** - **32**:52
In this Torah portion, Moses recites a song to the Children of Israel that serves as testimony of their covenant with YeHoVaH. YeHoVaH tells Moses to head up Mount Nebo to find his final resting place.

Reading 54 *"And This Is The Blessing"* (Vezot Haberakhah) Deuteronomy **33:1** - **34:12**
In this Torah portion, Moses gives the tribes of Israel a final blessing and dies at the age of **120**. The Children of Israel mourn and begin to follow Joshua, their new leader.

-End Torah Readings for Deuteronomy-

CHAPTERS 1- 10

Chapter 1

Moses speaks: We journeyed from Horeb and you would not go up to take the land, so YeHoVaH said, "This generation will not live to see it."

Reading 44 begins

1 These are the words that Moses spoke to all Israel on this side of the Jordan in the wilderness, in the plain against the Red sea, between Paran, and Tophel, and Laban, and Hazeroth, and Dizahab. **2** (There are eleven days' journey from Horeb by the way of mount Seir to Kadeshbarnea.) **3** And it came to pass in the 40th year, in the 11th month, on the first day of the month, that Moses spoke to the children of Israel, according to all that **YeHoVaH** had given him in commandment to them; **4** After he had slain Sihon the king of the Amorites, which dwelt in Heshbon, and Og the king of Bashan, which dwelt at Astaroth in Edrei: **5** On this side of Jordan, in the land of Moab, Moses began to declare this law (instruction), saying, **6 YeHoVaH** our **Elohim** spoke to us in Horeb, saying, You have dwelt long enough in this mountain: **7** Break camp and advance into the hill country of the Amorites; go to all the neighboring peoples in the Arabah, in the mountains, in the western foothills, in the Negev and along the coast, to the land of the Canaanites and to Lebanon, as far as the great river, the Euphrates. **8** Behold, I have set the land before you: go in and possess the land which **YeHoVaH** swore to your fathers, Abraham, Isaac, and Jacob, to give to them and to their seed after them. **9** And I spoke to you at that time, saying, I am not able to bear you myself alone: **10 YeHoVaH** your **Elohim** has increased your numbers so that today you are as numerous as the stars in the sky.

11 YeHoVaH Elohim of your fathers make you a thousand times so many more as you are, and bless you, as he has promised you! **12** How can I myself alone bear your obstacles, and your burden, and your strife? **13** Take you wise men, and understanding, and known among your tribes, and I will make them rulers over you. **14** And you answered me, and said, The thing which you have spoken is good for us to do. **15** So I took the chief of your tribes, wise men, and known, and made them heads over you, captains over thousands, and captains over hundreds, and captains over fifties, and captains over tens, and officers among your tribes. **16** And I charged your judges at that time, saying, Hear the causes between your brethren, and judge righteously between every man and his brother, and the stranger that is with him. **17** You shall not be partial in judgment; but you shall hear the small as well as the great; you shall not be afraid of the face of man; for the judgment is **Elohim's**: and the cause that is too hard for you, bring it to me, and I will hear it. **18** And I commanded you at that time all the things that you should do. **19** And when we departed from Horeb, we went through that entire great and terrible wilderness, which you saw by the way of the mountain of the Amorites, as **YeHoVaH** our **Elohim** commanded us; and we came to Kadeshbarnea. **20** And I said to you, You have come to the mountain of the Amorites, which **YeHoVaH** our **Elohim** does give to us.

21 Behold, **YeHoVaH** your **Elohim** has set the land before you: go up and possess it, as **YeHoVaH** the **Elohim** of your fathers has said to you; fear not, neither be discouraged. **22** And you came near to me every one of you, and said, We will send men before us, and they shall search us out the land, and bring us word again by what way we must go up, and into what cities we shall come. **23** And the saying pleased me well: and I took twelve men of you, one of each tribe: **24** And they turned and went up into the mountain, and came to the valley of Eshcol, and searched it out. *25* And they took of the fruit of the land in their hands, and brought it down to us, and brought us word again, and said, It is a good land which **YeHoVaH** our **Elohim** does give us. *26* Notwithstanding you would not go up, but rebelled against the commandment of **YeHoVaH** your **Elohim**: *27* And you murmured in your tents, and said, Because **YeHoVaH** hated us, he has brought us forth out of the land of Egypt, to deliver us into the hand of the Amorites, to destroy us. *28* Whether we shall go up? our brethren have discouraged our heart, saying, The people are greater and taller than we; the cities are great and walled up to heaven; and moreover we have seen the sons of the Anakims there. *29* Then I said to you, Dread not, neither be afraid of them. *30* **YeHoVaH** your **Elohim** that goes before you, he shall fight for you, according to all that he did for you in Egypt before your eyes;

31 And in the wilderness, where you have seen how **YeHoVaH** your **Elohim** bare you, as a man does bear his son, in all the way that you went, until you came into this place. *32* Yet in this thing you did not believe **YeHoVaH** your **Elohim**, *33* Who went in the way before you, to search you out a place to pitch your tents, in fire by night, to show you by what way you should go, and in a cloud by day. *34* And **YeHoVaH** heard the voice of your words, and was angry, and swore, saying, *35* Surely there shall not one of these men of this evil generation see that good land, which I swore to give to your fathers. *36* except Caleb the son of Jephunneh; he shall see it, and to him will I give the land that he has traveled upon, and to his children, because he has wholly followed **YeHoVaH**. *37* Also **YeHoVaH** was angry with me for your sake, saying, You also shall not go in either. *38* But Joshua the son of Nun, which stands before you, he shall go in: encourage him: for he shall cause Israel to inherit it. *39* Moreover your little ones, which you said should be a prey, and your children, which in that day had no knowledge between good and evil, they shall go in, and to them will I give it, and they shall possess it. *40* But as for you, turn you, and take your journey into the wilderness by the way of the Red sea.

41 Then you answered and said to me, We have sinned against **YeHoVaH**, we will go up and fight, according to all that **YeHoVaH** our **Elohim** commanded us. And when you had girded on every man his weapons of war, you were ready to go up into the hill. *42* And **YeHoVaH** said to me, Say to them. Go not up, neither fight; for I am not among you; or you will be beaten before your enemies. *43* So I spoke to you; and you would not hear, but rebelled against the commandment of **YeHoVaH**, and went presumptuously up into the hill. *44* And the Amorites, which dwelt in that mountain, came out against you, and chased you, as bees do, and destroyed you in Seir, even to Hormah. *45* And you returned and wept before **YeHoVaH**; but **YeHoVaH** would not listen to your voice, nor give ear to you. *46* So you abode in Kadesh many days, according to the days that you abode there.

Chapter 2
They went into the wilderness. Thirty-eight years passed, then YeHoVaH told them to cross by Moab. He delivered Sihon the Amorite to us.

1 Then we turned, and took our journey into the wilderness by the way of the Red sea, as **YeHoVaH** spoke to me: and we went around mount Seir many days. *2* And **YeHoVaH** spoke to me, saying, *3* You have gone around this mountain long enough: turn you northward. *4* And command you the people, saying, You are to pass through the coast of your brethren the children of Esau, which dwell in Seir; and they shall be afraid of you: take you good heed to yourselves therefore: *5* Meddle not with them; for I will not give you of their land, no, not so much as a foot breadth; because I have given mount Seir to Esau for a possession. **6** You shall buy food of them for money, that you may eat; and you shall also buy water of them for money, that you may drink. **7** For **YeHoVaH** your **Elohim** has blessed you in all the works of your hand: he knows your walking through this great wilderness: these 40 years **YeHoVaH** your **Elohim** has been with you; you have **lacked nothing**. **8** And when we passed by from our brethren the children of Esau, which dwelt in Seir, through the way of the plain from Elath, and from Eziongaber, we turned and passed by the way of the wilderness of Moab. **9** And **YeHoVaH** said to me, disturb not the Moabites, neither contend with them in battle: for I will not give you of their land for a possession; because I have given Ar to the children of Lot for a possession. **10** The Emims dwelt there in times past, a people great, and many, and tall, as the Anakims;

11 Which also were accounted giants, as the Anakims; but the Moabites called them Emims. **12** The Horims also dwelt in Seir before time; but the children of Esau succeeded them, when they had destroyed them from before them, and dwelt in their stead; as Israel did to the land of his possession, which **YeHoVaH** gave to them. **13** Now rise up, said I, and get you over the brook Zered. And we went over the brook Zered. **14** And the space in which we came from Kadeshbarnea, until we came over the brook Zered, was 38 years; until all the generation of the men of war were wasted out from among the host, as **YeHoVaH** swore to them. **15** For indeed the hand of **YeHoVaH** was against them, to destroy them from among the host, until they were consumed. **16** So it came to pass, when all the men of war were consumed and dead from among the people, **17** That **YeHoVaH** spoke to me, saying, **18** You are to pass over through Ar, the coast of Moab, this day: **19** And when you come near over against the children of Ammon, disturb them not, nor meddle with them: for I will not give you of the land of the children of Ammon any possession; because I have given it to the children of Lot for a possession. **20** (That also was considered a land of giants: giants dwelt therein in old time; and the Ammonites call them Zamzummims;

21 A people great, and many, and tall, as the Anakims; but **YeHoVaH** destroyed them before them; and they succeeded them, and dwelt in their stead: **22** As he did to the children of Esau, which dwelt in Seir, when he destroyed the Horims from before them; and they succeeded them, and dwelt in their stead even to this day: **23** And the Avims which dwelt in Hazerim, even to Azzah, the Caphtorims, which came forth out of Caphtor, destroyed them, and dwelt in their stead. **24** Rise up, take your journey, and pass over the river Arnon: behold, I have given into your hand Sihon the Amorite, king of Heshbon, and his land: begin to possess it, and contend with him in battle. **25** This day will I begin to put the dread of you and the fear of you upon the nations that are under the whole heaven, who shall hear report of you, and shall tremble, and be in anguish because of you. **26** And I sent messengers out of the wilderness of Kedemoth to Sihon king of Heshbon with words of peace, saying, **27** Let me pass through your land: I will go along by the high way, I will neither turn to the right hand nor to the left. **28** You shall sell me food for money, that I may eat; and give me water for money, that I may drink: only I will pass through on my feet; **29** As the children of Esau which dwell in Seir, and the Moabites which dwell in Ar, did to me; until I shall pass over Jordan into the land which **YeHoVaH** our **Elohim** gives us. **30** But Sihon king of Heshbon would not let us pass by him: for **YeHoVaH** hardened his spirit, and made his heart obstinate, that he might deliver him into your hand, as appears this day.

31 And **YeHoVaH** said to me, Behold, I have begun to give Sihon and his land before you: begin to possess, that you may inherit his land. **32** Then Sihon came out against us, he and all his people, to fight at Jahaz. *33* And **YeHoVaH** our **Elohim** delivered him before us; and we killed him, and his sons, and all his people. *34* And we took all his cities at that time, and utterly destroyed the men, and the women, and the little ones, of every city, we left none to remain: *35* Only the cattle we took for a prey to ourselves, and the spoil of the cities which we took. *36* From Aroer, which is by the brink of the river of Arnon, and from the city that is by the river, even to Gilead, there was not one city too strong for us: **YeHoVaH** our **Elohim** delivered all to us: *37* Only to the land of the children of Ammon you came not, nor to any place of the river Jabbok, nor to the cities in the mountains, nor to whatever **YeHoVaH** our **Elohim** forbade us.

Chapter 3

Moses continues to speak. "YeHoVaH delivered Og of Bashan to us. I gave Gilead to Reuben, Gad and Manasseh. YeHoVaH said that I would not cross into the land."

1 Then we turned, and went up the way to Bashan: and Og the king of Bashan came out against us, he and all his people, to battle at Edrei. *2* And **YeHoVaH** said to me, Fear him not: for I will deliver him, and all his people, and his land, into your hand; and you shall do to him as you did to Sihon king of the Amorites, which dwelt at Heshbon. *3* So **YeHoVaH** our **Elohim** delivered into our hands Og also, the king of Bashan, and all his people: and we killed him until none was left. *4* And we took all his cities at that time, there was not a city which we did not take from them, 60 cities, all the region of Argob, the kingdom of Og in Bashan. *5* All these cities were fenced with high walls, gates, and bars; beside unwalled towns a great many. *6* And we utterly destroyed them, as we did to Sihon king of Heshbon, utterly destroying the men, women, and children, of every city. *7* But all the cattle, and the spoil of the cities, we took for a prey to ourselves. *8* And we took at that time out of the hand of the two kings of the Amorites the land that was on this side Jordan, from the river of Arnon to mount Hermon; *9* (Which Hermon the Sidonians call Sirion; and the Amorites call it Shenir;) *10* All the cities of the plain, and all Gilead, and all Bashan, to Salchah and Edrei, cities of the kingdom of Og in Bashan.

11 For only Og, king of Bashan remained of the remnant of giants; behold his bedstead was a bedstead of iron; is it not in Rabbath of the children of Ammon? nine cubits (a cubit = 20 inches) was the length, and four cubits the width of it, after the cubit of a man. *12* And this land, which we possessed at that time, from Aroer, which is by the river Arnon, and half mount Gilead, and the cities thereof, gave I to the Reubenites and to the Gadites. *13* And the rest of Gilead, and all Bashan, being the kingdom of Og, gave I to the half tribe of Manasseh; all the region of Argob, with all Bashan, which was called the land of giants. *14* Jair the son of Manasseh took all the country of Argob to the coasts of Geshuri and Maachathi; and called them after his own name, Bashanhavothjair, to this day. *15* And I gave Gilead to Machir. *16* And to the Reubenites and to the Gadites I gave from Gilead even to the river Arnon half the valley, and the border even to the river Jabbok, which is the border of the children of Ammon; *17* The plain also, and Jordan, and the coast thereof, from Chinnereth even to the sea of the plain, even the salt sea, under Ashdoespisgah eastward. *18* I commanded you at that time: "**YeHoVaH** your **Elohim** has given you this land to take possession of it. But all your able-bodied men, armed for battle, must cross over ahead of the other Israelites. *19* But your wives, and your little ones, and your cattle, (for I know that you have much cattle,) shall abide in your cities which I have given you; *20* Until **YeHoVaH** has given rest to your brethren, as well as to you, and until they also possess the land which **YeHoVaH** your **Elohim** has given them beyond Jordan: and then shall you return every man to his possession, which I have given you.

21 And I commanded Joshua at that time, saying, Your eyes have seen all that **YeHoVaH** your **Elohim** has done to these two kings: so shall **YeHoVaH** do to all the kingdoms that you pass. **22** You shall not fear them: for **YeHoVaH** your **Elohim** he shall fight for you.
Reading 44 ends

Reading 45 begins
23 And I asked **YeHoVaH** at that time, saying, **24** O Adonai **Elohim**, you have begun to show your servant your greatness, and your mighty hand: for what **Elohim** is there in heaven or in earth, that can do according to your works, and according to your might? **25** I pray you, let me go over, and see the good land that is beyond Jordan, that goodly mountain, and Lebanon. **26** But **YeHoVaH** was angry with me for your sakes, and would not hear me: and **YeHoVaH** said to me, Let it suffice you; speak no more to me of this matter. **27** Get you up into the top of Pisgah, and lift up your eyes westward, and northward, and southward, and eastward, and behold it with your eyes: for you shall not go over this Jordan. **28** But charge Joshua, and encourage him, and strengthen him: for he shall go over before this people, and he shall cause them to inherit the land that you shall see. **29** So we abode in the valley over against Bethpeor.

Chapter 4
*Now, Israel, hear the commandments and obey them. You heard YeHoVaH speak from the fire. Take care not to make idols. YeHoVaH is **Elohim**.*

1 Now therefore listen, O Israel, to the laws and to the judgments, which I teach you, for to do them, that you may live, and go in and possess the land that **YeHoVaH** the **Elohim** of your fathers gives you. **2 You shall not add to the word that I command you, neither shall you diminish anything from it,** that you may keep the commandments of **YeHoVaH** your **Elohim** that I command you. **3** Your eyes have seen what **YeHoVaH** did because of Baalpeor: for all the men that followed Baalpeor, **YeHoVaH** your **Elohim** has destroyed them from among you. **4** But you that did cleave to **YeHoVaH** your **Elohim** are alive, every one of you this day. **5** Behold, I have taught you laws and judgments, even as **YeHoVaH** my **Elohim** commanded me, that you should do so in the land where you go to possess it. **6** Keep therefore and do them; for this is your wisdom and your understanding in the sight of the nations, which shall hear all these laws (instructions), and say, Surely this great nation is a wise and understanding people. **7** For what nation is there so great, who has a god so nigh to them, as **YeHoVaH** our **Elohim** is in all things that we call upon him for? **8** And what nation is there so great, that has laws and judgments so righteous as all this law (instruction), which I set before you this day? **9** Only take heed to thyself, and keep your soul diligently, so you do not forget the things which your eyes have seen, and so they do not despair from your heart all the days of your life: but teach them your sons, and your sons' sons; **10** Especially the day that you stood before **YeHoVaH** your **Elohim** in Horeb, when **YeHoVaH** said to me, Gather me the people together, and I will make them hear my words, that they may learn to fear me all the days that they shall live upon the earth, and that they may teach their children.

11 And you came near and stood under the mountain; and the mountain burned with fire to the midst of heaven, with darkness, clouds, and thick darkness. **12** And **YeHoVaH** spoke to you out of the midst of the fire: you heard the voice of the words, but saw no likeness; only you heard a voice. **13** And he declared to you his covenant, which he commanded you to perform, even Ten Commandments; and he wrote them upon two tables of stone. **14** And **YeHoVaH** commanded me at that time to teach you law (instruction) and judgments that you might do them in the land where you go over to possess. *15* Take you therefore good notice to yourselves; for you saw no manner of resemblance on the day that **YeHoVaH** your **Elohim** spoke to you in Horeb out of the midst of the fire: *16* For fear that you corrupt yourselves, and make you a graven (carved out of stone, wood, or metal) image, the similarity of any figure, the likeness of male or female, *17* The likeness of any animal that is on the earth, the likeness of any winged bird that flies in the air, *18* The likeness of anything that creeps on the ground, the likeness of any fish that is in the waters beneath the earth: *19* And for fear that you lift up your eyes to heaven, and when you see the sun, and the moon, and the stars, even all the host of heaven, should be driven to worship them, and serve them, which **YeHoVaH** your **Elohim** has divided to all nations under the whole heaven. *20* But **YeHoVaH** has taken you, and brought you forth out of the iron furnace, even out of Egypt, to be to him a people of inheritance, as you are this day.

21 Furthermore **YeHoVaH** was angry with me for your sake, and swore that I should not go over Jordan, and that I should not go in to that good land, which **YeHoVaH** your **Elohim** gives you for an inheritance: *22* But I must die in this land, I must not go over Jordan: but you shall go over, and possess that good land. *23* Pay attention to yourselves, For fear that you forget the covenant of **YeHoVaH** your **Elohim**, which he made with you, and make you a graven (carved out of stone, wood, or metal) image, or the likeness of anything, which **YeHoVaH** your **Elohim** has forbidden you. *24* For **YeHoVaH** your **Elohim** is a consuming fire, even a jealous **Elohim**. *25* When you shall produce children, and children's children, and you shall have remained long in the land, and shall corrupt yourselves, and make a graven image, or the likeness of anything, and shall do evil in the sight of **YeHoVaH** your **Elohim**, to provoke him to anger: *26* I call heaven and earth to witness against you this day, that you shall soon utterly perish from off the land where you go over Jordan to possess it; you shall not prolong your days upon it, but shall utterly be destroyed. *27* And **YeHoVaH** shall scatter you among the nations, and you shall be left few in number among the heathen (a person who does not acknowledge **Elohim**), where **YeHoVaH** shall lead you. *28* And there you shall serve gods, the work of men's hands, wood and stone, which neither see, nor hear, nor eat, nor smell. *29* But if from then you shall seek **YeHoVaH** your **Elohim**, you shall find him, if you seek him with all your heart and with all your soul. *30* When you are in suffering, and all these things are come upon you, even in the latter days, if you turn to **YeHoVaH** your **Elohim**, and shall be obedient to his voice;

31 For **YeHoVaH** your **Elohim** is a merciful **Elohim**; he will not forsake you, neither destroy you, nor forget the covenant of your fathers which he swore to them. *32* For ask now of the days that are past, which were before you, since the day that **Elohim** created man upon the earth, and ask from the one side of heaven to the other, whether there has been any such thing as this great thing is, or has been heard like it? *33* Did ever people hear the voice of a god speaking out of the midst of the fire, as you have heard, and live? *34* Has any god ever tried to take for himself one nation out of another nation, by testing, by signs and wonders, by war, by a mighty hand and an outstretched arm, or by great and awesome deeds, like all the things **YeHoVaH** your **Elohim** did for you in Egypt before your very eyes? *35* Unto you it was shown, that you might know that **YeHoVaH** is **Elohim**; *there is no one else beside* him. *36* Out of heaven he made you to hear his voice, that he might instruct you: and upon earth he showed you his great fire; and you heard his words out of the midst of the fire. *37* And because he loved your fathers, therefore he chose their seed after them, and brought you out in his sight with his mighty power out of Egypt; *38* To drive out nations from before you greater and mightier than you are, to bring you in, to give you their land for an inheritance, as it is this day. *39* Know therefore this day, and consider it in your heart, that **YeHoVaH** is **Elohim** in heaven above, and upon the earth beneath: **there is none else**. **40** You shall keep therefore his laws (instructions), and his commandments, which I command you this day, that it may go well with you, and with your children after you, and that you may prolong your days upon the earth, which **YeHoVaH** your **Elohim** gives you, forever.

41 Then Moses severed three cities on this side Jordan toward the sun rising; **42** That the slayer might flee there, which should kill his neighbor accidentally, and hated him not in times past; and that fleeing to one of these cities he might live: **43** Namely, Bezer in the wilderness, in the plain country, of the Reubenites; and Ramoth in Gilead, of the Gadites; and Golan in Bashan, of the Manassites. **44** And this is the law (instruction) that Moses set before the children of Israel: **45** *These are the testimonies, and the* laws (instructions), *and the judgments, which Moses spoke to the children of Israel, after they came forth out of Egypt.* **46** On this side Jordan, in the valley over against Bethpeor, in the land of Sihon king of the Amorites, who dwelt at Heshbon, whom Moses and the children of Israel killed, after they came forth out of Egypt: **47** And they possessed his land, and the land of Og king of Bashan, two kings of the Amorites, which were on this side Jordan toward the sun rising; **48** From Aroer, which is by the bank of the river Arnon, even to mount Sion, which is Hermon, **49** And all the plain on this side Jordan eastward, even to the sea of the plain, under the springs of Pisgah.

Chapter 5
YeHoVaH makes his covenant with us: Have no other gods; Keep the Sabbath; Honor your parents. You shall do all that he has commanded. The Ten Commandments!

1 And Moses called all Israel, and said to them, Hear, O Israel, the laws (instructions) and judgments that I speak in your ears this day, that you may learn them, and keep, and do them. **2** **YeHoVaH** our **Elohim** made a covenant with us in Horeb. **3** **YeHoVaH** made not this covenant with our fathers, but with us, who are all of us here alive this day. **4** **YeHoVaH** talked with you face to face in the mount out of the midst of the fire, **5** I stood between **YeHoVaH** and you at that time, to show you the word of **YeHoVaH**: for you were afraid by reason of the fire, and went not up into the mount; saying, **6** I am your **Elohim**, which brought you out of the land of Egypt, from the house of bondage. **7** You shall have no other gods before me. **8** You *shall not* make you any graven (carved out of stone, wood, or metal) image, or *any likeness of anything that is in heaven above*, or that is in the earth beneath, or that is in the waters beneath the earth: **9** You *shall not bow down thyself to them, nor serve them*: for I **YeHoVaH** your **Elohim** am a jealous **Elohim**, visiting (hold to the same standard) the iniquity of the fathers upon the children to the third and fourth generation if they too hate me, **10** And showing mercy to thousands of them that love me and keep my commandments.

11 You shall not take the name of **YeHoVaH** your **Elohim** in vain (swear by falsely): for **YeHoVaH** will not hold him guiltless that takes his name in vain. **12** **Keep the Sabbath day** to sanctify it, as **YeHoVaH** your **Elohim** **has commanded you**. **13** Six days you shall labor, and do all your work: **14** *But the seventh day is the Sabbath of YeHoVaH your Elohim*: in it you shall not do any work, you, nor your son, nor your daughter, nor your manservant, nor your maidservant, nor your ox, nor your donkey, nor any of your cattle, nor your stranger that is within your gates; that your servants may rest as well as you. **15** And remember that you were a servant in the land of Egypt, and that **YeHoVaH** your **Elohim** brought you out then through a mighty hand and by a stretched out arm: therefore **YeHoVaH** your **Elohim** *commanded* you to **keep the Sabbath** day. *16* Honor your father and your mother, as **YeHoVaH** your **Elohim** has commanded you; that your days may be prolonged, and that it may go well with you, in the land which **YeHoVaH** your **Elohim** gives you. *17* You shall not kill. Neither shall you commit adultery. Neither shall you steal. Neither shall you bear false witness against your neighbor. *18* Neither shall you desire your neighbor's wife; neither shall you covet your neighbor's house, his field, or his manservant, or his maidservant, his ox, or his donkey, or anything that is your neighbor's. *19* These words **YeHoVaH** spoke to all your assembly in the mount out of the midst of the fire, of the cloud, and of the thick darkness, with a great voice: and he added no more. And he wrote them in two tables of stone, and delivered them to me. *20* And it came to pass, when you heard the voice out of the midst of the darkness, (as the mountain burn with fire,) that you came near to me, even all the heads of your tribes, and your elders;

21 And you said, Behold, **YeHoVaH** our **Elohim** has showed us his glory and his greatness, and we have heard his voice out of the midst of the fire: we have **seen this day that Elohim** *does talk with man, and he lives.* *22* Now therefore why should we die? for this great fire will consume us: if we hear the voice of **YeHoVaH** our **Elohim** any more, then we shall die. *23* For who is there of all flesh, that has heard the voice of the living **Elohim** speaking out of the midst of the fire, as we have, and lived? *24* Go you near, and hear all that **YeHoVaH** our **Elohim** shall say: and speak you to us all that **YeHoVaH** our **Elohim** shall speak to you; and we will hear it, and do it. *25* And **YeHoVaH** heard the voice of your words, when you spoke to me; and **YeHoVaH** said to me, I have heard the voice of the words of this people, which they have spoken to you: they have well said all that they have spoken. *26* O that there were such a heart in them, that they would fear me, and keep all my commandments always, that it might be well with them, and with their children forever! *27* Go say to them, Get you into your tents again. *28* But as for you, stand you here by me, and I will speak to you all the commandments, and the laws (instructions), and the judgments, which you shall teach them, that they may do them in the land that I give them to possess. *29* You shall observe to do therefore as **YeHoVaH** your **Elohim** has commanded you: you shall not turn aside to the right hand or to the left. *30* You shall walk in all the ways which **YeHoVaH** your **Elohim** has commanded you, that you may live, and that it may be well with you, and that you may prolong your days in the land that you shall possess.

Chapter 6

Hear, O Israel: YeHoVaH our Elohim is one. Love YeHoVaH with all your heart, soul and strength. Teach your children these commandments.

1 Now these are the commandments, the laws (instructions), and the judgments, which **YeHoVaH** your **Elohim** commanded to teach you, that you might do them in the land where you go to possess: *2* That you might fear **YeHoVaH** your **Elohim**, to keep all his laws (instructions) and his commandments, which I command you, you, and your son, and your son's son, **all the days of your life**; and that your days may be prolonged. *3* Hear therefore, O Israel, and observe to do it; that it may be well with you, and that you may increase mightily, as **YeHoVaH Elohim** of your fathers has promised you, in the land that flows with milk and honey. *4* *Hear, O Israel: **YeHoVaH** our **Elohim** is **One**: 5 And you shall love **YeHoVaH** your **Elohim** with all your heart, and with all your soul, and with all your might. 6 And these words, which I command you this day, shall be in your heart: 7 And you shall teach them diligently to your children, and shall* *talk of them when you sit in your house, and when you walk by the way, and when you lie down, and when you rise up. 8 And you shall bind them for a sign upon your hand, and they shall be as frontlets between your eyes. 9 And you shall write them upon the posts of your house, and on your gates.* (verses 4-9 is the **Shema;** a liturgical prayer, prominent in Jewish history and tradition, that is recited daily at the morning and evening services and expresses the Jewish people's ardent faith in and love of **Elohim.**) *10 And it shall be, when **YeHoVaH** your **Elohim** shall have brought you into the land that he swore to your fathers, to Abraham, to Isaac, and to Jacob, to give you great and goodly cities, which you build not,*

11 And houses full of all good things, which you do not fill, and wells dug, which you dig not, vineyards and olive trees, which you did not plant; when you shall have eaten and be full; 12 Then beware so you don't forget **YeHoVaH**, which brought you forth out of the land of Egypt, from the house of bondage. 13 You shall fear **YeHoVaH** your **Elohim**, and serve him, and shall swear by his name. 14 You shall not go after other gods, of the gods of the people which are around you; 15 For **YeHoVaH** your **Elohim** is a jealous **Elohim** among you or else the anger of **YeHoVaH** your **Elohim** be kindled against you, and destroy you from off the face of the earth. 16 You shall not tempt **YeHoVaH** your **Elohim**, as you tempted him in Massah. 17 You shall diligently keep the commandments of **YeHoVaH** your **Elohim**, and his testimonies, and his laws (instructions), which he has commanded you. 18 And you shall do that which is right and good in the sight of **YeHoVaH**: that it may be well with you, and that you may go in and possess the good land that **YeHoVaH** swore to your fathers. 19 To cast out all your enemies from before you, as **YeHoVaH** has spoken. 20 And when your son asks you in time to come, saying, What is meant by the testimonies, and the laws (instructions), and the judgments, which **YeHoVaH** our **Elohim** has commanded you?

21 Then you shall say to your son, We were Pharaoh's bondmen in Egypt; and **YeHoVaH** brought us out of Egypt with a mighty hand: 22 And **YeHoVaH** did great signs and wonders against Egypt, and against Pharaoh and all his house, before our eyes: 23 And he brought us out from there, that he might bring us in, to give us the land which he swore to our fathers. 24 And **YeHoVaH** commanded us to do all these laws, to fear **YeHoVaH** our **Elohim**, for our good always, that he might preserve us alive, as it is at this day. 25 And it shall be our righteousness, if we observe to do all these commandments before **YeHoVaH** our **Elohim**, as he has commanded us.

Chapter 7
Make no treaty with the nations of the land. You are a holy people, YeHoVaH has chosen you. He will drive out the nations before you.

1 When **YeHoVaH** your **Elohim** shall bring you into the land where you go to possess it, and has cast out many nations before you, the Hittites, and the Girgashites, and the Amorites, and the Canaanites, and the Perizzites, and the Hivites, and the Jebusites, seven nations greater and mightier than you; 2 And when **YeHoVaH** your **Elohim** shall deliver them before you; you shall utterly destroy them; you shall make no covenant with them, nor show mercy to them: 3 Neither shall you make marriages with them; your daughter you shall not give to his son, nor his daughter shall you take to your son. 4 For they will turn away your son from following me that they may serve other gods: so will the anger of **YeHoVaH** be kindled against you, and destroy you suddenly. 5 But thus shall you deal with them; you shall destroy their altars, and

break down their images, and cut down their groves, and burn their graven images with fire. *6* For you are a holy people to **YeHoVaH** your **Elohim**: **YeHoVaH** your **Elohim** has chosen you to be a special people to himself, above all people that are upon the face of the earth. *7* **YeHoVaH** did not set his love upon you, nor choose you, because you were more in number than any people; for you were the fewest of all people: *8* But because **YeHoVaH** loved you, and because he would keep the oath which he had sworn to your fathers, has **YeHoVaH** brought you out with a mighty hand, and redeemed you out of the house of bondmen, from the hand of Pharaoh king of Egypt. *9* Know therefore that **YeHoVaH** your **Elohim**, he is **Elohim**, the faithful **Elohim**, which keeps covenant and mercy with them that love him and **keep his commandments to a thousand generations**; *10* And repays them that hate him to their face, to destroy them: he will not be slack to him that hates him, he will repay him to his face.

11 You shall therefore keep the commandments, and the laws (instructions), and the judgments, which I command you this day, to do them.
Reading 45 ends

Reading 46 begins
12 Wherefore it shall come to pass, if you listen to these judgments, and keep, and do them, that **YeHoVaH** your **Elohim** shall keep to you the covenant and the mercy which he swore to your fathers: *13* And he will love you, and bless you, and multiply you: he will also bless the fruit of your womb, and the fruit of your land, your corn, and your wine, and your oil, the increase of your cattle, and the flocks of your sheep, in the land which he swore to your fathers to give you. *14* You shall be blessed above all people: there shall not be male or female barren among you, or among your cattle. *15* And **YeHoVaH** will take away from you all sickness, and will put none of the evil diseases of Egypt, which you know, upon you; but will lay them upon all them that hate you. *16* And you shall consume all the people which **YeHoVaH** your **Elohim** shall deliver you; your eye shall have no pity upon them: neither shall you serve their gods; for that will be a snare to you. *17* If you shall say in your heart, These nations are more than I; how can I dispossess them? *18* You shall not be afraid of them: but shall well remember what **YeHoVaH** your **Elohim** did to Pharaoh, and to all Egypt; *19* The great temptations which your eyes saw, and the signs, and the wonders, and the mighty hand, and the stretched out arm, whereby **YeHoVaH** your **Elohim** brought you out: so shall **YeHoVaH** your **Elohim** do to all the people of whom you are afraid. *20* Moreover **YeHoVaH** your **Elohim** will send the hornet among them, until they that are left, and hide themselves from you, be destroyed.

21 Do not be terrified by them, for **YeHoVaH** your **Elohim**, who is among you, is a great and awesome **Elohim**. *22* And **YeHoVaH** your **Elohim** will put out those nations before you by little and little: you may not consume them at once, lest the beasts of the field increase upon you. *23* But **YeHoVaH** your **Elohim** shall deliver them to you, and shall destroy them with a mighty destruction, until they be destroyed. *24* And he shall deliver their kings into your hand, and you shall destroy their name from under heaven: there shall no man be able to stand before you, until you have destroyed them. *25* The graven images of their **Elohim**s shall you burn with fire: you shall not desire the silver or gold that is on them, nor take it to you, or you be will be snared there: for it is an abomination (disgrace) to **YeHoVaH** your **Elohim**. *26* Neither shall you bring an abomination into your house, lest you be a cursed thing like it: but you shall utterly detest it, and you shall utterly abhor it; for it is a cursed thing.

Chapter 8

YeHoVaH led you in the wilderness and tested you. He is bringing you into a good land. Do not forget YeHoVaH or you shall perish.

1 All the commandments which I command you this day shall you observe to do, that you may live, and multiply, and go in and possess the land which **YeHoVaH** swore to your fathers. *2* And you shall remember all the way which **YeHoVaH** your **Elohim** led you these forty years in the wilderness, to humble you, and to prove you, to know what was in your heart, whether you would keep his commandments, or not. *3* And he humbled you, and suffered you to hunger, and fed you with manna, which you knew not, neither did your fathers know; that he might make you know that man does not live by bread only, but by every word that proceeds out of the mouth of **YeHoVaH** does man live. *4* Your clothes did not wear out and your feet did not swell during these forty years. *5* You shall also consider in your heart that, as a man disciplines his son, so **YeHoVaH** your **Elohim** disciplines you. *6* Therefore you shall keep the commandments of **YeHoVaH** your **Elohim**, to walk in his ways, and to fear him. *7* For **YeHoVaH** your **Elohim** brings you into a good land, a land of brooks of water, of fountains and depths that spring out of valleys and hills; *8* A land of wheat, and barley, and vines, and fig trees, and pomegranates; a land of olive oil, and honey; *9* A land where you shall eat bread without scarceness, you shall not lack anything in it; a land whose stones are iron, and out of whose hills you may dig brass. *10* When you have eaten and are full, then you shall bless **YeHoVaH** your **Elohim** for the good land that he has given you.

11 Beware that you forget not **YeHoVaH** your **Elohim**, in not keeping his commandments, and his judgments, and his laws (instructions), which I command you this day: *12* Otherwise when you have eaten and are full, and have built good houses, and dwelt therein; *13* And when your herds and your flocks multiply, and your silver and your gold is multiplied, and all that you have is multiplied; *14* Then your heart be lifted up, and you forget **YeHoVaH** your **Elohim**, who brought you forth out of the land of Egypt, from the house of bondage; *15* Who led you through that great and terrible wilderness, wherein were fiery serpents, and scorpions, and drought, where there was no water; who brought you forth water out of the rock of flint; *16* Who fed you in the wilderness with manna, which your fathers knew not, that he might humble you, and that he might prove you, to do you good at your latter end; *17* And you say in your heart, My power and the might of my hand has gotten me this wealth. *18* But you shall remember **YeHoVaH** your **Elohim**: for it is he that gives you power to get wealth, that he may establish his covenant which he swore to your fathers, as it is this day. *19* And it shall be, if you do at all forget **YeHoVaH** your **Elohim**, and walk after other **Elohim**s, and serve them, and worship them, I testify against you this day that you shall surely perish. *20* As the nations that **YeHoVaH** destroys before your face, so shall you perish; because you would not be obedient to the voice of **YeHoVaH** your **Elohim**.

Chapter 9

It is not for your righteousness that you will occupy the land. You rebelled and made the golden calf so I broke the tablets of the covenant.

1 Hear, O Israel: You are to pass over Jordan this day, to go in to possess nations greater and mightier than thyself, cities great and fenced up to heaven, *2* A people great and tall, the children of the Anakims, whom you know, and of whom you have heard say, Who can stand before the children of Anak! *3* Understand therefore this day, that **YeHoVaH** your **Elohim** is the one that goes over before you; as a consuming fire he shall destroy them, and he shall bring them down before your face: so shall you drive them out, and destroy them quickly, as **YeHoVaH** has said to you. *4* Speak not you in your heart, after that **YeHoVaH** your **Elohim** has cast them out from before you, saying, For my righteousness **YeHoVaH** has brought me in to possess this land: but for the wickedness of these nations **YeHoVaH** does drive them out from before you. *5* Not for your righteousness, or for the uprightness of your heart, do you go to possess their land: but for the wickedness of these nations **YeHoVaH** your **Elohim** does drive them out from before you, and that he may perform the word which **YeHoVaH** swore to your fathers, Abraham, Isaac, and Jacob. *6* Understand therefore, that **YeHoVaH** your **Elohim** gives you not this good land to possess it for your righteousness; for you are a stiff-necked people. *7* Remember, and forget not, how you provoked **YeHoVaH** your **Elohim** to anger in the wilderness: from the day that you did despair out of the land of Egypt, until you came to this place, you have been rebellious against **YeHoVaH**. *8* Also in Horeb you provoked **YeHoVaH** to wrath, so that **YeHoVaH** was angry with you to have destroyed you. *9* When I went up into the mount to receive the tables of stone, the tables of the covenant which **YeHoVaH** made with you, then I stayed in the mount 40 days and 40 nights, I neither did eat bread nor drink water: *10* And **YeHoVaH** delivered to me two tables of stone written with His finger; and on them was written according to all the words, which **YeHoVaH** spoke with you in the mount out of the midst of the fire in the day of the assembly.

11 And it came to pass at the end of 40 days and 40 nights, that **YeHoVaH** gave me the two tables of stone, even the tables of the covenant. *12* And **YeHoVaH** said to me, Arise, get you down quickly from here; for your people which you have brought forth out of Egypt have corrupted themselves; they are quickly turned aside out of the way which I commanded them; they have made them a molten image. *13* Furthermore **YeHoVaH** spoke to me, saying, I have seen this people, and, behold, it is a stiff-necked people: *14* Let me alone, that I may destroy them, and blot out their name from under heaven: and I will make of you a nation mightier and greater than they. *15* So I turned and came down from the mount, and the mount burned with fire: and the two tables of the covenant were in my two hands. *16* And I looked, and, behold, you had sinned against **YeHoVaH** your **Elohim**, and had made you a molten (from melted gold) calf: you had turned aside quickly out of the way that **YeHoVaH** had commanded you. *17* And I took the two tables, and cast them out of my two hands, and broke them before your eyes. *18* And I fell down before **YeHoVaH**, as at the first, 40 days and 40 nights: I did neither eat bread, nor drink water, because of all your sins which you sinned, in doing wickedly in the sight of **YeHoVaH**, to provoke him to anger. *19* For I was afraid of the anger and hot displeasure, that **YeHoVaH** was angry against you to destroy you. But **YeHoVaH** listened to me at that time also. *20* And **YeHoVaH** was very angry with Aaron to have destroyed him: and I prayed for Aaron also the same time.

21 And I took your sin, the calf which you had made, and burnt it with fire, and stamped it, and ground it very small, even until it was as small as dust: and I cast the dust thereof into the brook that descended out of the mountain. *22* And at Taberah, and at Massah, and at Kibrothhattaavah, you provoked **YeHoVaH** to anger. *23* Likewise when **YeHoVaH** sent you from Kadeshbarnea, saying, Go up and possess the land that I have given you; then you rebelled against the commandment of **YeHoVaH** your **Elohim**, and you believed him not, nor listened to his voice. *24* You have been rebellious against **YeHoVaH** from the day that I knew you. *25* Thus I fell down before **YeHoVaH** 40 days and 40 nights, as I fell down at the first; because

YeHoVaH had said he would destroy you. *26* I prayed therefore to *YeHoVaH*, and said, *O Adonai Elohim*, destroy not your people and your inheritance, which you have redeemed through your greatness, which you have brought forth out of Egypt with a mighty hand. *27* Remember your servants, Abraham, Isaac, and Jacob; look not to the stubbornness of this people, nor to their wickedness, nor to their sin: *28* Let not the land that you brought us out say, Because *YeHoVaH* was not able to bring them into the land which he promised them, and because he hated them, he has brought them out to slay them in the wilderness. *29* Yet they are your people and your inheritance, which you brought out by your mighty power and by your stretched out arm.

Chapter 10

YeHoVaH wrote on new tablets. What does YeHoVaH ask? That you fear him, walk in his ways, love him, serve him and keep his commands.

1 At that time *YeHoVaH* said to me, Cut you two tables of stone like the first, and come up to me into the mount, and make an ark of wood. *2* And I will write on the tables the words that were in the first tables that you broke, and you shall put them in the ark. *3* And I made an ark of shittim wood (probably the acacia tree), and hewed two tables of stone like to the first, and went up into the mount, having the two tables in my hand. *4* And he wrote on the tables, according to the first writing, the ten commandments, which *YeHoVaH* spoke to you in the mount out of the midst of the fire in the day of the assembly: and *YeHoVaH* gave them to me. *5* And I turned myself and came down from the mount, and put the tables in the ark that I had made; and there they be, as *YeHoVaH* commanded me. *6* And the children of Israel took their journey from Beeroth of the children of Jaakan to Mosera: there Aaron died, and there he was buried; and Eleazar his son ministered in the priest's office in his stead. *7* From then on they journeyed to Gudgod; and from Gudgod to Jotbath, a land of rivers of waters. *8* At that time *YeHoVaH* separated the tribe of Levi, to bear the ark of the covenant of *YeHoVaH*, to stand before *YeHoVaH* to minister to him, and to bless in his name, to this day. *9* That is why the Levites have no share or inheritance among their fellow Israelites; *YeHoVaH* is their inheritance, as *YeHoVaH* your *Elohim* told them. *10* And I stayed in the mount, according to the first time, 40 days and 40 nights; and *YeHoVaH* listened to me at that time also, and *YeHoVaH* would not destroy you.

11 And *YeHoVaH* said to me, Arise, take your journey before the people, that they may go in and possess the land, which I swore to their fathers to give to them. *12* And now, Israel, what does *YeHoVaH* your *Elohim* require of you, but to fear *YeHoVaH* your *Elohim*, to walk in all his ways, and to love him, and to serve *YeHoVaH* your *Elohim* with all your heart and with all your soul, *13* To keep the commandments of *YeHoVaH*, and his laws (instructions), which I command you this day for your good? *14* Behold, the heaven and the heaven of heavens is the *YeHoVaH*'s your *Elohim*, the earth also, with all that there is. *15* Only *YeHoVaH* had a delight in your fathers to love them, and he chose their seed after them, even you above all people, as it is this day. *16* Circumcise therefore your heart, and be no more stiff-necked. *17* For *YeHoVaH* your *Elohim* is *Elohim* of *Elohim*s and Lord of lords, the great *Elohim*, mighty and awesome, who shows no partiality and accepts no rewards. *18* He does execute the judgment of the fatherless and widow, and loves the stranger, in giving him food and clothes. *19* Love you therefore the stranger: for you were strangers in the land of Egypt. *20* Fear *YeHoVaH* your *Elohim* and serve him. Hold fast to him and take your oaths in his name.

21 He is your praise, and he is your *Elohim*, that has done for you these great and awesome things, which your eyes have seen. *22* Your fathers went down into Egypt with seventy persons; and now **YeHoVaH** your *Elohim* has made you like the stars of heaven in number.

CHAPTERS 11- 20

Chapter 11

You have seen all that YeHoVaH has done. Keep these commands so that you may live long in the land. A blessing and a curse are set before the people.

1 Therefore you shall love **YeHoVaH** your *Elohim*, and keep his instructions, and his laws (instructions), and his judgments, and his commandments, always. *2* Remember today that your children were not the ones who saw and experienced the discipline of **YeHoVaH** your *Elohim*: his majesty, his mighty hand, his outstretched arm *3* And his miracles, and his acts, which he did in the midst of Egypt to Pharaoh the king of Egypt, and to all his land; *4* And what he did to the army of Egypt, to their horses, and to their chariots; how he made the water of the Red sea to overflow them as they pursued after you, and how **YeHoVaH** has destroyed them to this day; *5* And what he did to you in the wilderness, until you came into this place; *6* And what he did to Dathan and Abiram, the sons of Eliab, the son of Reuben: how the earth opened her mouth, and swallowed them up, and their households, and their tents, and all the substance that was in their possession, in the midst of all Israel: *7* But your eyes have seen all the great acts of **YeHoVaH** which he did. *8* Therefore shall you keep all the commandments which I command you this day, that you may be strong, and go in and possess the land, where you go to possess it; *9* And that you may prolong your days in the land, which **YeHoVaH** swore to your fathers to give to them and to their seed, a land that flows with milk and honey. *10* For the land, where you go in to possess it, is not as the land of Egypt, from where you came out, where you sow your seed, and water it with your foot, as a garden of herbs:

11 But the land, where you go to possess it, is a land of hills and valleys, and drink water of the rain of heaven: *12* A land which **YeHoVaH** your *Elohim* cares for: the eyes of **YeHoVaH** your *Elohim* are always upon it, from the beginning of the year even to the end of the year. *13* And it shall come to pass, if you shall listen diligently to my commandments which I command you this day, to love **YeHoVaH** your *Elohim*, and to serve him with all your heart and with all your soul, *14* That I will give you the rain of your land in its due season, the first rain and the latter rain, that you may gather in your corn, and your wine, and your oil. *15* And I will send grass in your fields for your cattle, that you may eat and be full. *16* Take heed to yourselves, that your heart be not deceived, and you turn aside, and serve other *gods*, and worship them; *17* And then **YeHoVaH**'s wrath be kindled against you, and he shut up the heaven, that there be no rain, and that the land yield not her fruit; and you perish quickly from off the good land which **YeHoVaH** gives you. *18* Therefore shall you lay up these my words in your heart and in your soul, and bind them for a sign upon your hand, that they may be as frontlets between your eyes. *19* And you shall teach them your children, speaking of them when you sit in your house, and when you walk by the way, when you lie down, and when you rise up. *20* And you shall write them upon the doorposts of your house, and upon your gates: (the Shama)

21 That your days may be multiplied, and the days of your children, in the land which **YeHoVaH** swore to your fathers to give them, as the days of heaven upon the earth. *22* For if you shall diligently keep all these commandments which I command you, to do, to love **YeHoVaH** your **Elohim**, to walk in all his ways, and to cling to him; *23* Then will **YeHoVaH** drive out all these nations from before you, and you shall possess greater nations and mightier than yourselves. *24* Every place where the soles of your feet shall tread shall be yours: from the wilderness and Lebanon, from the river, the river Euphrates, even to the uttermost sea shall your coast be. *25* There shall no man be able to stand before you: for **YeHoVaH** your **Elohim** shall lay the fear of you and the dread of you upon all the land that you shall tread upon, as he has said to you.

Reading 46 ends

Reading 47 begins

26 Behold, I set before you this day a blessing and a curse; *27* A blessing, if you obey the commandments of **YeHoVaH** your **Elohim**, which I command you this day: *28* And a curse, if you will not obey the commandments of **YeHoVaH** your **Elohim**, but turn aside out of the way which I command you this day, to go after other **Elohim**s, which you have not known. *29* And it shall come to pass, when **YeHoVaH** your **Elohim** has brought you in to the land where you go to possess it, that you shall put the blessing upon mount Gerizim, and the curse upon mount Ebal. *30* Are they not on the other side of Jordan, by the way where the sun goes down, in the land of the Canaanites, which dwell in the level, open country over against Gilgal, beside the plains of Moreh?

31 For you shall pass over Jordan to go in to possess the land that **YeHoVaH** your **Elohim** gives you, and you shall possess it, and dwell there. *32* And you shall observe to do all the laws (instructions) and judgments that I set before you this day.

Chapter 12

Destroy the high places where the nations worship their gods. You shall bring your offerings at the place that YeHoVaH will choose.

1 These are the laws (instructions) and judgments, which you shall observe to do in the land, which **YeHoVaH Elohim** of your fathers gives you to possess, all the days that you live upon the earth. *2* You shall utterly destroy all the places, where the nations which you shall possess served their *gods*, upon the high mountains, and upon the hills, and under every green tree: *3* And you shall overthrow their altars, and break their pillars, and burn their groves with fire; and you shall cut down the graven images of their *gods*, and destroy the names of them out of that place. *4* You shall not do so to **YeHoVaH** your **Elohim**. *5* But to the place which **YeHoVaH** your **Elohim** shall choose out of all your tribes to put his name there, even to his habitation shall you seek, and there you shall come: *6* And there you shall bring your burnt offerings, and your sacrifices, and your tithes, and heave offerings of your hand, and your vows, and your freewill offerings, and the firstlings of your herds and of your flocks: *7* And there you shall eat before **YeHoVaH** your **Elohim**, and you shall rejoice in all that you put your hand to, you and your households, wherein **YeHoVaH** your **Elohim** has blessed you. *8* You shall not do after all the things that we do here this day; every man whatever is right in his own eyes. *9* For you are not as yet come to the rest and to the inheritance, which **YeHoVaH** your **Elohim** gives you. *10* But when you go over Jordan, and dwell in the land which **YeHoVaH** your **Elohim** gives you to inherit, and when he gives you rest from all your enemies all around, so that you dwell in safety;

11 Then there shall be a place which **YeHoVaH** your **Elohim** shall choose to cause his name to dwell there; there shall you bring all that I command you; your burnt offerings, and your sacrifices, your tithes, and the heave offering of your hand, and all your choice vows which you vow to **YeHoVaH**: **12** And you shall rejoice before **YeHoVaH** your **Elohim**, you, and your sons, and your daughters, and your menservants, and your maidservants, and the Levite that is within your gates; for as much as he has no allotment nor inheritance with you. **13** Take heed to yourself that you offer not your burnt offerings in every place that you see: **14** But in the place which **YeHoVaH** shall choose in one of your tribes, there you shall offer your burnt offerings, and there you shall do all that I command you. **15** Nevertheless, you may slaughter your animals in any of your towns and eat as much of the food as you want, as if it were gazelle or deer, according to the blessing **YeHoVaH** your **Elohim** gives you. Both the ceremonially unclean and the clean person may eat it. **16** Only you shall not eat the blood; you shall pour it upon the earth as water. **17** You may not eat within your gates the tithe of your corn, or of your wine, or of your oil, or the firstlings of your herds or of your flock, nor any of your vows which you vows, nor your freewill offerings, or heave offering of your hand: **18** But you must eat them before **YeHoVaH** your **Elohim** in the place which **YeHoVaH** your **Elohim** shall choose, you, and your son, and your daughter, and your manservant, and your maidservant, and the Levite that is within your gates: and you shall rejoice before **YeHoVaH** your **Elohim** in all that you put your hands to. **19** Take heed to yourself that you forsake not the Levite as long as you live upon the earth. **20** When **YeHoVaH** shall enlarge your border, as he has promised you, and you shall say, I will eat flesh, because your soul longs to eat flesh; you may eat flesh, whatsoever your soul lusts after.

21 If the place where **YeHoVaH** chooses to put his Name is too far away from you, you may slaughter animals from the herds and flocks **YeHoVaH** has given you, as I have commanded you, and in your own towns you may eat as much of them as you want. **22** Eat them as you would gazelle or deer. Both the ceremonially unclean and the clean may eat. **23** But be sure you do not eat the blood, because the blood is the life, and you must not eat the life with the flesh. **24** You shall not eat it; you shall pour it upon the earth as water. **25** You shall not eat it; that it may go well with you, and with your children after you, when you shall do that which is right in the sight of **YeHoVaH**. **26** Only your holy things which you have, and your vows, you shall take, and go to the place which **YeHoVaH** shall choose: **27** And you shall offer your burnt offerings, the flesh and the blood, upon the altar of **YeHoVaH** your **Elohim**: and the blood of your sacrifices shall be poured out upon the altar of **YeHoVaH** your **Elohim**, and you shall eat the flesh. **28** Observe and hear all these words which I command you, that it may go well with you, and with your children after you forever, when you do that which is good and right in the sight of **YeHoVaH** your **Elohim**. **29** When **YeHoVaH** your **Elohim** shall cut off the nations from before you, whether you go to possess them, and you succeed them, and dwell in their land; **30** After their destruction take care that you do not go in their ways, and that you do not give thought to their *gods*, saying, How did these nations give worship to their *gods*? I will do as they did. **31** You shall not do so to **YeHoVaH** your **Elohim**: for every abomination to **YeHoVaH**, which he hates, have they done to their *gods*; for even their sons and their daughters they have burnt in the fire to their *gods*.

Chapter 13

If a prophet or anyone else entices you away from YeHoVaH they must be put to death. If a town has turned away it must be destroyed.

1 Whatever I command you, observe to do it: you shall not add thereto, nor diminish from it. **2** If there arise among you a prophet, or a dreamer of dreams, and gives you a sign or a wonder, **3** And the sign or the wonder come to pass, that he spoke to you, saying, Let us go after other **Elohim**s, which you have not known, and let us serve them; **4** You shall not listen to the words of that prophet, or that dreamer of dreams: for **YeHoVaH** your **Elohim** tests you, to know whether you love **YeHoVaH** your **Elohim** with all your heart and with all your soul. **5** You shall walk after **YeHoVaH** your **Elohim**, and fear him, and keep his commandments, and obey his voice, and you shall serve him, and cling to him. **6** And that prophet, or that dreamer of dreams, shall be put to death; because he has spoken to turn you away from **YeHoVaH** your **Elohim**, which brought you out of the land of Egypt, and redeemed you out of the house of bondage, to thrust you out of the way which **YeHoVaH** your **Elohim** commanded you to walk in. So shall you put the evil away from your midst. **7** If your brother, the son of your mother, or your son, or your daughter, or the wife of your bosom, or your friend, which is as your own soul, entice you secretly, saying, Let us go and serve other *gods*, which you have not known, you, nor your fathers; **8** Namely, of the gods of the people which are round about you, near to you, or far off from you, from the one end of the earth even to the other end of the earth; **9** You shall not consent to him, nor listen to him; neither shall your eye pity him, neither shall you spare, neither shall you conceal him: **9** But you shall surely kill him; your hand shall be first upon him to put him to death, and afterwards the hand of all the people. **10** And you shall stone him with stones, that he die; because he has sought to thrust you away from **YeHoVaH** your **Elohim**, which brought you out of the land of Egypt, from the house of bondage.

11 And all Israel shall hear, and fear, and shall do no more any such wickedness as this is among you. **12** If you shall hear say in one of your cities, which **YeHoVaH** your **Elohim** has given you to dwell there, saying, **13** Certain men, the children of Belial, are gone out from among you, and have withdrawn the inhabitants of their city, saying, Let us go and serve other *gods*, which you have not known; **14** Then shall you enquire, and make search, and ask diligently; and, behold, if it be truth, and the thing certain, that such abomination is wrought among you; **15** You shall surely smite the inhabitants of that city with the edge of the sword, destroying it utterly, and all that is therein, and the cattle thereof, with the edge of the sword. **16** And you shall gather all the spoil of it into the midst of the street thereof, and shall burn with fire the city, and all the spoil thereof every speck, for **YeHoVaH** your **Elohim**: and it shall be a heap of rubble forever; it shall not be built again. **17** And there shall cling not of the cursed thing to your hand: that **YeHoVaH** may turn from the fierceness of his anger, and show you mercy, and have compassion upon you, and multiply you, as he has sworn to your fathers; **18** When you shall listen to the voice of **YeHoVaH** your **Elohim**, to keep all his commandments which I command you this day, to do that which is right in the eyes of **YeHoVaH** your **Elohim**.

Chapter 14

You may eat animals with cloven hooves that chew the cud. Bring a tithe from your fields to eat before YeHoVaH and for the Levites.

1 You are the children of **YeHoVaH** your **Elohim**: you shall not cut yourselves, nor make any baldness between your eyes for the dead. *2* For you are a holy people to **YeHoVaH** your **Elohim**, and **YeHoVaH** has chosen you to be a peculiar people to him, above all the nations that are upon the earth. *3* Do not eat any detestable thing. *4* These are the animals you **may** eat: the ox, the sheep, the goat, *5* the deer, the gazelle, the roe deer, the wild goat, the ibex, the antelope and the mountain sheep. *6* You may eat any animal that has a divided hoof and that chews the cud. *7* However, of those that chew the cud or that has a divided hoof you may not eat the camel, the rabbit or the hyrax. Though they chew the cud, they do not have a divided hoof; they are ceremonially unclean for you. *8* And the **swine**, because it divides the hoof, yet chews not the cud, it is unclean to you: you shall **not** eat of their flesh, nor touch their dead carcass. *9* These you **shall** eat of all that are in the waters: all that have fins and scales shall you eat: *10* And whatsoever does not have fins and scales you may **not** eat; it is unclean to you.

11 Of all clean birds you shall eat. *12* But these are they of which you shall **not** eat: the eagle, and the ossifrage (a vulture), and the ospray (a large Hawk), *13* And the glede (a bird of prey), and the kite (a bird of prey like an owl), and the vulture after his kind, *14* And every raven after his kind, *15* And the owl, and the night hawk, and the cuckow (like a seagull), and the hawk after his kind, *16* The little owl, and the great owl, and the swan, *17* And the pelican, and the gier eagle (a vulture), and the cormorant (aquatic bird), *18* And the stork, and the heron after her kind, and the lapwing (slow wingbeat), and the bat. *19* And every creeping thing that flies is unclean to you: they shall not be eaten. *20* But of all clean birds you may eat,

21 you shall **not** eat of anything that dies of itself: you shall give it to the stranger that is in your gates, that he may eat it; or you may sell it to an foreigner: for you are a holy people to **YeHoVaH** your **Elohim**. You shall not cook a goat in its mother's milk. (Yes, you can eat meat and cheese together) *22* **You shall truly tithe all the increase of your seed that the field brings forth year by year.** *23* And you shall eat before **YeHoVaH** your **Elohim**, in the place which he shall choose to place his name there, the tithe of your corn, of your wine, and of your oil, and the firstlings of your herds and of your flocks; that you may learn to fear **YeHoVaH** your **Elohim** always. *24* And if the way be too long for you, so that you are not able to carry it; or if the place be too far from you, which **YeHoVaH** your **Elohim** shall choose to set his name there, when **YeHoVaH** your **Elohim** has blessed you: *25* Then shall you turn it into money, and bind up the money in your hand, and shall go to the place which **YeHoVaH** your **Elohim** shall choose: *26* And you shall bestow that money for whatsoever your soul lusts after, for oxen, or for sheep, or for wine, or for *strong drink*, or for whatsoever your soul desires: and you shall eat there before **YeHoVaH** your **Elohim**, and you shall rejoice, you, and your household, *27* And the Levite that is within your gates; you shall not forsake him; for he has no pare (allotment) nor inheritance with you. *28* At the end of three years you shall bring forth all the tithe of your increase the same year, and shall lay it up within your gates: *29* And the Levite, (because he has no allotment nor inheritance with you,) and the stranger, and the fatherless, and the widow, which are within your gates, shall come, and shall eat and be satisfied; that **YeHoVaH** your **Elohim** may bless you in all the work of your hand which you do.

Chapter 15

Every seven years you shall cancel debts. Hebrew slaves shall go free in the seventh year. Set apart every firstborn male animal.

1 At the end of every seven years you shall make a release. *2* And this is the manner of the release: Every creditor that lends anything to his neighbor shall release it; he shall not demand it of his neighbor, or of his brother; because it is called **YeHoVaH**'s release. *3* Of a foreigner you may demand it again: but that which is yours with your brother, your hand shall release; *4* Except when there shall be no poor among you; for **YeHoVaH** shall greatly bless you in the land which **YeHoVaH** your **Elohim** gives you for an inheritance to possess it: *5* Only if you carefully listen to the voice of **YeHoVaH** your **Elohim**, to observe to do all these commandments which I command you this day. *6* For **YeHoVaH** your **Elohim** blesses you, as he promised you: and you shall lend to many nations, but you shall not borrow; and you shall reign over many nations, but they shall not reign over you. *7* If there be among you a poor man of one of your brethren within any of your gates in your land which **YeHoVaH** your **Elohim** gives you, you *shall not harden your heart, nor shut your hand from your poor brother.* *8* But you shall open your hand wide to him, and shall surely lend him sufficient for his need, in that which he wants. *9* Beware that there be not a thought in your wicked heart, saying, The seventh year, the year of release, is at hand; and your eye be evil against your poor brother, and you give him not; and he cry to **YeHoVaH** against you, and it be sin to you. *10* You shall surely give him, and your heart shall not be grieved when you give to him: because that for this thing **YeHoVaH** your **Elohim** shall bless you in all your works, and in all that you put your hand to.

11 For the poor shall *never* cease out of the land: therefore I command you, saying, *You shall open your hand wide to your brother, to your poor, and to your needy, in your land.* *12* And if your brother, a Hebrew man, or a Hebrew woman, be sold to you, and serve you six years; then in the seventh year you shall let him go free from you. *13* And when you send him out free from you, you shall not let him go away empty: *14* You shall furnish him liberally out of your flock, and out of your floor, and out of your winepress: of that which **YeHoVaH** your **Elohim** has blessed you, you shall give to him. *15* And you shall remember that you were a slave in the land of Egypt, and **YeHoVaH** your **Elohim** redeemed you: therefore I command you this thing today. *16* And it shall be, if he say to you, I will not go away from you; because he loves you and your house, because he is well with you; *17* Then you shall take an aul (pointed tool), and thrust it through his ear to the door, and he shall be your servant forever. And also to your maidservant you shall do likewise. *18* It shall not seem hard to you, when you send him away free from you; for he has been worth a double hired servant to you, in serving you six years: and **YeHoVaH** your **Elohim** shall bless you in all that you do. *19* All the firstling males that come of your herd and of your flock you shall sanctify to **YeHoVaH** your **Elohim**: you shall do no work with the firstling of your bullock, nor shear the firstling of your sheep. *20* You shall eat it before **YeHoVaH** your **Elohim** year by year in the place that **YeHoVaH** shall choose, you and your household.

21 And if there be any blemish therein, as if it be lame, or blind, or have any ill blemish, you shall not sacrifice it to **YeHoVaH** your **Elohim**. *22* You are to eat it in your own towns. Both the ceremonially unclean and the clean person may eat it, as if it were gazelle or deer. *23* Only you shall not eat the blood thereof; you shall pour it upon the ground as water.

Chapter 16
Moses continues to review YeHoVaH's commands and laws (instructions). Celebrate the Passover in the month of Abib. Celebrate the Feast of Weeks (Shavuot/Pentecost) and the Feast of Booths (Tabernacles/Sukkot). Appoint judges in all your towns.

1 Observe the month of Abib, and keep the **Passover** to **YeHoVaH** your **Elohim**: for in the month of Abib **YeHoVaH** your **Elohim** brought you forth out of Egypt by night. *2* You shall therefore sacrifice the Passover to **YeHoVaH** your **Elohim**, of the flock and the herd, in the place that **YeHoVaH** shall choose to place his name there. *3* You shall eat no leavened bread with it; seven days shall you eat unleavened bread therewith, even the bread of affliction; for you came forth out of the land of Egypt in haste: that you may remember the day when you came forth out of the land of Egypt all the days of your life. *4* For seven days let no leaven be used through all your land; and nothing of the flesh which is put to death in the evening of the first day is to be kept through the night till morning. *5* You may not sacrifice the Passover within any of your gates, which **YeHoVaH** your **Elohim** gives you: *6* But at the place which **YeHoVaH** your **Elohim** shall choose to place his name in, there you shall sacrifice the Passover at evening, at the going down of the sun, at the season that you came forth out of Egypt. *7* And you shall roast and eat it in the place which **YeHoVaH** your **Elohim** shall choose: and you shall turn in the morning, and go to your tents. *8* Six days you shall eat unleavened bread: and on the *seventh day* shall be a solemn assembly to **YeHoVaH** your **Elohim**: you shall do no work therein. *9* Seven weeks shall you number to you: begin to number the seven weeks from such time as you begin to put the sickle to the corn. *10* And you shall keep the **feast of Weeks** to **YeHoVaH** your **Elohim** with a tribute of a freewill offering of your hand, which you shall give to **YeHoVaH** your **Elohim**, according as **YeHoVaH** your **Elohim** has blessed you:

11 And you shall rejoice before **YeHoVaH** your **Elohim**, you, and your son, and your daughter, and your manservant, and your maidservant, and the Levite that is within your gates, and the stranger, and the fatherless, and the widow, that are among you, in the place which **YeHoVaH** your **Elohim** has chosen to place his name there. *12* And you shall remember that you were a servant in Egypt: and you shall observe and do these laws (instructions). *13* You shall observe the **feast of tabernacles (booths/Sukkot)**seven days, after that you have gathered in your corn and your wine: *14* And you shall rejoice in your feast, you, and your son, and your daughter, and your manservant, and your maidservant, and the Levite, the stranger, and the fatherless, and the widow, that are within your gates. *15* Seven days shall you keep a solemn feast to **YeHoVaH** your **Elohim** in the place which **YeHoVaH** shall choose: because **YeHoVaH** your **Elohim** shall bless you in all your increase, and in all the works of your hands, therefore you shall surely rejoice. *16* Three times in a year shall all your males appear before **YeHoVaH** your **Elohim** in the place which he shall choose; in the feast of unleavened bread (Passover), and in the feast of **Weeks (Shavuote/Pentecost)**, and in the feast of tabernacles (booths): and they shall not appear before **YeHoVaH** empty: *17* Every man shall give as he is able, according to the blessing of **YeHoVaH** your **Elohim** which he has given you.

Reading 47 ends

Reading 48 begins
18 Judges and officers shall you make in all your gates, which **YeHoVaH** your **Elohim** gives you, throughout your tribes: and they shall judge the people with just judgment. *19* You shall not extort judgment; you shall not respect persons, neither take a gift (bribe): for a gift does blind the eyes of the wise, and pervert the words of the righteous. *20* That which is altogether just shall you follow, that you may live, and inherit the land which **YeHoVaH** your **Elohim** gives you.

21 You shall not plant a grove of any trees near to the altar of **YeHoVaH** your **Elohim**, which you shall make. *22* Neither shall you set up any image; which **YeHoVaH** your **Elohim** hates.

Chapter 17
Anyone who breaks the covenant shall be put to death. Go to the priests with hard decisions. Appoint the king that YeHoVaH chooses by the standards set by YeHoVaH.

1 No ox or sheep that has a mark on it or is damaged in any way may be offered to **YeHoVaH** your **Elohim**: for that is an abomination to **YeHoVaH** your **Elohim**. *2* If there be found among you, within any of your gates which **YeHoVaH** your **Elohim** gives you, man or woman, that has formed wickedness in the sight of **YeHoVaH** your **Elohim**, in disobeying his covenant, *3* And has gone and served other *gods*, and worshipped them, either the sun, or moon, or any of the host of heaven, which I have not commanded; *4* And it be told you, and you have heard of it, and enquired diligently, and, behold, it be true, and the thing certain, that such abomination is formed in Israel: *5* Then shall you bring forth that man or that woman, which has committed that wicked thing, to your gates, even that man or that woman, and shall stone them with stones, till they die. *6* At the mouth of two witnesses, or three witnesses, shall he that is worthy of death be put to death; but at the mouth of *one* witness he shall *not* be put to death. *7* The hands of the witnesses shall be first upon him to put him to death, and afterward the hands of all the people. So you shall put the evil away from among you. *8* If you are not able to give a decision as to who is responsible for a death, or who is right in a cause, or who gave the first blow in a fight, and there is a division of opinion about it in your town: then go to the place marked out by **YeHoVaH** your **Elohim**; *9* And you shall come to the priests the Levites, and to the judge that shall be in those days, and enquire; and they shall show you the sentence of judgment: *10* And you shall do according to the sentence, which they of that place which **YeHoVaH** shall choose shall show you; and you shall observe to do according to all that they inform you:

11 According to the sentence of the law (instruction) which they shall teach you, and according to the judgment which they shall tell you, you shall do: you shall not decline from the sentence which they shall show you, to the right hand, nor to the left. *12* And the man that will assume he is right, and will not listen to the priest that stands to minister there before **YeHoVaH** your **Elohim**, or to the judge, even that man shall die: and you shall put away the evil from Israel. *13* All the people will hear and be afraid, and will not be disapproving again. *14* When you have come to the land which **YeHoVaH** your **Elohim** gives you, and shall possess it, and shall dwell therein, and shall say, I will set a king over me, like other nations around me; *15* You shall in any way set him king over you, whom **YeHoVaH** your **Elohim** shall choose: one from among your brethren shall you set king over you: you may *not* set a stranger over you, which is not your brother. *16* But he shall *not* multiply horses to himself, nor cause the people to return to Egypt, to the end that he should multiply horses: forasmuch as **YeHoVaH** has said to you, You shall from this time forth return no more that way. *17* Neither shall he multiply wives to himself, that his heart turns not away: neither shall he greatly multiply to himself silver and gold. *18* And it shall be, when he sits upon the throne of his kingdom, that he shall write him a copy of this law (instruction) in a book out of that which is before the priests the Levites: *19* And it shall be with him, and he shall read therein all the days of his life: that he may learn to fear **YeHoVaH** his **Elohim**, to keep all the words of this law (instruction) and these laws (instructions), to do them: *20* That his heart be not lifted up above his brethren, and that he turn not aside from the commandment, to the right hand, or to the left: to the end that he may prolong his days in his kingdom, he, and his children, in the midst of Israel.

Chapter 18

The priests shall eat the offerings made by fire. You shall not practice divination (predicting the future). YeHoVaH will raise up a prophet (Joshua) from among you.

1 The priests the Levites, and all the tribe of Levi, shall have no possession, or inheritance with Israel: they shall eat the offerings of **YeHoVaH** made by fire, and his inheritance. *2* Therefore shall they have no inheritance among their brethren: **YeHoVaH** is their inheritance, as he has said to them. *3* And this shall be the priest's due from the people, from them that offer a sacrifice, whether it be ox or sheep; and they shall give to the priest the shoulder, and the two cheeks, and the jaw. *4* The first-fruit also of your corn, of your wine, and of your oil, and the first of the fleece of your sheep, shall you give him. *5* For **YeHoVaH** your **Elohim** has chosen him *'out of all your tribes'*, to stand to minister in the name of **YeHoVaH**, him and his sons forever. *6* And if a Levite come from any of your gates out of all Israel, where he traveled, and come with all the desire of his mind to the place which **YeHoVaH** shall choose; *7* Then he shall minister in the name of **YeHoVaH** his **Elohim**, as all his brethren the Levites do, which stand there before **YeHoVaH**. *8* They shall have like portions to eat, beside that which comes of the sale of his belongings. *9* When you come into the land which **YeHoVaH** your **Elohim** gives you, you shall not learn to do after the disgrace of those nations. *10* There shall not be found among you any one that makes his son or his daughter to pass through the fire, or that uses telling of the future, or an observer of times, or an enchanter (a magician; sorcerer), or a witch.

11 Or a charmer, or a consulter with familiar spirits, or a wizard, or a necromancer (the practice of communicating with the dead). *12* For all that do these things are a shameful action to **YeHoVaH**: and because of these abominations **YeHoVaH** your **Elohim** does drive them out from before you. *13* You shall be perfect with **YeHoVaH** your **Elohim**. *14* For these nations, which you shall possess, listened to observers of times, and to diviners: but as for you, **YeHoVaH** your **Elohim** has not suffered you so to do. *15* **YeHoVaH** your **Elohim** will raise up to you a Prophet (Joshua) *from the **midst of you**, of **your brethren**, like to me; to him you shall listen; *16* According to all that you desire of **YeHoVaH** your **Elohim** in Horeb in the day of the assembly, saying, Let me not hear again the voice of **YeHoVaH** my **Elohim**, neither let me see this great fire any more, that I die not. *17* And **YeHoVaH** said to me, They have well-spoken that which they have spoken. *18* I will raise them up a Prophet (Joshua) *from among their brethren*, like to you, and will put my words in his mouth; and he shall speak to them all that I shall command him. *19* And it shall come to pass, that whosoever will not listen to my words that he shall speak in my name, I will require it of him. *20* But the prophet, who shall presume to speak a word in my name, which I have not commanded him to speak, or that shall speak in the name of other gods, even that prophet shall die.

21 And if you say in your heart, How shall we know the word which **YeHoVaH** has not spoken? *22* When a prophet speaks in the name of **YeHoVaH**, if the thing follow not, nor come to pass, that is the thing which **YeHoVaH** has not spoken, but the prophet has spoken it presumptuously: you shall not be afraid of him.

Chapter 19

Set aside three cities so that anyone who kills accidentally may flee there. A matter must be established by a minimum of two or three witnesses.

1 When **YeHoVaH** your **Elohim** has cut off the nations, whose land **YeHoVaH** your **Elohim** gives you, and you succeed them, and dwell in their cities, and in their houses; *2* You shall separate three cities for you in the midst of your land, which **YeHoVaH** your **Elohim** gives you to possess. *3* You shall prepare you a way, and divide the coasts of your land, which **YeHoVaH** your **Elohim** gives you to inherit, into three areas, that every slayer may flee there. *4* And this is the case of the slayer, which shall flee there, that he may live: Whoever kills his neighbor ignorantly, whom he hated not in time past; *5* As when a man goes into the wood with his neighbor to hew wood, and his hand fetches a stroke with the axe to cut down the tree, and the head slips from the helve, and lands upon his neighbor, that he die; he shall flee to one of those cities, and live: *6* In case the avenger of the blood pursue the slayer, while his heart is hot, and overtake him, because the way is long, and slay him; whereas he was not worthy of death, inasmuch as he hated him not in time past. *7* Therefore I command you, saying, You shall separate three cities for you. *8* And if **YeHoVaH** your **Elohim** enlarge your coast, as he has sworn to your fathers, and give you all the land which he promised to give to your fathers; *9* If you shall keep all these commandments to do them, which I command you this day, to love **YeHoVaH** your **Elohim**, and to walk ever in his ways; then shall you add three cities more for you, beside these three: *10* That innocent blood be not shed in your land, which **YeHoVaH** your **Elohim** gives you for an inheritance, and so blood be upon you.

11 But if any man hate his neighbor, and lie in wait for him, and rise up against him, and wound him mortally that he die, and flees into one of these cities: *12* Then the elders of his city shall send and fetch him there, and deliver him into the hand of the avenger of blood, that he may die. *13* Your eye shall not pity him, but you shall put away the guilt of innocent blood from Israel, that it may go well with you. *14* You shall not remove your neighbor's landmark, which they of old time have set in your inheritance, which you shall inherit in the land that **YeHoVaH** your **Elohim** gives you to possess it. *15* One witness shall *not* rise up against a man for any iniquity, or for any sin, in any sin that he sins: at the mouth of two witnesses, or at the mouth of three witnesses, shall the matter be established. *16* If a false witness rise up against any man to testify against him that which is wrong; *17* Then both the men, between whom the controversy is, shall stand before **YeHoVaH**, before the priests and the judges, which shall be in those days; *18* And the judges shall make diligent inquisition: and, behold, if the witness be a false witness, and has testified falsely against his brother; *19* Then shall you do to him, as he had thought to have done to his brother: so shall you put the evil away from among you. *20* And those which remain shall hear, and fear, and shall henceforth commit no more any such evil among you.

21 And your eye shall not pity; but life shall go for life, eye for eye, tooth for tooth, hand for hand, foot for foot.

Chapter 20

When you go to war, do not be afraid; YeHoVaH is with you. As you go to attack a city, offer peace first but if refused then destroy all the men by the sword.

1 When you go out to battle against your enemies, and see horses, and chariots, and a people more than you, be not afraid of them: for **YeHoVaH** your **Elohim** is with you, which brought you up out of the land of Egypt. *2* And it shall be, when you come near to the battle, that the priest shall approach and speak to the people, *3* And shall say to them, Hear, O Israel, you approach this day to battle against your enemies: let not your hearts be faint, fear not, and do not tremble, neither be you terrified because of them; *4* For **YeHoVaH** your **Elohim** is he that goes with you, to fight for you against your enemies, to save you. *5* And the officers shall speak to the people; saying, What man is there that has built a new house, and has not dedicated it? let him go and return to his house, in case he die in the battle, and another man dedicate it. *6* And what man is he that has planted a vineyard, and has not yet eaten of it? let him also go and return to his house, in case he die in the battle, and another man eat of it. *7* And what man is there that has betrothed a wife, and has not taken her? let him go and return to his house, lest he die in the battle, and another man take her. *8* And the officers shall speak further to the people, and they shall say, What man is there that is fearful and fainthearted? let him go and return to his house, lest his brethren's heart faint as well as his heart. *9* And it shall be, when the officers have made an end of speaking to the people that they shall make captains of the armies to lead the people.

Reading 48 ends

Reading 49 begins
10 When you come near to a city to fight against it, then proclaim peace to it.

11 And it shall be, if it makes you answer of peace, and open to you, then it shall be, that all the people that is found therein shall be tributaries to you, and they shall serve you. *12* And if it will make no peace with you, but will make war against you, then you shall besiege it: *13* And when **YeHoVaH** your **Elohim** has delivered it into your hands, you shall smite every male there with the edge of the sword: *14* But the women, and the little ones, and the cattle, and all that is in the city, even all the spoil thereof, shall you take to yourself; and you shall eat the spoil of your enemies, which **YeHoVaH** your **Elohim** has given you. *15* Thus shall you do to all the cities that are very far off from you, which are not of the cities of these nations. *16* But of the cities of these people, which **YeHoVaH** your **Elohim** does give you for an inheritance, you shall leave alive nothing that breathes: *17* But you shall utterly destroy them; namely, the Hittites, and the Amorites, the Canaanites, and the Perizzites, the Hivites, and the Jebusites; as **YeHoVaH** your **Elohim** has commanded you: *18* That they teach you not to do after all their abominations, which they have done to their **Elohim**s; so should you sin against **YeHoVaH** your **Elohim**. *19* When you shall besiege a city a long time, in making war against it to take it, *you shall not destroy the trees* thereof by forcing an axe against them: for you may eat of them, and you shall not cut them down (*for the tree of the field is man's life*) to employ them in the siege: *20* Only the trees which you know that they be not trees for fruit, you shall destroy and cut them down; and you shall build barricades against the city that make war with you, until it be subdued.

CHAPTERS 21- 30

Chapter 21
If a dead body is found, the city elders must cleanse the guilt. Give your eldest son his portion. A rebellious son shall be stoned.

1 If one be found slain in the land which **YeHoVaH** your **Elohim** gives you to possess, lying in the field, and it be not known who has slain him: *2* Then your elders and your judges shall come forth, and they shall measure to the cities which are round about him that is slain: **3** And it shall be, that the city which is next to the slain man, even the elders of that city shall take a heifer, which has not been worked with, and which has not drawn in the yoke; **4** And the elders of that city shall bring down the heifer to a rough valley, which is neither eared nor sown, and shall strike off the heifer's neck there in the valley: **5** And the priests the sons of Levi shall come near; for them *YeHoVaH* your *Elohim* has chosen to minister to him, and to bless in the name of *YeHoVaH*; and by their word shall every controversy and every stroke be tried: **6** And all the elders of that city, that are next to the slain man, shall wash their hands over the heifer that is beheaded in the valley: **7** And they shall answer and say, Our hands have not shed this blood, neither have our eyes seen it. **8** Be merciful, O *YeHoVaH*, to your people Israel, whom you have redeemed, and lay not innocent blood to your people of Israel's charge. And the blood shall be forgiven them. **9** So shall you put away the guilt of innocent blood from among you, when you shall do that which is right in the sight of *YeHoVaH*. **10** When you go forth to war against your enemies, and *YeHoVaH* your *Elohim* has delivered them into your hands, and you have taken them captive,

11 And sees among the captives a beautiful woman, and have a desire to her, that you would have her for your wife; **12** Then you shall bring her home to your house, and she shall shave her head, and cut her nails; **13** and put aside the clothes she was wearing when captured. After she has lived in your house and mourned her father and mother for a full month, then you may go to her and be her husband and she shall be your wife. **14** And it shall be, if you have no delight in her, then you shall let her go where she will; but you shall not sell her at all for money, you shall not make merchandise of her, because you have humbled her. **15** If a man have two wives, one beloved, and another hated, and they have born him children, both the beloved and the hated; and if the firstborn son be hers that was hated: **16** Then it shall be, when he makes his sons to inherit that which he has, that he may not make the son of the beloved firstborn before the son of the hated, which is indeed the firstborn: **17** But he shall acknowledge the son of the hated for the firstborn, by giving him a double portion of all that he has: for he is the beginning of his strength; the right of the firstborn is his. **18** If a man have a stubborn and rebellious son, which will not obey the voice of his father, or the voice of his mother, and that, when they have disciplined him, and will not listen to them: **19** Then shall his father and his mother lay hold on him, and bring him out to the elders of his city, and to the gate of his place; **20** And they shall say to the elders of his city, This our son is stubborn and rebellious, he will not obey our voice; he is a glutton, and a drunkard.

21 And all the men of his city shall stone him with stones, that he die: so shall you put evil away from among you; and all Israel shall hear, and fear. **22** And if a man have committed a sin worthy of death, and he be put to death, and you hang him on a tree: **23** His body shall not remain all night upon the tree, but you shall in any wise bury him that day; (for he that is hanged is accursed of *Elohim*;) that your land be not defiled, which *YeHoVaH* your *Elohim* gives you for an inheritance.

Chapter 22

If you find your neighbor's ox you shall return it. If a man falsely claims that his new wife was not a virgin he shall be punished. The laws (instructions) for marriage and promiscuity (sexual relations) are given.

1 You shall not see your brother's ox or his sheep go astray, and hide thyself from them: you shall in any case bring them again to your brother. *2* And if your brother be not near to you, or if you know him not, then you shall bring it to your own house, and it shall be with you until your brother seek after it, and you shall restore it to him again. *3* In like manner shall you do with his donkey; and so shall you do with his clothes; and with all lost things of your brother's, which he has lost, and you have found, shall you do likewise: you may not hide thyself. *4* You shall not see your brother's donkey or his ox fall down by the way, and hide thyself from them: you shall surely help him to lift them up again. *5* ***The woman shall not wear that which pertains to a man, neither shall a man put on a woman's garment: for all that do so are an abomination to YeHoVaH your Elohim.*** *6* If a bird's nest chance to be before you in the way in any tree, or on the ground, whether they be young ones, or eggs, and the mother sitting upon the young, or upon the eggs, you shall not take the mother with the young: *7* But you shall let the mother go, and take the young to you; that it may be well with you, and that you may prolong your days. *8* When you build a new house, then you shall make a parapet (safety walls or rails) for your roof, that you bring not blood upon your house, if any man falls from there. *9* Do not plant two kinds of seed in your vineyard; if you do, not only the crops you plant but also the fruit of the vineyard will be defiled. *10* You shall not plow with an ox and a donkey together (not equally yoked).

11 You shall not wear a garment of different sorts, as of woolen and linen together. *12* You shall make you fringes upon the four quarters of your garment, that you cover yourself. *13* If any man take a wife, and go in to her, and hate her, *14* And give occasions of speech against her, and bring up an evil name upon her, and say, I took this woman, and when I came to her, I found her not a maid (virgin): *15* Then shall the father of the damsel, and her mother, take and bring forth the tokens of the damsel's virginity to the elders of the city in the gate: *16* And the damsel's father shall say to the elders, I gave my daughter to this man for his wife, and he hates her; *17* Now he has slandered her and said, 'I did not find your daughter to be a virgin.' But here is the proof of my daughter's virginity." Then her parents shall display the cloth before the elders of the town, *18* And the elders of that city shall take that man and punish him; *19* They shall fine him a hundred shekels of silver and give them to the young woman's father, because this man has given an Israelite virgin a bad name. She shall continue to be his wife; he must not divorce her as long as he lives. *20* But if it is found to be true, and the tokens of virginity be not found for the damsel:

21 she shall be brought to the door of her father's house and there the men of her town shall stone her to death. She has done an outrageous thing in Israel by being promiscuous while still in her father's house. You must purge the evil from among you. *22* If a man be found lying with a woman married to another husband, then they shall both die, both the man that lay with the woman, and the woman: so shall you put away evil from Israel. *23* If a damsel that is a virgin be betrothed to a husband, and a man find her in the city, and lie with her; *24* Then you shall bring them both out to the gate of that city, and you shall stone them with stones that they die; the damsel, because she cried not, being in the city; and the man, because he has humbled his neighbor's wife: so you shall put away evil from among you. *25* But if a man finds a betrothed damsel in the field, and the man force her, and lie with her: then the man only that lay with her shall die. *26* But to the damsel you shall do nothing; there is in the damsel no sin worthy of death: for as when a man rises against his neighbor, and slays him, even so is this matter: *27* For he found her in the field, and the betrothed damsel cried, and there was none to hear and save her. *28* If a man find a damsel that is a virgin, which is not betrothed, and lay hold on her, and lie with her, and they be found; *29* he shall pay her father fifty shekels of silver. He must marry the young woman, for he has violated her. He can never divorce her as long as he lives. *30* A man is not to marry his father's wife; he must not dishonor his father's bed.

Chapter 23

No Ammonite shall enter the assembly of YeHoVaH. When you go out to war the camp must be holy. Be careful to do what you have vowed to YeHoVaH .

1 No one who has been emasculated (castrated) by crushing or cutting may enter the assembly of **YeHoVaH**. *2* No one born of a forbidden marriage nor any of their descendants may enter the assembly of **YeHoVaH**, not even in the tenth generation.. *3* An Ammonite or Moabite shall not enter into the congregation of **YeHoVaH**; even to their tenth generation shall they not enter into the congregation of **YeHoVaH** forever: *4* Because they met you not with bread and with water in the way, when you came forth out of Egypt; and because they hired against you Balaam the son of Beor of Pethor of Mesopotamia, to curse you. *5* Nevertheless **YeHoVaH** your **Elohim** would not listen to Balaam; but **YeHoVaH** your **Elohim** turned the curse into a blessing to you, because **YeHoVaH** your **Elohim** loved you. *6* You shall not seek their peace nor their prosperity all your days forever. *7* You shall not hate an Edomite; for he is your brother: you shall not hate an Egyptian; because you were a stranger in his land. *8* The children that are born of them shall enter into the congregation of **YeHoVaH** in their third generation. *9* When the armies go forth against your enemies, then keep you from every wicked thing. *10* If any man among you becomes unclean through anything which has taken place in the night, he is to go out from the tent-circle and keep outside it:

11 But when evening comes near, let him take a bath: and after sundown he may come back to the tents. *12* Let there be a place outside the tent-circle to which you may go; *13* And have among your arms a spade; and when you have been to that place, let that which comes from you be covered up with earth: *14* For Adonai your **Elohim** is walking among your tents, to keep you safe and to give up into your hands those who are fighting against you; then let your tents be holy, so that he may see no unclean thing among you, and be turned away from you *15* You shall not deliver to his master the servant which is escaped from his master to you: *16* He shall dwell with you, even among you, in that place which he shall choose in one of your gates, where it likes him best: you shall not oppress him. *17* No Israelite man or woman is to become a shrine prostitute. *18* You must not bring the earnings of a female prostitute or of a male prostitute into the house of **YeHoVaH** your **Elohim** to pay any vow, because **YeHoVaH** your **Elohim** detests them both. *19* You shall not lend with interest to your brother; interest of money, interest of food, interest of anything that is lent with interest: *20* To a stranger you *may* lend with interest; but to your brother you shall *not* lend with interest: that **YeHoVaH** your **Elohim** may bless you in all that you set your hand to in the land when you go to possess it.

21 When you shall vow a vow to **YeHoVaH** your **Elohim**, you shall not slack to pay it: for **YeHoVaH** your **Elohim** will surely require it of you; and it would be sin in you. *22* But if you shall forbear to vow, it shall be no sin in you. *23* That which is gone out of your lips you shall keep and perform; even a freewill offering, according as you have vowed to **YeHoVaH** your **Elohim**, which you have promised with your mouth. *24* When you come into your neighbor's vineyard, then you may eat grapes your fill at your own pleasure; but you shall not take any extra.

25 When you come into the standing corn of your neighbor, then you may pluck the ears with your hand; but you shall not move a sickle to your neighbor's standing corn.

Chapter 24
If a man divorces his wife he cannot remarry her. Do not withhold wages to those you hire. Leave the remnants of your harvest for widows and orphans.

1 When a man has taken a wife, and married her, and it come to pass that he no longer find any favor in his eyes, because he has found some uncleanness in her: then let him write her a bill of divorcement, and give it in her hand, and send her out of his house. **2** and if after she leaves his house she becomes the wife of another man, **3** And if the latter husband hate her, and write her a bill of divorcement, and gives it in her hand, and sends her out of his house; or if the latter husband die, which took her to be his wife; **4** Her former husband, which sent her away, may *not* take her again to be his wife, after that she is defiled; for that is disgrace before **YeHoVaH**: and you shall not cause the land to sin, which **YeHoVaH** your **Elohim** gives you for an inheritance. **5** When a man has taken a new wife, he shall not go out to war, neither shall he be charged with any business: but he shall be free at home one year, and shall cheer up his wife which he has taken. **6** Do not take a pair of millstones—not even the upper one—as security for a debt, because that would be taking a person's livelihood as security. **7** If a man be found stealing any of his brethren of the children of Israel, and makes merchandise of him, or sells him; then that thief shall die; and you shall put evil away from among you. **8** Take heed in the plague of leprosy that you observe diligently, and do according to all that the priests, the Levites shall teach you: as I commanded them, so you shall observe to do. **9** Remember what **YeHoVaH** your **Elohim** did to Miriam by the way, after that you came forth out of Egypt. **10** When you do lend your brother anything, you shall not go into his house to fetch his pledge.

11 You shall stand outside, and the man to whom you do lend shall bring out the pledge outside to you. **12** And if the man be poor, you shall not sleep one night with his pledge: **13** In any case you shall deliver him the pledge again when the sun goes down, that he may sleep in his own clothes, and bless you: and it shall be righteousness to you before **YeHoVaH** your **Elohim**. **14** You shall not oppress a hired servant that is poor and needy, whether he be of your brethren, or of your strangers that are in your land within your gates: **15** At his day you shall give him his hire, neither shall the sun go down upon it; for he is poor, and sets his heart upon it: for he may cry against you to **YeHoVaH**, and it be sin to you. **16** The fathers shall not be put to death for the children, neither shall the children be put to death for the fathers: every man shall be put to death for his own sin. **17** You shall not pervert the judgment of the stranger, nor of the fatherless; nor take a widow's clothes to pledge: **18** But you shall remember that you were a slave in Egypt, and **YeHoVaH** your **Elohim** redeemed you there: therefore I command you to do this thing. **19** When you cut down your harvest in your field, and have forgotten a sheaf in the field, you shall not go again to fetch it: it shall be for the stranger, for the fatherless, and for the widow: that **YeHoVaH** your **Elohim** may bless you in all the work of your hands. **20** When you beat your olive tree, you shall not go over the boughs again: it shall be for the stranger, for the fatherless, and for the widow.

21 When you gather the grapes of your vineyard, you shall not gather it again: it shall be for the stranger, for the fatherless, and for the widow. **22** And you shall remember that you were a slave in the land of Egypt: therefore I command you to do this thing.

Chapter 25

A judge may give up to forty lashes. If a man dies and has no son, his brother shall marry his widow. You shall have honest weights.

1 If there be a controversy between men, and they come to judgment, that the judges may judge them; then they shall justify the righteous, and condemn the wicked. *2* And it shall be, if the wicked man be worthy to be beaten, that the judge shall cause him to lie down, and to be beaten before his face, according to his fault, by a certain number. *3* Up to 40 lashes he may give him, but not exceed: lest, if he should exceed, and beat him above these with many lashes, then your brother should seem evil to you. *4* You shall not muzzle the ox when he treads out the corn. *5* If brothers are living together and one of them dies without a son, his widow must not marry outside the family. Her husband's brother shall take her and marry her and fulfill the duty of a brother-in-law to her. *6* And it shall be, that the firstborn whom she bears shall succeed in the name of his brother that is dead, that his name be not put out of Israel. *7* However, if a man does not want to marry his brother's wife, she shall go to the elders at the town gate and say, "My husband's brother refuses to carry on his brother's name in Israel. He will not fulfill the duty of a brother-in-law to me." *8* Then the elders of his city shall call him, and speak to him: and if he stand to it, and say, I like not to take her; *9* Then shall his brother's wife come to him in the presence of the elders, and take his shoe from off his foot, and spit in his face, and shall answer and say, So shall it be done to that man that will not build up his brother's house. *10* And his name shall be called in Israel, The house of him that has his shoe loosed.

11 If two men are fighting and the wife of one of them comes to rescue her husband from his assailant, and she reaches out and seizes him by his private parts, *12* you shall cut off her hand. Show her no pity. *13* You shall not have in your bag diver's weights, a great and a small. *14* Do not have two differing measures in your house—one large, one small. *15* But you shall have a perfect and just weight, a perfect and just measure shall you have: that your days may be lengthened in the land which **YeHoVaH** your **Elohim** gives you. *16* For all that do such things, and all that do anything unrighteous, are an abomination to **YeHoVaH** your **Elohim**. *17* Remember what Amalek did to you by the way, when you came forth out of Egypt; *18* How he met you by the way, and killed the furthest back of you, even all that were feeble behind you, when you were faint and weary; and he feared not **Elohim**. *19* Therefore it shall be, when **YeHoVaH** your **Elohim** has given you rest from all your enemies round about, in the land which **YeHoVaH** your **Elohim** gives you for an inheritance to possess it, that you shall blot out the remembrance of Amalek from under heaven; you shall not forget it.

Reading 49 ends

Chapter 26

Bring the first-fruits of the land to YeHoVaH. Bring a tithe in the third year and say to YeHoVaH, "Look down and bless your people."

Reading 50 begins

1 And it shall be, when you come into the land which **YeHoVaH** your **Elohim** gives you for an inheritance, and possess it, and dwell therein; *2* That you shall take of the first of all the fruit of the earth, which you shall bring of your land that **YeHoVaH** your **Elohim** gives you, and shall put it in a basket, and shall go to the place which **YeHoVaH** your **Elohim** shall choose to place his name there. *3* And you shall go to the priest that shall be in those days, and say to him, I profess this day to **YeHoVaH** your **Elohim**, that I come to the country that **YeHoVaH** swore to our fathers to give us. **4** And the priest shall take the basket out of your hand, and set it down before the altar of **YeHoVaH** your **Elohim**. **5** And you shall speak and say before **YeHoVaH** your **Elohim**, A Syrian ready to perish was my father, and he went down into Egypt, and lived there with a few, and became there a nation, great, mighty, and populous: **6** And the Egyptians evil overtook us, and afflicted us, and laid upon us hard bondage: **7** And when we cried to **YeHoVaH Elohim** of our fathers, **YeHoVaH** heard our voice, and looked on our affliction, and our labor, and our oppression: **8** And **YeHoVaH** brought us forth out of Egypt with a mighty hand, and with an outstretched arm, and with great terribleness, and with signs, and with wonders: **9** And he has brought us into this place, and has given us this land, even a land that flows with milk and honey. **10** And now, behold, I have brought the first-fruits of the land, which you, O **YeHoVaH**, have given me. And you shall set it before **YeHoVaH** your **Elohim**, and worship before **YeHoVaH** your **Elohim**:

11 And you shall rejoice in every good thing which **YeHoVaH** your **Elohim** has given to you, and to your house, you, and the Levite, and the stranger that is among you. **12** When you have made an end of tithing all the tithes of your increase the third year, which is the year of tithing, and have given it to the Levite, the stranger, the fatherless, and the widow, that they may eat within your gates, and be filled; **13** Then you shall say before **YeHoVaH** your **Elohim**, I have brought away the hallowed things out of my house, and also have given them to the Levite, and to the stranger, to the fatherless, and to the widow, according to all your commandments which you have commanded me: I have not transgressed your commandments, neither have I forgotten them. **14** I have not eaten thereof in my mourning, neither have I taken away any thereof for any unclean use, nor given any thereof for the dead: but I have listened to the voice of **YeHoVaH** my **Elohim**, and have done according to all that you have commanded me. **15** Look down from your holy habitation, from heaven, and bless your people Israel, and the land that you have given us, as you swore to our fathers, a land that flows with milk and honey. **16** This day **YeHoVaH** your **Elohim** has commanded you to do these laws (instructions) and judgments: you shall therefore keep and do them with all your heart, and with all your soul. **17** You have affirmed **YeHoVaH** this day to be your **Elohim**, and to walk in his ways, and to keep his laws (instructions), and his commandments, and his judgments, and to listen to his voice: **18** And **YeHoVaH** has affirmed you this day to be his set apart people, as he has promised you, and that you should keep all his commandments; **19** And to make you high above all nations which he has made, in praise, and in name, and in honor; and that you may be a holy people to **YeHoVaH** your **Elohim**, as he has spoken.

Chapter 27
Write the law (instruction) on large stones. The Levites will say, "Cursed is anyone who does not keep the law," and the people will reply, "Amen."

1 And Moses with the elders of Israel commanded the people, saying, Keep all the commandments which I command you this day. **2** And it shall be on the day when you shall pass over Jordan to the land which **YeHoVaH** your **Elohim** gives you, that you shall set up great stones, and plaster them with plaster: **3** And you shall write upon them all the words of this law (instruction), when you are passed over, that you may go in to the land which **YeHoVaH** your **Elohim** gives you, a land that flows with milk and honey; as **YeHoVaH Elohim** of your fathers has promised you. **4** Therefore it shall be when you go over Jordan that you shall set up these stones, which I command you this day, in mount Ebal, and you shall plaster them with plaster. *5* And there shall you build an altar to **YeHoVaH** your **Elohim**, an altar of stones: you shall not lift up any iron tool upon them. *6* You shall build the altar of **YeHoVaH** your **Elohim** of whole stones: and you shall offer burnt offerings thereon to **YeHoVaH** your **Elohim**: *7* And you shall offer peace offerings, and shall eat there, and rejoice before **YeHoVaH** your **Elohim**. *8* And you shall write upon the stones all the words of this law (instruction) very plainly. *9* And Moses and the priests the Levites spoke to all Israel, saying, Take heed, and listen, O Israel; this day you become the people of **YeHoVaH** your **Elohim**. *10* You shall therefore obey the voice of **YeHoVaH** your **Elohim**, and do his commandments and his laws (instructions), which I command you this day.

11 And Moses charged the people the same day, saying, *12* These shall stand upon mount Gerizim to bless the people, when you come over to Jordan; Simeon, and Levi, and Judah, and Issachar, and Joseph, and Benjamin: *13* And these shall stand upon mount Ebal to curse; Reuben, Gad, and Asher, and Zebulun, Dan, and Naphtali. *14* And the Levites shall speak, and say to all the men of Israel with a loud voice, *15* "Cursed is anyone who makes an idol—a thing detestable to **YeHoVaH**, the work of skilled hands—and sets it up in secret." Then all the people shall say, "Amen!" *16* Cursed be he that sets light by his father or his mother. And all the people shall say, *Amen*. *17* Cursed be he that removes his neighbor's landmark. And all the people shall say, *Amen*. *18* Cursed be he that makes the blind to wander out of the way. And all the people shall say, *Amen*. *19* Cursed be he that perverts the judgment of the stranger, fatherless, and widow. And all the people shall say, *Amen*. *20* "Cursed is anyone who sleeps with his father's wife, for he dishonors his father's bed." Then all the people shall say, "Amen!"

21 Cursed be he that lies with any animal. And all the people shall say, *Amen*. *22* Cursed be he that lies with his sister, the daughter of his father, or the daughter of his mother. And all the people shall say, *Amen*. *23* Cursed be he that lies with his mother-in-law. And all the people shall say, *Amen*. *24* Cursed be he that kills his neighbor secretly. And all the people shall say, *Amen*. *25* Cursed be he that takes reward to slay an innocent person. And all the people shall say, *Amen*. *26* Cursed be he that confirms not all the words of this law (instruction) to do them. And all the people shall say, *Amen*.

Chapter 28
If you obey YeHoVaH He will bless you above all nations; if not, you will be cursed and YeHoVaH will send a nation to destroy you.

1 And it shall come to pass, if you shall listen diligently to the voice of **YeHoVaH** your **Elohim**, to observe and to do all his commandments which I command you this day, that **YeHoVaH** your **Elohim** will set you on high above all nations of the earth: *2* And all these blessings shall come on you, and overtake you, if you shall listen to the voice of **YeHoVaH** your **Elohim**. *3* Blessed shall you be in the city, and blessed shall you be in the field. *4* Blessed shall be the fruit of your body, and the fruit of your ground, and the fruit of your cattle, the increase of your cattle, and the flocks of your sheep. *5* Blessed shall be your basket and your store. *6* Blessed shall you be when you come in, and blessed shall you be when you go out. *7* **YeHoVaH** shall cause your enemies that rise up against you to be destroyed before your face: they shall come out against you one way, and flee before you seven ways. *8* **YeHoVaH** shall command the blessing upon you in your storehouses, and in all that you set your hand to; and he shall bless you in the land which **YeHoVaH** your **Elohim** gives you. **9** **YeHoVaH** shall establish you a holy people to himself, as he has sworn to you, if you shall keep the commandments of **YeHoVaH** your **Elohim**, and walk in his ways. **10** And all people of the earth shall see that you are called by the name of **YeHoVaH**; and they shall be afraid of you.

11 And **YeHoVaH** shall make you abundant in goods, in the fruit of your body, and in the fruit of your cattle, and in the fruit of your ground, in the land that **YeHoVaH** swore to your fathers to give you. **12** **YeHoVaH** shall open to you his good treasure, the heaven to give the rain to your land in his season, and to bless all the work of your hand: and you shall lend to many nations, and you shall not borrow. **13** And **YeHoVaH** shall make you the head, and not the tail; and you shall be above only, and you shall not be beneath; if that you listen to the commandments of **YeHoVaH** your **Elohim**, which I command you this day, to observe and to do them: **14** And you shall not go aside from any of the words which I command you this day, to the right hand, or to the left, to go after other gods to serve them. **15** But it shall come to pass, if you will not listen to the voice of **YeHoVaH** your **Elohim**, to observe to do all his commandments and his laws (instructions) which I command you this day; that all these curses shall come upon you, and overtake you: **16** Cursed shall you be in the city, and cursed shall you be in the field. **17** Cursed shall be your basket and your store. **18** Cursed shall be the fruit of your body, and the fruit of your land, the increase of your cattle, and the flocks of your sheep. **19** Cursed shall you be when you come in, and cursed shall you be when you go out. **20** **YeHoVaH** shall send upon you cursing, aggravation, and rebuke, in all that you set your hand to for to do, until you be destroyed, and until you perish quickly; because of the wickedness of your doings, whereby you have forsaken me.

21 **YeHoVaH** shall make the pestilence cling to you, until he has consumed you from off the land, wherever you go to possess it. **22** **YeHoVaH** shall destroy you with consumption, and with a fever, and with an inflammation, and with an extreme burning, and with the sword, and with blasting, and with mildew; and they shall pursue you until you perish. **23** And your heaven that is over your head shall be brass, and the earth that is under you shall be iron. **24** **YeHoVaH** shall make the rain of your land powder and dust: from heaven shall it come down upon you, until you be destroyed. **25** **YeHoVaH** shall cause you to be obsessed before your enemies: you shall go out one way against them, and flee seven ways before them: and shall be removed into all the kingdoms of the earth. **26** And your carcass shall be food to all birds of the air, and to the beasts of the earth, and no man shall fight them away. **27** **YeHoVaH** will strike you with the spoil of Egypt, and with the emerods (hemorrhoids), and with the scab, and with the itch, here you cannot be healed. **28** **YeHoVaH** shall strike you with madness, and blindness, and astonishment of heart: **29** And you shall grope at noonday, as the blind gropes in darkness, and you shall not prosper in your ways: and you shall be only oppressed and spoiled evermore, and no man shall save you. **30** You shall betroth (engaged) a wife, and another man shall lie with her: you shall build a house, and you shall not dwell therein: you shall plant a vineyard, and shall not gather the grapes thereof.

31 Your ox shall be slain before your eyes, and you shall not eat thereof: your donkey shall be violently taken away from before your face, and shall not be restored to you: your sheep shall be given to your enemies, and you shall have no one to rescue them. **32** Thy sons and your daughters shall be given to another people, and your eyes shall look, and fail with longing for them all the day long; and there shall be no might in your hand. **33** The fruit of your land, and all your labors, shall a nation that you know not eat up; and you shall be only oppressed and crushed always: **34** So that you shall be mad for the sight of your eyes that you shall see. **35** *YeHoVaH* shall strike you in the knees, and in the legs, with a sore botch (inflammatory sore) that cannot be healed, from the sole of your foot to the top of your head. **36** *YeHoVaH* shall bring you, and your king which you shall set over you, to a nation which neither you nor your fathers have known; and there shall you serve other gods, wood and stone. **37** And you shall become astonishment, a proverb, and a byword, among all nations whither *YeHoVaH* shall lead you. **38** You shall carry much seed out into the field, and shall gather but little in; for the locust shall consume it. **39** You shall plant vineyards, and dress them, but shall neither drink of the wine, nor gather the grapes; for the worms shall eat them. **40** You shall have olive trees throughout all your coasts, but you shall not anoint thyself with the oil; for your olive shall cast its fruit away.

41 You shall produce sons and daughters, but you shall not enjoy them; for they shall go into captivity. **42** All your trees and fruit of your land shall the locust consume. **43** The stranger that is about you shall get up above you very high; and you shall come down very low. **44** He shall lend to you, and you shall not lend to him: he shall be the head, and you shall be the tail. **45** Moreover all these curses shall come upon you, and shall pursue you, and overtake you, till you be destroyed; because you listen not to the voice of *YeHoVaH* your *Elohim*, to keep his commandments and his laws (instructions) which he commanded you: **46** And they shall be upon you for a sign and for a wonder, and upon your seed forever. **47** Because you served not *YeHoVaH* your *Elohim* with joyfulness, and with gladness of heart, for the abundance of all things; **48** Therefore shall you serve your enemies which *YeHoVaH* shall send against you, in hunger, and in thirst, and in nakedness, and in want of all things: and he shall put a yoke of iron upon your neck, until he has destroyed you. **49** *YeHoVaH* shall bring a nation against you from far, from the end of the earth, as swift as the eagle flies; a nation whose tongue you shall not understand; **50** A hard-faced nation, who will have no respect for the old or mercy for the young:

51 And he shall eat the fruit of your cattle, and the fruit of your land, until you are destroyed: which also shall not leave corn, wine, or oil, or the increase of your cattle, or flocks of your sheep, until he has destroyed you. **52** And he shall besiege you in all your gates, until your high and fenced walls come down, throughout all your land: and he shall besiege you in all your gates throughout all your land, which *YeHoVaH* your *Elohim* has given you. **53** Because of the suffering your enemy will inflict on you during the siege, you will eat the fruit of the womb, the flesh of the sons and daughters *YeHoVaH* your *Elohim* has given you. **54** So that the man that is tender among you, and very delicate, his eye shall be evil toward his brother, and toward his wife, and toward the remnant of his children which he shall leave: **55** So that he will not give to any of them of the flesh of his children whom he shall eat: because he has nothing left him in the siege, and in the straightness, where your enemies shall distress you in all your gates. **56** The tender and delicate woman among you, which would not adventure to set the sole of her foot upon the ground for delicateness and tenderness, her eye shall be evil toward her husband, and toward her son, and toward her daughter, **57** the afterbirth from her womb and the children she bears. For in her dire need she intends to eat them secretly because of the suffering your enemy will inflict on you during the siege of your cities. **58** If you will not observe to do all the words of this law (instruction) that are written in this book, that you may fear this glorious and fearful name, *YeHoVaH* your *Elohim*; **59** Then *YeHoVaH* your *Elohim* will make your punishment, and the punishment of your seed, a thing to be wondered at; great punishments and cruel diseases stretching on through long years. *60* Moreover he will bring upon you all the diseases of Egypt, which you were afraid of; and they shall cleave to you.

61 Also every sickness, and every plague, which is not written in the book of this law (instruction), will **YeHoVaH** bring upon you, until you be destroyed. *62* And you shall be left few in number, whereas you were as the stars of heaven for multitude; because you would not obey the voice of **YeHoVaH** your **Elohim**. *63* And it shall come to pass, that as **YeHoVaH** rejoiced over you to do you good, and to multiply you; so **YeHoVaH** will rejoice over you to destroy you, and to bring you to nothing; and you shall be plucked from off the land where you go to possess it. *64* And **YeHoVaH** shall scatter you among all people, from the one end of the earth even to the other; and there you shall serve other gods, which neither you nor your fathers have known, even wood and stone. *65* And among these nations shall you find no ease, neither shall the sole of your foot have rest: but **YeHoVaH** shall give you there a trembling heart, and failing of eyes, and sorrow of mind: *66* And your life shall hang in doubt before you; and you shall fear day and night, and shall have no assurance of your life: *67* In the morning you will say, If only it was evening! And at evening you will say, If only morning would come! Because of the fear in your hearts and the things which your eyes will see. *68* And **YeHoVaH** shall bring you into Egypt again with ships, by the way where I spoke to you, You shall see it no more again: and there you shall be sold to your enemies for slaves, and no man shall buy you.

Chapter 29
You have seen all that YeHoVaH has done so keep this covenant. If you break it the land will be cursed and YeHoVaH will uproot you.

1 These are the words of the covenant, which **YeHoVaH** commanded Moses to make with the children of Israel in the land of Moab, beside the covenant that he made with them in Horeb. *2* And Moses called to all Israel, and said to them, You have seen all that **YeHoVaH** did before your eyes in the land of Egypt to Pharaoh, and to all his servants, and to all his land; *3* The great temptations which your eyes have seen, the signs, and those great miracles: *4* Yet **YeHoVaH** has not given you a *heart to know, and eyes to see, and ears to hear,* to this day. *5* And I have led you forty years in the wilderness: your clothes are not aged old upon you, and your shoe is not worn old upon your foot. *6* You have not eaten bread, neither have you drank wine or strong drink: that you might know that I am **YeHoVaH** your **Elohim**. *7* And when you came to this place, Sihon the king of Heshbon, and Og the king of Bashan, came out against us to battle, and we killed them: *8* And we took their land, and gave it for an inheritance to the Reubenites, and to the Gadites, and to the half tribe of Manasseh.
Reading 50 ends

Reading 51 begins
9 Keep therefore the words of this covenant, and do them, that you may prosper in all that you do. *10* You stand this day all of you before **YeHoVaH** your **Elohim**; your captains of your tribes, your elders, and your officers, with all the men of Israel,

11 Your little ones, your wives, and your stranger that is in your camp, from the worker of your wood to the drawer of your water: *12* That you should enter into covenant with **YeHoVaH** your **Elohim**, and into his oath, which **YeHoVaH** your **Elohim** makes with you this day: *13* That he may establish you today for a people to himself, and that he may be to you an **Elohim**, as he has said to you, and as he has sworn to your fathers, to Abraham, to Isaac, and to Jacob. *14* Neither with you only do I make this covenant and this oath; *15* But with him that stands here with us this day before **YeHoVaH** our **Elohim**, and also with him that is not here with us this day: *16* For you know how we have dwelt in the land of Egypt; and how we came through the nations which you passed by; *17* And you have seen their outrageous idols, wood and stone, silver and gold, which were among them: *18* So that there may not be among you any man or woman or family or tribe whose heart is turned away from the **Adonai** our **Elohim** today, to go after other gods and give them worship; or any root among you whose fruit is poison and bitter sorrow; *19* If such a man, hearing the words of this oath, takes comfort in the thought that he will have peace even if he goes on in the pride of his heart, taking whatever chance may give him: *20* **YeHoVaH** will not spare him, but then the anger of **YeHoVaH** and his jealousy shall smoke against that man, and all the curses that are written in this book shall lie upon him, and **YeHoVaH** shall blot out his name from under heaven.

21 And **YeHoVaH** shall separate him to evil out of all the tribes of Israel, according to all the curses of the covenant that are written in this book of the law (instruction): *22* So that the generation to come of your children that shall rise up after you, and the stranger that shall come from a far land, shall say, when they see the plagues of that land, and the sicknesses which **YeHoVaH** has laid upon it; *23* And that the whole land is brimstone, and salt, and burning, that it is not sown, nor bears, nor any grass grows there, like the overthrow of Sodom, and Gomorrah, Admah, and Zeboim, which **YeHoVaH** overthrew in his anger, and in his wrath: *24* Truly all the nations will say, Why has **YeHoVaH** done so to this land? what is the reason for this great and burning wrath? *25* Then men shall say, Because they have forsaken the covenant of **YeHoVaH Elohim** of their fathers, which he made with them when he brought them forth out of the land of Egypt: *26* For they went and served other gods, and worshipped them, gods whom they knew not, and whom he had not given to them: *27* And the anger of **YeHoVaH** was kindled against this land, to bring upon it all the curses that are written in this book: *28* And **YeHoVaH** rooted them out of their land in anger, and in rage, and in great resentment, and cast them into another land, as it is this day. *29* The secret things belong to **YeHoVaH** our **Elohim**: but those things that are revealed belong to us and to our children forever, that we may do all the words of this law (instruction).

Chapter 30
When you return to YeHoVaH he will have compassion; he will circumcise your heart. He has set before you life and death, a blessing and a curse: Choose life.

1 And it shall come to pass, when all these things are come upon you, the *blessing and the curse*, which I have set before you, and you shall call them to mind among all the nations, where **YeHoVaH** your **Elohim** has driven you, *2* And shall return to **YeHoVaH** your **Elohim**, and shall obey his voice according to all that I command you this day, you and your children, with all your heart, and with all your soul; *3* So that **YeHoVaH** your **Elohim** will turn your captivity, and have compassion upon you, and will return and gather you from all the nations, where **YeHoVaH** your **Elohim** has scattered you. *4* Even if you have been banished to the most distant land under the heavens, from there **YeHoVaH** your **Elohim** will gather you and bring you back. *5* And **YeHoVaH** your **Elohim** will bring you into the land that your fathers possessed, and you shall possess it; and he will do you good, and multiply you above your fathers. *6* And **YeHoVaH** your **Elohim** *will circumcise your heart* (your heart belongs to **Elohim** alone), and the heart of your seed, to love **YeHoVaH** your **Elohim** with all your heart, and with all your soul, that you may live. **7** And **YeHoVaH** your **Elohim** will put all these curses upon your enemies and on them that hate you, which persecuted you. **8** And you shall return and obey the voice of **YeHoVaH**, and do all his commandments that I command you this day. **9** And **YeHoVaH** your **Elohim** will make you plentiful in every work of your hand, in the fruit of your body, and in the fruit of your cattle, and in the fruit of your land, for good: for **YeHoVaH** will again rejoice over you for good, as he rejoiced over your fathers: **10** If you shall listen to the voice of **YeHoVaH** your **Elohim**, to keep his commandments and his laws (instructions) which are written in this book of the law (Torah), and if you turn to **YeHoVaH** your **Elohim** with all your heart, and with all your soul.

11 For this commandment that I command you this day, **it is not hidden from you**, neither is it far off. **12** It is not in heaven, that you should say, Who shall go up for us to heaven, and bring it to us, that we may hear it, and do it? **13** Neither is it beyond the sea that you should say, Who shall go over the sea for us, and bring it to us, that we may hear it, and do it? **14** But the word is very near to you, in your mouth, and in your heart, that you may do it. **15** See, I have set before you this day life and good, and death and evil; **16** In that I command you this day to love **YeHoVaH** your **Elohim**, to walk in his ways, and to keep his commandments and his laws (instructions) and his judgments, that you may live and multiply: and **YeHoVaH** your **Elohim** shall bless you in the land where you go to possess it. **17** But if your heart turn away (be hardened), so that you will not hear, but shall be drawn away, and worship other **Elohim**s, and serve them; **18** I denounce to you this day, that you shall surely perish, and that you shall not prolong your days upon the land, where you pass over Jordan to go to possess it. **19** This day I call the heavens and the earth as witnesses against you that I have set before you life and death, blessings and curses. Now choose life, so that you and your children may live and that you may love **YeHoVaH** your **Elohim. 20** That you may love **YeHoVaH** your **Elohim**, and that you may obey his voice, and that you may cling to him: for he is your life, and the length of your days: that you may dwell in the land which **YeHoVaH** swore to your fathers, to Abraham, to Isaac, and to Jacob, to give them.
Reading 51 ends

CHAPTERS 31- 34

Chapter 31
Joshua will cross ahead of you. Read the law (instruction) *every seven years. YeHoVaH said, "The people will surely turn away." He tells Moses to write a song as a witness."*
Reading 52 begins

1 And Moses went and spoke these words to all Israel. **2** And he said to them, I am 120 years old this day; I can no more go out and come in: also **YeHoVaH** has said to me, You shall not go over this Jordan. **3 YeHoVaH** your **Elohim**, he will go over before you, and he will destroy these nations from before you, and you shall possess them: and Joshua, he shall go over before you, as **YeHoVaH** has said. **4** And **YeHoVaH** shall do to them as he did to Sihon and to Og, kings of the Amorites, and to the land of them, whom he destroyed. **5** And **YeHoVaH** shall give them up before your face, that you may do to them according to all the commandments that I have commanded you. **6** Be strong and of a good courage, fear not, nor be afraid of them: for

YeHoVaH your **Elohim**, he is the one that does go with you; he will not fail you, nor forsake you. **7** And Moses called to Joshua, and said to him in the sight of all Israel, Be strong and of a good courage: for you must go with this people to the land which **YeHoVaH** has sworn to their fathers to give them; and you shall cause them to inherit it. **8** And **YeHoVaH** is he that does go before you; he will be with you, he will not fail you, neither forsake you: fear not, nor be dismayed. **9** And Moses wrote this law (instruction), and delivered it to the priests the sons of Levi, which bare the ark of the covenant of **YeHoVaH**, and to all the elders of Israel. **10** And Moses commanded them, saying, At the end of every seven years, in the solemnity of the year of release, in the *feast of tabernacles*,

11 When all Israel has come to appear before **YeHoVaH** your **Elohim** in the place that he shall choose, you shall read this law (instruction) before all Israel in their hearing. **12** Gather the people together, men and women, and children, and your stranger that is within your gates, that they may hear, and that they may learn, and fear **YeHoVaH** your **Elohim**, and observe to do all the words of this law (instruction): **13** And that their children, which have not known anything, may hear, and learn to fear **YeHoVaH** your **Elohim**, as long as you live in the land where you go over Jordan to possess it. **14** And **YeHoVaH** said to Moses, Behold, your day approaches that you must die: call Joshua, and present yourselves in the tabernacle of the congregation, *that I may give him a charge.* And Moses and Joshua went, and presented themselves in the tabernacle of the congregation. **15** And **YeHoVaH** appeared in the tabernacle in a pillar of a cloud: and the pillar of the cloud stood over the door of the tabernacle. **16** And **YeHoVaH** said to Moses: "You are going to rest with your ancestors, and these people will soon prostitute themselves (sell their integrity or give it willingly) for an unworthy purpose to the foreign **Elohim**s of the land they are entering. They will forsake me and break the covenant I made with them. **17** Then my anger shall be kindled against them in that day, and I will forsake them, and I will hide my face from them, and they shall be devoured, and many evils and troubles shall befall them; so that they will say in that day, Have not these evils come upon us, because our **Elohim** is not among us? **18** And I will surely hide my face in that day for all the evils that they shall have created, in that they are turned to other gods. **19** Now therefore write you (Moses) this song for you, and teach it the children of Israel: put it in their mouths, that this song may be a witness for me against the children of Israel. **20** For when I shall have brought them into the land which I swore to their fathers that flows with milk and honey; and they shall have eaten and filled themselves, and grown fat; then will they turn to other **Elohim**s, and serve them, and provoke me, and break my covenant.

21 And it shall come to pass, when many evils and troubles are befallen them, that this song shall testify against them as a witness; for it shall not be forgotten out of the mouths of their children: for I know their imagination (intensions) which they go about, even now, before I have brought them into the land which I swore. **22** Moses therefore wrote this song the same day, and taught it the children of Israel. **23** And he gave Joshua the son of Nun a charge, and said, Be strong and of a good courage: for you shall bring the children of Israel into the land which I swore to them: and I will be with you. **24** *And it came to pass, when Moses had finished writing the words of this law (instruction) in a book (Torah), until they were finished,* **25** That Moses commanded the Levites, which carried the ark of the covenant of **YeHoVaH**, saying, **26** Take this book of the law (Torah), and put it in the side of the ark of the covenant of **YeHoVaH** your **Elohim**, that it may be there for a witness against you. **27** For I know your rebellion, and your stubbornness: behold, while I am yet alive with you this day, you have been rebellious against **YeHoVaH**; and how much more after my death? **28** Gather to me all the elders of your tribes, and your officers, that I may speak these words in their ears, and call heaven and earth to record against them. **29** For I know that after my death **you will utterly corrupt yourselves**, and turn aside from the way which I have commanded you; and evil will befall you in the latter days; because you will do evil in the sight of **YeHoVaH**, to provoke him to anger through the work of your hands. **30** And Moses spoke in the ears of all the congregation of Israel the words of this song, until their completion.

Reading 52 ends

Chapter 32

The Song of Moses as YeHoVaH commanded him to write and teach the children of Israel.
Reading 53 begins

1 "Listen, O you heavens, and I will speak; and hear, O earth, the words of my mouth. **2** My doctrine shall drop as the rain, my speech shall distil as the dew, as the small rain upon the tender herb, and as the showers upon the grass: **3** because I will publish the name of **YeHoVaH**: ascribe you greatness to our **Elohim**. **4** He is the Rock, his work is perfect: for all his ways are judgment: a **Elohim** of truth and without iniquity, just and right is he. **5** They have corrupted themselves, their spot is not the spot of his children: they are a perverse and crooked generation. **6** Do you thus seek retaliation **YeHoVaH**, O foolish people and unwise? is not he your father that has bought you? has he not made you, and established you? **7** Remember the days of old, consider the years of many generations: ask your father, and he will show you; your elders, and they will tell you. **8** When the Most High divided to the nations their inheritance, when he separated the sons of Adam, he set the bounds of the people according to the number of the children of Israel. **9** For **YeHoVaH**'s portion is his people; *Jacob* is the lot of his inheritance. **10** He found him in a desert land, and in the waste howling wilderness; he led him about, he instructed him, he kept him as the apple of his eye.

11 As an eagle stirs up her nest, flutters over her young, spreads abroad her wings, takes them, bears them on her wings: **12** So **YeHoVaH** alone did lead him, and there was no strange **Elohim** with him. **13** He made him ride on the high places of the earth, that he might eat the increase of the fields; and he made him to suck honey out of the rock, and oil out of the flinty rock; **14** Butter of cattle, and milk of sheep, with fat of lambs, and rams of the breed of Bashan, and goats, with the fat of kidneys of wheat; and you did drink the pure blood of the grape. **15** But Israel grew fat, and kicked: you are grown thick, you are covered with fatness; then he forsook **Elohim** which made him, and lightly esteemed the Rock of his salvation. **16** They provoked him to jealousy with strange gods, with disgrace they provoked him to anger. **17** They sacrificed to devils, not to **Elohim**; to gods whom they knew not, to new gods that came, whom your fathers feared not. **18** Of the Rock that begat you, you are unmindful, and have forgotten **Elohim** that formed you. **19** And when **YeHoVaH** saw it, he detested them, because of the annoying of his sons, and of his daughters. **20** And he said, I will hide my face from them, I will see what their end shall be: for they are a very perverse generation, children in whom there is no faith.

21 They have moved me to jealousy with that which is not **Elohim**; they have provoked me to anger with their vanities: and I will move them to jealousy with those which are not a people; I will provoke them to anger with a foolish nation. **22** For a fire is kindled in my anger, and shall burn to the realm of the dead below, and shall consume the earth with her increase, and set on fire the foundations of the mountains. **23** I will heap mischief upon them; I will spend my arrows upon them. *24* They shall be burnt with hunger, and devoured with burning heat, and with bitter destruction: I will also send the teeth of beasts upon them, with the poison of serpents of the dust. *25* The sword without, and terror within, shall destroy the young man and the virgin, the babies also with the man of gray hairs. *26* I said, I would scatter them into corners, I would make the remembrance of them to cease from among men: *27* Were it not that I feared the wrath of the enemy, for fear that their adversaries should behave themselves strangely, and for fear they should say, Our hand is high, and **YeHoVaH** has not done all this. *28* For they are a nation void of counsel, neither is there any understanding in them. *29* O that they were wise, that they understood this that they would consider their later end! *30* How would it be possible for one to overcome a thousand, and two to send ten thousand in flight, if their rock had not let them go, if **YeHoVaH** had not given them up?

31 For their rock is not as our Rock, even our enemies themselves being judges. *32* For their vine is of the vine of Sodom, and of the fields of Gomorrah: their grapes are grapes of gall, their clusters are bitter: *33* Their wine is the poison of dragons, and the cruel venom of venomous snakes. *34* Is not this laid up in store with me, and sealed up among my treasures? *35* To me belongs vengeance and compensation; their foot shall slide in due time: for the day of their disaster is at hand, and the things that shall come upon them make quickness. *36* For **YeHoVaH** shall judge his people, and repent himself for his servants, when he sees that their power is gone, and there is none left. *37* And he shall say, Where are their gods, their rock in whom they trusted, *38* which did eat the fat of their sacrifices, and drank the wine of their drink offerings? let them rise up and help you, and be your protection. *39* See now that I, even I, am he, **and *there is no Elohim with me***: I kill, and I make alive; I wound, and I heal: neither is there any that can deliver out of my hand. *40* For I lift up my hand to heaven, and say, I live forever.

41 If I make sharp my shining sword, and my hand is outstretched for judging, I will give punishment to those who are against me, and their right reward to my haters. *42* I will make my arrows drunk with blood, and my sword shall devour flesh; and that with the blood of the slain and of the captives, from the beginning of revenges upon the enemy. *43* Rejoice, O you nations, with his people: for he will avenge the blood of his servants, and will render vengeance to his adversaries, and will be merciful to his land, and to his people." (End of the song of Moses) *44* And Moses came and spoke all the words of this song in the ears of the people, he, and Joshua the son of Nun. *45* And Moses ended speaking all these words to all Israel: *46* And he said to them, Set your ears to all the words which I testify among you this day, which you shall command your children to observe to do, all the words of this law (instruction). *47* For it is not a vain thing for you; because it is your life: and through this thing you shall prolong your days in the land, where you go over Jordan to possess it. *48* And **YeHoVaH** spoke to Moses that same day, saying, *49* Get you up into this mountain Abarim, to mount Nebo, which is in the land of Moab, that is over against Jericho; and behold the land of Canaan, which I give to the children of Israel for a possession: *50* And die in the mount where you go up, and be gathered to your people; as Aaron your brother died in mount Hor, and was gathered to his people:

51 Because you trespassed against me among the children of Israel at the waters of MeribahKadesh, in the wilderness of Zin; *because* you sanctified me not in the midst of the children of Israel. *52* Yet you shall see the land before you; but you shall not go there to the land which I give the children of Israel."
Reading 53 ends

Chapter 33
Moses blesses Israel before his death.

Reading 54 begins

1 And this is the blessing, that Moses the man of **Elohim** blessed the children of Israel before his death. *2* "**YeHoVaH** came from Sinai, and rose up from Seir to them; he shined forth from mount Paran, and he came with 10,000 set-apart (sacred) ones: from his right hand went a fiery law for them. *3* Yea, he loved the people; all his saints are in your hand: and they sat down at your feet; every one shall receive of your words. *4* Moses commanded us a law, even the inheritance of the congregation of Jacob. *5* And he was king in Israel, when the heads of the people and the tribes of Israel were gathered together. *6* Let *Reuben* live, and not die; and let not his men be few. *7* And this is the blessing of *Judah*: and he said, Hear, **YeHoVaH**, the voice of Judah, and bring him to his people: let his hands be sufficient for him; and be you a help to him from his enemies. *8* And of *Levi* he said, Let your Thummim and your Urim be with your faithful one, whom you didst prove at Massah, and with whom you did strive at the waters of Meribah; *9* Who said to his father and to his mother, I have not seen him; neither did he acknowledge his brethren, nor knew his own children: for they have observed your word, and kept your covenant. *10* They shall teach Jacob your judgments, and Israel your law: they shall put incense before you, and whole burnt sacrifice upon your altar.

11 Bless, **YeHoVaH**, his strength, and accept the work of his hands; destroy the loins of those that rise against him, and of those that hate him, that they rise not again. *12* And of *Benjamin* he said, The beloved of **YeHoVaH** shall dwell in safety by him; and **YeHoVaH** shall cover him all the day long, and he shall dwell between his shoulders. *13* And of *Joseph* he said, Blessed of **YeHoVaH** be his land, for the precious things of heaven, for the dew, and for the deep that lies beneath, *14* And for the precious fruits brought forth by the sun, and for the precious things put forth by the moon, *15* And for the chief things of the ancient mountains, and for the precious things of the lasting hills, *16* And for the precious things of the earth and fullness thereof, and for the good will of him that dwelt in the (burning) bush: let the blessing come upon the head of Joseph, and upon the top of the head of he that was separated from his brethren. *17* His glory is like the firstling of his bull, and his horns are like the horns of *unicorns* (or wild ox): with them he shall push the people together to the ends of the earth: and they are the 10,000's of Ephraim, and they are the thousands of Manasseh. *18* And of *Zebulun* he said, Rejoice, Zebulun, in your going out; and, Issachar, in your tents. *19* They will send out the word for the people to come to the mountain, taking there the offerings of righteousness: for the store of the seas will be theirs, and the secret wealth of the sand. *20* And of *Gad* he said, Blessed be he that enlarges Gad: he dwells as a lion, and tears the arm with the crown of the head.

21 And he provided the best for himself, because there, in a portion of the lawgiver, was he seated; and he came with the heads of the people, he executed the justice of **YeHoVaH**, and his judgments with Israel. *22* And of *Dan* he said, Dan is a lion's cub: he shall leap from Bashan. *23* And of *Naphtali* he said, O Naphtali, satisfied with favor, and full with the blessing of **YeHoVaH**: possess you the west and the south. *24* And of *Asher* he said, Let Asher be blessed with children; let him be acceptable to his brethren, and let him dip his foot in oil. *25* Thy shoes shall be iron and brass; and as your days, so shall your strength be. *26* There is none like to the **Elohim** of Israel, who rides upon the heaven in your help, and in his excellency on the sky. *27* The eternal **Elohim** is your refuge, and underneath are the everlasting arms: and he shall thrust out the enemy from before you; and shall say, Destroy them. *28* Israel then shall dwell in safety alone: the fountain of Jacob shall be upon a land of corn and wine; also his heavens shall drop down dew. **29** Happy are you, O Israel: who is like to you, O people saved by **YeHoVaH**, the shield of your help, and who is the sword of your excellency! and your enemies shall be found liars to you; and you shall tread upon their high places. (End of Moses' blessing)

Chapter 34
Moses climbs Mount Nebo. There YeHoVaH showed him the Promised Land. Then Moses died. No prophet has arisen in Israel like Moses.

1 And Moses went up from the plains of Moab to the mountain of Nebo, to the top of Pisgah, which is over against Jericho. And **YeHoVaH** showed him all the land of Gilead, to Dan, **2** And all Naphtali, and the land of Ephraim, and Manasseh, and all the land of Judah, to the utmost sea,

3 And the south, and the plain of the valley of Jericho, the city of palm trees, to Zoar. **4** And **YeHoVaH** said to him, This is the land which I swore to Abraham, to Isaac, and to Jacob, saying, I will give it to your seed: I have caused you to see it with your eyes, but you shall not go over there. **5** So Moses the servant of **YeHoVaH** died there in the land of Moab, according to the word of **YeHoVaH**. **6** And **YeHoVaH** put him to rest in the valley in the land of Moab opposite Beth-peor: but no man has knowledge of his resting-place to this day. **7** And Moses was 120 years old when he died: his eye was not dim, nor his natural force abated. **8** And the children of Israel wept for Moses in the plains of Moab thirty days: so the days of weeping and mourning for Moses were ended. **9** And Joshua the son of Nun was full of the spirit of wisdom; for Moses had laid his hands upon him: and the children of Israel listened to him, and did as **YeHoVaH** commanded Moses. **10** And there arose not a prophet since in Israel like Moses, whom **YeHoVaH** knew face to face,

11 In all the signs and the wonders, which **YeHoVaH** sent him to do in the land of Egypt to Pharaoh, and to all his servants, and to all his land, **12** And in all that mighty hand, and in all the great terror which Moses showed in the sight of all Israel.

Reading 54 ends

Thus ends the Book of Deuteronomy   Praise **YeHoVaH**

True Name Torah Version

◆ ◆ ◆

SUMMARY

The Word of YeHoVaH is the most solemn in the World. It has no equal: past, present, or future. We either take it for what it is or we don't. We can't add to or take from His Word to change it to our liking. We can't that is, without defying Him. Anyone who feels they have that power will answer to YeHoVaH on judgement day if not before.

If after reading the Torah completely you in any way feel that YeHoVaH was only speaking to the Jews or that His laws were only temporary or that He gave the power of attorney to someone else to change them, then you too will answer to YeHoVaH on judgement day if not before.

His Word is not something you can read once and think you know it. Read it and re-read it and re-read it. You will gain something new every time. It's a living Word: meaning that there are messages for everyone that apply to you in different ways. You simply have to read and believe, and let YeHoVaH guide you.

When you read without any pre-conceived notions and without blinders, you will see the Truth, the whole Truth, and nothing but the Truth, so help you YeHoVaH.

If you have questions please contact us at: Questions@TorahPublications.com

Printed in Great Britain
by Amazon